D1175388

**Individual Differences in
Language Ability and
Language Behavior**

PERSPECTIVES IN
NEUROLINGUISTICS and PSYCHOLINGUISTICS

Harry A. Whitaker, Series Editor
DEPARTMENT OF PSYCHOLOGY
THE UNIVERSITY OF ROCHESTER
ROCHESTER, NEW YORK

HAIGANOOSH WHITAKER and HARRY A. WHITAKER (Eds.).
Studies in Neurolinguistics, Volumes 1, 2, and 3

NORMAN J. LASS (Ed.). Contemporary Issues in Experimental Phonetics

JASON W. BROWN. Mind, Brain, and Consciousness: The Neuropsychology
of Cognition

SIDNEY J. SEGALOWITZ and FREDERIC A. GRUBER (Eds.). Language Development and Neurological Theory

SUSAN CURTISS. Genie: A Psycholinguistic Study of a Modern-Day "Wild
Child"

JOHN MACNAMARA (Ed.). Language Learning and Thought

I. M. SCHLESINGER and LILA NAMIR (Eds.). Sign Language of the Deaf:
Psychological, Linguistic, and Sociological Perspectives

WILLIAM C. RITCHIE (Ed.). Second Language Acquisition Research: Issues
and Implications

PATRICIA SIPLE (Ed.). Understanding Language through Sign Language
Research

MARTIN L. ALBERT and LORAINE K. OBLER. The Bilingual Brain: Neurophysiological and Neurolinguistic Aspects of Bilingualism

HAIGANOOSH WHITAKER and HARRY A. WHITAKER (Eds.). Studies in Neurolinguistics, Volume 4

TALMY GIVON. On Understanding Grammar

CHARLES J. FILLMORE, DANIEL KEMPLER and WILLIAM S-Y. WANG (Eds.).
Individual Differences in Language Ability and Language Behavior

In preparation

JEANNINE HERRON (Ed.). Left-Handedness, Brain Organization, and
Learning

FRANCOIS BOLLER and MAUREEN DENNIS (Eds.). Auditory Comprehension: Clinical and Experimental Studies with the Token Test

Individual Differences in Language Ability and Language Behavior

Edited by

CHARLES J. FILLMORE
Department of Linguistics
University of California, Berkeley
Berkeley, California

DANIEL KEMPLER
Department of Linguistics
University of California, Los Angeles
Los Angeles, California

WILLIAM S-Y. WANG
Project on Linguistic Analysis
University of California, Berkeley
Berkeley, California

ACADEMIC PRESS   NEW YORK   SAN FRANCISCO   LONDON   1979

A Subsidiary of Harcourt Brace Jovanovich, Publishers

Social Science Research Council
Committee on Sociolinguistics

Members, 1978–1979

Allen D. Grimshaw, *co−chairman*
Dell Hymes, *co−chairman*
Charles A. Ferguson
Charles J. Fillmore
Shirley Brice Heath
Hugh Mehan
Joel Sherzer

David L. Szanton, *staff*

COPYRIGHT © 1979, BY ACADEMIC PRESS, INC.
ALL RIGHTS RESERVED.
NO PART OF THIS PUBLICATION MAY BE REPRODUCED OR
TRANSMITTED IN ANY FORM OR BY ANY MEANS, ELECTRONIC
OR MECHANICAL, INCLUDING PHOTOCOPY, RECORDING, OR ANY
INFORMATION STORAGE AND RETRIEVAL SYSTEM, WITHOUT
PERMISSION IN WRITING FROM THE PUBLISHER.

ACADEMIC PRESS, INC.
111 Fifth Avenue, New York, New York 10003

United Kingdom Edition published by
ACADEMIC PRESS, INC. (LONDON) LTD.
24/28 Oval Road, London NW1   7DX

Library of Congress Cataloging in Publication Data
Main entry under title:

Individual differences in language ability and language
    behavior.

    Includes bibliographies.
    1. Psycholinguistics. 2. Language and languages— —
Variation. 3. Language acquisition. I. Fillmore,
Charles F. II. Kempler, Daniel. III. Wang,
William S −Y., 1933–
BF455.I46   155.2'2   78–20044
ISBN 0–12–255950–9

PRINTED IN THE UNITED STATES OF AMERICA

79 80 81 82   9 8 7 6 5 4 3 2 1

Contents

18

Locating the Frontier between Social and Psychological Factors in Linguistic Variation   327

W. Labov

List of Contributors

Numbers in parentheses indicate the pages on which the authors' contributions begin.

JOHN B. CARROLL (13), The L.L. Thurstone Psychometric Laboratory, The University of North Carolina at Chapel Hill, Chapel Hill, North Carolina 27514

DAVID CRYSTAL (167), Department of Linguistic Science, University of Reading, Whiteknights, Reading RG6 2AA, England

RUTH S. DAY (57), Department of Psychology, Duke University, Durham, North Carolina 27706

ROBERT EFRON (245), Neurophysiology–Biophysics Research Laboratories, Veterans Administration Medical Center, Martinez, California 94553, and Department of Neurology, University of California Medical Center, Davis, California 95616

CHARLES A. FERGUSON (189), Department of Linguistics, Stanford University, Stanford, California 94305

CHARLES J. FILLMORE (85), Department of Linguistics, University of California, Berkeley, Berkeley, California 94720

LILY WONG FILLMORE (203), Department of Education, University of California, Berkeley, Berkeley, California 94720

PAUL FLETCHER (167), Department of Linguistic Science, University of Reading, Whiteknights, Reading RG6 2AA England

JOHN H.V. GILBERT (229), The Phonetics Laboratory, Division of Audiology and Speech Sciences, University of British Columbia, Vancouver, British Columbia, Canada

HENRY GLEITMAN (103), Department of Psychology, University of Pennsylvania, Philadelphia, Pennsylvania 19174

LILA GLEITMAN (103), Graduate School of Education, University of Pennsylvania, Philadelphia, Pennsylvania 19174

HAROLD GOODGLASS (253), Psychology Research, Veterans Administration Hospital, Boston, Massachusetts 02130

JOHN J. GUMPERZ (305), Department of Anthropology, University of California, Berkeley, Berkeley, California 94720

CURTIS HARDYCK (261), Institute of Human Learning, University of California, Berkeley, Berkeley, California 94720

DELL HYMES (33), Graduate School of Education, University of Pennsylvania, Philadelphia, Pennsylvania 19174

HARRY J. JERISON (277), Department of Psychiatry, University of California, Los Angeles, Los Angeles, California 90024

W. LABOV (327), Department of Linguistics, University of Pennsylvania, Philadelphia, Pennsylvania 19174

WALLACE E. LAMBERT (47), Department of Psychology, McGill University, Montreal, Quebec, Canada

JERRE LEVY* (289), Department of Psychology, University of Pennsylvania, Philadelphia, Pennsylvania 19174

HILARY NAYLOR (261), Institute of Human Learning, University of California, Berkeley, Berkeley, California 94720

JOHN ROBERT ROSS (127), Department of Linguistics and Philosophy, Massachusetts Institute of Technology, Cambridge, Massachusetts 02139

REBECCA M. SMITH (261), Department of Social Welfare, University of California, Los Angeles, Los Angeles, California 90024

DEBORAH TANNEN (305), Department of Linguistics, Georgetown University, Washington, DC 20007

---

* PRESENT ADDRESS: Department of Behavioral Sciences, University of Chicago, Chicago, Illinois 60637.

Preface

The typical descriptive paradigm for mainstream linguistics has been built on the fiction of the homogeneous speech community; except for obvious questions of dialect, individual variation in language has been peripheral to the interests of scholars working within this paradigm. Now, however, enough has been discovered about the nature and extent of individual variation in linguistic abilities and behavior to make it clear that linguistics needs methods and theories which take heterogeneity in language as a starting assumption. The collection of articles found in this book is an argument for locating concern with individual differences at the center of the study of language.

The chapters in this volume were selected to elucidate the various dimensions of linguistic ability and behavior along which individuals can differ from each other, the development of techniques by which individuals can be measured along such dimensions, and inquiry into the correlation of such measures with biological, psychological, and cultural parameters. The fields represented in these chapters seemed to us to be just those needed for laying the groundwork for a major effort in this area.

The book is divided into five sections. The first section contains three chapters which describe previous treatments of linguistic variation in psychology and anthropology. The authors stress continuity between past and present investigations, and place recent work in a historical perspective. The second section consists of four chapters which discuss variation in verbal fluency and in speakers' judgments. Both experimental and theoretical viewpoints are taken. The chapters in the third section focus on the origins, patterns, and functions of differences in language acquisition. The chapters cover abnormal development, phonetic and phonological development, and second language learning. Section four is made up of five investigations of the neurophysiological substrates of linguistic variation. These authors correlate linguistic variability with differences in the biology of perception and cerebral organization. A comparative examination of brain size variability places the topic of neurolinguistic variation in an evolutionary light. The final section contains two chapters which look at language in its social setting. The linguistic correlates of social differences, in both individuals and groups, are analyzed.

Such diverse perspectives endow this volume with a rather explicit interdisciplinary approach to the study of language variation. The necessarily wide range of interests touched upon, we feel, is essential for a preliminary understanding of the factors that can account for the diversity of observable language behavior. As a volume presenting pioneering research in a newly emerging area of language study, the work contained in this compendium should be of interest to linguists, psychologists, and ethnographers, as well as educators and clinicians. The level of sophistication of each chapter is geared for an audience with some familiarity of linguistics and psychology, but is not forbidding to a reader with a familiarity with any one of the fields touched upon. The volume integrates a broad variety of interests at a level which people from all relevant fields can appreciate, rather than presenting an in-depth view from a single perspective.

It is our hope that this broadly based survey into the questions of language variation will stimulate new research which will lead us closer to a coherent and integrated view of language ability and language behavior.

Acknowledgments

For the funding of this project we are indebted to the efforts of Dr. David Jenness and the Sociolinguistics Committee of the Social Science Research Council (SSRC) and to Dr. James Kavanagh of the National Institute for Child Health and Human Development (NICHD) through whose offices the needed money was granted by NICHD to SSRC for sponsorship. We would also like to thank Marcy Darnovsky for her time and ingenuity devoted to organizing this project.

Introduction

CHARLES J. FILLMORE
DANIEL KEMPLER
WILLIAM S -Y. WANG

People can differ greatly, and sometimes obviously, in the ways they use and control their language. Even with the same communicative goals, speakers will vary in many ways in their language performance, whether it is in the choice of words or intonation patterns, in the pacing of their utterances or in turn-taking strategies, or in the coherence or effectiveness of the total performance. We have wondered how such individual differences should be understood; in particular, we have wanted to learn how such differences could be seen as relating to social, psychological, or biological parameters. In what ways does personality determine, and in what ways is personality determined by, an individual's language resources? How and why do cultures value language fluency differently? How does our own culture identify, assess, and cultivate language ability? Does the observed variation in language ability have any basis in biological equipment? There is a sizeable literature documenting significant differences across individuals, from the whorls and ridges on the skin of

1

Individual Differences in Language Ability and
Language Behavior

Copyright © 1979 by Academic Press, Inc.
All rights of reproduction in any form reserved.
ISBN 0-12-255950-9

the fingers, to the mechanics of the heart, to the chemistry of the glands, to the structure of the cerebral cortex (e.g., Williams, 1967). It seems reasonable to raise the question of how much of what we see as language differences can be traced to observable variation in personal hardware. If such biological differences for language should exist, what, we need to ask, is the function of such variation in the evolution of the species?

Many language differences are readily noticeable. Our nontechnical vocabulary is replete with terms which recognize such differences: words like *gabby, articulate, tongue-tied, verbose,* etc. The kinds of personal variation in language use designated by such terms, which are distinct from the sorts of differences treated in the study of dialectal and idiolectal variation, have never been part of the traditional concern of linguistics. Furthermore, in recent decades, mainstream linguistics has been captivated by such illusory notions as those of the "ideal speaker–hearer" and the "homogeneous speech community" (e.g., Chomsky, 1965). There is every sign now that our discipline is reexamining the usefulness of these "convenient idealizations." An interest in language variation and the ethnography of speaking, as well as the emergence of more realistic views of the purpose of grammar writing, all lead quite inevitably to questions of the source and nature of the differences we see in language behavior and linguistic abilities (cf. Weinreich, Labov, and Herzog, 1968).

It became clear to us fairly early on that if we wished to be able to pose the right questions about language ability variation, we needed not only to rid ourselves of the methodological commitments that underlay the assumption of the "ideal speaker–hearer," we also had to be wary even of such a comparatively uncontroversial notion as that of the "normal" speaker–hearer. The possibility of defining norms of performance and ability, it became clear, has to depend on empirical data concerning the exact nature and range of observable individual differences. In particular, it seemed important to balance the accumulated knowledge of the "normal" experimental subject—the college sophomore—with expertise on at least four others: the child, the nonnative, the language impaired, and the linguistically self-conscious, that is, the intellectual. The questions we found ourselves confronting clearly reached beyond linguistics, or any other single discipline. We were led, in short, to the idea of a broad-based interdisciplinary compendium on individual differences in language ability and language behavior.

Our first task in defining the scope of the project was to identify the relevant issues and to consider which research disciplines offered data, insights, and methodologies that could contribute to the study of the kinds of individual variation in language behavior that interested us. Various areas of recent and ongoing research impressed us as particularly pertinent. Carroll's well-known analysis of the major components of language ability offered a valuable starting point toward defining the issues.

Day's reports on the differences between "language-bound" and "language-optional" characteristics of her subjects provided us with some immediate experimental dimensions of language ability, both for perception and for production. The Gleitmans' experiments with paraphrasing suggested ways of sorting people according to their access to the productive resources of English, and in particular to their metalinguistic awareness of the word-formational and syntactic possibilities of this language. The decades of important observations on the impaired language of aphasics on the part of Goodglass and his colleagues suggested that the quest for biological substrates, at least for the obvious cases, was not altogether without hope. Ferguson's developmental studies of the various "routes" children follow in the acquisition of phonology suggested ways of explaining how and why adult phonologies differ as they do. On a larger, phylogenetic, scale, Jerison's study of the role of variation in evolution could be seen as suggesting how the range of individual variation in the species might have functioned in the evolution of human cognitive and linguistic abilities. And recent ethnographic studies illustrate how language variation functions in discourse and social interaction, leading us to realize the need to discover just what kinds of social realities language differences reflect or create.

These were some of the areas of inquiry that seemed particularly fertile for the study of individual differences. By confronting the results and viewpoints represented in such an array of studies, we hoped to create something from which a coherent picture of the range of linguistic behavior could emerge.

An interdisciplinary approach offers the comprehensive overview necessary for a seminal effort of this kind. By soliciting contributions from various fields, we hoped that the end product would be accessible to readers of varied academic backgrounds. Accordingly, the authors who accepted the invitation were asked to shape their presentation to a new, broader audience than typically exists in the specialized fields being sampled. The resulting combination of articles in this volume can, we hope, give students the chance to explore methodological approaches of other disciplines, and, in general, afford readers the opportunity to gain new perspectives, new vantage points, from which to view an area of common interest.

A decision to juxtapose scholarly works from different scientific perspectives inevitably presents most readers with problems of intelligibility. Each author necessarily brings to the topic his or her own ideas on identifying the relevant questions, choosing the appropriate descriptive terms and explanatory principles, evaluating the data, and so on. Indeed, all the contributors agree that the study of individual differences is essential, but as might be expected, they all have their own unique ideas on what exactly the study of individual differences in language should be about. We think, therefore, that it may be of some use at this point to attempt to characterize for the reader some of the individual perspectives represented in the chapters to follow.

The most obvious differences are to be found in research methodology and presentation style. Since methodological stances are in a large part determined, or at least constrained, by the scope and topic of investigation, such diversity can be easily tolerated and generally appreciated. For example, it seems clear that only a controlled experimental approach could be suitable for the kind of psychophysical study seen in the chapter by Efron, and equally obvious that a more ethological approach, involving observations of language behavior in a naturalistic setting, was necessary for L. Fillmore's language acquisition project. We also find that research results can be presented in very different forms. For instance, while Day and Labov present their results in quantitative terms, the chapters by C. Fillmore and Hymes are better suited for a prose-style delivery. Investigators differ greatly in the data they use for analysis: Although Labov uses natural connected discourse, Efron uses dichotic chords; Hardyck, Naylor, and Smith use reaction time measures for conclusions regarding linguistic processing; and the Gleitmans ask informants for their metalinguistic judgments. And finally, the subject pool may give the best idea of the diversity of the work contained in this volume. Some authors did not make use of experimental subjects (C. Fillmore; Hymes). Among the subject pools used for the research reported here we find college sophomores (Day), accomplished bilinguals (Lambert), "normal" children (Ferguson), language delayed children (Crystal and Fletcher), adult aphasics (Goodglass), split-brain patients (Levy), young second-language learners (L. Fillmore), several classifications of "normal" adults (Gleitmans), accomplished linguists (Ross), and even australopithecines and nonhuman primates (Jerison).

Perhaps the ultimate value of such a collection of articles is exactly this juxtaposition of divergent inquiries. It is this heterogeneity in perspective and methodology which can stimulate thought and induce authors to formulate their objectives for a new audience and possibly, in some cases, to clarify their objectives to themselves.

The concrete advantages of juxtaposing chapters that differ in style, perspective, and topic of interest may be best illustrated with an example. For instance, Efron reports "ear dominance" for pitch, documenting that when two tones of a dichotic chord are presented at equal intensity, for one-half of the normal population the pitch of the tone presented to the right ear is distinctly more salient in the chord, for the other half of the population the left ear tone is more salient. Efron's success in identifying a response variable that consistently defined a group difference was a tangible result that served as a model for one kind of evidence in the study of individual differences. Although there was no obvious direct connection between Efron's findings and the sorts of linguistic differences we started out looking for, it is clear that many researchers would be eager to take his findings as a standard for the kinds of results we would all like to be able to document.

Approaching the subject from a different perspective, Ross asked colleagues and friends to take part in an experiment in which they were asked to give "grammaticality," "confidence," and "liberality" judgements on a list of "interesting" sentences (see appendix of Ross's chapter). The results, once analyzed, illustrated quite graphically that if what we mean by "English" is the set of sentences which all native speakers agree are grammatical, then English is very small, consisting of only "uninteresting" sentences like *The cat is on the mat.* There was very little agreement among Ross's informants on the grammatical status of the example sentences, but there were regularities in the set of judgements nevertheless. It appears to be the case that there are a number of syntactic continua, governed by implicational laws, such that if a speaker accepts a sentence at a distance X from the core (along any of these continua), he must accept any sentence more centrally positioned on the same continuum. Ross also believes that speakers may tacitly know of the existence of such continua, and may even have some notion of their own approximate "locations" on these continua with respect to other speakers of the same language.

The clear, dichotomous results reported by Efron for "ear dominance" in pitch perception stand in sharp contrast with the wide-ranging responses that informants gave to Ross's questions. Although this can be little more than an article of faith at present, it is possible that this difference is largely attributable to the fact that while Efron was eliciting an ability that is "elementary," Ross was confronting an ability that is highly "complex." It may turn out in future research that (a) most complex abilities associated with language can be teased apart into sets of elementary abilities, and (b) most elementary abilities can be shown to differ across individuals in relatively simple and discrete ways.

Within the same perspective, we may conjecture that people can be divided into groups more neatly along the dimensions of the elementary abilities, since here the scales and the units are relatively well-defined. However, for the highly complex abilities that we usually associate with language behavior, the multiple dimensions involved partition people into numerous different subsets, in ways that do not necessarily correspond with other criteria of grouping, such as handedness, age, educational background, etc. These subsets, as a result, would appear to be reflected in differences across individuals rather than groups.

Just as the dissimilarity between Efron's and Ross's chapters brings to the foreground the issue of "group" versus "individual" differences, we feel that the combination of contrasting approaches seen in this volume should provide a starting point for research into language variation. We hope that these pages will stimulate new research which begins to coordinate and supplement the findings reported here into a coherent and integrated view of language ability and language behavior.

CHAPTER SUMMARIES

Three chapters, those by Carroll, Hymes, and Lambert, present histories of the treatment of individual differences in language study. Carroll's chapter most clearly represents the psychometricians' perspective: the quantitative study of abilities, educational achievements, personality styles, attitudes, and other human traits and characteristics. The chapter goes into some detail regarding the history and development of psychometrics—with particular attention given to Thurstone's 1938 *Primary Mental Abilities*. This nicely illustrates the type of results yielded by such factor analytic studies and the difficulties of interpretation they often entail. The relevance of such studies to linguistic, psycholinguistic, and sociolinguistic research is examined. Finally, Carroll turns to review his own research on the Modern Language Aptitude Test which contributes to the prediction of success in learning foreign languages. Several of the test items and resulting "factors" (e.g., grammatical knowledge, verbal factor) of linguistic ability are discussed.

Hymes traces the current interest in individual variation back to Sapir's writings of the late 1920s and 1930s. He then outlines several reasons to study such differences: The inclusion of individual differences is necessary for completeness in any language description; individual differences can be an added resource in problems of language analysis; they can shed light on differences that are considered social problems; and individual differences offer a "vantage point" from which to consider questions of method and theory in the study of language in general. The last sections of Hymes' chapter are devoted to a discussion of the "social meaning" of such individual differences as seen in ethnographic studies by sociologists and anthropologists. This discussion is extended to explore how these investigations shed light on more general questions of language theory. In Hymes' words, in the larger context of the present collection, the chapter "attempts to establish the concern with individual differences as something central to linguistics."

Lambert addresses the treatment of individual differences from a slightly different perspective: He reviews the traditions in psycholinguistic research which differentially emphasize looking at subgroup comparisons versus looking at truly individual differences. He compares both of these perspectives to the long standing tradition that focuses attention on the universal aspects of language and psychology. This qeneral discussion touches on the contrast of perspectives developed in linguistics as opposed to those cultivated in psychology; Lambert explores the reason for these attitudes with reference to specific research tactics, problems and results. Several illustrative examples demonstrate the uses of "subgroup" and "individual" data in data analysis. Lambert's own research on bilingualism provides excellent instances of how subgroups are used in experimental paradigms, and how individuals and new subgroups emerge in the process of research.

Four chapters present discussions of how individuals access, use, and judge their language. The contributions by Day and C. Fillmore explore variation in fluency while Ross (discussed above) and the Gleitmans deal with variation that reveals itself through speakers' judgements.

Day approaches the subject of fluency from an empirical framework based on her past research with "language-bound" and "language-optional" subjects. In various experiments designed to assess fluency, Day discovers only minor differences in response quantity with respect to the two groups. However, detailed analyses of the types of responses given by the subjects reveal certain "organizing principles" by which responses are produced. It seems that two subjects can be equally fluent (i.e., give the same number of responses) but they may access their language by different modes. For instance, one person may attain fluency by accessing information that is organized on spatial principles, another may give the same number of responses but have accessed the material in a more linguistic–phonetic manner. Such results have implications for reevaluating old data on verbal fluency as well as for creating new standardized tests for assessing fluency, taking into account the extent to which subjects rely on various forms of mental representation.

The first sections of Filmore's chapter examine how language variation in general has been dealt with in theoretical linguistics—paying particular attention to the generativist school and the restricted usefulness of notions like "competence" and "performance." Fillmore then outlines possible dimensions of fluency in language, distinguishing ways in which people appear fluent: for example, ready access to the language's lexical and syntactic resources, the ability to have appropriate things to say in a wide range of contexts, the ability to be creative and imaginative in language use, etc. The sources of such fluency differences are discussed along with some research possibilities suggesting a more empirical framework on which to base further claims about verbal fluency.

The Gleitmans' chapter reports and interprets their experimental findings on individuals' ability to give judgements about language as compared with findings of individuals' ability to use language in discourse. These differences are compared across populations (social, educational, and developmental), between individuals and with tasks of different levels (i.e., semantic, syntactic, and phonological judgements). The Gleitmans' data suggest that judgemental (metalinguistic) functions in language are separable from language functions. Individual differences, they propose, occur more noticeably at the judgemental level than at the speech and comprehension level.

Several chapters deal with individual differences in language acquisition. Crystal and Fletcher approach the investigation of individual language disabilities with their "profile analysis"—an empirical method of assessment and remediation of language disorders. The paper summarizes the linguistic motivation and actual framework of the profile analysis— including an explanation of the "descriptive," "developmental," and "longitudinal" components of typical language profiles. Several case studies of language delay, along with specific profiles, are discussed. These language profiles provide a systematic, linguistically sound method of making individual language disabilities accessible for assessment and treatment. Hopefully, this procedure will introduce a "greater measure of control over the nature of therapist–patient interaction, thus helping to build up the professional confidence that clinical work badly needs."

Ferguson, in his review of phonological development, discusses in some detail several types of strategies for the acquisition of sounds. For example, children exhibit preference strategies where they favor or disfavor a particular sound or class of sounds; "word-shaping" and "alternate paths" are other strategies widely exhibited by young children. Ferguson suggests that analogs to these individual learning strategies and types also exist in adult phonologies. The logical extension of such a stand is summed up by Ferguson: "If an individual's phonology at any point in his lifetime represents the accumulated effects of individual processes of acquisition, then THE phonology of a language variety—the normal object of phonologists' study—is a composite of individual phonologies in which the shared structure inevitably has indeterminacies, fuzzy boundaries, and both dialectal and idiosyncratic variation. Which is to say that phonology is like syntax, lexicon, and all the rest of human language."

L. Fillmore's chapter documents individual language acquisition strategies as demonstrated by young children learning a second language. In her naturalistic study of five Spanish-speaking children acquiring English, Fillmore found that various cognitive strategies and personal characteristics of the individuals combine to produce vastly different individual rates and degrees of success in the task of learning a second language. For instance, Fillmore noticed that individuals are differently disposed to take the necessary steps to insure the learning of the second language. Therefore a child who seeks out the company of speakers of the new language will be more successful than a child who avoids speakers of the new language. Similar individual differences emerge from children's differential tendencies to be playful and experimental with language. Fillmore nicely demonstrates that these social and personal aspects of the language learner account for much of the variation in language learning and must be considered if we are to explain the process (and the variation) in acquiring a second language.

Gilbert's chapter reviews the experimental evidence that bears on the issue of individual differences in the acquisition of phonetics of the child's first language. He gives special attention to the literature that sheds light on the variation which distinguishes perception and production in phonetic acquisition. Gilbert maintains that the bulk of the evidence supports his hypothesis that "the child perceives speech in terms of the adult system, but the production is affected by motor difficulties." In addition, individual children vary considerably in the strategies they use while still achieving their goals of communication. Whether or not the degree of variability decreases over time remains undetermined in the present literature.

Biological aspects of language variation are explored by: Efron (summarized above); Goodglass; Hardyck, Naylor, and Smith; Levy; and Jerison. Goodglass discusses two types of deficits in aphasia: selective disorders of syntax (or "agrammatism") and selective disorders of lexical retrieval (or "anomia"). Within subject variability (i.e., agrammatics' fluctuating ability to produce the correct target sentence and anomics' enhanced ability to find target words more easily when given the initial syllable as a cue) suggest that "in both domains (lexical and syntactic) there is some residual knowledge, even when aphasia prevents recovery of this knowledge. Partial knowledge is often sufficient for recognizing when an utterance—lexical or syntactic—sounds correct."

Two contributions, one by Hardyck, Naylor, and Smith, and one by Levy, report experimental investigations of cerebral lateralization effects in language processing. Hardyck, Naylor, and Smith, using "normal" subjects, ran experiments testing individuals' tendencies to assign names to abstract figures and their ability to recognize a variety of those figures presented in either the right or left visual field. The results are interpreted to indicate that lateralization effects are not present under conditions where new information is evaluated on every trial. Based on handedness data of the subjects and their performance on the tasks, Hardyck, Naylor, and Smith conclude that differences in cerebral lateralization were nonetheless present among their subjects; for example, they found superior ability at providing verbal coding for difficult information among left-handed subjects.

Levy's experiments made use of split-brain patients' performance on tasks to draw conclusions about language processing in normals. The studies described in this chapter focus on the language abilities of the right hemisphere. Levy outlines three specific deficiencies seen in the language system of apes and the human right hemisphere, thereby summarizing the abilities of the human left hemisphere which enable humans alone to utilize a "true language system."

Jerison addresses the question of individual differences from an evolutionary and biological point of view. By comparing the variation in human brain size to brain size variation within other species, Jerison concludes that the amount of variation found in human brain size is exactly what one expects of brains in mammals. He consequently suggests that we consider the "individual differences in human language ability as representing the normal variability of a brain in a species under natural selection." In short, "human language is unique, but its variability is not."

Sociolinguistic investigations of individual differences are presented by Labov and by Gumperz and Tannen. Gumperz and Tannen explore a new method for establishing exactly what knowledge is shared by individual speakers for successful communication to take place. Their approach, detailed in this chapter, is to analyze misunderstandings in simple conversational exchanges, thereby illuminating what conversational meaning was (not) shared and discovering the origin of the misinterpretation. Through this type of study, Gumperz and Tannen can recover the shared sociocultural knowledge used in conversation and, consequently, shed light on how groups are formed, and how and why linguistic differences are maintained.

Labov, in his chapter, reviews with the perspective of individual differences, some of his data on social dialects in New York City and Philadelphia. This chapter reveals what individual differences can mean in the context of sociolinguistic patterns. Labov includes examples of subjects who, by virtue of their individuality, provide clear prototypes for phenomena he has previously documented. He also discusses the meaning of individual deviance from language patterns and suggests patterns in his subjects similar to those discussed by Day (this volume), along with speculations about what these individual abilities might indicate about more general language capacities, for instance, the processes of learning to read or learning a second language.

REFERENCES

Chomsky, N. *Aspects of a theory of syntax*. Cambridge, Massachusetts: M.I.T. Press, 1965.

Weinreich, U., Labov, W., and Herzog, M. I. Empirical foundations for a theory of language change. In *Directions for Historical Linguistics*. University of Texas Press, 1968. Pp. 95–188.

Williams, R. J. *You are extraordinary*. New York: Random House, 1967.

I

THE TREATMENT OF INDIVIDUAL DIFFERENCES

1

Psychometric Approaches to the Study of Language Abilities

JOHN B. CARROLL

Among the more striking ways in which individuals differ are those noted in their learning and use of language. Either from everyday experiences or from more systematic observational procedures, such as psychological and educational tests, we can gain such facts as the following: Children differ in the rate at which they acquire their native language. Students in school differ in the rate at which they master various language-related skills such as reading and writing. Adults who have had apparently similar linguistic and educational backgrounds differ in speech style and fluency, in ability to comprehend speech and written language, and in ability to learn a foreign language.

In this chapter I propose to introduce a few of the major findings concerning these differences in language abilities and consider their possible relevance for linguistic, psycholinguistic, and sociolinguistic inquiries. At one point I will focus on studies in which I have attempted to investigate the nature of certain linguistic abilities that have attracted my interest.

13

Individual Differences in Language Ability and Language Behavior

Copyright © 1979 by Academic Press, Inc.
All rights of reproduction in any form reserved.
ISBN 0-12-255950-9

Individual differences in language abilities, certainly in performance but also, I think, in inferred "competence," have for many years received much attention from psychologists, particularly from those who specialize in the development, application, and interpretation of psychological and educational measurements. For convenience, I shall speak of these people as "psychometricians," although this term has often been used in a narrow sense, referring to technicians who administer and interpret tests on a more or less routine basis in school, clinical, or industrial settings.

Some of the investigation of language abilities has been done, almost unwittingly, in connection with the development of so-called "intelligence" tests; in fact, traditional classifications of intelligence tests refer to them as either "language" or "nonlanguage" tests, or as either "verbal" or "nonverbal" tests. There is some confusion in terminology here, in that sometimes the distinction refers to whether the *content* of the tests consists of language materials, and sometimes it refers to whether the *instructions* for the test are verbal or nonverbal. Although it may be useful to inquire what relations there may be between language abilities and performance on various kinds of intelligence tests, I would at the same time urge caution and even skepticism about some of the concepts of intelligence that are found in psychological writings or that are commonly held by the public, for example, the notion that intelligence is a very general kind of ability, that an individual's intelligence is fixed and immutable, and that intelligence is determined primarily by genetic factors.

My own view of these matters would emphasize that mental abilities (including language abilities) are quite diverse, that they often reflect rather specific kinds of environmental and educational influences, that they probably differ in the degree to which they are subject to change through learning and various kinds of intervention, and that the methodological problems in identifying and quantifying their possible genetic determinants are so exceedingly difficult that at the present time one cannot draw firm conclusions about the extent to which they are genetically determined. The psychological investigation of mental abilities is at its soundest if it remains at a purely descriptive level; explanatory adequacy will come only very slowly.

In pointing out, above, that psychometricians have been concerned with the observation and measurement of language abilities, I used the terms *competence* and *performance*—terms that will not be unfamiliar to linguists. It appears to me that there is at least a close analogy between the concepts underlying these terms in linguistics and certain concepts that have been developed in psychometric theory. For example, one of the basic theorems of psychometrics is that the observed score on a test (the performance) is an additive function of the "true score" (the hypothetical measure of competence) and an "error" that could be ascribed to any one or more of a large number of specific and extraneous influences (Lord and

Novick, 1968). Similarly, the notion of a "factor" in the psychometric methodology known as factor analysis (Harman, 1976) is essentially the notion of a particular kind of inferred competence that is said to "explain" variance in certain test performances. A principal goal of psychometric methodology is to design tests, observations, and data-handling procedures such that variance due to error is minimized, and variance due to underlying ability or competence is maximized, in a relative sense.

Note, however, that there is possibly a difference between linguistic and psychometric notions of "ability" or "competence." As in any science that involves measurement, the existence of variation among observations—whether within individuals (at different times or under different testing conditions) or among individuals in a defined sample—is essential for the success of any psychometric investigation. In contrast, one has the impression that in linguistics the notion of "competence" assumes no variation among speakers, that is, that in a defined speech community all speakers attain the "same" basic competence with the language. At least in the case of Chomsky's "ideal native speaker" we have no competence to *measure*—we have only a competence to *describe*. Despite its title, *An Integrated Theory of Linguistic Ability*, a book by Bever, Katz, and Langendoen (1976) contains little if any mention of individual differences or variation in linguistic ability. It is gratifying to note, however, that the papers in the present volume seem to start from the assumption that even individuals in the same speech community can differ in their linguistic competence, that is, in precisely what rules of language govern their communicative behavior.

At the same time, it seems desirable, as I have pointed out previously (Carroll, 1968), to develop a much more elaborate theory of competences and performances than is available in contemporary linguistics and psycholinguistics if one is to deal adequately with linguistic abilities. The customary distinction between competence and performance merely draws attention to what the individual knows about the language, in contrast to how the individual uses that knowledge in actual communication, and (on the side of performance) to the factors that may affect that use on a particular occasion (the individual's state of health and alertness, momentary distractions, and the like, all of which may result in speech or writing that is in some way deviant from the output of an "ideal native speaker"). It seems necessary to extend the notion of competence to describe a whole range of competences (with emphasis on the plural), not only those having to do with implicit knowledge of language rules, but also those having to do with the characteristic abilities of speakers (or writers) to use their linguistic knowledge to produce effective communications, to retrieve particular types of linguistic knowledge when called for, or to adapt their speech or writing styles to the demands of different occasions. There are different classes of language rules, for example, phonological, syntactic, lexicosemantic, orthographic, and sociolinguistic, with respect to which individuals may differ in their implicit knowledge. Likewise, there may be diverse kinds of communication tasks with respect to which individuals differ in their characteristic approaches, modes of adaptation, and capabilities of performance. While it is not within the province of psychometrics to develop an adequate theory of linguistic competences and performances, certain methodologies of psychometrics could make a contribution to the empirical validation of such a theory.

THE PLACE OF PSYCHOMETRICS IN PSYCHOLOGY

Broadly defined, psychometrics is devoted to the quantitative study of behavior and the methodologies for pursuing such study. Psychometric methodology can be utilized in many settings, for example, in psychophysics and other branches of experimental psychology, where the investigator may be concerned not only with the reliability of observations but also with the attempt to fit mathematical models to data. Within psychometrics, however, there has been a dominant interest in the quantitative study of abilities, educational achievements, personality styles, attitudes, and other human traits and characteristics. Literally thousands of psychological and educational tests have been developed to measure these characteristics, and while one may have various misgivings about such tests, they would appear to have had considerable practical utility. For this reason, psychometrics has often been viewed as an area of applied rather than theoretical psychology. This subdiscipline, evolved by a small band of devoted scholars, has for much of its history enjoyed almost an independent existence, having little contact with developments in other branches of psychology.

Nevertheless, at least a few psychometricians have been interested in using the psychometrics of mental tests in the study of theoretical questions in psychology. In fact, while so-called cognitive psychology seems to have had only a recent rebirth among experimental psychologists, psychometrics may be said to have begun, and to have continued up to the present time, with an interest in the properties of the human mind— witness the title of a work by one of the founders of psychometrics, Francis Galton (1822–1911), *Inquiries into Human Faculty and Its Development* (1883). It is not widely recognized, even among psychologists, that the well-known British psychometrician, Charles Spearman (1863–1945)—the proponent of a "g" or "general" factor of intelligence—was as much interested in the theoretical analysis of cognitive processes as he was in the measurement of intelligence (Spearman, 1923). Likewise, L. L. Thurstone (1887–1955), the chief American developer of factor analysis—

one of the principal methodologies of psychometrics—had an abiding faith that factor analysis could be valuable, at least in an exploratory and descriptive phase, in the study of mental processes (Thurstone, 1935). A number of contemporary disciples of Spearman and Thurstone, like J. P. Guilford (1967), R. B. Cattell (1971), and J. Horn (1976), have continued to insist on the usefulness of factor analysis in the building of psychological theories, because it seeks to identify the basic parameters and dimensions of variations in behavior.

Factor analysis, to be sure, is only one of the methodological tools of psychometrics, and its use depends upon the development and refinement of satisfactory measures of ability and other attributes of behavior, a problem that is the subject matter of still another branch of psychometrics called the theory of tests (Lord and Novick, 1968). At times, the technical problems inherent in psychometric methods have drawn psychometricians into purely mathematical inquiries that are far removed from substantive problems of mental processes of human behavior. In the following discussion I will almost completely ignore technical problems and focus on what factor-analytic studies seem to have disclosed about language abilities. Also, I shall have little to say about longitudinal studies of the development of language abilities, primarily for the reason that there are relatively few such studies of any value, using adequately differentiated concepts of these abilities.

FACTOR-ANALYTIC STUDIES OF LANGUAGE ABILITIES

Factor analysis is essentially a method of analyzing the interrelations among a series of measures applied to a defined set of objects (usually, human individuals, but not necessarily) in order to disclose the smallest number of "factors" or inferred dimensions of underlying variability (in ability, personality, performance, or whatever else is being measured), that will explain, according to a mathematical model, the significant variation and covariation among the measurements. Obviously, there must be reliable variation, and at least some covariation, in the data in order to make a factor analysis successful and meaningful. A number of factor-analytic models are available, but most psychometricians have favored, for theoretical or practical reasons, linear models that focus on explaining covariation among measurements in a maximally parsimonious way.

For present purposes, let us first consider in fair detail a classic factor-analytic study conducted by Thurstone (1938) and published in a monograph entitled *Primary Mental Abilities*. The word *primary* in this title is to be taken in a technical sense, rather than in the sense that the abilities identified were regarded as being of paramount importance. Thurstone developed a battery of 57 psychological tests and administered it to 240 college students. The tests were designed so that the tasks or items included on any one test were relatively homogeneous in type. For example, one test—a vocabulary test—required examinees to identify, by selecting appropriate synonymous expressions, the meanings of a series of English words; another type of vocabulary test required them to supply words fitting given definitions (the number of letters in the desired word, and its initial letter, being given as clues); another test required the subject to think of, and write down, as many words as possible that begin and end with specified letters. The kinds of tasks were for the most part drawn from typical intelligence tests; some had verbal content, others involved arithmetical computations or quantitative reasoning, and still others involved perception and mental manipulation of geometric figures and designs. Some tests were specially designed to measure hypothesized varieties of abilities. The essential purpose was to see how these tasks would be classified by the statistical analysis.

A possible outcome, of course, could have been that all the measurements were highly correlated—at least to the extent permitted by their reliabilities. Such an outcome would have confirmed Spearman's hypothesis of a "general factor" of intelligence, that is, a unitary dimension of ability that "explains" performance on all intellectual tasks. This was not, however, the outcome. Although there were high intercorrelations among some clusters of test variables, a substantial number of intercorrelations were near zero, and when the factor-analysis results were obtained, Thurstone concluded that at least 13 independent factors or dimensions were required to yield a satisfactory account of the covariation among the tests. After further processing of the results (by "rotation to simple structure") to produce parsimonious descriptions of the tests, he believed he could interpret seven of these factors with assurance, and make tentative interpretations for some of the rest. In this process, the tests that best measured each of the factors were examined, and the interpretation of a factor was then made by trying to decide what elements of content or of psychological process appeared to be common to all the tests that measured the factor, and at the same time were uniquely present in the tests of that factor. When interpretations could not be made with certainty, there was the prospect of testing various possible interpretive hypotheses in further studies, using more carefully refined and differentiated measurements.

Thurstone's study was performed shortly before 1938, some years prior to the further development of factor-analytic procedures and the advent of fast computers to make these analyses more feasible. In discussing the results of this study, I use the reanalysis of Thurstone's data published by Kaiser (1960); the interpretations made possible by this reanalysis are generally similar to Thurstone's, but are more complete (more factors appear interpretable) and more refined.

To clear the ground, I will first mention several factors in Thurstone's study that would not normally be thought of as corresponding to language abilities, even though tests of these factors might conceivably involve language processes. They can be identified as Space (the ability to perceive and mentally operate on visually presented spatial configurations), Number (the ability to make rapid and accurate arithmetical computations), Associative Memory (the ability to learn and remember a series of arbitrary associations), and Recognition Memory (the ability to recognize which of a series of stimuli have been previously presented). Their interest in the present context consists only in the fact that they were found to be largely independent of the language ability factors that I shall mention momentarily.

Next, I mention a group of factors that involve various kinds of verbal reasoning processes; they were named, respectively, as Induction, Deduction or Syllogistic Reasoning, Quantitative Reasoning, Classification, and Numerical Estimation. The tests of these factors contain verbal material, but these factors are independent of the two or three factors that could properly be identified as types of language abilities, that is, abilities reflecting differential acquisition of language, or differential facility in language use.

One of these latter factors is the so-called Verbal factor. In his own analysis, Thurstone identified it as having to do with "ideas and the meanings of words," and called it "Verbal Relations." In the Kaiser re-analysis it comes out much more clearly as involving mainly extent of vocabulary, and ability to produce or comprehend connected discourse containing difficult or abstract concepts. The variables that best and most uniquely measure the factor are a difficult multiple-choice vocabulary test, two reading comprehension tests, and the judged quality of a short theme that the examinee was required to write on an assigned topic. Many other tests also measured this factor, but they were not in every case "pure" tests of the Verbal factor, for they also measured some other factor or factors. However, to the extent that they measured the Verbal factor, they required the examinee to draw upon his general competence with English, particularly, his implicit knowledge of the lexicosemantic rules of the language.

The appearance of this Verbal factor in such a battery of tests will probably not surprise anyone. It simply represents the extent to which the individual can exhibit a knowledge of the more advanced reaches of English vocabulary, handle the concepts and relations that are likely to be conveyed in prose of substantial difficulty, and produce prose that is well written according to the standards of English composition teaching. Note, however, that this kind of verbal ability is apparently little related, at least in the sample studied by Thurstone, to factors involving inference, reasoning, or other general "mental operations," when abilities in these reasoning processes are measured in such a way as not to challenge the examinee's knowledge of difficult and infrequent words and expressions. The relatively low correlation, confirmed in other studies, of verbal ability with reasoning abilities, makes one inclined to be skeptical about the concept of a factor of "general intelligence." Many intelligence tests are loaded with materials involving language abilities, mixed in with materials testing reasoning ability. Consequently, a moderately high score on an intelligence test could reflect either the presence of high verbal ability, accompanied by mediocre reasoning ability, or the presence of good reasoning abilities accompanied by mediocre language knowledge.

A second type of language ability that looms quite large in Thurstone's data is a little more puzzling, but nevertheless intriguing. Thurstone called it, somewhat misleadingly, Word Fluency, but no simple phrase would be adequate to describe it. We have to consider the actual tasks that are found to measure it. One such task is an anagrams task: the subject has to make up as many words as he can, within a certain time-limit, from the letters in the word GENERATIONS. Another task is to think of, and write down within a time limit, as many words as possible that begin with the letter S and end with the letter L. There are various other tasks that involve rapidly discovering words fitting certain orthographic or semantic criteria. Not unexpectedly, a spelling test is one of those measuring the factor, but it is somewhat surprising that a so-called Grammar test also appears—actually a test requiring the examinee to evaluate the "correctness" of various sentences in terms of highly traditional criteria (e.g., the sentence *Everyone put their hands up* is to be marked incorrect).

The difficulties in interpreting this factor illustrate those frequently encountered. The tests measuring the factor are not very highly intercorrelated, but they are sufficiently correlated to suggest that they are linked by something in common. This "something in common" need not be unitary—it could be a composite of elements that happen to co-occur in the tests, or at least that co-occur in the sample of persons tested. What is this common thread, in the present case? Is it merely the result of the learning of orthographic conventions, in school or otherwise? If so, does the Grammar test appear because people who learn correct spelling are also those who are likely to learn traditional canons of grammatical correctness? Or is there a more basic ability here—a special facility in calling up words from one's lexicon to fit set criteria, or a special kind of memory for materials organized according to orthographic criteria? These questions could be answered only by designing further studies in which these different elements might be disentangled. Actually, various subsequent studies have indicated that there are at least several different abilities here: (a) knowledge of English orthographic conventions; (b) knowledge of canons of grammatical correctness; (c) facility in calling up isolated words and unrelated ideas; (d) facility in utilizing learned associations in what Tulving (1972) has called semantic memory. Even now, however, the exact structure and differentiation of these abilities remains somewhat unclear (Ekstrom, 1973).

One further language ability identified in Kaiser's reanalysis was left uninterpreted by Thurstone. It appears strongly in only two tests, respectively called Rhythm and Sound Grouping. The Rhythm test measures the ability to identify a line of poetry that does not have the same meter as three others; Sound Grouping asks the subject to identify a word that does not rhyme with three others, as in the quadruplet *comb, foam, home,* and *come.* (Both these tests are in printed format.) Again we are presented with difficulties of interpretation: Is the underlying ability related to some capacity to handle certain characteristics of speech sounds, or is it simply an ability to identify the odd member of a set? In this particular case, later studies yield little further information, because these tests have not been frequently included in the test batteries.

Up to this point I have focused attention on the Thurstone primary mental abilities study to illustrate the kinds of information that factor analysis studies can give and the kinds of difficulties of interpretation they often entail. Since Thurstone's day there have been numerous factor-analytic studies that have included various kinds of language ability tests. I cannot review here the wealth of detail in these studies; a preliminary attempt to do so was included in my chapter (Carroll, 1971) in a book on language learning edited by Carroll Reed. Relevant information is also contained in treatises on the results of factor-analytic studies (Cattell, 1971; Guilford, 1967). Although some of the results are fairly clear, for example, the well-nigh universal confirmation of a "verbal" or vocabulary factor, the total output of these studies is far from satisfying. As yet, few studies have employed the most technically advanced procedures of analysis. A more serious defect, however, is that the studies, and the designs of the tests and variables employed, reflect little sophistication, on the part of the investigators, in matters of linguistics, psycholinguistics, or sociolinguistics. As a simple example of this, note that almost all studies are based on group-administered, printed tests that require respondents to be able to read. Individual differences in reading ability, which are of considerable extent even in college students, are therefore inevitably confounded with possibly more basic abilities pertaining to language in its spoken form. It is difficult for me to say to what extent the "verbal" factor identified in numerous studies is in reality a factor associated only with written language, although at least one study (Spearritt, 1962) that explored verbal abilities in both spoken and written modes suggested that verbal ability cuts across both these modes. As another example, note that we have few if any studies that explore syntactic skills as they might be described by a linguist.

Questions can and have been raised about the ecological validity or relevance of the language abilities disclosed in the available psychometric studies. It is clear that the verbal ability factor that is measured by vocabulary and reading comprehension tests is relevant to many activities in educational institutions, at all levels; it is probably also relevant to the adult's ability to comprehend either spoken or printed verbal materials of all types encountered in daily life, and to the adult's ability to produce effective communications with respect to sophistication and complexity in lexicon and syntax. The ecological validity of some of the other factors of language ability that have been identified is more in question. Some of them may in fact be pertinent only to the rather specialized language performances required in certain psychological tests or procedures. Nevertheless, I deem it important to establish what kinds of language abilities can be demonstrated to exist, regardless of their possible relevance outside the testing room or laboratory, because until the existence of such abilities is well established, their possible ecological validity cannot even be determined. It is conceivable, however, that some of the more important language abilities can be established only through studies of language performances in realistic, nontesting situations.

The theory and technology for performing appropriate and wide-ranging studies of language abilities is now available, on the one hand from psychometrics, and on the other hand from linguistics and psycholinguistics. Obviously, interdisciplinary efforts would be not only desirable but also necessary. I should, however, enter a note of caution: Factor-analytic studies are major enterprises, usually requiring large amounts of testing time from fairly large numbers of respondents. If the tests require individual administration, or if they involve extensive recording, transcription, coding, and analysis of subjects' responses or verbal productions, the amount of time, labor, and expense required can become very substantial.

THE POSSIBLE RELEVANCE OF LANGUAGE ABILITY STUDIES FOR LINGUISTIC, PSYCHOLINGUISTIC, AND SOCIOLINGUISTIC RESEARCH

The immediately obvious conclusion that emerges from studies of language abilities is that users of a language differ among themselves enormously both in their implicit knowledge of language rules and in their ability to use that knowledge in language performances. In view of this, the possible existence, or even the possible theoretical description, of anything like an "ideal native speaker" is moot. Would the "ideal native speaker" be a person who has the highest possible levels of competence in *all* the language abilities that can be demonstrated? Can we even assert that there is necessarily a value, to the individual or to society, in having a "high" level of competence on some kind of language ability, or in approaching the status of an "ideal native speaker"? If we restrict attention to the "verbal ability" factor as defined above, precisely what language rules would constitute the sum total of knowable facts about the language? Would this consist of all the language facts that could be conceivably compiled in grammars and dictionaries of the language? Asked in this way, the question virtually answers itself, in the negative. Linguists are already too well aware of facts about language variation and change. It would be impossible to define, even in principle, the characteristics of an "ideal native speaker" because one would face the problem of what set of language facts would constitute the implicit knowledge of such a speaker.

On the other hand, the assumption of psychometric approaches to the measurement of language abilities is that one can define, at least on a probabilistic basis, some common core of facts and rules about a "standard" form of a language that are ordinarily learned or acquired together by educated speakers of the language; the verbal ability factor disclosed in psychometric studies measures, in effect, the extent to which the individual knows this common core of language facts and rules. It is possible that linguistic studies should take account of an informant's verbal ability, considered in this way. For example, there may be systematic relations between an individual's verbal ability and the grammatical acceptability, to that individual, of particular modes of expression. It has sometimes been noted that linguists' intuitions about acceptability or grammaticality seem to differ somewhat from those of the general populace, possibly stemming from the fact that linguists tend to be highly educated in some form of standard language. It would be desirable to obtain acceptability judgments from a more representative sample of speakers, with controls for psychometrically determined verbal ability.

To the extent that sociolinguistic studies involve observation of speakers interacting in communication situations, it would be desirable to consider the possible relevance of various kinds of language abilities. For example, the relative dominance of persons in a dyadic interchange may interact with verbal fluency factors. Persuasive speech styles are possibly a function of abilities in organizing verbal expression and retrieving appropriate verbal memories. So little research in this area has attempted to take account of individual differences in language abilities and styles that it is difficult at this point to specify what lines of investigation would be most promising, but I have the feeling that such investigations would be very productive.

STUDIES OF SPECIFIC LANGUAGE ABILITIES
INVOLVED IN FOREIGN LANGUAGE APTITUDE
TESTS

As a further illustration of the kinds of results obtained in psychometric studies and the problems in interpreting these results, I now introduce an account of a study in which I have been engaged, over the past several years, in an attempt to investigate the nature of certain striking individual differences that I have observed in measuring aptitudes for learning foreign languages among speakers who have already acquired English as a native language. Some of the outcomes have a bearing on remarks I have made in the course of the above overview of findings and implications of factor-analytic studies of language abilities.

Some years ago, with my associate Stanley Sapon, I developed a test (Carroll and Sapon, 1959), called the *Modern Language Aptitude Test* (MLAT), that has been successfully used in selecting people for foreign language training, for example in the Peace Corps (Hobbs, 1963; Krug, 1962). When I developed this test, actually a battery of five subtests, I was mainly interested in identifying tasks that were highly predictive of success in foreign language learning, with little concern for what these tasks actually measured. I could not resist the temptation, however, to speculate about the nature of the abilities measured by the subtests of the battery. I was particularly interested in three of them, Parts 2, 3, and 4 of the battery.

Part 2, entitled "Phonetic Script," presents the task of learning to identify the transcriptions of certain English phonemes. The transcription system used is actually that of Trager and Smith (1951), familiar to many linguists but presumably unfamiliar to the typical college student or adult who might happen to take the MLAT. Subjects are told that they will hear a series of nonsense syllables spoken on a tape recording, while they observe the transcriptions of these syllables on their answer sheets. They are told that the sounds of the syllables correspond in a one-to-one fashion to the graphic symbols of the transcription. From this audiovisual presentation, they are to try to learn what sounds are represented by each graphic symbol. For example, the first item presents the following syllables in both auditory and visual forms:

/ tik   tiyk   tis   tiys /

This item introduces the phonemic and transcriptional contrast between /i/ and /iy/, also the opportunity to learn the transcriptions of the phonemes /t/, /k/, and /s/. Later items gradually introduce a number of other contrasts, with the corresponding transcriptions. Periodically, the subject has to go back to the beginning of a block of five items he has just heard; for each item, he is presented with just one spoken syllable, and asked to mark the transcription for that syllable. For example, in Item 4, which shows the following syllables on the answer sheet:

/   kas   kaws   kaz   kawz   /

the subject has to indicate the correct transcription for the spoken syllable /kawz/. Many subjects erroneously mark /kaws/, not having recognized or learned the phonemic and transcriptional contrast between /s/ and /z/.

At one time I speculated that the test tapped an ability to form associations between sounds and graphic symbols, because scores on this test were correlated with performance on tests in which subjects learned Devanagari or Mongolian script, but certain kinds of evidence subsequently persuaded me that it might be a test of the ability to identify phonetic units and remember them over a period of time. For example, I noted that individuals with low scores on this test had difficulty identifying sounds in foreign languages and even in repeating foreign language words after a 10-sec period of performing an interfering task. I therefore regarded the test as one of what I called phonetic coding ability, that is, the ability to store a phonetic entity in memory and later retrieve it.

The nature of Part 3, entitled "Spelling Clues," can best be explained by presenting a sample item:

luv

- A. *carry*
- B. *exist*
- C. *affection*
- D. *wash*
- E. *spy*

Subjects are told that their task is to recognize the key word, *luv*, as a "disguised" spelling of *love*, and then find the alternative corresponding most closely in meaning to *love*—in this case, *affection*. The test has 50 items of this type, and subjects are told to work rapidly. Scores tend to correlate with those on Part 2; thus the test seems to measure somewhat the same ability that is tested in Part 2, whatever that may be. I persuaded myself that that ability might still be the "phonetic coding ability" postulated above, because the ability to recognize disguised spellings might depend upon some kind of memory for the orthographic coding conventions of English spelling. Because of the speededness of the test, scores might also be a function of a general factor of work-speed that has been found in factorial studies (Lord, 1956), and since many of the items utilize comparatively infrequent and unfamiliar words, its scores could be expected to be partly a function of vocabulary knowledge, that is, the "verbal factor."

Like Part 3, Part 4, called "Words in Sentences," is a printed test.

Subjects are told that it is a test of their ability "to understand the function of words and phrases in sentences." The task is explained to them through a series of sample items, the first of which is the following (with the accompanying explanation):

LONDON is the capital of England.
He liked to go fishing in Maine.
  A   B   C   D   E

In the first sentence, which we will call the **key** *sentence,* LONDON *is printed in capital letters. Which word in the second sentence does the same thing in* **that** *sentence as* LONDON *does in the* **key** *sentence? The right answer is the word "he," because the key sentence is about "London," and the second sentence is about "he."*

Essentially the test is one of solving "grammatical analogies"; its 45 items present a wide variety of syntactic phenomena. It is not "speeded," that is, nearly all subjects finish the test within the 15-min time limit. It is to be noted that performance on the test does not involve any use or knowledge of grammatical terminology. I speculated that the test measures a special kind of "grammatical sensitivity," that is, sensitivity to grammatical functions of linguistic elements in sentences, quite apart from any formal knowledge of grammar.

All these tests contribute materially to the prediction of success in learning foreign languages (Carroll, 1962).

In the series of studies I have conducted over the past two years, I attempted to determine what essential traits or abilities these tests measured, and to form more precise descriptions of these traits in terms of psychological processes and/or acquired memories. For this purpose, I designed or selected a rather large group of test tasks that I thought might measure, in purer form, the abilities that the MLAT subtests measured. My studies went through pilot phases in which I sought to refine the tests or screen out those that did not promise to serve my purposes. The results I report here pertain to a series of 38 variables derived from tests, questionnaires, and other data on a group of 72 University of North Carolina students who volunteered to be subjects in response to an advertisement promising a nominal payment, along with information on certain test results, for their participation. The tests given required a total of approximately 5 hours. Many of them had to be administered individually or in small groups seated at computer terminals, sometimes with a tape cassette machine so that oral responses could be recorded. Space does not permit giving detailed descriptions of the tests, and I can report only selected results.

Overall, the correlations among the 38 variables appeared to be best accounted for by a factor solution with 11 distinct, uncorrelated factors. Some of these factors, however, made little or no contribution to the explanation of the variance on the MLAT.

Of special concern were the results relating to my hypothesis of a "phonetic coding ability" that would explain performance on Parts 2 and 3 of the MLAT. In a pilot study, I had found indications of both an *auditory* phonetic coding factor and a *visual*, or alphabetic coding factor. Performance on Part 2, Phonetic Script, was explained predominantly by the auditory coding factor, and performance on Part 3, Spelling Clues, was explained by the visual coding factor. The auditory coding factor was measured by several experimental tasks, including two memory span or free recall tasks in which the stimuli were phonetic nonsense syllables, and a task analogous to that devised by Peterson and Peterson (1959) in which subjects have to repeat, at a signal, an auditory stimulus (a sequence of 2 or 3 phonemic nonsense syllables) which they have heard just before having to perform an interfering task (reading a series of numbers aloud). The visual memory coding factor was measured by tasks in which subjects had the opportunity to remember stimuli in terms of alphabetic spellings (either presented directly in the visual stimuli, or imposed on auditory stimuli by the subjects).

In the main study, several factors in the phonetic or alphabetic coding domain emerged, but their identification was not as clear as it had appeared to be in the pilot studies (possibly because the pilot studies capitalized on chance correlations arising from the small size of the sample tested). Furthermore, the manner in which these factors accounted for variance in the Phonetic Script and Spelling Clues subtests of the MLAT was somewhat different from what had appeared in the pilot studies.

The single factor that seemed to account for most of the reliable variance in *both* Parts 2 and 3 of the MLAT was one that reflected the individual's ability to spell correctly, to recognize words spelled correctly, and to recognize deviant spellings as possibly making correct English words if pronounced according to the more frequent orthographic rules of English. The critical tests were among those devised by Baron and Strawson (1976) to measure a difference between what they called "Phonecians" and "Chinese," that is, college-age English-speaking subjects who do, or do not, respectively, have a superior knowledge of English orthographic rules and use them in reading. There was also, however, a test that reflected an ability to recognize that certain phonemic nonsense syllables have *not* been used in a preceding free-recall memory task, and also a test of a person's ability correctly to read aloud words with "disguised spelling" drawn from the stimuli used in Part 3 of the MLAT. Clearly, some sort of ability to handle phonetic–orthographic material is indicated here, but this factor failed to appear on several tasks that had been specially de-

signed to measure ability to encode and retrieve phonetic material. Instead, these tests defined other factors, which showed low or vanishing
correlations with the two phonetic tests of the MLAT.

One of these factors was particularly intriguing, and possibly related to
the visual or alphabetic coding factor that had appeared in the pilot
studies. It was measured principally by two kinds of tests. One of these
was adapted from a task studied by Crowder (1971). Four versions of this
memory span test were used. In one version ("alphabetic vowels") the
subject heard series of seven syllables like:

/ gay giy gey gay gow giy gey /

after which the syllables were to be repeated aloud in the correct order.
Note that the vocalic nuclei of the syllables in this item are the names of
the vowel letters I E A I O I A; thus a subject had an opportunity to encode
the stimuli in terms of these alphabetic names. In another version of the
task ("phonemic vowels") the syllables were drawn from the set
/ gæ gə gu ge /, where none of the vocalic nuclei directly represented
alphabetic letter names. A third version ("mixed vowels") used syllables
drawn from both the alphabetic and non-alphabetic sets. A fourth version
used syllables contrasting only in their consonants, drawn from the set
/ba da ga/. The factor was measured most clearly by the versions that
contained alphabet-named vowels, somewhat less by the phonemic vowel
version, and hardly at all by the consonant version. The factor was also
represented in several scores derived from the Peterson–Peterson task,
described above, in which subjects had to remember phonemic nonsense
syllables and repeat them at the end of an interfering task. It is conceivable
that the more successful subjects on this task were those who adopted a
strategy of coding the stimuli in terms of an alphabetic encoding.

At the same time, it is to be noted that many of the tests that loaded
highest on this factor were those involving immediate memory for *vocalic*
sounds. It is possible that the factor represents a special ability to deal
with *vocalic* as opposed to consonant sounds. (In a pilot study, a "vowel
bias" factor had been suggested; there was a significant correlation of
vowel–consonant difference scores over written and oral versions of the
Crowder task; that is, some subjects consistently did better with vowels
than consonants.)

At this point I can only say that the definition and structure of various
abilities concerned with phonetic and orthographic materials is unclear.
That large individual differences in test performance can be observed is
not in doubt, but only further studies, with more differentiated types of
tasks, can promise to elucidate the nature of the abilities involved, and we
are far from being able to say much about how these individual differences arise—whether, that is, they are the result of special learning experiences or of inherent constitutional traits.

Let me now turn to the results regarding the hypothesized factor of grammatical sensitivity. Some aspects of these results are very clear. Scores on Part 4, Words in Sentences, of the MLAT are highly correlated with a test of knowledge of grammatical functions and with a self-rating of knowledge about grammar. In the grammatical knowledge test, subjects were asked to identify sentence elements in terms of named grammatical functions (appositive, auxiliary, verb, direct object or accusative, indirect object or dative, etc.). It might appear, then, that this factor represents nothing more than *acquired* grammatical knowledge. On the other hand, consider the fact that this factor showed virtually no correlation with any information, elicited from the subjects on a questionnaire, on how much teaching of formal grammar they had had in school or elsewhere, and when they had acquired any knowledge they had. As a matter of fact most respondents indicated that they had had considerable formal training in grammar, but it appears many had forgotten what they had learned, if indeed they had ever learned it. Furthermore, the grammatical knowledge test showed a significant correlation ($r = .30; p < .05$) with scores on a test of verbal reasoning. It therefore seems possible that high scores in the Grammatical Knowledge factor reflect a capacity for learning grammatical facts that is related to other cognitive capacities. The factor was also related to the correctness of judgments of the "completeness" of one class of sentences (the "D" sentences) studied by Maclay and Sleator (1960) in their investigation of judgments of grammaticalness.

The Grammatical Knowledge factor proved **not** to be related to several other tasks that, it had been thought, might measure some aspect of grammatical sensitivity. One such task was an adaptation of a task used by Sachs (1967) in demonstrating that people on the average have good memory for sentence meaning but poor memory for exact sentence form. In my study, high performers on the grammatical knowledge tests did no better than low performers in detecting, in a paragraph memory test, whether sentences had been changed from active to passive, or vice versa. The possibility still exists, of course, that significant correlates of grammatical knowledge could be found in tests of various cognitive abilities or in certain kinds of speech and writing performances that were not included in my study.

The Verbal factor that is often found in studies of cognitive abilities appeared in my study as well. It was measured by a test of advanced vocabulary knowledge, the Verbal score of the Scholastic Aptitude Test (admissions scores for the subjects being available from university records), and to some extent the Mathematical score of that test. It also showed up, as expected, in the Spelling clues subtest of the MLAT. Of most interest in the present context was the fact that the Verbal factor was also measured by a task (studied by MacKay and Bever, 1967) of perceiving lexical and syntactic ambiguities. Subjects with low Verbal factor scores tended to fail to see the "obvious" ambiguities in certain types of sentences, or to correctly disambiguate them. This evidence adds to our knowledge of the nature of linguistic abilities: It says that the Verbal factor pertains not only to knowledge of vocabulary, but also to ability to have a kind of metalinguistic awareness concerning the possible interpretations of quite common forms of expression.

REFERENCES

Baron, J., and Strawson, C. Use of orthographic and word-specific knowledge in reading words aloud. *Journal of Experimental Psychology: Human Perception and Performance*, 1976, *2*, 386–393.

Bever, T. G., Katz, J. J., and Langendoen, D. T. *An integrated theory of linguistic ability*. New York: Crowell, 1976.

Carroll, J. B. The prediction of success in intensive foreign language training. In R. Glaser (Ed.), *Training research and education*. Pittsburgh: University of Pittsburgh Press, 1962.

Carroll, J. B. The psychology of language testing. In A. Davies (Ed.), *Language testing symposium: A psycholinguistic approach*. London: Oxford University Press, 1968.

Carroll, J. B. Development of native language skills beyond the early years. In C. Reed (Ed.), *Language learning*. New York: Appleton-Century-Crofts, 1971.

Carroll, J. B., and Sapon, S. M. *Modern language aptitude test*. (Test, manual, stimulus tape, keys, etc.) New York: The Psychological Corporation, 1959.

Cattell, R. B. *Abilities: Their structure, growth, and action*. Boston: Houghton Mifflin, 1971.

Crowder, R. G. The sound of vowels and consonants in immediate memory. *Journal of Verbal Learning and Verbal Behavior*, 1971, *10*, 587–596.

Ekstrom, R. B. Cognitive factors: Some recent literature. Princeton: Educational Testing Service, July 1973. (Technical Report PR-73-30.)

Galton, F. *Inquiries into human faculty and its development*. London: Macmillan, 1883.

Guilford, J. P. *The nature of human intelligence*. New York: McGraw-Hill, 1967.

Harman, H. H. *Modern factor analysis* (Third Edit.). Chicago: University of Chicago Press, 1976.

Hobbs, N. A psychologist in the Peace Corps. *American Psychologist*, 1963, *18*, 47–55.

Horn, J. L. Human abilities: A review of research and theory in the early 1970's. *Annual Review of Psychology*, 1976, *27*, 437–485.

Kaiser, H. F. Varimax solution for primary mental abilities. *Psychometrika*, 1960, *25*, 153–158.

Krug, R. E. *An analysis of eighteen Peace Corps projects*. Pittsburgh: American Institute for Research, 1962.

Lord, F. M. A study of speed factors in tests and academic grades. *Psychometrika*, 1956, *21*, 31–50.

Lord, F. M., and Novick, M. R. *Statistical theories of mental test scores*. Reading, Massachusetts: Addison-Wesley, 1968.

MacKay, D. G., and Bever, T. G. In search of ambiguity. *Perception and Psychophysics*, 1967, *2*, 193–200.

Maclay, H., and Sleator, M. D. Responses to language: Judgments of grammaticalness. *International Journal of American Linguistics*, 1960, *26*, 275–282.

Peterson, L. R., and Peterson, M. J. Short-term retention of individual verbal items. *Journal of Experimental Psychology*, 1959, *54*, 157–173.

Sachs, J. S. Recognition memory for syntactic and semantic aspects of connected discourse. *Perception and Psychophysics*, 1967, *2*, 437–442.

Spearman, C. *The nature of 'intelligence' and the principles of cognition.* London: Macmillan, 1923.

Spearritt, D. *Listening comprehension—A factorial analysis.* Melbourne: Australian Council for Educational Research, 1962.

Thurstone, L. L. *The vectors of the mind.* Chicago: University of Chicago Press, 1935.

Thurstone, L. L. *Primary mental abilities.* Chicago: University of Chicago Press, 1938. (*Psychometric Monographs,* No. 1.)

Trager, G. L., and Smith, H. L., Jr. *An outline of English structure.* Norman, Okla.: Battenburg Press, 1951. (*Studies in Linguistics, Occasional Papers,* No. 3.)

Tulving, E. Episodic and semantic memory. In E. Tulving and W. Donaldson (Eds.), *Organization of memory.* New York: Academic Press, 1972.

2

Sapir, Competence, Voices

DELL HYMES

Individual differences should be of fundamental importance in the study of language and in linguistic theory. We can hope that this volume will help to establish this point, and even to catalyze greater involvement of linguists in the working out of its implications. I should like to suggest three points which seem to me important to the success of such a development. One is historical, one is sociological, and one, in a sense, is poetic.

1.

If we look for precedent for the concerns of the conference in linguistics in the United States, the principal candidate, I think, is the effort of Sapir

Individual Differences in Language Ability and
Language Behavior

Copyright © 1979 by Academic Press, Inc.
All rights of reproduction in any form reserved.
ISBN 0-12-255950-9

to sketch an approach to language that he called "psychiatric or personalistic (Sapir, 1938, SWES p. 573)."[1]

Although Sapir was in the forefront of the movement to establish discovery of pattern as central to linguistics, he came to feel keenly the limitations of such work if divorced from other concerns. He came to believe that the separation of "grammar," "culture," and "society" from each other as objects of study, however rigorous each in their own right, was part of an estrangement of the human sciences from human beings. The "many kinds of segmental scientists of man (Sapir, 1939, SWES p. 578)" could, he thought, find unity in a discipline that would take as its starting point the interactions of individuals with each other, and the meanings that cultural and linguistic patterns come to have for those who acquire and use them, a discipline that would not allow itself "to forget the experienced unity of the individual" (Sapir, 1918, SWES p. 492; 1932, SWES p. 515; 1939, SWES p. 581).

Among Sapir's immediate circle, only Stanley Newman seems to have implemented his concern at the time (Newman, 1938, 1939, 1941, and 1944). The impulse given by Sapir may be said to have reemerged about 1950 with the development of lines of work christened as "paralinguistics," "kinesics," "proxemics," and with study of discourse in psychiatric sessions, by such scholars as Trager, Smith, Hockett, McQuown, Birdwhistell, Bateson, Sarles, and others. Men such as Trager, Birdwhistell, and Hall indeed were conscious of working out implications of a perspective enunciated by Sapir. [Trager's introduction to his contribution to the Sapir memorial volume (Trager, 1941) is instructive in this regard. It makes clear the logic of a development to encompass all patterned phenomena of sound, stemming from the principle enunciated at the end of Sapir's "Sound patterns in language" (1925); Trager (1958) further indicates this connection in his synthesis of work to that point in paralinguistics.]

These lines of work have continued and influence some studies of discourse today, but whereas they were begun as developments out of linguistics, largely by linguists, they have found themselves at the periphery of linguistics, if not quite outside it, from the standpoint of the conception dominating the discipline.

Of course, it is not the case that a concern with individual differences

---

[1] Sapir's major papers are collected in D. G. Mandelbaum (ed.), *Selected Writings of Edward Sapir* (Berkeley: University of California Press, 1968, here abbreviated "SWES." Page numbers following this abbreviation refer to page numbers within this volume. Some relevant quotations are given on pp. 207–208 of my *Foundations in Sociolinguistics* (Philadelphia: University of Pennsylvania Press, 1974); on the course that led to the approach, found in writings of the last decade of Sapir's life, see the section on Sapir in my "Linguistic method of ethnography," in P. Garvin (ed.), *Method and theory in linguistics* (The Hague: Mouton, 1970), 294–325.

and a concern with communicative patterns beyond the edge of grammar must go together. Indeed, as Sapir insisted, in "Speech as a personality trait" (1927), individual differences require a knowledge of sociocultural commonalties and codes to be properly recognized as such and calibrated. There is much of a purely "cultural pattern" sort to be done in the investigation of paralinguistics, kinesics, proxemics, and such. But the initial impetus from Sapir, and the ties with psychiatry, made questions of personality and individual differences at home in the ambience created by these efforts. They have not been so at home in efforts focused on universals of structures, especially when accompanied by a disparagement of actual speech and a substitution of introspection for observation as a method of work.

In sum, if there is a significant precedent for concern with individual differences on the part of linguists, there is little continuity with that precedent. The Sapir of "Sound patterns in language" has been restored to professional consciousness, but not the Sapir of "Speech as a personality trait," "The unconscious patterning of behavior in society," "Cultural anthropology and psychiatry," and "Why cultural anthropology needs the psychiatrists" (SWES 533–43, 544–559, 509–521, 569–577, respectively; originally published 1927, 1927, 1932, 1938, respectively). If the present volume helps to establish concern with individual differences as something *central* to linguistics, it will have accomplished something novel.

This history is worth examination for the bearing it may have on the prospects of the present effort. A full consideration would require examination of the general course of linguistics as a discipline, which of course is not feasible. [In "American structuralism" (Hymes and Fought, 1976), I attempt, with John Fought, a view of the historiography of the subject.] The history does suggest a lesson. For the study of individual differences in language to flourish, linguists must participate with others in research whose methods and contexts of explanation go beyond those of conventional linguistics. The makeup of this volume of course reflects such a conception, a conception which is widely shared today. It seems likely, however, that the attraction of narrow linguistic methods and contexts of explanation must always remain very strong. There is so much that one can do without raising questions of individual differences, there is so much motivation to do so in terms of the tradition of the study of language, there is so much practical and scientific pressure for results stated in terms of whole languages and large populations. And for many languages there is nothing much one can do about individual differences, except to note them as qualifications on the sources of the data; such is the case with the work on Wasco Chinook, now virtually extinct, by Michael Silverstein (1974) and myself (Hymes, 1975). Perhaps the present surge of interest will not succeed in institutionalizing itself.

The difficulty may seem to have been already overcome through the widespread integration of linguistic and psychological research. That indeed does go a long way to overcome the difficulty. There seems to me, however, to be two further dimensions of integration that are necessary. One I can present in terms of data and theoretical understandings, the other I can only express as a glimpsed possibility.

These two dimensions seem to fall into place within a series of reasons for being interested in individual differences in language behavior and linguistic ability.

One reason might be a view of individual differences as residual. Once common patterns are known, individual differences remain. Attention to them would be a matter of completeness.

Another reason might be a view of individual differences as an added resource. Problems in the analysis of language may be solved, or better understood, if individual differences are taken into account. Attention to them would be a matter of scientific advance in the study of other topics.

A third reason might be a view of individual differences as a social problem. A good many children and adults show differences that are considered problems by others, themselves, or both. A sounder grasp of individual differences in general could contribute to the treatment of these problems. Scientific advance and social relevance would go together.

A fourth reason might be a view of individual differences as a vantage point from which to consider questions of method and theory in the study of language in general. This would be to give individual differences foundational status.

In the next section I shall try to indicate that successful study of individual differences must include the social meaning of such differences, and hence a method of work, ethnography, cultivated in sociology and anthropology. I shall also try to indicate that successful study, especially for the third reason, must include a perspective often called "critical." Social meaning and critical perspective seem to me in turn to imply the possibility and importance of work motivated by the fourth reason, which I will take up in the last section.

2.

The fundamental methodological principle in the study of language is that of form–meaning covariation. Each advance in the systematic study of language seems to involve fresh recognition of the force of that principle. The very birth of an independent profession was associated with the systematization of the principle in the study of speech sounds, hitherto divided between a separate phonetics and a plurality of individual language (and language-family) phonologies. The success of generative syntax and the opening up of the study of speech acts, pragmatics, and the like, seem to involve recognition that an existing level of study was inadequate to certain kinds of systematic form–meaning covariation. Sapir's "Sound patterns in language" seems to be the first articulation of what is involved. What appear to be identical patterns may turn out to be different, what appear to different may turn out to be alike, once the communicative relevance of the elements of the patterns is established.

It is my impression that the force of this principle is not universally recognized in the study of individual differences at the present time. For example, some studies of development of language in children make use of Mean Length of Utterance (MLU) as a criterion. Perhaps this measure correlates with things of interest. It certainly does not touch the processes of development themselves. One and the same length of utterance may come about for a variety of reasons, having to do with intentions and meanings, favored styles, norms and genres, and for that matter, ability. The longer utterance may sometimes be the less cogent. In the course of development children are acquiring and using a system of speaking, of acts, routines, and genres. Perhaps in a given case length of utterance is itself subject to social evaluation, in which case of course to study it would be to study directly children's ability to master a norm of their community. Otherwise, study of mean length of utterance seems simply to divert attention from what is going on. (The argument here is parallel to Chomsky's argument against stochastic models of syntax. That is, quantitative measures in principle cannot capture the qualitative relationships that underly the phenomena. Phenomena that are quantitatively equivalent may be qualitatively distinct (see Chomsky, 1957).

There may be a general difficulty here. Measures used in the study of individual differences may miss what is meaningful, and they may imply a meaningfulness that is alien and even prejudicial. It may be that any measures imply a notion of normal development. If communities differ in what is considered normal development, abnormality may be found where none exists. In all such work it is probably not possible to escape wholly the influences of our own backgrounds, social assumptions, and preferences. Our society is one in which "secondary and tertiary" responses to language— the addressing of which Bloomfield (1944) believed a major justification for the existence of a science of linguistics—are rife. As is well known, bilingualism has often been associated with handicap; differences due to dialect are often treated as differences in intelligence; and speech therapy may be invoked where the problem is not one of disability but variability. Liberality with regard to religion and sex does not seem to extend to speech, and evaluation of individual differences in speech may well be built into our culture as a subtle but pervasive instrument of hegemony. Were everyone to speak only English, and only standard English, there might still be an industry of deploring the decline of the language and discriminating the faults of most of us. In such a society one can not avoid the consequences that one's findings, methods, and very choice of problem may have a social meaning.

So far as I can see, there is no privileged position from which to view this issue. The difficulty is built into the subject, and all that can be asked is openness to challenge and critical reflection. Ultimately, critical reflection involves consciousness of one's conception of ideal kinds of speaker and ideal kinds of speech community, and acceptance of the commitments entailed. The uncomfortable result may be awareness that our own values about differences do not agree with those of people we wish to study or with those of people who might fund our research. Let me suggest examples, none of which are intended to be invidious, but only to indicate the pervasiveness of the issue. The genetic bases of language competence must be investigated, yet one can be wary of a tendency in periods of political conservatism to favor biological explanations of problems that have social causes. The impulse of a liberal, especially one of anthropological background, may be to perceive a situation in terms of the rights of a subordinated group, but the variety of language behavior one appreciates and defends may be offensive to many in the group itself, when publicly noticed. One's impulse to defend a traditional language may align one with the right of the community political spectrum against what a sector of the working class perceives to be its interest.

Many will identify their perspective with that of some community or sector of a community; many will find no conflict between their perspective and that of sources of funds. The healthiest thing would be for there to exist a critical, self-conscious discussion of the ways in which linguistic differences become defined as social problems, a discussion independent both of government and other funding agencies, and of particular groups. International perspective would be particularly helpful, both with regard to societal processes underlying the definition of problems, and with regard to what kinds of relationship may in fact obtain between differences and their social meanings. Some recent writing has shown too ready a generalization of experience limited to a part of our own society.

Probably most of us would have assumed that status and verbal correctness would coincide; the lower the status, the lower the evaluation of the form of speech. A striking case in contrast is that of the Wolof of Senegal, brilliantly analyzed by Judith Irvine (1974). There, activeness is associated with lowness of status, and the cultivated forms of public speech are assigned to a caste-like, almost outcast group, the griots. The association of activity, including speech, with low status is carried to the point that the traditional king was expected to speak with mistakes of grammar and pronunciation, showing how far beneath him was mere outward form. (I recall an analogous phenomenon among the Ashanti of Nigeria.)

Again, direct and referentially relevant speech has seemed so fundamental as to be taken as not only a norm of our own society, but of societies in general. Among the Malagasy of Madgascar, as analyzed by Elinor Keenan (1976), direct and referentially relevant speech is officially disvalued, and considered characteristic of women. Valued speech, associated with men, is indirect. It is assumed that one should provide others with no more information than one can not avoid giving, so as not to be held responsible for the consequences.

Being away from books and notes, I cannot elaborate such examples. To do so would be in the pattern of Boas (1911), who in the course of defining what he called an "analytic" approach to grammar demolished established linguistic universals of the time, universals too narrowly based in European experience. We can use a dose of Boas these days, but let me suggest a further step. [To pursue the allusion, it is a step in the pattern of Sapir, whose *Language* (1921) summed up the insights of the Boasian "analytic" approach as applied to American Indian languages, and went on to suggest a positive general linguistics in terms of typological configurations (and in later papers, in terms of hierarchies, scales, alternative realizations of common functions.] Studies such as those of Irvine and Keenan indicate both specific differences and general dimensions. The Wolof and the Malagasy are not wholly different from our own society, but the analogous phenomena here have different social place and meaning. Vis-à-vis the Wolof king: Presidents of the United States have been known to employ a disvalued grammatical form, such as -in' (instead of -ing), or tell their audience that a learned word just used had had to be looked up. The Wolof king, of course, differentiates himself from those below him, the American president suggests he is not that different at all. Again, vis-à-vis the Malagasy public norm of indirect, referentially evasive speech: We ourselves may criticize a general or ambassador who offends allies by saying what he thinks, and the phenomenon of the "public position" distinct from actual views is commonplace at all levels of our society. As with the Malagasy, the express purpose is to avoid consequences, but whereas in Malagasy the indirectness is a recognized ideal and norm of everyday life, in the United States it is not. The norm is there, but it is not publicly accepted, except apparently in the breach. Indirect or evasive speech of officials, though essential to some situations, is often publicly scorned. (Whereas among the Malagasy, it is direct speech, though essential to some situations, that is stigmatized.)[2]

---

[2] Such examples bear on the cooperative principle of Grice, and the four maxims he associates with it: be informative as possible, be truthful, be relevant, be clear. These maxims are true to a mainstream tendency of American culture, and to what Gouldner has called the emerging "culture of critical discourse" of intellectuals and intelligentsia (1978). The referentially evasive speech of Malagasy males, however, patently conflicts with the principle, particularly the maxim, be informative. Now, many scholars find the maxims useful, and point out that they need not be always observed. The maxims are not descriptive, but underlying. When people depart from the maxims in what they say, one still interprets what

There is reason to believe that societies differ not only in kinds of speech that are valued and disvalued, but also in the relative importance of speech itself. This is to me the most interesting question of all about language. What have people made of it? What has it come to mean to them? In the nature of the case, individual differences are universally given and universally evaluated, but the evaluations, the meanings and the patterns into which they fit, are not given, but historically, socially devised. What then do a given set of people make of differences? What differences do they notice, what ignore? What differences do they stigmatize or seek to repress, what tolerate, what encourage and cultivate? Given abilities with regard to the use of language which there is reason to think universal, what is their relative place?

In this regard the methodological approach of John Roberts (1972) is of great utility. It provides a way to integrate differences among cultures with differences among individuals. In brief, Roberts examines cross-cultural data to infer correlates and underlying motivation for the development of expressive forms, including such interactional uses of language as riddling and interrogation. He reasons that if the hypothesis as to the reason for the presence of the practice (and associated ability) as a salient form in some cultures and not others is valid, it should also explain individual differences within a single society. If a certain set of conditions brings about institutionalization of riddling, high individual involvement in riddling should have the same explanation.

The approach is independent of Roberts's particular sociopsychological theory of expressive behavior. It could be applied to the dimensions of speaking style which Alan Lomax (1977) believes he has identified cross-culturally in recent research.

In sum, the results of ethnography in other cultures provide necessary perspective on what is universal, what variable, in language behavior. They provide a basis on which accurate typologies of the kinds of configuration that exist can be built, analogous to the sort of general linguistics one associates with Sapir, Jakobson, Greenberg, and others. They can be

---

they say as a departure. That is well and good for a cultural context in which "be informative" can reasonably be said to be an underlying norm. But Malagasy men would find conversational implicature invited, not when a man was not informative, but when he was. When a Malagasy man is referentially evasive, he is observing the common norm. It is contradictory to impose the principle "be informative" on such conduct, as if, for Malagasy men, to observe a norm is to flout one.

Cultural realities can be reconciled with the usefulness that the maxims appear to have by changing their linguistic form. They are not maxims, but dimensions; not imperatives, but nouns. Human cultures universally orient their norms of discourse to the dimensions of informativeness, truthfulness, relevance, clarity. The choices they make in terms of those dimensions, the values and norms they consider ecology, history, experience to justify and require, that,they inculate in the young and expect from their fellows—these vary in configurations that are interesting to discover and, one can hope, possible to explain.

joined with investigation of individual differences in a search for explanatory theory. Finally, and most important of all perhaps, ethnography is essential to study of the much-abused, but necessary notion, competence.

My criticism of Chomsky's use of "competence" (Chomsky, 1965) may be familiar, and in any case there is no time or space to review it here. The point is simply that "competence" is the normal and natural word for the abilities of individuals. The difficulty with Chomsky's use was that the term was, in effect, redefined so as to apply only to a part of the abilities of a person, and so as to imply an equation between the object of theory that bore the name "English" and individual abilities. (So much force did this redefinition have for a time that more than one intelligent scholar, wanting to recognize the differences between Chomsky's "competence" and the abilities of individuals, felt compelled to resort to other terms for the latter.) We know, of course, that the abilities of individuals are both more and less than was implied by Chomsky's notion: more, in that they comprise more than grammar, often more than a single variety or indeed language; less, in that it is in the nature of the social division of labor and the contingency of experience that the systematic potential of the language as a whole exceeds the command of any one person. It seems to me desirable to reinstitute the term "competence" in the study of individual differences. What a person is able or not able to do, after all, is at the heart of much of the interest in the subject, where individual differences as a social problem are concerned. And when we are forced to reflect on our assumptions about ideals of speech and an ideal speech community, it is about an ideal distribution, or organization, of competencies that we must think.

It should be obvious that personal competence in language can not be assessed by fit or lack of fit to a preconceived model, or by tests in a single type of situation. The common problem of education in our country is that the verbal abilities of children are assessed in settings which do not represent the true range of their competence. Ethnographic observation and participation in the range of settings in which the children participate is necessary, if schools, and researchers like ourselves, are to have an accurate knowledge, both of the competence and of the meaning to those who have it, of its various elements.

Again, individual differences in verbal ability are often the basis of success or failure, or degree of success, in a variety of settings and careers. We know little about the patterns of verbal ability required, or expected, in the institutions and professions of our society. We need sometimes to look at our society as if it were West Africa or New Guinea, or perhaps the traditional Chinese Empire, congeries of curious, puzzling, intriguing ways of life and ways of speaking, which, with patience, we may come to understand.

3.

The anthropologist Robert Redfield once said that the difference between himself and a colleague, in their separate studies of a certain village,
was that the colleague had asked, "From what do they suffer?," and he,
"What makes them happy?" These poles may apply to the study of individual differences in language and ability. A great deal of the attention to
the subject comes, I suppose, from concern with differences that are
considered defects, from disability rather than ability. Much of recent
linguistics appears to have been neutral: Wind up the grammar, so to
speak, and if other things don't get in the way, all will be fine. It is from
students of traditions other than our own that we hear most often of
marvelous things that certain speakers can do.

I would like to suggest, very briefly, a way in which a critical perspective on our assumptions and expectations about language ability, and an
ethnographic approach focused on individual competence, can come together as a basis for work of value both to a theory of language and to
society. Let me take the narrative use of language as an example.

In the elementary sense of coherent discourse, of the creation of text,
narrative ability is apparently universal. Halliday (1977) has focused upon
it in his account of the language development of his son, Nigel; Elinor
Keenan (1974) has found it one of the five elementary uses of language in
the speech of her twin sons. It is an ability, however, which is very
differently shaped in different social settings. In our own society it is
subject to complex evaluation, encouragement, and discouragement.
Among older people at Warm Springs Reservation there still exists what
might be called a "narrative view of the world"—often it seems as if
everyday life is essentially a resource for narrative reshaping of significant
incident, according to traditional norms of presentation (including direct
quotation as against reported speech). Much in our schools and professions seems to discourage personal narrative. Courtney Cazden has observed this in her own experience as a teacher at Harvard (see Cazden and
Hymes, 1978). The word "anectodal" is often pejorative, often preceded
by "merely." Yet it would be a false picture to think of narrative orientation, a folk orientation, as being wholly superceded by a bureaucratic
orientation toward references, numbers, concepts, etc. Ethnography of
any room in which decisions are made would be likely to show a significant role for the telling case, the apt anecdote, the strip of narrative that
makes consideration concrete. Despite the apparatus with which judgment is often surrounded, judgment is often affected by concrete images,
what Burke (1945, pp. 59–61, 323–325) calls "representative anecdotes,"
and narrative is their generic source. Consider further what it means to
become an accepted member of a profession or any other guildlike group.
Commonly it means to share the narrative tradition, what in women we

call "gossip" and in men "shoptalk," the lore of one's mentors and in time, of one's own career. Would someone be accepted as a member of your profession who was ignorant of all such anecdote and took no part in its exchange?

All this suggests that narrative is an essential part of any self-conscious group, and that its acceptability is highly constrained. Social hierarchy may ensure the perpetuation of narrative, yet diminish its quality. An employer can have an audience without winning it by skill, while all around the country community narrative artistry perhaps dies out for lack of audience, its occasions gone, its competition from various media too severe.

I do not know this to be true. The point is simply to illustrate a possibility I do believe to be true, namely, that a universal use of language, a universally present ability, may be differently shaped, not only in terms of pattern, but also in terms of quality. A universal frame of reference, so conceived, can be used critically. It seems to me that it must be so used with regard to a society such as our own. Where and what are the satisfactions possible through uses of language? What factors encourage, what discourage them? What configurations of individual ability and skill are fostered, what frustrated? Where are there abilities that lack occasion? Where occasions to which ability can not or does not rise? It may be ethnographic blinders and bias that leads me to think more readily of Indian people than of whites, when it is a question of people to be remembered for their gifts with language, as memorable voices. Even our intellectual classes continue to stereotype traditional societies as lacking individuality, but those of us who have worked closely with such cultures are often blinded by the blaze of individuality in them. The range of difference in occupation, activity, etc., to be sure, is less. But if by individuality one is willing to mean a strong, rich sense of personal identity, of personal voice, then an Indian reservation often seems richer than the nearby towns. This is a quality of "primitive" life on which Stanley Diamond (1963) has written very well. It seems to depend on conditions hard to come by in our own society.

This sort of comparison is old in social science, going by various names (Gemeinschaft—Gesellschaft; folk–urban; genuine–spurious culture; etc.). It can be easily abused. Nevertheless, it is important to a study of individual differences that includes a study of the conditions for the realization of competence, as something not simply triggered by social environment but intimately shaped by it, and differentially realized along various dimensions. A critical approach to individual differences as matters of competence and social meaning perhaps comes to this: What is the relation between the present distribution and organization of individual competence in our society, and the distribution and organization that we should like to see? And how might one get from the one to the other? In terms of voices: Difference of voice is given naturally, but not realization of voice. One way to think about a society is in terms of the voices it has and might have.[3]

REFERENCES

Bloomfield, L. Secondary and tertiary responses to language. *Language*, 1944, *20*, 45–55.

Boas, F. Introduction to *Handbook of American Indian Languages*, Bulletin of the Bureau of American Ethnology, Vol. 40, Part I, 1911.

Burke, K. *A Grammar of Motives*. New York: Prentice-Hall, 1945.

Cazden, C. and Hymes, D. Narrative thinking and story-telling rights: A folklorist's clue to a critique of education. *Keystone Folklore* Quarterly, 1978, *22:* 21–36.

Chomsky, N. *Aspects of the Theory of Syntax*. Cambridge: M.I.T. Press, 1965.

Chomsky, N. *Syntactic Structures*. The Hague: Mouton, 1957.

Diamond, S. The search for the primitive. In I. Galdston (Ed.), *Man's Image in Medicine and Anthropology*. New York: International Universities Press, 1963. Pp. 62–115.

Gouldner, A. W. The new class project. *Theory and Society*, 1978, *6:* 153–204, 343–390.

Halliday, M. A. *Learning How to Mean: Explorations in the Development of Language*. New York: Elsevier-North Holland, 1977.

Hymes, D. From space to time in tenses in Kiksht. *International Journal of American Linguistics*, 1975, 41, 313–329.

Hymes, D. and Fought, J. American structuralism. In T. A. Sebeok (Ed.), *Current Trends in Linguistics*, Vol. XIII, The Hague: Mouton, 1976.

Hymes, V. The ethnography of linguistic intuitions at Warm Springs. LACUS, 1976, *2.*

Irvine, J. Strategies of status manipulation in the Wolof greeting. In R. Bauman and J. Sherzer (Eds.), *Explorations in the Ethnography of Speaking*. Cambridge University Press, 1974, Pp. 167–191.

Keenan, E. Conversational competence in children. *Journal of Child Language*, 1974, *1*, 163–183.

Keenan, E. The universality of conversational postulates. *Language in Society*, 1976, *5*, 67–80.

Lomax, A. A stylistic analysis of speaking. *Language in Society*, 1977, *6*, 15–47.

Newman, S. and Mather, V. Analysis of spoken language of patients with affective disorders. *American Journal of Psychiatry*, 1938, *94*, 913–942.

Newman, S. Personal symbolism in language patterns. *Psychiatry*, 1939, *2*, 177–182.

Newman, S. Behavior patterns in linguistic structure: A case study. In L. Spier, A. I. Hallowell, and S. S. Newman (Eds.), *Language Culture and Personality*. Menasha, Wisconsin: Banta, 1941. Pp. 94–106.

Newman, S. Cultural and psychological features in English intonation. *Transactions of the New York Academy of Sciences*, 1944, *7*, 45–54.

Roberts, J. M. and Forman, M. L. Riddles: Expressive models of interrogation. In J. Gumperz and D. Hymes (Eds.), *Directions in Sociolinguistics: the Ethnography of Communication*. New York: Holt, Rinehart, and Winston, 1972.

Sapir, E. Representative Music. *The Musical Quarterly*, 1918, *4*, 161–167. [Reprinted in D.

---

[3]I cannot close without having once mentioned "Abnormal types of speech in Nootka" (SWES p. 179–196), the classic precedent for a concern with individual differences, defects, and social stereotypes in speech. So far as I know, there is no study of comparable care and fullness for any community within the United States. Let me also mention "The ethnography of linguistic intuitions at Warm Springs" by Virginia Hymes (1976), in which the social meaning of individual differences is shown to condition linguistic analysis proper.

Mandelbaum (Ed.), *Selected Writings of Edward Sapir*, Berkeley: University of California Press, 1968. Pp. 490–495.]

Sapir, E. *Language*. New York: Harcourt, Brace, and Co., 1921.

Sapir, E. Sound patterns in language. *Language*, 1925, *1*, 37–51. [Reprinted in D. Mandelbaum (Ed.), *Selected Writings of Edward Sapir*, Berkeley: University of California Press, 1968. Pp. 33–45.]

Sapir, E. Speech as a personality trait. *American Journal of Sociology*, 1927, *32*, 892–905. [Reprinted in D. Mandelbaum (Ed.), *Selected Writings of Edward Sapir*, Berkeley: University of California Press, 1968. Pp. 533–543.]

Sapir, E. The unconscious patterning of behavior in society. Originally published in E. S. Drummer (Ed.), *The Unconscious: A Symposium*. New York: Knopf, 1927. Pp. 114–142. [Reprinted in D. Mandelbaum (Ed.), *Selected Writings of Edward Sapir*, Berkeley: University of California Press, 1968. Pp. 544–559.

Sapir, E. Cultural anthropology and psychiatry. *Journal of Abnormal and Social Psychology*, 1932, *27*, 229–242. [Reprinted in Mandelbaum (Ed.), *Selected Writings of Edward Sapir*, Berkeley: University of California Press, 1968. Pp. 509–521.]

Sapir, E. Why cultural anthropology needs the psychiatrist. *Psychiatry*, 1938, *1*, 7–12. [Reprinted in D. Mandelbaum (Ed.), *Selected Writings of Edward Sapir*, Berkeley: University of California Press, 1968. Pp. 569–577.]

Sapir, E. Psychiatric and cultural pitfalls in the business of getting a living. *Mental Health* Publication No. 9, American Association for the Advancement of Science, 1939. [Reprinted in D. Mandelbaum (Ed.), *Selected Writings of Edward Sapir*, Berkeley: University of California Press, 1968. Pp. 578–589.]

Silverstein, M. Dialectal developments in Chinookan tense-aspect systems: An areal-historical analysis. Memoir 29, *International Journal of American Linguistics*, 1974.

Trager, G. Introduction to L. Spier, A. I. Hallowell and S. S. Newman (Eds.), *Language Culture and Personality*. Menasha, Wisconsin: Banta, 1941.

Trager, G. Paralinguistics: A first approximation. *Studies in* Linguistics, 1958, 13, 1–12. [Reprinted in D. Hymes (Ed.), *Language in Culture and Society*. New York: Harper and Row, 1964.]

3

The Treatment of Individual Differences in Psycholinguistic Research

WALLACE E. LAMBERT

Since the turn of this century when psychology broke itself loose, more or less, from philosophy, it has given a good deal of attention to the matter of individual differences, and slowly certain approaches have become standardized. As I see it, psychologists nowadays are uncomfortable with two extreme positions taken on this topic: on the one hand, *universalism,* where the focus is on similarities rather than differences between individuals, and on the other hand, *individualism,* where the focus is on individual uniqueness. They are more comfortable with *subgroups* or clusters of individuals who are believed to form a subgroup of one sort or another making them distinctive and contrastive with reference to some other subgroup or subgroups. I am using universalism here in the philosophical tradition of searching for universal features of behavior common to all humans, what Gordon Allport (1968) called the search for "simple and sovereign theories" of man's human nature. This tradition, exemplified by thinkers like Hobbes, Spencer, Le Dantec and Bentham

47

Individual Differences in Language Ability and
Language Behavior

Copyright © 1979 by Academic Press, Inc.
All rights of reproduction in any form reserved.
ISBN 0-12-255950-9

(see Allport, 1968), is worrisome because it gives too free a reign to logic and persuasiveness and leaves no room for empirical documentation whenever claims are made about the universal nature of behavior. (This logical-persuasive approach to behavioral universals has been severely criticized because of its speculativeness, but it really deserves no more criticism, I feel, than the modern trend in psychology to overemphasize a "hypothetical deductive approach" that draws models from physics and physiology so freely that psychology becomes no more than a type of applied human engineering.) A more important critique, I feel, is the built-in limitation to the value of searching for universals in behavior. Granted that there may be facets of behavior common to all humans, these facets become less interesting than others that might account for the obvious subgroup differences one finds in the real world, differences, for example, in the advantages of life that some people enjoy and others do not or differences in the treatment some people receive in societies that others do not. For the psychologist, then, it is much more interesting to focus on such subgroups of humanity, the "some people" versus "others," and try to figure out what underlies these differences.

At the other extreme, psychologists veer away from individualism in the form professed, for example, by the dedicated clinician who, in his attempts to be as faithful as possible to the unique features of the individual, too often becomes atheoretical or counterproductive with regard to theory development. To explain each exemplar's uniqueness, the individualist must rely either on common sense or on whatever structural models have been passed on to him in his training. He is thereby more prone than most of us—and it is more than just a matter of degree—to find pretty much what he expects to find in his attempts to understand the individual; and he is unlikely to contribute to new theoretical models. Of course, if the clinician were to start searching in a systematic way for recurrences of behavior distinctive to subgroups of exemplars, he would become indistinguishable from the experimentally minded psychologist since then he too would be essentially involved in the study of some recurrent process or another.

There is an apparent inconsistency here because the psychologist's preoccupation with subgroup comparisons is usually based on a belief that the processes to be discovered are themselves *universal*, for example, "achievement need" in McClelland's thinking (McClelland, 1961), or "Machiavellianism" in Christie's (Christie and Geis, 1970). At the same time an experimentally minded researcher might choose to study the development or *change* of some recurrent process, and he might do this by focusing on *an individual* and studying him through time, much as Roger Barker does in his research on human ecology and the processes he refers to as "settings" and "responsible roles" (Barker, 1960). These inconsistencies stem from two uses of the term universal: The processes are believed to be universal, although varying in magnitudes through time and from place to place, at the same time as the behavior of individuals and sub-groups everywhere is believed to vary as a function of each of the processes, much as any biological characteristic varies. As I see it, by addressing himself to subgroup comparisons, the researcher has a means of teasing out and testing the roles played by various recurrent processes, alone and in combination, and also testing each process for its universality.

Incidentally, the psychologist's belief in the universality of psychological processes is shared by many behavioral scientists, I find, linguists included, and this is probably what Chomsky—with his strong belief in the universality of linguistic mechanisms—means when he refers to himself as a psychologist of language. The parallel with linguistics is very close when psychologists study phenomena cross-nationally, for then the "surface" differences from nation to nation in the expression of, say, the perceptual constancies, intelligence, or achievement motivation are assumed to have a common "deep-structure" foundation. But in each national setting there will still be socially significant subgroup differences in intelligence or in need achievement, and theory development requires that these differences be explained, starting within one national setting and then testing cross-nationally. The disciplines differ at the point where linguists become more interested in the structure of language whereas psychologists seem more interested in the processes associated with language, as in systems of social communication, or in the processes associated with perception rather than the structure of perception, per se.

At the start of a program of research, the subgroups compared may simply be clusters of individuals judged to be extreme, for example, "highs" versus "lows," on some loosely defined dimension such as helpfulness, affiliation, Machiavellianism, or smartness in school. The subgroups may also be natural ones like boys versus girls; first-borns versus later-borns; those with middle versus lower social class backgrounds; blacks versus whites; or bilinguals versus monolinguals. Starting with a two-group minimum, the subgroups can, of course, be made more precise and more numerous through subdivisions, but the minimum itself permits the researcher to start exploring for dependable contrasts in behavioral outputs. In this way, some hypothetical construct—that is, the researcher's new idea for a major psychological process which, in turn, leads him to select particular groups to be compared—can be put to the behavioral test, and the search can be started for antecedent events or conditions that are hypothesized to account for the fact that some individuals have more and some less of the hypothesized factor. For instance, David McClelland (1961) started with the hypothetical construct "achievement need," and by comparing subgroups of "high" and "low" need achievers (as judged by observers or as reflected by scores on objective measures), he has been able to describe in a splendid fashion how differences in need achievement affect behavior in various ways (in tests of learning, persistence, preoccupation with standards of excellence, etc.) and how different degrees of achievement need are generated by socializers who place different emphasis on early independence training, on the Protestant ethic, etc. Robert Gardner and I (Gardner and Lambert, 1972) used the same basic paradigm in our attempts to map out the behavioral consequences and the antecedent conditions associated with two forms of motivation—instrumental versus integrative orientations toward foreign people—and the differential effects these orientations can have in the case of learning a foreign language.

To the extent that different degrees of the hypothesized factor do affect behavior, they can be said to "count." The researcher spends a good deal of his time determining the conditions under which his hypothesized construct counts and it is also his responsibility to determine the conditions under which the construct stops counting. There is, in other words, a responsibility on the part of the researcher to set the limits on whatever new construct he proposes and to differentiate its effects from those of other already established constructs. The point is that he is helped in these tasks by making subgroup comparisons.

Often when the hypothesized comparison fails to count, the theoretical consequences of the failure of predicted outcomes can be very instructive. For instance, in a recent study at McGill, Gary Cziko (1975) found, contrary to expectations, that children from "middle" and "working" class backgrounds (that is, children whose fathers were professionals versus those whose fathers were skilled and semiskilled blue collar workers) did *not* differ in I.Q., in scholastic achievement, or in progress made in immersion programs (where a foreign or second language is used as the medium of instruction). These unexpected outcomes force one to qualify and limit the effects social class is thought to have on academic performance and measured intelligence. This example suggests that the usual dampening effects of lower social class may be due mainly to very low social class background factors, but not, apparently, to membership in the solid "working class."

It can also happen that nondifferences between subgroups can count behaviorally, and these cases are especially instructive to the researcher. For example, in a recent set of studies, we selected subgroups of children who were actually alike in terms of measured intelligence and scholastic potential but whose styles of speech differed enough so that teachers placed them into their own subgroups, seeing one cluster—those with less prestigious speech styles—as less intelligent and less gifted scholastically than the other, and assigning grades accordingly (Frender, Brown, and Lambert, 1970; Frender and Lambert, 1972). Since there were *no* such subgroup differences in terms of objective tests of intelligence or academic achievement, this research suggests to us that variations in speaking styles can count a great deal in the judgments teachers (and others) make of children's abilities, often counting more heavily than actual differences in ability (Seligman, Tucker, and Lambert, 1972).

Let me close by illustrating with ongoing research how we are currently using subgroup comparisons in the study of bilingualism. I will simply give short summaries of two current research studies that a group of us at McGill have underway, both having to do with the relation of language function to cerebral activity. The fuller reports are available on request.

The first study, titled "Language processing strategies of bilinguals: A Neurophysiological study" (Genesee *et al.*, 1976) is derived from our earlier research on the distinction between "compound" and "coordinate" forms of bilingualism. In the present study we compared three subgroups: *infant bilinguals* whose bilinguality dated from early infancy; *childhood bilinguals* who became bilingual at about 5 years of age; and *adolescent bilinguals* who became bilingual at secondary school age only. At the time of testing, all subjects were in their early twenties and all were perfectly balanced in their skills with English and French. The experimental procedure was a simple language recognition task in which the subject had merely to press a reaction time button to indicate whether each of a series of words, presented monaurally through earphones, was French or English. At the same time, EEG activity in the left and right hemispheres was monitored, using the latest electronic equipment and the wisdom about these brain matters that one can find in abundance around McGill. Measures were taken of the latencies of EEG reactions—put technically: Averaged Evoked Reactions were measured and latencies to N_1, to P_2, and N_1–N_2 peak to peak amplitudes were calculated. These are commonly accepted indices of the neural activities that accompany the early stages of perceptual processing of incoming information. They are extremely rapid, occurring within 75–100 msec after the presentation of a stimulus, much in advance of the button push which takes 800–1000 msec. Briefly, what we found was that these processing latencies were much faster in the left than in the right hemisphere for the "early" bilinguals (the infant and childhood subgroups), but faster in the right than in the left hemisphere for the adolescent bilinguals. This statistically very clear difference, indicating a left hemisphere preference for early bilinguals and a right hemisphere preference for later bilinguals, held up regardless of the ear of input of the stimulus material and regardless of the language input. It was also true that the adolescent bilinguals were much faster in their neurological processing than were the early bilinguals. We are inclined to interpret these findings in terms of strategy differences: The early bilinguals seem to rely more on (or have a proclivity for) a left hemisphere-based strategy, one that draws on what we believe to be a more semantic or analytic form of processing while the adolescent subgroup seems to have a proclivity for a right hemisphere-based strategy, one relying more on a gestalt-like or melodic form of processing. To explore one implication of this interpretation, we recalled our subjects and presented them with a somewhat more demanding task: to repeat aloud each word as it appeared monaurally through the earphones. We reasoned that this task would require a deeper level of processing, one closer to a semantic analysis, and thus more likely to involve the left hemisphere. If this were true, the early bilinguals should react more rapidly because of their left hemisphere proclivity whereas the adolescent subgroup should be at a disadvantage because the stimulus information would have to be transferred from the favored right hemisphere to the left for final processing. Using a voice key to register reaction times, these expectations were supported: The vocal reaction times were significantly shorter for the early bilingual subgroups. In sum, these findings that seem to relate language learning experiences to cerebral processing styles, fit well with other behavioral distinctions already found between early and late bilinguals. We are ready now to start making finer subgroup differentiations.

The final illustration, very much a pilot study, starts out by examining bilinguals as a group, but then ends up with fascinating subgroups. The paper is titled: "Visual field and cerebral hemisphere preferences of bilinguals" (Hamers and Lambert, 1976) and it addresses itself to the question of whether the bilingual's two languages are both "controlled" by the same cerebral hemisphere. Fifteen balanced French–English bilinguals (all right-handed) were asked to identify words, presented in a mixed series, as being French or English. The words were presented through the left and the right *visual fields,* and reaction times were recorded. We found that 12 of the 15 bilinguals identified the language of verbal material faster when it was presented in the right rather than the left visual field as one would expect because the right visual field is believed to have stronger connections with the left hemisphere, the one supposedly more involved with language processing. Still, 3 subjects identified more rapidly via the left visual field. Thus, 13 subjects supported a "both languages on the same side" principle, but two interesting cases turned up: They demonstrated a greater facility in processing one language on one side of the brain and a greater facility with the other language on the other side of the brain. We have found then one subgroup providing support for Penfield's belief that one hemisphere only (usually the left hemisphere) is dominant for both languages of the bilingual person, but also a fascinating subgroup, albeit small, that goes counter to that belief. Needless to say we will be following both these subgroups in much more detail.

REFERENCES

Allport, G. W. The historical background of modern social psychology. In G. Lindzey and E. Aronson (Eds.), *The handbook of social psychology,* Vol. 1, Reading, Massachusetts: Addison-Wesley, 1968.

Barker, G. R. Ecology and motivation. In M. R. Jones (Ed.), *The Nebraska symposium on motivation.* Lincoln: University of Nebraska Press, 1960.

Christie, R. and Geis, F. L. *Studies in Machiavellianism.* New York: Academic Press, 1970.

Cziko, G. The effects of different French immersion programs on the language and academic skills of children from various socioeconomic backgrounds. Unpublished Master's thesis, McGill University, Psychology Department, 1975.

Frender, R., Brown, B., and Lambert, W. E. The role of speech characteristics in scholastic success. *Canadian Journal of Behavioral Science,* 1970, *2,* 299–306.

Frender, R., and Lambert, W. E. Speech style and scholastic success: The tentative relationships and possible implications for lower social class children. In R. Shuy (Ed.), *Georgetown University Round Table on Languages and Linguistics: Sociolinguistics, current trends and Propects.* Washington, D. C.: Georgetown University Press, 1972, *25,* 237–271.

Gardner, R. C., and Lambert, W. E. *Attitudes and motivation in second-language learning.* Rowley, Massachusetts: Newbury House, 1972.

Genesee, F., Hamers, J., Lambert, W. E., Mononen, L., Seitz, M., and Starck, R. Language processing strategies of bilinguals: A Neurophysiological study. Mimeographed, McGill University, Psychology Department, 1976.

Hamers, J. F., and Lambert, W. E. Visual field and cerebral hemisphere preferences in bilinguals. Mimeographed, McGill University, Psychology Department, 1976.

McClelland, D. C. *The achieving society.* New York: Van Nostrand Reinhold, 1961.

Seligman, C. R., Tucker, G. R., and Lambert, W. E. The effects of speech style and other attributes on teachers' attitudes toward pupils. *Language in Society,* 1972, *1,* 131–142.

II

LANGUAGE USE AND LANGUAGE JUDGMENTS

4

Verbal Fluency and the Language-Bound Effect

RUTH S. DAY

The proverbial person in the street, if asked to describe how individuals differ in "language ability," would probably say something about fluency. Some people talk easily while others say less and/or speak in a slower, more halting fashion. This contrast in general verbal fluency is built into many of our expectations concerning different sorts of individuals. Say that we ask various people a simple question, such as, "How many people work for you?" We might expect a disc jockey to go on and on about how "it depends on what kind of show we're doing, whether 'oldies-but-goodies' or current 'top-forty' tunes, because a lot of our old records are worn out so someone has to go get better copies from collectors, and it also depends on whether we're having guest artists because then someone has to dig up background material (unless I know them and can just ad-lib), and of course if I'm tired then someone has to stand in view and signal me when to do commercials, and then there are those days when. . . ." In

Individual Differences in Language Ability and
Language Behavior

Copyright © 1979 by Academic Press, Inc.
All rights of reproduction in any form reserved.
ISBN 0-12-255950-9

contrast, when a native from the state of Maine is asked how many people work for him, he might say "'bout half" (Starbird, 1977, p. 475).

What kinds of people are highly fluent? Various investigators have argued that fluent individuals are more intelligent or creative than others (see Murphy, 1973, for an evaluation of these positions). However, verbal fluency could reflect, in part, the extent to which a person usually relies on linguistic representations of objects and events rather than other forms of representation.

Recent work suggests that individuals may indeed differ in the extent to which they rely on linguistic structures (Day, 1969, 1977a). Some appear to be language-bound (LB): They perceive and remember events in language terms even when this approach leads them into misperceptions and distorted memories. Others appear to be language-optional (LO): They can use language structures or set them aside, depending on task demands. Classification of individuals as LB or LO is based on a temporal order judgment (TOJ) task involving fusible dichotic items. On a typical trial, an utterance such as BANKET is presented to one ear over earphones while LANKET is presented to the other ear. One of these items begins slightly before the other (by 50–125 msec) and the subject is asked to report "which sound" (phoneme) began first. LBs usually report hearing /b/ first even when /l/ led by a considerable interval; thus they report hearing what their language allows, namely /bl/ in initial position but not /lb/. In contrast, LOs report the correct phoneme no matter which led; they can set aside linguistic rules concerning phoneme sequence and accurately perceive the events as presented. The LB effect is not based primarily on an effort to achieve meaningful percepts (as in BLANKET) since LBs still have difficulty with nonsense items such as BA/LA or GORIGIN/LORIGIN. However they do judge temporal order accurately when fusions can occur in either order (e.g., GAS/GAP can be fused into GASP or GAPS) or when no fusions are possible (e.g., BA/GA cannot be fused into either BGA or GBA). Thus LBs have trouble only when phonological rules of their language are violated by the temporal arrangements of the stimuli.

The LB–LO distinction extends beyond the domain of dichotic listening experiments to a wide variety of perception and memory tasks. For example, the two groups differ in their ability to remember a list of spoken digits (Day, 1973a), translate everyday words into a "secret language" (Day, 1973b), and find words embedded in a matrix of letters (Day, 1974). In each case, LBs appear to rely more heavily on linguistic structures while LOs are not bound by them. The empirical contrasts do not appear to be based on quantitative differences in overall intelligence levels, since the two groups achieve comparable scores on both the Scholastic Aptitude Test and a standard intelligence test (Day, 1977b). Instead, LBs and LOs may process information in qualitatively different ways, perhaps by developing and then relying on different kinds of mental structures or by using existing structures in different ways.

There are several different ways to view the LB–LO distinction. For example, LBs could be "bound" by heavy reliance on schemas in general, rather than just language schemas in particular. Nevertheless, since LBs clearly rely more heavily on language across a variety of cognitive tasks, it makes sense to ask whether they have an advantage in situations that explicitly require heavy use of linguistic skills and which show large individual differences, such as verbal fluency.

The present series of experiments was designed to study the fluency of LBs and LOs. Short of eavesdropping on daily conversations, it can be difficult to assess an individual's general level of fluency. Asking people to "just talk" about a general topic in the laboratory setting can make otherwise fluent individuals turn fairly silent. Therefore, it was useful to reduce task demands by having subjects simply recite items that belong to a given category, such as words that begin with the letter "B" or types of vegetables. Admittedly this approach yields response protocols that are impoverished relative to everyday speaking. Nevertheless it has been used extensively by other investigators (see Horn, 1976, for a recent review) and evidently does tap fluency capabilities. We used this basic technique but extended its generality by varying the level of category constraint, mode of response, and time interval (as described below). The primary measure of interest was the sheer number of items produced during a specified time interval. The way in which subjects produced these words was also of interest, for two individuals could produce the same number of items yet do so in very different ways.

GENERAL METHOD

Since all three experiments used a common set of methods, a general overview is provided here. Additional details are given later as each category is considered.

Subjects

The 144 subjects were students from the introductory cognition course at Yale University who met certain a priori criteria: They were right-handed, had no history of hearing trouble, and spoke English as their native language. Each experiment drew on different editions of the course taught over a 4-year period, thereby permitting replication across different samples of subjects. All subjects were classified as LB or LO on the basis of the criterion TOJ task. In Experiment I there were 16 LBs (11 males, 5 females) and 21 LOs (16 males, 5 females); in Experiment II there were 26 LBs (14 males, 12 females) and 26 LOs (12 males, 14 females); and in Experiment III there were 25 LBs (16 males, 9 females) and 30 LOs (12 males and 18 females).

Category Constraints

Four levels of category constraints were studied which placed increasing demands on the production process. The distribution of these constraint levels across the three experiments is shown in Figure 4.1, along with the actual categories used. At the Word Form level, subjects produced words that began with the letter "B." Since they did not have to consider the syntactic or semantic status of these words, this task made relatively few demands on finding appropriate responses. At the Word Content level, subjects gave items that belong to a particular content category, such as Cities, Flowers, or States of the United States ("USA"). Ordinarily such categories might be viewed as representing semantic constraints. However since some of them could be represented in spatial form as well (e.g., States), both types of constraints were pooled to represent a broad concept of word "content" as opposed to word "form." At the Sentence level, subjects produced responses based on word form, word content, and syntactic factors. They gave four-word sentences in which the first letter of each successive word was always W-C-E-D, as in WASHINGTON CROSSED EVERY DELAWARE and WHEN CAN EDITH DANCE? At the Interpre-

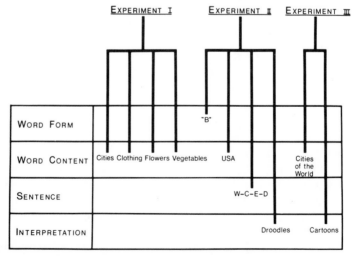

Figure 4.1.   Categories studied in each experiment, based on four levels of constraints.

tation level, subjects looked at drawings and gave verbal interpretations of them. There were two categories at this level. In one, the stimuli were Droodles as shown in Figure 4.2 (see p. 63), which were selected from a study by Bower, Karlin, and Dueck (1975). Although Figure 4.2 gives representative interpretations for the Droodles, a caption was given to the subjects only for the sample item; the remaining eleven test figures were drawn on 5" × 8" cards without captions. In the Cartoon category, subjects provided a caption for a *New Yorker* cartoon (August 23, 1976, p. 25) which depicted a middle-aged, mustachioed man reclining on a terrace balcony, feet over the ledge, while a woman peered at him from behind. The original caption was, "In some deep, ineffable way, Bob, you change when you put on your Earth shoes," but it was removed from the copy shown to the subjects.

Procedure

Subjects were asked to produce as many items as possible for each category, and to do so as rapidly as they could.

Mode of Response

Some individuals are notably taciturn around other people yet are highly fluent when they write. Others show the reverse pattern of fluency. Furthermore, otherwise orally fluent people could become tongue-tied when faced with a tape recorder in the laboratory setting. Since mode of response could interact with the LB–LO distinction, both written and oral modes were used. Subjects in Experiments I and III gave written responses, which enabled us to test 5–6 subjects at the same time. Subjects in Experiment II gave oral responses, so they had to be tested individually; their responses were tape recorded and later transcribed.

Time per Category

Some individuals might be highly fluent even under severe time constraints while others might need more time to achieve high fluency scores. Since such effects could also interact with the LB–LO distinction, a wide range of response intervals was used. For administrative reasons, it was not feasible to use all of these intervals for each category. The cumulative number of responses given by each subject was obtained at more than one interval[1] for most categories: 5 sec, 15 sec, and 1 min for "B" and USA; 30

[1]Cumulative responses for intermediate time intervals were obtained by circling the last item given at the appropriate times. For subjects who used the written mode (Experiments I and III, the experimenter told them when to circle, while for those who used the oral mode (Experiment II), the experimenter timed the taped responses and circled the appropriate item on the corresponding transcript.

sec and 5 min for Cities, Clothing, Vegetables, and Flowers; 1, 2, and 3 min for Cities of the World and the Cartoon; 15 sec for Droodles;[2] and 1 min for W-C-E-D.

Task Order

It was not always possible or useful to counterbalance the order in which the categories were presented to the subjects.[3] Therefore the three experiments did differ somewhat in their task order conventions, but it seems highly unlikely that such differences could have any bearing on the LB–LO distinction.

Presentation of category constraints

Subjects were told to stop giving items at the end of the allotted interval for each category. In Experiment I, they were also told to turn the page for the next category, and the category name was printed at the top of each page. In Experiment II, the experimenter said aloud that the category was "States of the United States" and "words that begin with the letter 'B,' the second letter of the alphabet." For the Sentence constraint, subjects were given a more detailed explanation along with sample sentences for another set of letters: "A-M-E-C" could be ALL MICE EAT CHEESE, ARISTOTE-LIANS MAKE EXCELLENT COMICS, etc. Then they were told to use the letters "W-C-E-D" and were given a reminder card with these letters on it. For Droodles, subjects saw the sample Droodle shown in Figure 4.2 and were given two possible interpretations: THE EARLY BIRD WHO CAUGHT A VERY STRONG WORM and BALLET DANCERS IN A SPOT-LIGHT. They were asked whether they could "see" both interpretations and were told that each figure has several possible interpretations, none of which is "correct." Each card was then held in view for the allotted interval. The Cities category of Experiment I was expanded to Cities of the World in Experiment III in order to increase our capability to determine whether subjects used spatial constraints (e.g., foreign versus domestic

---

[2]Most pilot subjects immediately gave an interpretation or two for each Droodle, but then fell into a glassy-eyed silence. Since they gave few if any responses after 15 sec had elapsed, responses were limited to this interval in the present study.

[3]Since all categories in Experiment I were based on a constraint level that generally elicits many responses (Word Content), the order of categories was counterbalanced across subjects within each group (LB, LO). In order to reduce the chances that subjects would become tongue-tied when giving oral responses in Experiment II, a fixed test order was used for all subjects, beginning with the easiest categories (USA, "B") and followed by the more difficult ones (W-C-E-D, Droodles). Pilot work for Experiment III suggested that subjects were able to produce items for Cities of the World and the Cartoon with roughly comparable ease, so the order of these categories was counterbalanced. However, unlike Experiments I and II, Experiment III was included in the initial session designed to identify subjects as LB or LO; since their status with respect to this distinction was not known at the time of testing, category counterbalancing could not be achieved within the two subject groups.

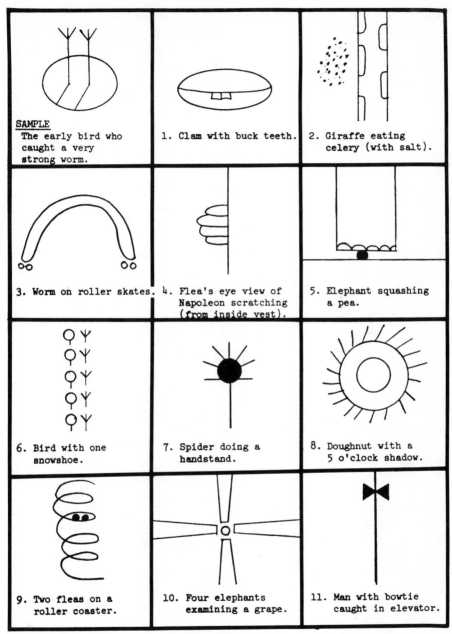

SAMPLE
The early bird who caught a very strong worm.

1. Clam with buck teeth.

2. Giraffe eating celery (with salt).

3. Worm on roller skates.

4. Flea's eye view of Napoleon scratching (from inside vest).

5. Elephant squashing a pea.

6. Bird with one snowshoe.

7. Spider doing a handstand.

8. Doughnut with a 5 o'clock shadow.

9. Two fleas on a roller coaster.

10. Four elephants examining a grape.

11. Man with bowtie caught in elevator.

Figure 4.2. Droodles used in Experiment II. Items #1–11 served as stimuli and were shown without captions.

cities). They were also told to write down only those cities that are "fairly well-known, recognizable to most educated people," since previous subjects listed cities such as AVON, WEATOGUE, FARMINGTON, SIMSBURY, which might well have existed somewhere (in this case, in northwestern Connecticut) or could have been pure fabrications. For the Cartoon each subject was given a copy of the captionless cartoon and was asked to write as many captions as possible.

RESULTS AND DISCUSSION

General Analysis Approach

Three general types of measures were examined. The most straightforward was the sheer quantity of responses produced. A second set of measures was designed to determine the extent to which subjects relied on phonetic, semantic, spatial, syntactic, or commonality principles to generate their responses. A final set was concerned with the quality of responses for those categories that permitted a fair amount of ingenuity, namely, W-C-E-D, Droodles, and the Cartoon.

All sets of measures were evaluated by analyses of variance. Since the groups factor (LB, LO) was of primary interest in this work, detailed statistical information is provided for this distinction in the text; all results that met at least the $p < .05$ level of statistical reliability are reported, along with multiple comparisons that met the same reliability criterion (as evaluated by the Newman-Keuls procedure). Although the sex of the subjects and amount of time elapsed also served as factors in some of the analyses, these factors did not change the interpretation of the LB–LO findings based on the group factor alone; therefore only a brief overview of reliable findings is provided for them at the end of the appropriate sections. The analyses were performed separately for each of the categories since the three experiments used different configurations of time intervals, levels of category constraints, and task orders. Because of these minor differences in method, it was not possible to make certain cross-experiment comparisons in a completely rigorous way. Fortunately none of these was important for the primary concerns of this research.

Response Quantity

The number of items produced in fluency tasks presumably reflects the ease with which people can "think of" verbal exemplars of a given category. A given item was counted only once per subject in analyses of response quantity, even though the person might have given it more than once. Since the few repetitions that did occur yielded an interesting LB–LO distinction, they are also described.

Repetitions

Repetitions occurred on 2% of responses for "B" and 3% for USA, both of which involved the oral response mode. There was no reliable difference between LBs and LOs for "B," but LBs gave more repetitions (4%) than LOs (2%) for USA [$F(1,48) = 4.14, p < .05$]. Since USA readily lends itself to a spatial representation, this finding suggests that LOs may have relied more heavily on a mental map of the United States and "crossed off" each state as they said it, while LBs had a less accurate mental image, less careful spatial bookkeeping practices, or relied almost exclusively on language-oriented methods for naming states. Repetitions did not occur for the remaining categories, all of which used the written response mode.

Unique Responses

The cumulative number of unique responses produced by LBs and LOs for each category is shown in Figure 4.3. Casual inspection of this figure shows a striking lack of differences between the two groups. Statistical analyses confirm this impression since for nine of the ten categories there

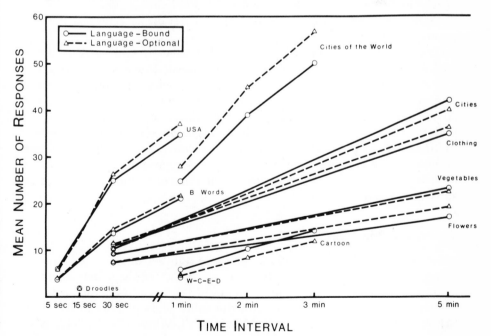

Figure 4.3. Mean number of cumulative responses produced by language-bound and language-optional individuals for all categories and time intervals.

were no reliable group differences. For the remaining category, Cities of the World, LOs produced more items than LBs: 56.8 and 50.0, respectively [$F(1,51) = 6.29; p < .05$]. It is notable that LOs again excelled in another category that readily permits a spatial representation.

Effects of Sex and Elapsed Time

To date about 1000 subjects have taken the criterion TOJ experiment and no reliable sex differences in the LB–LO distinction have been observed. Nevertheless sex was included as a factor in the present analyses because of two well-known facts: women tend to achieve higher scores on verbal fluency tests and men achieve higher scores on spatial ability tests. Analyses of response quantity reflected these facts, since females gave more responses for Clothing, Flowers, and Vegetables, while males gave more responses for one of the categories that readily lends itself to a spatial representation, Cities of the World. Therefore, the relative lack of differences between LBs and LOs in response quantity described above cannot be attributed to statistical "floor" or "ceiling" effects since differences occurred readily for a repartitioning of the same data by sex. Sex differences were important for the LB–LO distinction itself in only one case: LB males gave more repetitions than LO males for USA while the two subsets of females gave comparable amounts.

As the amount of elapsed time increased, subjects achieved reliably higher cumulative response levels for all ten categories. This increase was the typical one of decreasing gains, as illustrated by additional analyses for "B" which showed that subjects gave a mean of 4.1 items during the first 5 sec and 1.3 during the last 5 sec. The elapsed time factor was important for the LB–LO distinction in only one of the categories: the advantage of LOs in producing items for Cities of the World increased with the passage of time. Reliable differences between males and females in four categories (described above) also became greater with the passage of time. Since elapsed time did not alter the presence or direction of LB–LO differences in response quantity, it was not included as a factor in subsequent analyses.

Generating Principles

Two individuals could produce the same number of items for a given category yet do so in very different ways. For example, when asked to name States of the United States, one might rely on a linguistic principle and select items that all begin with the same phoneme, as in MAINE, MASSACHUSETTS, MICHIGAN, MISSISSIPPI, MISSOURI, MONTANA. Someone else might turn to spatial principles and generate states by regional location, as in MAINE, NEW HAMPSHIRE, VERMONT, MASSACHUSETTS, RHODE ISLAND, CONNECTICUT. In order to study how

LBs and LOs generated items in the fluency tasks, we examined five types of generating principles: phonetic, semantic, spatial, syntactic, and commonality.

Phonetic Clusters

For categories at the Word Content level, successive pairs of responses were scored as a phonetic cluster if they shared the same initial phoneme. Thus the sequence PARSNIPS, PEAS, POTATOES, SQUASH, BROCCOLI, BEANS has three phonetic clusters, two based on /p/ and one on /b/. Since the category at the Word Form level already specified that items begin with /b/, successive pairs were scored in terms of the following consonant (if any) and/or the first vowel. A clustering measure was obtained for each subject in each category, computed as (Number of Clusters)/(Total Responses−1). The same measure was later used for other types of clustering, as described below.

If indeed LBs generally rely more heavily on linguistic structures than LOs, then we might expect them to achieve higher phonetic clustering scores. This result did occur, but for only one of the seven cases examined, as shown in Table 4.1. Given a category that readily lends itself to a spatial representation, Cities of the World, LBs turned more readily to a linguistic principle to generate their responses [$F(1,51) = 5.51, p < .05$].

Semantic Clusters

It was often difficult to establish criteria for identifying semantic clusters. For example, responses in the Vegetable category could be generated according to color, whether "leafy" or "rooty," whether usually eaten raw or cooked, or according to a wide variety of other properties. Even within fairly clear-cut distinctions, assignment of particular items was often troublesome; for example, is CABBAGE red or green? In view of these problems, semantic cluster scores were obtained only for selected categories, one each at the Word Form and Word Content levels. For "B" a fairly exhaustive clustering measure was obtained by using all semantic distinctions that could be identified in the protocols. In most cases the items within a semantic subcategory were all from the same syntactic class, as in BABOON, BOBCAT, BADGER and BARK, BITE. Sometimes there was a syntactic shift, as in BISHOP, BERKELEY, or BUBBLE, BURST; however, since such cases involve a semantic link as well, they were included in the tally of semantic clusters. Identification of semantic clusters for Clothing were limited to four subcategories: types (e.g., underwear), function (e.g., belt, suspenders), location on body (e.g., head, torso, hands), and occasions when worn (e.g., at bedtime, to formal affairs, for cold weather).

If the language-binding process occurs at linguistic levels other than

TABLE 4.1

Reliance on Generating Principles for Categories at the Word Form and Word Content Levels[a,b,c]

	Type of Principle			
	Phonetic	Semantic	Spatial	Commonality
Word Form				
"B"	.20 (.17)	.19 (.25)*	—	6.1 (6.9)
Word Content				
Cities	.07 (.08)	—	.25 (.22)	10.3 (10.2)
Clothing	.05 (.07)	.46 (.51)	—	16.3 (15.5)
Flowers	.04 (.03)	—	—	13.1 (12.5)
Vegetables	.08 (.08)	—	—	18.7 (18.7)
USA	.09 (.14)	—	.44 (.47)[d]	39.6 (38.8)*
			.64 (.64)[e]	
Cities of the World	.07 (.05)*	—	.28 (.30)	19.1 (18.9)

* $p < .05$.

[a] Descriptions of the measures used are provided in the text.

[b] Mean values are given separately for LBs and LOs (in parentheses).

[c] Empty cells indicate that the analysis was not appropriate or that the scoring would require too many arbitrary decisions.

[d] Adjacency clusters

[e] Regional clusters

those closely connected to the sound stream (phonetic, phonological), then we might expect LBs to achieve higher semantic clustering scores. However, Table 4.1 shows that there was no reliable difference between the two groups for Clothing, and the opposite result occurred for "B": LOs gave a greater proportion of semantic clusters for this category [$F(1,48) = 4.52, p < .05$]. Thus, although "B" required subjects to focus at least part of their attention at the phonetic level, LOs turned to other means to generate their responses.

Spatial Clusters

Cities and Cities of the World were examined in terms of a single spatial criterion, foreign versus domestic cities. For USA, a stringent adjacency criterion required that successive pairs of states share a common geographical border in order to be counted as a spatial cluster. An additional regional analysis was more lenient in that it only required that pairs be from the same general region (Northeast, South, Midwest and Plains, or West). It did not seem appropriate to look for spatial clusters in the remaining categories, even though some quasi-spatial distinctions could be conjured up for some of them (e.g., Vegetables that are put together in "dishes" such as salads or succotash).

If indeed LOs form and/or use spatial representations more readily than

LBs, then we might expect them to achieve higher spatial clustering scores. However, there was no reliable difference between the two groups in the cases examined, as shown in Table 4.1.

Syntactic Repetition

In W-C-E-D, subjects sometimes used the same syntactic structure for several sentences. For example, one subject preserved the Adjective-Noun-Verb-Noun pattern in this sequence: WHITE CHEESE EXHIBITS DISTASTE, WHITE CARNATIONS EAT DALMATIONS, WIDER COURSE-LOADS EXCLAIM DIRGES, WHOLE CARROTS EXUDE DE-TERMINATION. Since subjects produced far fewer responses in W-C-E-D than in the Word Form and Word Content categories, a cluster analysis was not attempted. Instead, a more lenient syntactic repetition score was obtained for each subject, which was evaluated as the mean number of sentences s/he gave per syntactic pattern.

If the language-binding effect extends to tasks involving simple syntactic processes, then we might expect LBs to achieve higher syntactic repetition scores. However, Table 4.2 shows that LBs and LOs did not differ reliably in this measure. Whether the two groups would differ in more complex tasks involving syntactic competence remains an open question.

TABLE 4.2

Reliance on Generating Principles for Categories at the Sentence and Interpretation Levels[a,b,c]

	Type of Principle[d]	
	Syntactic	Commonality
Sentence		
W-C-E-D	1.45 (1.75)	72.9 (64.1)
Interpretation		
Droodle #1	—	21.3 (20.7)
Droodle #2	—	16.6 (17.2)
Droodle #3	—	8.9 (10.9)
Droodle #4	—	33.9 (35.3)
Droodle #5	—	33.2 (30.2)
Droodle #6	—	26.2 (21.2)
Cartoon	—	0.7 (0.7)

[a] Descriptions of the measures used are provided in the text.

[b] Mean values are given separately for LBs and LOs (in parentheses).

[c] Empty cells indicate that the analyses were not appropriate.

[d] None of the LB–LO contrasts reached the $p < .05$ level of reliability.

Commonality

Within each category, some responses were given by many subjects while others were uncommon. If individual subjects explicitly and persistently searched for highly common items, the number of items they produced would be restricted as the supply of common items became diminished. Alternatively, if they searched for unusual items, they would eventually achieve higher response levels.[4] Since commonality does not involve a partitioning of a category into subsets based on specific organizing principles (e.g., phonetic, semantic, spatial), it represents an alternative way to generate items. In order to study commonality we constructed a hierarchy for each category consisting of the responses given by all subjects and their respective frequencies of occurrence. Then we computed a commonality score for each subject based on the mean frequency of items that he produced for that category.

The commonality analyses netted some LB–LO differences at the Word Form and Word Content levels, as shown in Table 4.1. Although LOs had a somewhat higher commonality for "B," this difference did not meet the conventional level of reliability [$F(1,48) = 2.97, p < .10$]. This marginal finding is mentioned only because LOs also gave more semantic clusters for this same category, as mentioned above. Of the six categories at the Word Content level, only one yielded reliable group differences: LBs had higher commonality scores for USA [$F(1,48) = 5.40, p < .05$]. Again, given a category with an obvious spatial aspect, LBs turned to a nonspatial principle to generate their responses.

For W-C-E-D a slightly different measure of commonality was used. The frequency of occurrence was obtained for all individual words. The commonality index for each sentence was then the sum of those for the words it contained. Sentences varied widely in their commonality indices, as illustrated by these examples: WHITE CATS EAT DOUGHNUTS (123) and WILD STRAWBERRIES EXCEED DOORSTEPS (4). There was no reliable difference between LBs and LOs in their mean sentence commonality scores, as shown in Table 4.2.

Droodles were evaluated in terms of the commonality of the main object seen in each drawing. The complete response hierarchies are given in the Appendix, in order to show the wide range of objects seen and to provide an interesting set of normative data for other potential Droodle inves-

---

[4]Other investigators view unusualness as a by-product of response quantity (e.g., see Wallach, 1976). Here we acknowledge the empirical relationship found elsewhere, but entertain the possibility that an explicit search for items of a given commonality (high or low) can affect eventual levels of response quantity. Since correlations do not indicate causality, it is not clear which manner of speaking is more appropriate. However, for convenience in making contact with the literature on organization and memory, we will talk about the effect of commonality *on* response quantity.

tigators. Since it was a very time-consuming task to construct these hierarchies, only Droodles #1–6 were examined. LBs and LOs did not differ in mean commonality scores for any of the Droodles, as shown in Table 4.2.

Captions for the Cartoon were scored in terms of their general topic, such as "interruptions," "lazy bum," or "hanky-panky." Since the sorting of captions into general topics involved some arbitrary decisions, the dependent measure used was the proportion of sentences that subjects produced based on the dozen most common topics, rather than a mean commonality score. LBs and LOs did not differ in this measure, as shown in Table 4.2.

Sex Differences

Sex differences occurred in only three of the 29 analyses of generating principles. These cases provided an interesting comparison with the response quantity results. For Clothing and Flowers, males had higher commonality scores yet produced fewer responses, while for Cities of the World, females had higher commonality scores and fewer responses. Therefore reliance on commonality was not compatible with achieving high performance levels in these cases. Sex differences had implications for the LB–LO distinction in only one analysis of generating principles: for Droodle #3, LO females relied more heavily on commonality that LB females, but the two subsets of males did not differ in this regard. Sex differences did not affect the findings for LBs and LOs in the other 28 analyses of generating principles.

Overview of Generating Principles

Of the 29 analyses performed to study the extent to which subjects used various generating principles, only three yielded reliable LB–LO differences. While these reliable results (all at $p < .05$) could be chance occurrences, they form an interesting pattern, especially when considered along with the results for response quantity. LBs had trouble with two spatial categories. For Cities of the World they gave fewer responses and also turned more heavily than LOs to a linguistic generating principle (phonetic clustering). For USA, they gave more repetitions and also relied more heavily on another nonspatial generating principle (commonality). LOs, on the other hand, gave more semantic clusters and had marginally higher commonality scores for "B." Therefore perhaps LOs, in some sense, had trouble using the stated phonetic constraint and hence turned to other means to generate their responses. Conceivably, they might have relied on spatial distinctions for this category, but there was no obvious way to identify such clusters in the response protocols.

Relationships Between Generating Principles and
Response Quantity

Reliance on organizing principles usually helps people produce more items. For example, studies involving free recall of word lists generally find a positive correlation between performance (response quantity) and various measures of clustering (e.g., Bousfield, 1953; Tulving, 1962). Subjects in the present fluency experiments involving single words produced items from whatever storage systems they had prior to entering the laboratory rather than from experimenter-given lists. Nevertheless, since both types of experiments involve free recall, it seems reasonable to expect positive performance-clustering correlations in the present data. However the analyses conducted suggest that this relationship can be affected by the status of both the categories and the clustering measures as linguistic or spatial, as well as by the status of subjects as LB or LO. The analyses were confined to three categories that emphasize phonetic, semantic, and spatial factors, respectively: "B," Clothing, and USA. Correlations were obtained for all subjects combined and for subsets of LBs and LOs.

Defining a category in phonetic terms yielded several surprising findings. For "B," the more phonetic clustering subjects used, the fewer items they produced, yielding an unexpected negative correlation ($r = -.34$, p $<.05$). A negative correlation also occurred for semantic clusters in this same category ($r = -.42, p <.01$). One interpretation of these results is that "B" was so constrained at the outset that further constraints introduced by reliance on organizing principles restricted the number of items subjects could produce. However it is not useful to offer this or any interpretation as a general principle, since the same pattern of results did not occur for subsets of LB and LO subjects. The negative correlation for phonetic clusters held only for LOs ($r = -.55$, p $<.01$) while no reliable relationship occurred for LBs ($r = -.06$, p $>.10$). A similar pattern emerged for semantic clusters, since LOs showed a negative correlation ($r = -.51$, p $<.01$) while LBs did not ($r = -.36$, p $>.10$). Given that both groups achieved comparable performance levels for "B," the fact that LOs achieved lower performance levels when they relied on clustering principles suggests that they may indeed have had more difficulty generating items for a category defined in phonetic terms. No matter how we interpret the difference in outcomes for the two groups of subjects for "B," one fact remains clear: If we wanted to know simply whether organization helps performance in a phonetic category, and did not know the status of subjects as LB or LO, then we might well come to different conclusions depending on the relative proportions of the two types of subjects we happened to have in our sample.

The expected positive correlation between performance and clustering did occur for two of the cases studied. Reliance on semantic clustering was associated with high performance scores for the largely semantic Clothing category ($r = .63$, $p <.001$), and for spatial clustering in the potentially spatial USA category ($r = .66$, $p <.001$). Comparable results occurred for subsets of LBs and LOs in these cases. The fact that there was no reliable correlation between phonetic clustering and performance in either category suggests that organization may help only when the type of clustering principle used "matches" the nature of the category in terms of the semantic–spatial distinction. This interpretation is tentative, given that the categories in the present experiments did not lend themselves readily to all three types of representation; since it was not a straightforward matter to identify semantic clusters for USA nor spatial clusters for Clothing, no attempt was made to do so.

High clustering scores suggest that subjects searched for items within systematic partitions of a given category. High commonality scores, on the other hand, do not reflect this same kind of organizing process. Instead, they reflect the extent to which subjects gave items that were at the top of some "cognitive deck," without regard to sophisticated organizing schemes. Since the number of highly common items in a category is limited, then subjects who explicitly and persistently searched for highly common items might achieve lower performance levels. This expectation occurred for Clothing ($= -.78$, $p <.001$) and for USA ($r = -.79$, $p <.001$). Since these two categories yielded positive correlations between performance and their "matched" form of clustering as described above, it appears that clustering and commonality can be incompatible. This notion is supported by the fact that there was a negative correlation between semantic clustering and commonality for Clothing ($r = -.63$, $p <.001$) and between spatial clustering and commonality for USA ($r = -.39$, $p <.01$). While this negative correlation held up for LBs and LOs for Clothing, only LBs showed it for USA ($r = -.53$, $p <.01$) while LOs showed no reliable relationship ($r = -.30$, $p >.10$). Thus LOs were free to use both spatial and commonality principles in USA, while for LBs the use of one principle evidently limited the use of the other. There was no reliable relationship between commonality and phonetic clustering in any of the three categories studied for all subjects combined nor for subsets of LBs and LOs.

Although the present experiments were not explicitly designed to study the relationship between organization and recall, the findings may have implications for general methods used to study this issue. If an investigator is interested in the role of a particular parameter (e.g., list length) in the organization–recall relationship, then it might be useful to take into account whether the type of clustering measure obtained "matches" the categories studied, control for word commonality across lists, and have knowledge of the status of subjects as LB or LO.

Response Quality

Categories at the Sentence and Interpretation levels provided more opportunity for subjects to be innovative. Although response quality is admittedly an elusive entity, some responses clearly seemed to be "better" than others. For example, MOBILE MCDONALD'S ARCH is a more captivating caption for Droodle #3 than is SNAKE. Two general approaches were taken to assess response quality. First, subjective assessments were made by raters who judged the "goodness" of the obtained responses. Then factors that appeared to contribute to these subjective goodness measures were selected and studied in more objective ways. Mean scores for all measures are given in Table 4.3; a description of the specific measures used for each category is given below.

W-C-E-D

Fifteen new students produced a few of their own sentences for W-C-E-D in order to become familiar with the constraints of this task. Then they rated the "overall creativity or inventiveness" of the sentences produced by the original LBs and LOs, using a 5-point scale that ranged from "not creative" (1) to "very creative" (5). They were asked to establish their own criteria for creativity and to apply them in a consistent way.

TABLE 4.3
Response Quality for Categories at the Sentence and Interpretation Levels[a,b,c]

		Objective Measures		
	Subjective Measures	Syntactic Violations	Semantic Violations	Pragmatic Violations
Sentence	Creativity			
W-C-E-D	2.1 (2.2)	.04 (.03)	.17 (.18)	.45 (.30)*
		Perspective		Figure–Ground
Interpretation	Goodness	Commonality		Commonality
Droodle #1	2.7 (3.5)***	—		—
Droodle #2	3.1 (3.3)	40.2 (41.3)		—
Droodle #3	2.3 (2.9)*	—		—
Droodle #4	2.9 (3.1)	—		22.6 (21.9)
Droodle #5	3.0 (3.5)**	—		—
Droodle #6	3.0 (3.4)	—		—
				3rd Person
Cartoon	Humorous	Specific Terms		Perspective
	.12 (.18)	.14 (.30)**		.22 (.14)

* $p < .05$
** $p < .01$
*** $p < .001$
[a] Descriptions of the measures used are provided in the text.
[b] Mean values are given separately for LBs and LOs (in parentheses).
[c] Empty cells indicate that the analyses were not appropriate.

Mean creativity ratings for sample sentences were: WILL CORRUPTION END DYNASTIES? (3.7), WILLIAM CHASES EVERYONE'S DAUGHTER (2.8), and WHY COME EAT DOGS? (1.5). LBs and LOs did not differ in mean creativity scores.

In postsession interviews with the raters, many said that their evaluations were based in part on whether the responses were "good English sentences." Further study of the sentences showed that they sometimes violated normal English in terms of syntactic, semantic, and/or pragmatic conventions. For example, WILL CANDY ENTER DOOR? clearly violates English syntax. WHY CAN'T EVERYTHING DRINK? violates a semantic convention since EVERYTHING implies nonliving as well as living objects and DRINK implies an activity performed by living organisms (usually animals). Of course in more poetic usages most everything could DRINK, as in THE WET BARN DRINKS THE SUN'S RAYS; however, if ordinary semantic agreement rules were violated, the sentence was scored as a semantic violation. Pragmatic problems arose in sentences such as WOMEN CARRY EXCELLENT DOGS. Why do they carry only excellent dogs? What is the difference between excellent and nonexcellent dogs? Why do they carry dogs at all, anyway? Of course one could imagine a fantasy world in which such a sentence "makes sense;"[5] however if unusual circumstances were required to comprehend a sentence, it was scored as a pragmatic violation. Each sentence was scored as acceptable or unacceptable in terms of all three types of conventions, syntactic, semantic, and pragmatic. The proportion of sentences that violated each of these conventions were .04, .18, and .37, respectively, $[F(2,96) = 47.11, p < .001]$.

LBs and LOs gave comparable proportions of syntactic and semantic violations, but LBs made greater use of pragmatic violations $[F(2,96) = 3.38, p < .05]$. There are contrasting ways to view this finding. LBs may have found the task difficult and therefore violated pragmatic conventions out of desperation. Alternatively, they may have violated these conventions deliberately in order to be inventive (at least to themselves, if not to the raters). If so, then perhaps LBs can more readily find interpretations for expressions involving unusual pragmatic usage. While the string, WILD STRAWBERRIES EXCEED DOORSTEPS, simple does not make sense to some people, others readily understand that some strawberries are so wild that they even grow up over obstacles such as doorsteps. Perhaps the ability to understand that WOMEN CAN EAT DIFFERENCES and that WHITE COLORS EXHIBIT DIETING is related to the LB phenomenon. Since the status of the raters as LB or LO was not known, this question cannot be resolved from the present data.

[5]For example, on some far planet, dogs might be rulers and differ in social status ("excellence") according to breed, while among humans women have such high status that they have the honor of carrying the more exalted dogs in stately processions. Admittedly, this scenario is a bit far-fetched but it could exist in some science fiction or fantasy world.

Droodles

Five new students examined the sample Droodle and its caption (Figure 4.2). Then they examined each of the captionless test Droodles and rated the interpretations given by the original LBs and LOs along a 5-point scale from "poor" (1) to "excellent" (5). They were asked to consider whether the caption accounted for all or only part of the figure; whether it did so in an integrated rather than enumerative way; whether it was reasonable, interesting, or amusing; and whether it was in some way abstract rather than a literal description of lines. Since this was a fairly demanding task, the raters evaluated only Droodles #1–6, which involved a total of 563 captions. Mean goodness ratings varied widely across captions, as shown by these examples from Droodle #1: A HAMBURGER THAT SWALLOWED A GOPHER (5.0), TWO SHEETS HANGING ON A LINE AS SEEN THROUGH A PORTHOLE (4.8), and FOOTBALL (1.2).

LOs produced reliably better captions for Droodle #1 [$F(1,48) = 19.84, p <.001$], #3 [$F(1,48) = 4.87, p <.05$], and #5 [$F(1,48) = 7.5, p <.01$]. Thus LOs excelled in a category that involves perception of spatial relations. Additional analyses were performed to determine whether LOs viewed the figures from more perspectives or perceived more figure–ground relationships.

Most of the Droodles yielded descriptions viewed from a single perspective. However Droodle #2 permitted several different perspectives. For example, it was sometimes viewed from the side (as in TREE WITH A SWARM OF INSECTS BY IT) or from above (as in STREET WITH CARS PARKED ALONG IT AND BUSHES ON ONE SIDE). Evidently it takes a certain amount of spatial flexibility to spontaneously view the same drawing from more than one perspective. In order to study this type of spatial flexibility, the responses for Droodle #2 were categorized in terms of the perspective they implied. Perspective commonality scores where then obtained for each subject according to the same methods used for the commonality analyses described above. LBs and LOs did not differ in these scores.

There was little variation in figure–ground relationships in the responses for most Droodles. However Droodle #4 permitted many different configurations depending on the interpretation of its vertical line. For example, the line could establish a large figure on the right with smaller objects protruding from behind it (as in GUY CARRYING PILLOWS; PARROT ESCAPING DOWN THE STREET), a large figure on the left with small objects in front of it (as in A JELLO MOLD THAT SOMEONE THREW AGAINST THE WALL AND IT STUCK), a continuous figure with a seam in the middle (as in PERSON PUTTING HANDS FROM OCEAN LAST TIME AS DROWNING), a thin figure in the middle (FLAGS ON LINE), or, when rotated 90°, a small figure perpendicular to a large one (A

CACTUS ON THE HORIZON). Figure–ground commonality scores were computed, but LBs and LOs did not differ in this measure. Thus the advantage that LOs had in producing good Droodle captions was not based on a greater ability to spontaneously take alternative perspectives or form alternative figure–ground relationships.

Cartoon

Most of the Cartoon captions were quite pedestrian: GORGEOUS DAY; DINNER'S READY; WANT ANOTHER DRINK DEAR? Some were possibly funny: IF I'D MARRIED A TALL MAN WE'D HAVE TO GET A LARGER TERRACE; WHEN HE ASKED ME TO SLIP INTO SOMETHING MORE COMFORTABLE I DIDN'T KNOW HE MEANT A DEEP SLEEP; YOU'LL NEVER BELIEVE IT BUT OUR SON WANTS TO GO TO YALE; IF JERRY BROWN WINS WILL WE HAVE TO GIVE ALL OF THIS UP? A highly experienced viewer of *New Yorker* cartoons carefully studied all 727 captions (without knowing whether LBs or LOs produced them), and then selected those that seemed humorous enough to appear in that magazine. LBs and LOs did not differ reliably in the proportion of humorous captions they produced.

Sometimes the use of very specific terms increased the cleverness of the Cartoon captions. For example, compare CAPTAIN KANGAROO JUST CAME ON—DO YOU WANT IT IN COLOR versus COME IN DEAR, THE TV SHOW IS STARTING; or DOES THAT CLOUD LOOK TO YOU LIKE CARAVAGGIO's *BACCHUS* versus IT LOOKS LIKE RAIN. Each sentence was scored for the presence or absence of specific terms (excluding the man's name which was usually GEORGE or HARRY and items to be fixed which were often LAWNMOWERS or TOILETS). LOs gave a higher proportion of captions with specific terms than LBs [$F(1,51) = 11.51, p < .01$]. Given that the two groups gave a comparable proportion of humorous captions, LBs evidently used other means for being funny. Further study of the captions suggested that they did so by relying more on a general conception of the scene rather than by plugging in some funny words.

Most captions were made from the woman's perspective (STOP OM-ING HAROLD, THE MCFINTONS ARE HERE). A few were from the man's perspective (WILL YOU GO BACK INTO THE HOUSE AND STOP NAGGING ME). Perhaps the most interesting set of captions came from the perspective of a third party (CAPITALIST WARMONGERS IDLE ABOVE THE PROLETARIAT; EXISTENTIAL ENNUI IN THE MODERN CITY). LBs and LOs gave a comparable proportion of their responses from this third-person perspective.

Sex Differences

Males and females differed in only two of the 15 analyses of response quality. For unknown reasons, females had higher perspective commonality scores for one of the Droodles (#2) while males gave a higher proportion of humorous captions for the cartoon. In two of the Droodles (#1 and #5) that yielded reliable LB–LO differences in goodness ratings, LO males had higher goodness scores than LB males but the two subsets of females did not differ from each other. Thus the LB–LO distinction was more important for males than for females in these cases.

Overview of Response Quality

The assessments of response quality yielded some interesting differences between LBs and LOs. The superiority of LOs in giving good captions for the Droodles suggests that they were better able to synthesize spatial relationships among the lines in the drawings. This finding complements those from previous analyses showing that LOs handled other spatial categories with greater ease (i.e., they gave more responses for Cities of the World and had fewer repetitions for USA). Although the two groups did not differ in the rated quality of their responses for W-C-E-D or the Cartoon, other analyses suggested that they may have achieved these scores in different ways. LBs may have relied more heavily on "deeper conceptualizations" for both categories. In W-C-E-D they violated pragmatic conventions more often; the resulting sentences require more conceptualization (e.g., of surrounding circumstances or metaphorical interpretations) in order to comprehend them. In producing Cartoon captions, LBs gave fewer specific terms in order to achieve a comparable level of humorousness as LOs, which suggests that they relied more heavily on an overall conceptualization of the scene rather than on a more "surface" selection of funny terms.

GENERAL DISCUSSION

Basic Findings

Since individuals classified as LB on the basis of the dichotic fusion TOJ experiment rely heavily on language structures in many situations, it might seem reasonable to expect them to produce more responses than LOs in verbal fluency experiments. There was, however, little evidence to support this expectation in the present data. In fact, analyses of response quantity were most notable for their lack of reliable differences between LBs and LOs over a wide range of experimental variables, including level of category constraint, verbal versus written response mode, and duration of response interval. Failure to find LB–LO differences in response quantity was not based on statistical "floor" effects for difficult categories or "ceiling" effects for easy categories since a repartitioning of the same data yielded several reliable differences in terms of the male–female distinction. Whether LBs and LOs have differential fluency in more complex situations, such as connected discourse, remains an open question. It is important that we avoid becoming bound by the "language-bound" term; that is, because the people we call LB show a greater dependence on language in some tasks, it does not follow that they must excel at all tasks involving linguistic competence. Instead, we must take into account the nature of the processing demanded by a given task. Many of the tasks that distinguish LBs and LOs require perception or production of linguistic material that violates ordinary rules of the language. For example, in the criterion TOJ experiment, subjects must perceive a sequence of phonemes that is not permitted in English in order to achieve high accuracy scores. Fluency experiments pose different requirements such as prior knowledge of items that belong to a given category, availability of these items through past usage, and effective retrieval processes for locating the appropriate items in memory.

The only category that did yield a reliable LB–LO difference in response quantity suggested that the status of the categories as primarily linguistic or potentially spatial may be important. The fact that LOs gave more responses for a category that readily lends itself to a spatial representation is consonant with the fact that LOs also tend to achieve higher scores on standard tests of spatial relations. The linguistic–spatial distinction was also important in analyses of generating principles and response quality. In fact, this distinction enables us to construct a fairly comprehensive and cohesive overview of the reliable effects that occurred across the different types of analyses performed.

LBs often had difficulty with categories that readily lend themselves to a spatial representation. For Cities of the World, they produced fewer responses than LOs and turned more readily to a nonspatial method (phonetic clustering) to generate their responses. For USA, LBs were more likely to forget that they had already given a particular item, and again they turned more readily to a nonspatial means (commonality) to produce their responses. When confronted with simple line drawings (Droodles), LBs often gave captions that were of inferior quality.

On the other hand, LBs may have had subtle advantages in some of the more linguistically complex categories. Although both groups produced a comparable proportion of humorous captions for the Cartoon, LBs did so by forming a more general conception of the situation, while LOs relied on a more "surface" technique of inserting specific terms. LBs also violated pragmatic conventions more readily in W-C-E-D, and the resulting sentences require more general conceptualization in order to comprehend them. The possibility that LBs may have formed "deeper" conceptualizations for these more complex and heavily linguistic categories is tentative, since additional studies are needed to test this notion in an explicit way.

Ordinarily, subjects who rely more heavily on organizational principles in free recall situations produce more items. In the present data there were several cases where LBs and LOs produced a comparable number of items, yet one group relied more heavily on generating principles. Therefore it may be that reliance on such principles helped to compensate for a relatively deficient category representation and/or retrieval capability. This view represents a departure from the traditional interpretation of the role of organization in memory (see for example, Crowder, 1976, for a discussion of this issue). Both views suggest that organization helps recall; however, the present view is that organization can bring potentially inferior performance up to an adequate level as well as enable adequate performance to become superior. The present data also suggest that the well-known positive correlation between organization and response quantity can be affected by the linguistic–spatial nature of both the category itself and the clustering measures used, as well as by the status of subjects as LB or LO.

Although the present studies were not originally designed to study the linguistic–spatial distinction, its emergence as an important factor complements the outcomes of other experiments. For example, in a visual word search experiment (Day, 1974), LBs relied more heavily on linguistic representation and LOs on spatial representation. Thus, no matter whether the general format of an experiment emphasized visual representation (as in the word search experiment) or linguistic representation (as in fluency experiments), each group retained a stronger reliance on a particular form of representation. Furthermore, LOs often excel in tests of spatial relations. Since there is considerable evidence that linguistic information is processed primarily in the left cerebral hemisphere of the brain (e.g., Suddert-Kennedy and Shankweiler, 1970), while spatial information is processed primarily in the right hemisphere (e.g., Kimura, 1967), the present data suggest that LBs and LOs may differ in the extent to which they rely on these two types of brain systems. A subsequent paper presents data concerning hemispheric function for LBs and LOs.

Implications for the General Study of Verbal Fluency

The present work holds some possible implications for the general study of verbal fluency. Most fluency studies emphasize response quantity as the dependent measure and perhaps include commonality and the number of semantic categories used as well. It may also be useful to examine internal aspects of response organization since the present data demonstrate that the same number of responses can be produced according to different kinds of organizing principles. Attention might also be paid to the status of the categories as primarily linguistic or potentially spatial; otherwise, results could reflect the extent to which subjects can rely on the form(s) of representation best suited to the given categories, rather than more general fluency capabilities. Furthermore, since there are more LBs than LOs in the general population, then norms for standardized tests involving fluency could favor subjects who usually rely heavily on linguistic representations and penalize those of comparable intellectual ability who work better with other forms of representation.[6] In fact we could probably increase or decrease a given individual's fluency score by giving a heavy dose of categories that do or do not lend themselves to the form of representation the person uses best.

Fluency studies often disagree concerning the number of subfactors that compose a general fluency "ability." Such discrepancies occur even when the studies emanate from the same research group (e.g., see Wallach, 1970). Perhaps the nature of the matchings between subjects and categories studied in these investigations is partly responsible for the different results. For example, if we had comparable proportions of LBs and LOs in our sample, and both linguistic and spatial categories, then we might find something like the verbal and figural subfactors proposed by Murphy (1973). If, however, we had other configurations of subjects and categories, such as mostly LBs and all linguistic categories, then other subfactors might emerge. The subject-category matching problem could also be involved in various correlational disputes, such as the controversy concerning whether fluency reflects intelligence or is independent of it (see Murphy, 1973, for an overview of this issue). In fact, the existence of general patterns of cognition, such as those represented by the LB–LO distinction, could account in part for discrepancies that investigators obtain concerning factors and subfactors across a wide range of psychometric "abilities."

Comprehensiveness of the Present Investigation

Relative to our informal observations of the fluency of people in everyday life, the present work is admittedly narrow: Rarely, if ever, do we make such assessments by having people recite as many words as they can in a brief time interval. While it might be more "ecologically valid" to have subjects just talk freely, such an approach has many inherent methodological difficulties. However, given the considerable amount of work needed to analyze the well-constrained data reported here, an exhaustive study of fluency might prove to be more exhausting than enlightening. Nevertheless, the present work is more comprehensive than most studies

---

[6] As mentioned above, the LB–LO distinction itself does not appear to be based on differences in general intelligence. Evidently LBs and LOs achieve intelligent behavior in different ways.

of fluency in terms of the types of dependent measures, categories, modes of response, and subjects examined.

The present findings have not been related to the large body of fluency research reported in the psychometric literature (see Wallach, 1970 and Horn, 1976 for relevant reviews). In the temporary absence of data from LBs and LOs based on a full array of tests typically used in psychometric investigations, it seems best to defer that discussion to a later time.

Conclusion

LBs and LOs do not appear to possess gross differences in quantitative aspects of verbal fluency. However the two groups of subjects may achieve fluency in different ways, depending on the nature of the constraints imposed by a given category. Various aspects of the present data suggest that LBs have more difficulty with categories that readily lend themselves to a spatial representation, while LOs have more difficulty with those based on phonetic constraints.

ACKNOWLEDGMENTS

This chapter was written while the author was a Fellow at the Center for Advanced Study in the Behavioral Sciences. The writing was supported by the National Institutes of Mental Health (5 T32 MH14581-02), the Office of Naval Research (N00014-77-G-0079, NR 154–378), and the Spencer Foundation, while the research itself was supported by the Office of Naval Research (N00014-75-C-0967, NR 154–378) and the Center for the Study of Education at Yale. A preliminary version of this paper appeared as an ONR Technical Report (May, 1977).

A number of people contributed to this work, including Jane Weissman who transcribed the oral response tapes in Experiment II and provided many preliminary data tabulations, Lynne Alvarez who conducted most of the statistical analyses, Cynthia Joyce who helped in many ways, and Ray Jordon who was always standing by.

APPENDIX A.

Complete Response Hierarchies for the Main Object in Selected Droodles (Listed by Object and Frequencies of Occurrence).

Droodle #1
1. Football 42
2. Mouth 14
3. Clam 13
4. Hamburger 12
5. Vehicle 12
6. Egg . . . . : 9
7. Wash on line 7
8. Creature 3
9. Dish 2
10. Unique responses (N = 10) 1
Total 124
Droodle #2
1. Giraffe 30
2. Street 14
3. Tree 12
4. Snake 9
5. Building 5

Appendix A. *continued*

6. Microscope scene 5	8. Unique responses (N = 19) 1
7. Pole, post 4	Total 88
8. Unique responses (N = 9) 1	Droodle #5
Total 88	1. Elephant 49
Droodle #3	2. Window shade 11
1. Snake, worm 19	3. Curtain (on stage) 10
2. Rainbow 18	4. Something on ball 7
3. Arch......................... 8	5. View through window 6
4. Ribbon....................... 7	6. Seats in movie theater 3
5. Creature 6	7. Trapeze 2
6. Headphones 4	8. Unique responses (N = 7) 1
7. Hotdog 2	Total 95
8. Handle....................... 2	Droodle #6
9. Unique responses (N = 13) 1	1. Trees 38
Total 79	2. Birds 20
Droodle#4	3. Lollipops..................... 15
1. Hand 51	4. (Unidentified) tracks........... 3
2. Bird 5	5. Dancers...................... 2
3. Indian 3	6. Balloons 2
4. Hotdogs 3	7. Flowers 2
5. Cactus 3	8. Peace signs 2
6. Bananas 2	9. Unique responses (N = 3) 1
7. Tombstones 2	Total 87

REFERENCES

Bousfield, W. A. The occurrence of clustering in the recall of randomly arranged associates. *Journal of General Psychology*, 1953, *49*, 229–240.

Bower, G. H., Karlin, M. B., and Dueck, A. Comprehension and memory for pictures. *Memory and Cognition*, 1975, *3*, 216–220.

Crowder, R. G. *Principles of Learning and Memory*. Hillsdale, New Jersey: Erlbaum, 1976.

Day, R. S. Temporal order judgments in speech: Are individuals language-bound or stimulus-bound? Paper presented at the 9th meeting of the Psychonomic Society, St. Louis, November, 1969. (Also in Haskins Laboratories *Status Report*, 1970, SR-21/22, 71–87.)

Day, R. S. Digit-span memory in language-bound and stimulus-bound subjects. *Journal of the Acoustical Society of America*, 1973(a), *54*, 287(A). (Also in Haskins Laboratories *Status Report*, 1973, SR-34, 127–139.)

Day, R. S. On learning "secret languages." Paper presented at the Eastern Psychological Association meeting, Washington, D.C., May, 1973(b). (Also in Haskins Laboratories *Status Report*, 1973, SR-34, 141–150.)

Day, R. S. Differences between language-bound and stimulus-bound subjects in solving word search puzzles. *Journal of the Acoustical Society of America*, 1974, *55*, 412(A).

Day, R. S. Systematic individual differences in information processing. In Research Frontiers section of P. G. Zimbardo and F. L. Ruch, *Psychology and Life*. Glenview, Illinois: Scott, Foresman, 1977a. Pp. 5A–5D.

Day, R. S. Intelligence and the language-bound effect. ONR Technical Report #2 (N00014-75-C-0967, NR 154-378), July, 1977b.

Horn, J. L. Human abilities: A review of research and theory in the early 1970s. *Annual Review of Psychology*, 1976, *36*, 437–485.

Kimura, D. Dual functional asymmetry of brain in visual perception. *Neuropsychologia*, 1967, *4*, 275–285.

Murphy, R. T. *Investigations of a Creativity Dimension*. Princeton, New Jersey: Educational Testing Service, RB-73-12, 1973.

Studdert-Kennedy, M. and Shankweiler, D. P. Hemispheric specialization for speech. *Journal of the Acoustical Society of America*, 1970, *48*, 579–594.

Starbird, E. A way of life called Maine. *National Geographic*, 1977, *151*, 727–757.

Tulving, E. Subjective organization in free recall of "unrelated" words. *Psychological Review*, 1962, *69*, 344–354.

Wallach, M. A. Creativity. In P. H. Mussen (Ed.), *Carmichael's Manual of Child Psychology*, Third edition. New York: Wiley, 1970. Pp. 1211–1272.

Wallach, M. A. Tests tell us little about talent. *American Scientist*, 1976, *64*, 57–63.

5

On Fluency

CHARLES J. FILLMORE

In what follows, I sketch out, from a linguistic point of view, a number of perspectives on individual differences in language ability and language behavior, together with a preliminary formulation of a set of research questions which these perspectives bring to mind.

1. THE GENERATIVIST POSITION

I would like to begin my remarks by saying something about how questions of language variation sometimes get formulated within theoretical linguistics, especially within the generativist school.

Language behavior—accompanied by certain kinds of user judgments concerning the effect, meaning, well-formedness, appropriateness-to-context, etc., of that behavior—comprises the essential source of data for the student of language. Out of the complex of language behavior,

85

Individual Differences in Language Ability and
Language Behavior

Copyright © 1979 by Academic Press, Inc.
All rights of reproduction in any form reserved.
ISBN 0-12-255950-9

the linguist chooses as his main object of study the products of that behavior—that is, the utterances, the texts produced by the speakers. In fact, the creation of the discipline of scientific linguistics began with the invention and elaboration of notations and descriptive frameworks for language products.

As a first approximation, the goal of linguistic analysis, from the generative point of view, can be expressed as that of representing whatever regularities are observable in language products as rules ascribable to the language's speakers. These rules are seen as forming the grammar of the speaker's language; it is through the employment of this grammar that the speaker produces behavior of the kind the analyst observes.

When the linguist's goal is stated in that way—in a way which implies a direct relationship between the properties of the grammar and the nature of the linguistic products—it is one which, in principle, cannot be achieved. It has become necessary, therefore, to propose an important idealization, an idealization by which a speaker's knowledge of the forms and rules of his language is distinguished from his use of that knowledge in the process of speaking. This knowledge is taken by the generativist as something that can be represented as an integrated system comprising rules and a repertory of the forms on which the rules are believed to operate. The study of language use, then, requires consideration of the speaker's memorial access to the rules and forms he is taken as knowing, the processing strategies he follows while producing sentences in accordance with the rules of his grammar, his degree of practice and familiarity with the grammatical rules and the lexical forms in his language, the force of competing demands on his attention, and so on.

The distinction I have just drawn is essentially the distinction Noam Chomsky (e.g., Chomsky, 1965) has made current between competence and performance. The distinction is analogous to, though not identical with, a distinction familiar to workers in the behavioral sciences between ability and behavior. I shall assume that the competence–performance distinction is a familiar one and that the kinds of examples with which the distinction is usually illustrated and motivated need not be repeated here.

The distinction I am referring to, it should be pointed out, can be drawn either when describing a single individual's idiosyncratic linguistic knowledge and behavior, or it can be extended to fit descriptions of grammars and behavior in a whole linguistic community. Application of the distinction to a whole speech community works best, of course, under the assumption that the grammars of the members of that community are identical.

The most common research strategy linguists use in determining or justifying claims about the nature of a speaker's competence, that is, in discovering the details of his grammar, is that of comparing utterance types which are grammatical (being "in" the language), with others which are ungrammatical, and deriving from these observations hypotheses about specific grammatical rules—the rules, namely, which allow the grammatical sentences and disallow the ungrammatical ones. As a way of exemplifying the kind of strategy I have in mind, we might notice that among the speakers of the version of English we are examining, all of them accept as fully grammatical sentences like (1) and (2)

(1)   *Nobody had ever seen it.*
(2)   *Never had anybody seen it.*

while none of them will accept sentences (3) or (4)

(3)   **Anybody had never seen it.*
(4)   **Ever had nobody seen it.*

On the basis of these examples, and a few dozen more pages of analogous evidence, the linguist is likely to decide that the grammar of this language must provide for a distinction between related forms of words such that some of them are "negation-incorporated" (*nobody, never*) and others are "negative-environment-selected" (*anybody, ever*), and that the grammar must be constructed in such a way that for any sentence in the language which has more than one of these words, only the first one in line—only the leftmost one—can be of the "negation-incorporated" type. This could be accomplished by imputing to the grammar a rule of Negation Incorporation which applies, after all decisions about the order of elements in the sentence have been made, to the leftmost of such words in a sentence, and which determines the negation-incorporated form of the word (see Fillmore, 1967; Klima, 1964).

2. LANGUAGE VARIABILITY

This kind of research can, as I suggested, be carried out in the first instance using a single subject. But when we need to convince ourselves that the judgments we are getting from our lone informant are valid ones, we frequently appeal to a community of speakers and look for consensus. As anyone knows who has ever made such inquiry, however, speakers perversely disagree among themselves about what is grammatical in their language; some of the principal sources of suffering and dispute within generative linguistics have been over ways of coming to terms with such realities.

The lack of consensus about the acceptability of given linguistic forms permits a number of interpretations: It could be (a) that the grammarian's interview questions were badly put; (b) that the informants were tired or uncooperative; or (c) that some of the informants are simply insensitive to the realities of their own language, it being important to find informants whose judgment can be trusted. (After all, the theory of language ought not to be dependent on an assumed uniformity of metalinguistic judgments among the speakers of a language.)

A fourth possibility, of course, is (d) that the disagreeing speakers are actually speakers of different languages (different dialects or idiolects, if you prefer), and that the grammars of the languages they speak are demonstrated, precisely on the basis of the observed differences in grammaticality judgments, as being distinct.

In many cases one or more of the first three possibilities will turn out to be correct. Alternative ways of eliciting data from native speakers can often be devised that will reveal structures that were originally not discerned. Informants are more alert at some times than at others; and some informants have greater metalinguistic awareness than others. Often enough, however, it will be the fourth or "different dialect" explanation that is correct. To take an uncontroversial case, whenever we find that speakers of English differ in their pronunciation of a word like *either,* we have no reason whatever to believe that the elicitation instrument was inadequate or that we have here evidence of some kind of "measurement error." The fact is that the word is pronounced in one way in some dialects, in another way in other dialects.

Elicitation procedure defects and dialect differences are sources of observational differences with which linguists are completely familiar, even though it is not always easy to tell the difference between them. There is a third kind of explanation for language behavior differences: Individuals can differ from each other with respect to how well, how successfully, they can manage the language they speak. For initially quite good reasons, this kind of explanation has almost never played a role in linguistic inquiry. Where it is recognized at all, it is generally reserved for explaining the language behavior of the very young, the foreign, or the speech-impaired. Yet I would like to suggest that some respect should be given to the idea that there are levels of linguistic accomplishment, along various dimensions, that distinguish "normal" speakers from each other, and that such differences form a continuum with such clear cases as those of children and the speech-impaired.

The kinds of competence differences which we observe with this third kind of speaker variation—here I am using the word "competence" in its technical sense—are in many cases unlike those which lend themselves to familiar dialect-geographical techniques; second, the "competence–performance" distinction appears to be a confused one, one which cannot be maintained in all areas of language use; and third, the concepts of homogeneity and variation in language can be seen to apply equally as well to competence as to performance.

It is often extremely difficult to acquire fully reliable data on individual variation in language. Fairly precise methods are available for discovering facts about the nature of variation in phonology, but in a number of other areas the problem of getting good data and reaching correct conclusions about them is a serious one. To take a fairly trivial example, consider the effort I once made to find out how people interpret the word *heartburn*. I asked a number of people to tell me what kinds of experiences they associate with the word, and I got strikingly different answers from all of them; pain behind the breastbone, an event in or around the heart, a bubbling in the throat, some kind of event in the stomach, bitter juices flowing out of the esophagus, and so on. The problem in interpreting such data is that of deciding whether the word *heartburn* names different experiences, different health conditions, for these different individuals (in which case we could find the data useful in an argument about the noncomparability of private-experience vocabulary across individuals), or whether the word designates thoroughly comparable experiences for all of the subjects, the differences in their responses having to do with the (mis)information they have on the nature of the bodily event, or their (in)ability to sense what is going on inside them whenever they are suffering this condition. In the one case we have a fact about variability in the meaning of a word; in another case we do not. And it is not obvious how we can find out which of these positions is correct.

The difficulty in the less experimental studies of language variation then is that we cannot easily know what the facts we find are evidence for, and therefore we cannot know what model of explanation for the variation is appropriate. If we add to all this a general confusion regarding the concepts of competence and performance among people who deal professionally with the structure and function of language, the picture comes to look very gloomy indeed.

3. TWO SENSES OF "COMPETENCE"

If in nonexperimental research these notions are sometimes confused, we ought to be able to find clarity in the camp of researchers in psycholinguistics, the people who need to be most careful about such matters. We do not, however, always find such clarity where it is needed most. In a recently published textbook on experimental psycholinguistics there is a single paragraph on the nature of individual differences in language. Just by way of demonstrating how easily the competence notion can get confused, I reproduce that paragraph here. (Numbering of the sentences was added.)

[1] When we compare people's speech, we often find differences in vocabulary, in pronunciation, and in "grammar," as well as differences in style and communica-

tive clarity. [2] Do these differences in linguistic performance reflect differences in linguistic competence? [3] Differences in linguistic competence, that is, a speaker's "knowledge" of the grammatical rules of a language, could come about in two ways. [4] First, people could differ in terms of how well they had acquired the "correct" rules of their language. [5] Second, people could differ with respect to the particular rules their particular languages have. [6] But, as we noted in Chapter 5, we have not yet been able to specify fully the linguistic competence of young children, let alone that of adults. [7] Our best guess, given what we know about language, is that differences among people in their levels of linguistic competence are either trivial or nonexistent. [8] This conclusion applies to differences among people who speak the same language, as well as to differences among people who speak different languages. [9] Hundreds of languages have been studied, yet no one has found a "primitive" language or a language that could be regarded as less complex or less effective than any other. [from Glucksberg, S. and Danks, J., *Experimental Psycholinguistics*, © 1975, Halstead Press, New York, p. 154.]

We have in this paragraph what I see as a serious equivocation with the word "competence," equivocation between its technical sense in linguistics, and its everyday interpretation according to which it is the nominalization of the gradable property "competent (at such and such)." It would seem that because of a slip from one of its senses to the other, the question that gets asked at the beginning of the passage is not the question that gets answered at the end.

We are told in sentence [1] of "differences in vocabulary, in pronunciation and in 'grammar,' as well as in style and communicative clarity," and here we are likely to interpret what is to the left and what is to the right of the phrase "as well as" as references to competence and performance respectively. Then in sentence [2] we are asked to consider whether these differences in performance should be explained as differences in competence. In sentence [3] we are informed that differences in competence can come about in two ways; yet the two sentences that follow tell us rather about two possible senses of the word competence. What we are told in sentence [4] uses competence in the nontechnical way; and what we are told in sentence [5] uses it in the technical way. In sentence [7] we learn that people do not differ from each other in terms of their "levels of linguistic competence" (nontechnical sense). The conclusion that we are apparently led to in sentence [8], though this is never spelled out, must be that differences in behavior are due to differences in linguistic competence (technical sense). The rest of the chapter containing this paragraph discusses areal and social dialects, apparently bearing out my interpretation of the authors' conclusions. But the problem we started out with, as far as I can tell, was a problem of individual differences in both competence and performance.

The point that needs to be made is that some differences between individuals in their linguistic productions are to be explained in terms of differences in their internalized grammars; others must be explained in terms of the strategies individuals prefer to use or the linguistic mechanisms they are most practiced with in their internalized grammars. The study of individual differences in language ability and language behavior, however, does not begin and end with a description of these competence and performance differences. In particular, it may be that certain differences in speakers' linguistic competence might be due to differences in their ability to acquire the community's language (differences which might be biological, social, personal–psychological, random, or whatever), while differences in speakers' language performance might be relatable to differences in memory skills, processing speed, personality factors of many kinds, social skills, experience—in short, almost any of the ways in which human individuals can differ from each other.

An interesting consequence of Chomsky's choice of the English word "competence" for the concept he needed to introduce is that the resulting two senses of the word—the senses on which equivocation and confusion are so easy—are key concepts in the two opposing models for describing and explaining linguistic individual differences. One sense is appropriate in the tradition of differential psychology, with its efforts to describe individual differences according to measurements on various linear-scale abilities, aptitudes or achievements. The other sense is appropriate in the tradition of linguistics, where the effort has been to explain language differences in terms of differences in the grammars which speakers have internalized.

4. THE COMPETENCE–PERFORMANCE DISTINCTION

The first suggestion I wish to make is that both types of individual differences—differences in both types of "competence"—exist and that one of the main tasks of the student of language variation is that of determining which explanatory model is appropriate for which kind of variation data. The second suggestion—certainly not new with me—is that the distinction between competence and performance may not be as important for a larger understanding of language behavior as some scholars have considered it to be. It is a distinction which is most helpful when talking about a world in which language is produced solely for the sake of producing language. In a situation in which language use plays an essential role in a speaker's engagement in a matrix of human actions, however, the distinction seems not to be particularly helpful.

As a way of illustrating this second point, consider the importance of demonstrated knowledge of "formulaic expressions" in ordinary judgments about a speaker's degree of mastery of a language. "Formulaic expressions" are "memorized" rather than "generated" in the sense that they are fixed expressions whose interpretations and functions could not be predicted by somebody who merely knew the grammar and the vocabulary of the language. They are not "memorized" in the way that a poem or a credo is memorized, but rather are learned in close association with the situations in which their use is appropriate (Bolinger, 1976). Thus the ability to know when to use such expressions as:

(5)   *It's my turn.*
(6)   *All in favor say "aye"!*
(7)   *Speak of the devil.*
(8)   *Let me be the first to congratulate you.*
(9)   *Don't tell a soul.*
(10)   *Anybody home?*
(11)   *Plenty more where that came from.*
(12)   *It takes one to know one.*
(13)   *We'll hate each other in the morning.*

involves more than a knowledge of these expressions as such, more than merely having them as part of a repertory of linguistic forms, and it is more than what we usually think of as knowing an expression and its "meaning." Rather, it is knowledge of the appropriateness of each of these expressions to possibly highly specific contextual settings. That being the case, the difference between knowing linguistic forms and knowing when to use them—the difference between "knowing that" and "knowing how," the difference, in short, between competence and performance—becomes a really fine one in this domain of language use. (In order to give these opinions some perspective, I should explain that I believe a very large portion of a person's ability to get along in a language consists in the mastery of formulaic utterances. I shall have more to say about knowledge of formulaic expressions in Section 6.)

5. DIMENSIONS OF FLUENCY

We need to distinguish, then, between HOW people speak their language and HOW WELL people speak their language. In the rest of this paper I would like to consider seriously this second question. Ability to get along in a language involves both production and reception; in choosing language fluency as my subject, I have decided to concentrate on the production end.

The word "fluency" seems to cover a wide range of language abilities, these individually perhaps best described with terms like articulateness, volubility, eloquence, wit, garrulousness, etc. Taking these concepts as hints, but without organizing my discussion around definitions of them, I would like to survey, very informally, a number of the ways in which we judge speakers to be fluent in their language.

One kind of fluency is simply the ability to talk at length with few pauses, the ability to fill time with talk. A person who is fluent in this way does not have to stop many times to think of what to say next or how to phrase it. Some of the best examples of this kind of fluency can be found among the people who make their living as disc jockeys or sports announcers.

A second kind of fluency is the ability to talk in coherent, reasoned, and "semantically dense" sentences. The main ingredient in this kind of ability appears to be a mastery of the semantic and syntactic resources of the language. William Buckley is one example of the kind of speaker I have in mind. Noam Chomsky is another. Such people can say easily and in a compact and careful way what they wish to say; they tend not to fill discourse with lots of semantically empty material.

A third kind of fluency is the ability to have appropriate things to say in a wide range of contexts. A person who is fluent in this sense always says the right thing, is verbally at ease in many different kinds of conversational settings. A person who in not fluent in this way may be quite at home in certain familiar and intimate settings, but becomes tongue-tied in the presence of strangers or whenever confronted with an unexpected crisis of human interaction. A good public example of this kind of fluency might be Barbara Walters.

A fourth kind of fluency is the ability some people have to be creative and imaginative in their language use, to express their ideas in novel ways, to pun, to make up jokes, to attend to the sound independently of the sense, to vary styles, to create and build on metaphors, and so on. The impression you have with this kind of speaker is that he does very rapid preediting of what he says, that he is quickly able to look over a large range of alternative ways of responding to a situation and chooses the one that sounds most sonorous or clever. My memory of the Harvard linguist Joshua Whatmough is that he was like this; Mort Sahl, in a very different way, is another example of what I have in mind.

The maximally gifted wielder of language, then, is somebody who has all of these abilities.

6. SOURCES OF FLUENCY DIFFERENCES

It is obvious from the preceding that many distinct kinds of knowledge and skills enter into the formation of fluency in speech. Let me try in this section to itemize some of these.

First of all there is simply the speaker's knowledge of fixed linguistic forms, represented as the size and character of the speaker's repertory of morphemes, words, idioms, and fixed phrases. When we say that somebody knows lots of such units—lots of words, say—we have in mind not only the phonetic or graphic form of the units, but also their meanings and their contexts of appropriate use.

In this first case the source of fluency differences is seen as a difference in degrees of mastery of listable material. Some people know more words than other people, and can therefore express more easily and more directly the ideas that are associated with those words. Vocabulary size estimators have traditionally been among the major instruments of fluency evaluation in differential psychology.

It should be pointed out that what distinguishes people is not the total size of their vocabularies, but their particular areas of vocabulary elaboration. One person may be very knowledgeable in the vocabulary of the parts and workings of an automobile, and another may know a great deal of terminology for describing and classifying the shapes of printed letters of the alphabet, each knowing nothing of the other's special interests. If vocabulary knowledge is to be represented quantitatively, the measure must be relativized to particular semantic domains.

Some qualifications are necessary when talking about knowledge of vocabulary as a measure of fluency. Sometimes a person acquires a large vocabulary as a kind of compensation for a lack of verbal fluency in other ways. Furthermore, beyond a certain point size of vocabulary loses its advantages. Perhaps fluency in monologue could be enhanced by a speaker's knowing thoroughly and using frequently all of the nonobsolete words in Webster's Third, but not fluency in dialogue. Dialogue cannot really be considered fluent if only one participant understands what is being said.

In addition to linguistic forms on the level of morphemes, words, and idioms, there are various kinds of formulaic expressions—clichés, bromides, proverbs, greetings, leave-taking and other politeness formulas—for which, as was mentioned earlier, what must be learned is simultaneously an expression and the kind of context in which the expression serves a function.

In considering language fluency we can see that the use of speech formulas cuts two ways. On the one hand we regard somebody as nonfluent who relies overmuch on formulaic responses to situations. We take that as meaning that he is unable to respond creatively to small differences or novelties in situations. On the other hand, we regard as capable and fluent the person who has a large repertory of ready-made responses to a wide range of situations. The measure we need, in short, is not merely one of repertorial size: Having lots of formulas is not well described as an ability if the speaker is trapped by them.

Cultures differ a great deal in the life-situations for which formulaic expressions are provided and in which their use is welcomed (Tannen and Öztek, 1977). Contexts in which English-speaking people in the majority culture at any rate, generally feel nonfluent, and feel uncomfortable about their nonfluency, include the funeral. In more traditional societies, in the situation where a visitor comes to say something to the bereaved, there are many expected things to say, and the conversations can be both fluent and comforting to both parties. An anthropologist friend who recently had occasion to observe the language used in an American funeral reports that the most frequently used consoling expression was

(14)   *There's just nothing to say at a time like this.*

That is a most eloquent expression of the need for formulaic language. One of the reasons, in addition to the more obvious one, for our sense of awkwardness and inadequacy at a funeral is, I think, that this is an occasion in which we feel most severely the sense of not being able to say the right thing.

In addition to knowledge of linguistic forms and knowledge of formulaic expressions and their appropriate contexts, the speaker of a language also needs to have control of a number of processes for creating new expressions. Speakers can differ in their knowledge of such processes, in their active mastery of them, and in their habitual use of them.

At one level we have the various processes of word-formation. For obvious reasons, people engaged professionally in intellectual activities are going to be more adept at forming new terms out of the word-forming resources of their language; others, I would guess, are more likely to limit themselves to what they have learned as ready-made words than to create new ones. In the case of English nominal compounds, Gleitman and Gleitman (1970) have shown that there are impressive differences across classes with respect to word-formation, at least in the ability to give "standard" interpretations of novel compounds.

This being so, we can then point out a clear difference between word-formation processes in a language and the generative apparatus for producing sentences. There is no doubt that essentially all speakers of a language are free to produce sentences they have never heard or produced before. Very few people, on seeing two blue rabbits in a fish-bowl, are going to be poorly equipped, linguistically, to express their experience, even though the sentence they would need to create for the task would undoubtedly be completely novel to them. A part of knowing a language, then, is knowing its syntactic devices for combining smaller units into larger structures, for producing novel words and sentences.

There is clearly, at least in the case of world languages like English, a large part of the syntax of a language that is not known and practiced equally by all speakers. This is especially true of syntactic devices that are keyed onto particular lexical items. Some of these are characteristic of particular domains, such as the lawyers' preposition *absent,* the logician's conjunction *such that,* or the *is to . . . as* construction favored by writers of the "Analogies" sections of intelligence tests, as in (15).

(15)   *A is to B as X is to what?*

Others are limited or rare in their use, but are not domain-restricted. For example, a part of knowing the word *respectively* is knowing the kind of "cross-serial dependencies" that must obtain between the two lists that the word indexes, as in (16).

(16)   *A and B did X and Y, respectively.*

Knowing the word *though,* to give another example, involves for some speakers, but presumably not all, a predicate-adjective fronting operation which the word is capable of triggering, as seen in Example (17):

(17)   *Impatient though Harry was to share his secret,*
                            he remained silent.

A great many examples of this kind could be added. It seems clear that speakers will differ with respect to their knowledge of these constructions, their active mastery of them, and, to be sure, their willingness to use them in public.

In any case, we can say that a supremely fluent speaker of English will have quick access to and practiced control of a great many of the language's special syntactic devices, and that he will be able to decide readily when it is appropriate or efficient to use them.

In addition to differences in access to and ability to manipulate these syntactic devices, speakers can be expected to differ in their habitual use of such devices, in their preference-rating of the language's syntactic means. People must surely differ in their tendencies to perform or to avoid multiple embeddings of clauses within clauses, to pronominalize backwards, to accumulate negations in the same clause, and so on.

Much was recently made of the claim that a person's "speech pattern" or favored language style is something that remains strongly constant across situational context. F. Lee Bailey wanted the court to take such a position in the trial of Patricia Hearst. His wish to have the testimony of Margaret Singer (psychologist and "stylometrist") accepted as evidence was so that he could persuade the jury that Miss Hearst's tape of 18 April was composed by Angela Atwood and that therefore its message should not be taken as a statement made by Miss Hearst. Counsellor Bailey's interpretation of Dr. Singer's testimony was that "the defendant was not the author because she was incapable of structuring her phrases that way [Anspacher, 1976, p. 338]." Clearly if the techniques of disputed-author research can be reliably extended to the way ordinary people talk, their results are bound to contribute to our understanding of the nature of individual differences in linguistic ability and behavior.

A part of the ability to speak a language consists in knowledge of the cognitive or semantic "schemata" for which the language has provided linguistic encodings. We know, for example, that the schema for a sea voyage has states which are coded with the expressions *on land* and *at sea,* and that the schema for travel by airplane has states codable with the expressions *on the ground* and *in the air.* Without knowing these larger schemata, we could not know the meanings of these expressions when we hear them. Clearly one source of individual differences in language behavior is the differential knowledge of the cognitive and interactional schemata for which linguistic encodings have been provided. People who do not know the schemata at all will not be able to make sense of any discourse which makes use of them. People who do not know the linguistic forms that are associated with the schemata will not be fluent in talking about them.

Here we are dealing with a very special kind of knowledge. A possible objection to regarding knowledge of schemata in a consideration of verbal fluency is that it represents knowledge about the world more than knowledge about language as such. But that, of course, could also be said of knowledge of vocabulary; and it is standard to allow estimates of vocabulary size serve as measures of fluency. Furthermore, since there are so many cases in which the same vocabulary item is involved in more than one semantic schema, it may be that measures of knowledge of schemata—however these could be obtained—would be a more careful index of verbal facility than measures of vocabulary size.

Another dimension to one's ability to speak a language is knowledge of the various interactional schemata for conversations. Probably, there are only trivial differences between speakers' knowledge of the character or typology of speech acts; but there may be great differences in people's mastery of the principles of indirect communication—the means by which one conveys information by uttering a curse, makes a statement by asking a question, and so on. Some such differences may go back to differences in social environment (families seem to differ a great deal in the kind of language typically used for directives); others, so it would seem from descriptions of schizophrenia, may be pathological.

A still different dimension to one's ability to speak fluently is the knowledge of discourse schemata, one important type of which is the story. The master storytellers of each culture have available to them not just a repertory of tales, but patterns of theme, development, transition, resolution, etc., so that even when telling a new tale spontaneously, the speaker or singer has in mind, in advance, many aspects of the format and structure of a tale that can provide guidance in the storytelling act. Simply put, knowing what kind of thing ought to occur next makes it easier for the storyteller to find something to fill that slot.

Another dimension to language mastery is the knowledge of the appropriateness of particular words, forms, syntactic constructions, etc., to particular kinds of settings. If we find that certain kinds of ceremonial language are used only on certain occasions, only in the presence of certain individuals, or only when certain topics are being treated, we learn to associate with such settings the pronunciations, words, and constructions we observe in them. At one level this kind of knowledge—knowledge of register and style—can be quite automatic and unconscious. At another level, we might become able to gain conscious control of the relationship between language choice and social context—that is, we might acquire a "metalinguistic" awareness of this connection. Having that, we can then use registers and styles in situations for which they are not strictly appropriate, or we can exploit our knowledge of registral and stylistic choices for creating (rather than just passively accepting) social occasions of particular kinds. A speaker with a wide-ranging registral competence is in many ways going to impress us as more fluent than a speaker lacking such competence.

7. RESEARCH POSSIBILITIES

Having assumed that the considerations introduced above are among the ingredients of a person's mastery of his language, or of a person's unique way of using his language, we can define a number of research questions that might lead us to a better understanding of the speaker's use of this remarkable tool. In most cases, I must admit, I do not have any feasible proposals on how the research can be carried out.

First of all, it would be important to devise measures of fluency—different measures for the different kinds of fluency we have been considering—these to be used both for ranking speakers and for ranking discourse samples. I suspect that some of these measures are going to be amenable to familiar testing paradigms, but others may require long and sensitive observations in naturalistic settings. Measures that are easiest to devise and administer may not always reflect the intuitively recognized kinds of fluency we have in mind; perhaps there might be ways of evaluating these measures for their validity by asking judges to rank the speakers, or the texts, intuitively, and to see whether any of our measures succeed in ranking them the same way.

Establishing a type–token ratio for lexical items in a large text might be a kind of measure of semantic density, but surely not a very sensitive one. The portion of completed to incomplete sentences might indicate something of the degree of planning a speaker can manage, but we will surely suffer at realizing the number of arbitrary decisions we would have to make in doing the scoring. (If I begin a sentence by saying *the* three times, does that count as two incomplete sentences? If I leave off saying a sentence before I have finished it—because I know that my addressee is able to finish it—does that count?) The ratio of word count or morpheme count to the performance duration of the text is another possibility that suggests itself, but this time we will suffer at the insensitivity of the measure to the difference between the disfluency of not being able to think of what to say next and the rhetorical decision to pause in order to let something important sink in. The best measure of all will probably be simply the assigned rankings by reliable judges; but it is unfortunately a measure whose ingredients cannot be easily studied; and it is hard to see how it could be made sensitive to the different kinds of fluency I have tried to establish earlier in these pages.

Once we have somehow established a way of measuring degrees of verbal fluency of speakers and of assigning fluency ratings to discourse samples, then we can try to determine, for people in general as well as for specific individuals, which settings and which topics enhance, and which inhibit, fluency in the various senses that I have discussed. One hears of children who are masters of insult, direction-giving, or storytelling in the playground who become almost mute in the examination room during a verbal fluency test interview; and we probably all know adults whose verbal fluency varies enormously depending on whether they are in a small group setting or standing before a large audience.

One possible value of the discovery of such contexts and topics is that they might make it possible to sort out the various kinds of fluency. I suspect that there are contexts in which speakers do best who rely on knowledge of formulaic expressions, and contexts in which speakers do best who have the best control of the creative processes of the language. A second value of such a study is that it might make it possible for us to situate the testing setting among these contexts as a kind of check on the validity of standard fluency testing. A third consequence of such research will be that it can lead us to an understanding of the difference between those enhancing and inhibiting contexts that separate persons from those that separate cultures. We will surely be saying something interesting and important about a culture if we can succeed in distinguishing those areas of life in which its members engage most willingly or least willingly in fluent conversation.

Another possible area of research is the analysis of the relative degrees of planning that underlie different kinds of discourse, and of individual differences in the degree of planning that speakers habitually engage in in their discourse. I believe that syntactic structures and discourse types can be analyzed according to the extent and the nature of the advance planning which their use and performance require, and that the speech patterns of individuals can then be seen to differ according to their use of these structures. (The use of the *respectively* construction would show one kind of planning in discourse; see Keenan, 1977.)

The study of individual differences in language reception will surely include differences relating to relative dependency on imaginal processes. Some subjects, it appears, make greater use of imagery in their sentence comprehension activities than others. On the production side, there may be important differences between people in the ways in which, or in the success with which, they create and sustain images for their listeners. I would guess that there might be a relation between the two traits; that is, I would guess that individuals who rely on imagery a great deal in comprehension would themselves produce discourse in which the creation and transformation of imagery was an important part—that, in other words, visualizers would communicate well with other visualizers.

An area of individual differences that I am currently particularly interested in is differential knowledge of speech formulas. As I said before, I believe that a large part of our ability to get along well in a language is our facility with formulaic expressions. It ought to be possible to test people's knowledge of formulas, their access to formulas in memory, their readiness to think of formulas in given relevant contexts, and so on. It would be possible to study trends in the use of formulas by noting which of them are more familiar to younger people than to older people, and vice versa; and it may be possible to discover something about cerebral function differences in the use of formulaic versus nonformulaic speech.

One individual difference in linguistic ability that is obvious to anybody who has tried to teach grammar, or linguistics, or a foreign language, is the difference in the ability to make accurate metalinguistic observations. Some people find it extremely difficult to make observations about their own language, or to perform linguistic tasks that require them to constrain their language in particular ways. It would be interesting to find out whether such differences have any bearing at all on other kinds of language ability differences.

One thing more that I would be particularly interested in pursuing is what happens when a speaker goes through a "spiel," a highly rehearsed linguistic performance. The subjects of such a study could be Yugoslav singers of tales, street-corner evangelists, tour guides, or stage comedians. One kind of interest would be in the degree of rigidity with which persons go through their acts: some are more likely than others to survive interruptions and deflections gracefully. Of possibly greater interest would be the apprenticeship process: who can learn it, who cannot, what stages the learners go through, what kinds of mistakes they make, and so on.

8. SUMMARY

The two senses of "competence" known to people familiar with recent theorizing on language parallel two approaches to the study of individual differences in language behavior. I choose to take seriously the notion that some people are more capable at their language than others, and I speak of this kind of variation as a variation in degrees of language fluency. It has seemed to me that there are many different ways of being fluent in a language. I have surveyed some of these. I have considered the problem of devising tests for measuring degrees of fluency, and I have introduced into such discussion my suspicion that many of these cannot simply be provided by adopting familiar methods in the psychology of testing. I have proposed a number of research questions whose exploration will depend on the prior discovery and adoption of reliable empirical ways of dealing quantitatively and qualitatively with fluency.

REFERENCES

Anspacher, C. *The Trial of Patty Hearst.* San Francisco: Great Fidelity Press, 1976.

Bolinger, D. Meaning and Memory. *Forum Linguisticum,* 1976, *1*, 1–14.

Chomsky, N. *Aspects of the Theory of Syntax.* Cambridge, Massachusetts: M.I.T. Press, 1965.

Fillmore, C. J. On the syntax of proverbs. *Glossa,* 1967, *1*, 91–125.

Gleitman, L. and Gleitman, H. *Phrase and Paraphrase: Some Innovative Uses of Language.* New York: Norton, 1970.

Glucksberg, S. and Danks, J. H. *Experimental Psycholinguistics.* New York: Halstead Press, 1975.

Keenan, Elinor. Why look at planned and unplanned discourse? In E. O. Keenan and T. Bennett (Eds.), *Southern California Occasional Papers in Linguistics.* University of Southern California, 1977.

Klima, Edward. Negation in English. In Jerry A. Fodor and Jerrold J. Katz (Eds.), *The Structure of Language: Readings in the Philosophy of Language.* Englewood Cliffs, N.J.: Prentice Hall, 1964. Pp. 246–323.

Tannen, D. and Öztek, P. Health to our mouths. Manuscript, 1977.

6

Language Use and Language Judgment

HENRY GLEITMAN
LILA GLEITMAN

During the past two decades, linguists in the tradition of generative grammar have made systematic use of their own "intuitions" as sources of data for understanding language organization. The term *intuition* refers to the basis for judgmental performances, in the terminology of these linguists. The judgments are usually restricted to a few topics: grammaticality, ambiguity, relatedness of sentences in form and meaning, and the like. The theories that are developed within generative grammar are, in the main, explanatory accounts of the structure of these judgments. This methodology is a familiar one in psychological studies, being in essence very little different from, say, judgments of brightness, hue, and saturation that are made in the color-vision laboratory. However, recently there have been a number of attacks on this method for studying language.

Sometimes the objections have come from within the cloisters of the grammarians themselves, and these are usually to the effect that the method lacks generality in one way or another, over the linguistic domain.

103

Individual Differences in Language Ability and Language Behavior

Copyright © 1979 by Academic Press, Inc.
All rights of reproduction in any form reserved.
ISBN 0-12-255950-9

After all, while it is plausible that all normally sighted men see alike and hence the visual judgments of one man are just like those of another, it is plain that all men do not speak alike. Thus some linguists have come face to face with the problem that their own judgmental performances do not accord too well with the judgments of the nonlinguist-in-the-street, even though he putatively speaks the "same" language. In fact, they sometimes even fail to dovetail with judgments from other linguists who are equally imbued with intuitive convictions (Ross, this volume; see also Gleitman and Gleitman, 1970). Another objection to the generality of theories based on intuition-derived judgments comes from the finding that these do not accord closely with data derived from naturalistic observation of speech; this result is sometimes said to show that the data source is biased and cannot be used to study human language *use* (Labov, this volume).

A different kind of attack on the intuitional approach has come mainly from psychologists studying nonjudgmental language tasks. Some objections center on the failure of derivational theories (such as that put forward by Brown and Hanlon, 1970) to organize tightly the naturalistic findings in language learning (Bever, 1970). Others concern the failure of these theories to account for the facts about language computations in real time, (for discussion, see Fodor and Garrett, 1966; Fodor, Bever, and Garrett, 1974).

In some quarters, the reaction to these complications has been to abandon all hope for learning about the mental organization of language by studying the structure of judgments. We have only to dig 30 or 40 years back into the history of language study to find that this scenario has been played out before. Surely the Bloomfieldian revolution was, in part, an attempt to get away from the enigmas of judgments and back to the "real" data of language: utterances said and heard by ordinary people (a group that clearly excludes academic linguists). Left to the social bigot were questions of "right" or "wrong" instances of language behavior. As E. A. Nida put it:

> If any judgments are to be passed upon the acceptability or so called correctness of some usage, these are left to the anthropologist and sociologist for an objective statement of the factors in the society which make certain persons more socially prominent and hence make their speech more acceptable, or to the man on the street, who is thoroughly accustomed to forming judgments upon the basis of his own egocentric attitudes and limited knowledge [Nida, 1949, p. 2].

In effect, many of the empiricists of a few decades ago evidently believed that no nonarbitrary formulation of notions of well-formedness, etc., were to be found, outside dialectology. Leonard Bloomfield more or less shared this view:

> The discrimination of elegant or "correct" speech is a byproduct of certain social conditions. The linguist has to observe it as he observes other linguistic phenomena, [but] this is only one of the problems of linguistics and, since it is not a fundamental one, it can be attacked only after many other things are known [Bloomfield, 1933, p. 22].

These voices from the past are reminiscent of recent comment to the effect that grammars constructed on judgmental bases are not psychologically "real"; are remote byways in the study of language; in short, are obscurantist and restrictive sources for a psychologically relevant study of language.

We do not agree that judgmental performances can be swept aside so easily in the search for an account of human language organization. The mental events that yield judgments are as relevant to the psychology of language, perhaps, as speech events themselves, even though the patterns of these two kinds of psychological response are demonstrably different. In any event, the burden of proof is on anyone who denies the psychological reality of linguistic judgments to explain their orderliness. In our view, the disparities between speech and comprehension on the one hand, and judgments on the other, require study and explication.

Accordingly, we have conducted a number of investigations into the ability of humans to give judgments about language, and compared these findings against individuals' abilities to use language in conversational exchange. Indeed, we too find differences in people's abilities to perform these two kinds of feat, differences that have to do with the ages and capacities of the subjects, and differences that have to do with the structure of the tasks that are put to them. But we do not consider such outcomes to be cause for dismay.

It always turns out that giving language judgments—retrieving and making use of one's intuitions—is relatively hard, compared to talking and understanding. Thus it is not surprising that we find extensive individual and population differences in performance on the harder judgmental tasks, compared to lesser differences in talking and understanding. We believe this is because judgmental performances require a higher order of self-consciousness than do speech performances. To give a language judgment, one must take a prior cognitive process (linguistic performance) as the object of a yet higher-order cognitive process (reflection about language performance or, as we have called it, *metalinguistic* performance) which may have properties of its own.

It is interesting that difficulties in forming judgments differ within the individual subject, depending on the level of language representation he must access for the task given to him. The *lower* the level of the language feature that must be attended to and focused on in any language-like task, the more difficult the task and the more variable the performance; also, the lower the level of the language feature that must be attended to, the later in development a child is able to perform the task. Meanings are easier to access for the sake of making judgments than syntactic forms, and syntax easier than phonology. Stated another way, it is hard to access language information in relatively raw, partly processed forms, and easier to access fully processed language (i.e., the information at the stage of processing when it has been meaningfully interpreted).

We believe these facts about people's performances in laboratory situations are relevant to a number of more interesting facts about their language use in everyday life; for example, their differing responsiveness to language embroidery in certain kinds of poetry and wit; and their differing likelihood of grasping the ideas behind phonographies (i.e., their ability to acquire alphabetic reading).

In the sections to follow, the structure of our findings on these topics is summarized. However, we do not believe we have unraveled, at anything like the required level of specificity, the sources of differential human behavior in the language domains we have looked at. We put forward this summary of interim outcomes for the purpose that they may invite further inquiry in related terms.

1. POPULATION DIFFERENCES IN METALINGUISTIC PERFORMANCE, IN THE PRESENCE OF RELATIVELY INVARIANT LINGUISTIC PERFORMANCE

It is obvious that there are large differences among normal adults, and between adults and children, with respect to the meaningful content of their speech. But differences among adults, and between adults and children, are smaller and more subtle with respect to their syntactic usage and their phonology. Even many retarded individuals and most 4-year-old normals achieve adequate syntactic form in their speech (Lenneberg, 1967) but they are not usually profound in what they say. These facts contrast with those for judgment-giving. At least for certain kinds of materials, we have found striking similarities across adults in the ability to think about and comment on semantic novelty in language, but enormous differences in the ability to think about and comment on surface syntactic novelty. In Section 1.1, we describe such outcomes in the context of paraphrasing tasks. The same principles describe the outcomes of classification tasks and ambiguity-detection tasks performed by younger and older children, described in Section 1.2. Finally, the same principles describe aspects of children's differing success in tasks related to the acquisition of alphabetic reading (Section 1.3).

1.1. Variation in Paraphrasing Skills among Adults

Gleitman and Gleitman (1970) and Geer, Gleitman, and Gleitman (1972) studied the abilities of adults to produce and recognize paraphrases of novel nominal sequences (compound nouns). The stimuli in the experiments generally consisted of sequences of three simple words. Two of the words were fixed nouns such as *bird* and *house*. The third word was another noun (such as *foot*) or a verb or adjective (such as *kill* or *black*); of course some of these words had alternate categorial status (e.g., *kill* can be used nominally). The three-word sequences were taped and presented orally, with either of two stress patterns (132 or 213 stress) that are common for compound nouns. As the words were combined in various orders, this procedure yielded some simple nominal phrases such as *black bird-house* and *black-bird house*, but it also yielded some sequences that are harder to interpret, such as *bird house-black* and *bird-black house*. After suitable instructions, subjects were asked to produce or recognize phrasal paraphrases of these sequences. That is, the subject is being asked to realize that a *black-bird house* is a *house for black-birds* or a *house where birds who are black live*.[1]

The task is, we believe, a relatively natural and transparent one with which to inquire whether people can think about the relatedness among sentences. Everybody has been asked, from time to time, to say something "in his own words." Thus it seems an easy matter, when asked for another phrase meaning the same as *black bird-house*, to respond "That's a bird-house painted black." Surely this is easy enough to do in the context of real conversation. Upon seeing a black bird-house, even for the first time, presumably an adult can say "Look: there's a black bird-house." No normal English-speaking adult would, we presume, say instead "Look! there's a bird-house black!"

[1]A question immediately arises whether subjects can discriminate among the stress patterns of contextless compounds. It is well known that the stress effects are subtle, and are often ignored depending on the context in which the phrase is used (Bolinger and Gerstman, 1957). The question here is what the subject will do if there is no biasing context to guide him: Can he retrieve a meaning for these sequences guided solely by the meanings of the words and the rule-governed clues of stress and serial order? In this series of experiments, a number of precautions were taken so as to make the results interpretable. First, the stimuli were submitted to judges who had to determine the stress patterns, until a completely reliable tape of the stimuli was achieved. Second, subjects' responses were submitted to internal analysis to see whether, in general, they responded to "easy" instances in terms of the stress and order patterns. That is, if the subject responded identically to *black bird-house* and *black-bird house*, he was thrown out of the subject pool, because if he did this it was possible he simply did not understand the instruction in the experiment. Finally, in some versions of the experiment, the subject was asked to repeat the stimulus item after paraphrasing it. If the subject misrepeated the stimulus with any frequency he was removed from the subject pool (or, in one analysis his data were analyzed in terms of this problem, for it may have reflected a relevant memorial difficulty that could account for some of the population differences we found; see Geer, Gleitman, and Gleitman, 1972).

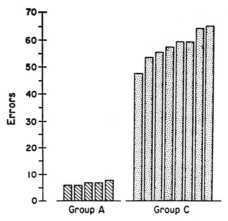

Figure 6.1. Forced-choice performance on a paraphrasing task by Ph.D. candidates (Group A) and clerical workers (Group C).

There were 144 stimulus items. As the Figure shows, the eight clerical workers in this version of the task came close to being wrong on half of them. That is, superficially, the performance of this group seems to be at chance levels. However, internal analyses of these results and those from a variety of other paraphrase tests reveals that both groups of subjects were highly systematic in their response styles, only they were different. Since scoring of "right" or "wrong" was in terms of syntactic, rather than semantic, analysis of the stimuli, the clerical group makes more of what we called "errors," but their performance was orderly nevertheless. Scoring in terms of plausibility or meaningfulness would approximately reverse the number of errors between the groups; that is, the *differences* between the groups in paraphrasing performance would be maintained. [From Gleitman, L. R., and Gleitman, H., *Phrase and paraphrase,* © 1970, W. W. Norton, New York, p. 133.]

Yet we found massive differences between two educational groups (clerical workers and Ph.D. candidates) in the ability to perform a variety of tasks related to paraphrasing compounds of this kind. On many occasions, the clerical workers *would* maintain that *bird-house black* was another way of saying *black bird-house,* contrary to what we believe their speech performance would be like. In fact, on a variety of paraphrasing tasks (even with simpler two-word compounds) there was no overlap at all in performance scores for members of the clerical and Ph.D. candidate groups. Figure 6.1 shows these population effects for a forced-choice task which required subjects to identify the correct paraphrases, from two choices, for three-word compound nouns.[2]

[2]It is of some interest that we could find no simple means to teach the clerical group to perform as the Ph.D. group performed. For instance, clerical workers listened to the stimuli over and over again, with feed-back as to correct choices and a financial reward for each correct choice made. Finally, their performance for a list of 72 stimuli came close to that of the uninstructed Ph.D. group. Then both groups were given a new, but closely equivalent, list of stimulus phrases from which to choose. Now the disparities in performance for the two groups appeared again, and in the same measure. Thus there is no easy way around the fact that these populations differed in their approach to paraphrasing.

A closer look at the findings reveals that the group differences were larger or smaller depending on the particular oddity in the stimulus phrase: The group differences were largely attributable to syntactic, not semantic, problems posed by the novel compound nouns. Thus the two groups paraphrased more or less equivalently such semantic oddities as *house foot-bird* ("a bird with large feet who lives in houses," or "a live-in livery-bird"). On the contrary, only the most educated group handled perceived syntactic oddity by changing the categorial assignments of words (e.g., *bird house-black* was paraphrased by an educated subject as "a blackener of houses who is a bird" and *eat house-bird* as "a house-bird who is very eat"). The response style of the clerical group was quite different. These subjects approached syntactic oddities by ignoring, rather than manipulating, their syntactic properties. *Bird house-black* was typically paraphrased by this group as "a black bird who lives in the house"; *eat house-bird* was paraphrased as "everybody is eating up their pet birds." In short, when taxed, the average group focused on meaning and plausibility, while the highly educated group focused on the syntax even when meaningfulness was thereby obscured (as in the response "a house-bird who is very eat").

Notice that the syntactic oddities in these materials posed greater problems than the semantic oddities for both groups; but also that the between-group differences were much greater for the syntactic oddities than for the semantic oddities. Manipulation and puzzle solving with low-level syntactic features seem to be attributes of linguistically talented people. This difference is apparent even in so far as one can show that the syntactic structures in question are handled adequately, in the context of normal speech and comprehension, by both populations.

Consider as an example Table 6.1 which lists the free paraphrases of both educational groups for the item *house-bird glass*. We can assume that every speaker of English, approximately, knows how to use *glass* both adjectivally (*a glass house*) and nominally (*a piece of glass; a glass to drink from*). Yet the less-educated subjects often interpreted *house-bird glass* as *glass house-bird*, a *house-bird made of glass*, or even as *glass bird-house*. Why not *glass used to make a house-bird* or *the glass used by the house-bird*, solutions which simultaneously resolve the semantic and syntactic properties of the stimulus item? (Notice particularly that there are no clear differences of semantic oddity for the two response types: Anyone who can conceive of and believe in a glass house-bird ought to be able to conceive of and believe in the glass which is used to manufacture such house-birds). But even in a forced-choice situation, when both options were displayed, the clerical group preferred the inversion still. The structure of these findings suggests that only the most-educated group will consider least-common categorial assignments for the component words of the stimuli (i.e., *glass* as noun rather than adjective) in this situation.

TABLE 6.1

Responses of Two Populations to the Task of Paraphrasing the Orally Presented Novel Compound, _house-bird glass_[a,b,c]

Responses of Seven Ph.D. Candidates
1.   glass for making house-birds
2.   a very small drinking cup used by a canary
3.   glass for house-birds
4.   glass for house-birds
5.   *a way of describing thickness of glass—glass as thick as (or in the shape of) glass of a bird-house
6.   glass that protects house-birds
7.   the glass that is produced by birds around the house

Responses of Seven Clerical Workers
1.   *a glass house-bird
2.   *house-bird that's in a glass
3.   a drinking glass or a cup made out of glass of a bird in a house
4.   *a bird that is made of glass
5.   *a special glass to use in a bird's house
6.   *a house-bird made from glass
7.   *a glass house-bird

[a] From Gleitman and Gleitman (1970).

[b] Hyphenation in the cited form represents the internal subcompound (i.e., the stress on this whole compound noun is 132).

[c] An asterisk marks the responses that fail to take into account the fact that the last word in such compounds is the head noun and thus must be the first (leftmost) noun in a paraphrase (a relative clause or prepositional phrase) that mirrors its syntactic and semantic properties. Thus the head noun of this compound is _glass_. For the internal sub-compound (_house-bird_), the same principle should apply: The rightmost noun (_bird_) in the compound is its head, and thus should appear in the leftmost position of a relative clause or prepositional phrase paraphrase of it. One Ph.D. candidate, but six clerical workers, err in applying this principle consistently, for this example. Similar performance disparities were observed for 144 similar stimuli, as well as in simplified (two-word) versions of them, and under a variety of task conditions.

In short, the clearest difference between these populations is in _focusing_ on the syntactic issues, accessing and manipulating language knowledge in a noncommunicative setting. Clearly this does not imply that adults are all equal in their ability to analyze complicated meanings in everyday life. But across a range broad enough to be of considerable psychological interest, all normal individuals can realize consciously that some expressions within their semantic compass (however limited this may be) are meaningless or odd in meaning. Everyone realizes that there is something peculiar about the sentence _George frightened the color green_ and can "fix it up" via some semantic change. But not everyone can focus on a syntactic anomaly and perform an appropriate syntactic manipulation to repair it, even if they are in productive control of the construction during ongoing conversational exchange. In this sense, meaning can be brought to conscious attention more readily than can syntactic form. Apparently, descending to phonological levels, the facts are similar. Jotto, Scrabble, anagrams, and cryptograms—all in part phonological puzzles—require skills that are probably unequally distributed in the population. One might conclude that puns are not the lowest form of humor after all.

The findings just presented seem to fit naturally with many experimental demonstrations that it is easier to remember and report on global semantic properties of heard or seen language than on its lower-level features. For example, Sachs (1967) and Fillenbaum (1966) demonstrated that subjects store the gist of connected discourse over indefinite periods of time but quickly lose hold of its exact syntactic form; Bransford and Franks (1971) in a quite different experimental setting showed essentially the same thing: When matters get complicated or time passes, linguistic stimuli are unavailable for verbatim report but the semantic facts remain. Reason dictates that phonological and syntactic analysis are implicated in the recovery of meaning from speech, but apparently these relatively early or "raw" stages of linguistic processing decay fairly quickly; perhaps this is why they are comparatively unavailable to reflection. Such familiar reading phenomena as the "eye–voice span" (Levin and Kaplan, 1970) and the word-superiority effect (e.g., Baron, in press) are probably subject to similar interpretation (for discussion, see Rozin and Gleitman, 1977).

1.2 Variations in Metalinguistic Performance as a Function of Developmental Level

The difficulty and variability of adult judgments about syntactic and phonological properties of their language are reflected in some aspects of development. Shatz (1972) and Gleitman, Gleitman, and Shipley (1972) asked children to detect and comment about anomalous sentences. The instructions were deliberately vague: "Tell me if these sentences are good or if they are silly." They found that children of 5 years typically were able to recognize and comment on matters of meaning and plausibility of the stimulus sentences. For example *The men wait for the bus* was rejected by some 5-year-old suburbanites on grounds that only children wait for busses. *The color green frightens George* was rejected on grounds that "green can't stand up and go 'Boo!'" But violations of syntax that scarcely affected meaningfulness went unnoticed by these kindergartners (examples are *Claire and Eleanor is a sister; Morning makes the sun to shine*), even though these children did not make such errors in their own spontaneous speech.

On the contrary, 7-year-olds usually accepted semantically odd or implausible sentences as "good" and "not silly." For example, a subject responded to *The color green frightens George* by saying "Doesn't frighten me, but it sounds OK." But these same subjects rejected meaningful but syntactically anomalous sentences. For example, in response to *Claire and Eleanor is a sister*, a 7-year-old commented "You can't use *is* there: Claire and Eleanor *are* sisters." Sometimes these verbally talented 7-year-olds, like the highly educated adults described earlier, manipulated the categorial content of anomalous sentences in considering their acceptability. As an example, in response to *Boy is at the door*, a subject said "If his name is *Boy*. You should—the kid is named *John*, see? *John* is at the door or *A* boy is at the door or *The* boy is at the door or *He's* knocking at the door." Table 6.2 shows how these subjects' judgments accorded with adults' judgments, for all the stimulus sentences in the investigation.

Overall, these findings suggest that the surface structure anomaly is harder for the kindergartner to spot than the meaning anomaly, while the syntactic anomaly becomes more salient to the 7-year-old in response to vague instructions about "good" and "silly" sentences.

We achieved essentially the same result in a task that requires the detection and report of ambiguity. Forty-eight children, ranging from 6 to 11 years, were asked to explicate verbal jokes, presented orally. Ambiguities that turned on word-meaning (e.g., the two interpretations of *bank*) or underlying structure (e.g., *Would you join me in a bowl of soup?*) were easiest for all age groups, and accessible even to the youngest subjects. But phonological deformations and segmentation ambiguities (e.g., *You ate 10 pancakes? How waffle!*) and surface-structure ambiguities (e.g., *Where would you go to see a man eating fish?*) were hardest for all age-groups, and almost uniformly inaccessible to the younger subjects (Hirsh-Pasek, Gleitman, and Gleitman, 1978). Similar findings have been reported by others (Fowles and Glanz, 1977; Kessel, 1970), though some investigators of similar issues (e.g., Shultz and Pilon, 1973) have classified the linguistic stimuli somewhat differently, and consequently interpret the developmental sequence differently also.

Summarizing, differences in the levels of linguistic analysis accessible to reflection at various ages contrast with the facts of speech acquisition: Children learn to *speak* with adequate syntactic form well before they express very complex thoughts, but they come to *notice* oddities of thought (that are within their compass) before oddities of syntax and phonology, even for instances where they have productive control. Many findings in the literature dovetail with our own on this topic. Children of age 5 can be taught the difference between the concepts "word" and "sentence" with little difficulty, but it is hard for them to distinguish among such concepts as "word," "syllable," and "sound" (Downing and Oliver, 1973). Children of ages 5 and 6 have some mild difficulty segmenting speech into words (Holden and MacGinitie, 1972) often failing to isolate connectives and determiners as separate words. They have greater difficulty in segmenting words into syllables (Rosner, 1974; Liberman *et al.*, 1974). And they have

TABLE 6.2

Conformance of Children's Judgments of Grammaticality to Those of Adults[a,b]

		Subjects' ages in years						
Example sentences	Adult judgment	5	5	6	7	7	7	8
1. *John and Mary went home.*	wf	+	+	+	+	+	+	+
2. *John went home and Mary went home.*	wf	+	+	+	+	+	+	+
3. *Two and two are four.*	wf	+	+	+	+	+	+	+
4. *Claire and Eleanor is a sister.*	d	−	−	+	+	+	+	+
5. *My sister plays golf.*	wf	+	+	+	+	+	+	+
6. *Golf plays my sister.*	d	+	+	+	+	+	+	+
7. *Boy is at the door.*	d	+	+	+	+	+	+	+
8. *I saw the queen and you saw one.*	d	−	−	−	−	+	+	+
9. *I saw Mrs. Jones and you saw one.*	d	+	+	+	+	+	+	+
10. *Be good!*	wf	+	+	+	+	+	−	+
11. *Know the answer!*	d	−	−	−	+	−	+	+
12. *I am eating dinner.*	wf	+	−	+	+	+	+	+
13. *I am knowing your sister.*	d	−	−	−	+	+	+	+
14. *I doubt that any snow will fall today.*	wf	+	−	+	+	+	−	+
15. *I think that any snow will fall today.*	d	−	−	+	+	+	+	+
16. *Claire loves Claire.*	wf/d							
17. *I do too.*	wf	+	−	+	−	+	+	+
18. *The color green frightens George.*	wf	−	+	+	−	−	+	−
19. *George frightens the color green.*	d	+	+	+	+	+	+	+
Total "+" judgments for all sentences		12	10	15	15	16	17	17

[a] Adapted from Gleitman, L. R., Gleitman, H., and Shipley, E. The emergence of the child as grammarian, *Cognition*, 1972, *1*(2/3), 137–152.

[b] Children were asked to judge a list of orally presented sentences as "good" or "silly," and these judgments were compared to those of adults. The adult judgments were provided by three independent judges who indicated whether each sentence was well-formed (wf) or deviant (d). The children's judgments are marked "+" if they agree with those of the adult and "−" if they do not, regardless of their explanations. Sentence 16 cannot be scored in this manner; whether or not it is deviant depends upon whether the same referent is assumed for both nouns. The names in Sentences 4 and 9 were chosen to be familiar; in Sentence 16 the child's own name was used.

the greatest difficulty of all in segmenting words or syllables into phonemes (Elkonen, 1973; Rosner and Simon, 1971; Gleitman and Rozin, 1973a). In sum, the lower the level of linguistic representation called for, the more difficult it is for young children to respond to noncommunicative linguistic activities in these terms. We have claimed (Rozin and Gleitman, 1977) that a major cognitive problem in reading can be viewed as a subpart of this more general problem of "metalinguistic" awareness, where large individual differences coexist with identical tacit linguistic knowledge. Some evidence for this claim follows.

1.3 Learning to Read Is Harder Than
Learning to Talk

One of the most striking examples of individual difference in language-like behavior is the acquisition of alphabetic reading. While a few individuals learn to read almost overnight and without instruction (Read, 1971), most require a substantial period of training, and a significant number fail to attain literacy even after years in school. The success and scope of reading acquisition varies as a function of intelligence (Singer, 1974; Thorndike, 1971), motivational and cultural factors (Downing, 1973), and internal differences in the nature of the writing system that is to be acquired (Gleitman and Rozin, 1973a; Rozin and Gleitman, 1977). This individual variation exceeds by orders of magnitude the differences that are observed in the acquisition of speech and comprehension of a first language.

Adequate speech is acquired over broad ranges of general intelligence; for example, spoken language of a character similar to that of normals emerges even among retardates, although progress is slower (Lenneberg, 1967; Lackner, 1976; Morehead and Ingram, 1976). Furthermore, despite many differences in cultural ambiance and differences in the languages that are being learned, normal children seem to pass through similar sequences of developmental accomplishments within the same narrow time-frame (Brown, 1973; Lenneberg, 1967; Slobin, 1973; 1975). Moreover, spoken language seems to emerge more or less equivalently under a variety of input content and presentation conditions; in both character and rate, language learning is remarkably insensitive to differences in the speech styles of caretakers (Newport, Gleitman, and Gleitman, 1977). Successful language-like communicative means are achieved even by children radically deprived of linguistic input (Herodotus, 460 B.C.; Feldman, Goldin-Meadow, and Gleitman, 1978). Finally, the spoken-language skills are resilient in early life, often surviving damage to the speech centers of the brain and to the speech apparatus (Lenneberg, 1967).

Summarizing, there are substantial differences among individuals both in acquisitional rate and in eventual level of attainment for written language, even though formal and specific training is usually available to the learner. In contrast, the similarities in rate and character of spoken language acquisition are striking, even though the conditions for acquisition are here variable and diffuse.

What account can be given for the fact that what appears to be the more general and complex task (learning to speak and understand) is less difficult and less variable than what appears to be a trivial derivative of this (learning to write and read a script based on a known spoken language by a learner who is certainly older and possibly wiser)? Clearly, the difference has only indirectly to do with the visual modality itself.

Manual–visual languages seem to be acquired in much the same way as spoken languages, by deaf children reared by signing parents (Newport and Ashbrook, 1977).

We believe that the major problem in learning to read has to do with the cognitive prerequisites to understanding alphabetic systems in particular: Properties of these orthographies require their users to become aware of and to focus attention on language in relatively raw or superficial representations, approximately at the level where *tap, apt,* and *pat* have the same components, only rearranged. Failure to achieve this fundamental insight about the nature of alphabets characterizes an overwhelming majority of individuals who do not achieve literacy (Firth, 1972; Liberman *et al.*, 1977; Calfee, Lindamood, and Lindamood, 1973). Thus the same approach that characterized our approach to the paraphrasing, ambiguity, and classification tasks seems useful in understanding the task of reading acquisition as well.

The aspiring reader is asked to reflect about language, and so to acquiesce in a number of judgments that make sense of alphabetic notation. The teacher asks him to realize that *pit* and *pat* start with "the same sound," that *pit* starts with what *tip* ends with, and that *pit* is decomposable into "p," "i," and "t." Such units are analyzed for spoken language acquisition without awareness, in terms of an evolutionarily old and highly evolved mental circuitry (for discussion in this evolutionary context, see Rozin, 1976); no conscious awareness or judgments are required. Prior evidence has been given that tasks that require judgments will pose greater difficulty than tasks that do not require judgments. Furthermore, we also have presented evidence that conscious recognition and awareness are especially hard to come by when the focus must be on molecular, rather than more molar, language representations. Taken together, these positions predict that learning to read should be harder and more variable than learning to talk, a fact we have just documented; furthermore, they predict that learning to read a script organized around word-meanings (a logography) should be easier than learning to read a script organized around phonology (a syllabary or alphabet), a claim which we document below (based on Gleitman and Rozin, 1977; Rozin and Gleitman, 1977).

1.3.1 Writing Systems, and the Acquisition of Reading

The natural history of writing reveals a conceptually orderly progression. Orthographic convention proceeds, almost uninterruptedly over time, in a single direction: At every advance, the number of symbols in the script decreases; concurrently, and as a direct consequence, the abstractness of the relations between the written symbols and the meanings increases. Pictographic scripts (which render "whole ideas") appeared earliest and were invented most frequently in separate cultural developments; abstract logographies (which render meaningful words) tend to be later, but still are frequent; syllabic scripts are yet later and rarer; the alphabet (phonemic writing) seems to have been invented but once, and latest (Gelb, 1952; Jefferey, 1961; and for a review see Gleitman and Rozin, 1977).

This succession of historical insights seems noncoincidental to us: The more analytic the unit, the harder it is to bring to conscious attention; and surely the invention of a script has to count as a prime case of self-conscious language manipulation. It was evidently easier to see that language consists of a sequence of words than that it consists of a sequence of sounds. It is of some interest here that many syntactic as well as phonological facts were ignored in the early writing systems: The Aegean logographies and syllabaries did not represent grammatical function words and morphemes very systematically, but only the "meaningful" substantives, verbs, etc. Given that these analytic insights were ultimately achieved, however, it does not seem surprising that each primitive script gave way in time to its more analytic successor. Obviously, if the number of symbols in the script is reduced, learning is broader and the problem of memorization is diminished during the course of attaining full literacy.

However, in the view of Rozin and Gleitman, decreasing the number of symbols in a script came at a cost. If the writing system abstracts away from the meanings it conveys, the decipherer will have to recover the meanings from the now encoded form in which they have been rendered. Learners of an alphabet are required to recognize, quite consciously, the phonological and syntactic substrata of language. On the suppositions sketched above, this ought to produce wide variability in the success of reading acquisition, and success ought to be correlated with the ability to give phonological judgments. There is much evidence in favor of this position.

Eimas et al., (1971) have shown that even 4-week-old infants can and will discriminate phonological properties of speech sounds relevant to language; they can discriminate, for example, between ba and pa. While humans are not the sole possessors of such discrimination skills (Kuhl and Miller, 1975) and although humans can also discriminate categorically among acoustic stimuli not relevant to speech (Cutting and Rosner, 1974), the findings of Eimas et al. clearly speak to the fact that the acoustic discriminative apparatus on which language learning is ultimately based are in place approximately from birth. But a well-known "reading-readiness test" (mis)named the Auditory Discrimination Test (Wepman, 1958) is based on the fact that some kindergartners cannot correctly say "different" or "same" in response to pairs of words that differ in one phonological segment (e.g., pat and bat) or are identical (e.g., pat and pat). From the demonstration of Eimas et al., we know that these 5-year-olds can hear the differences in such stimuli. They can even correctly repeat the stimulus items which they could not judge on the Wepman Test (Blank, 1968). Furthermore, the failing 5-year-olds do have the capacity to give judgments: they can correctly say "same" and "different" in response to written stimuli (e.g., they can discriminate between the visual displays BAT and PAT, and judge them to be "different," even though they cannot read them; Smith, 1974). Evidently the child who fails the Wepman test is very circumscribed in his deficits. His weakness appears only when he is asked to give a *judgment* about the sound properties of linguistic stimuli. Yet the Wepman test is a fairly useful predictor of early reading success, suggesting that the judgment faculty is implicated in learning to read.

In a similar vein, Firth (1972) has shown that groups of third graders matched for IQ, but differing in reading skills according to the estimates of their teachers, perform identically on such semantic tasks as guessing plausible completions of incomplete orally presented sentences; but the ability to provide consensual pronunciations for written nonsense words (such as *nide* or *prit*) appropriately classified these children in 98% of instances. It is of particular importance that the ability to perform word-segmentation and construction tasks continues to distinguish successful from unsuccessful readers all the way through twelfth grade (Calfee, Lindamood, and Lindamood, 1973; Rosner, 1972).

1.3.2. The Conceptual Demands of Orthographies

We have just argued that even at advanced stages and over a broad IQ range, the ability to think about phonology is a trait characteristic of good readers of alphabets. Rozin and Gleitman investigated this issue directly, by attempting to teach failing readers, and children with poor prognosis for reading acquisition, to read scripts of varying kinds. Their approach stemmed from the view that written language, for which there presumably exist no specific evolutionary adaptations, must be learned under the control of self-conscious, metalinguistic apparatus (whatever that may turn out to be). If so, the meaning-based scripts ought to pose less of a learning problem than the sound-based scripts, because of the relative difficulties of making judgments at these levels. Using a variety of notations, they attempted to teach logographies, syllabaries, and alphabets to Philadelphia-area school children.

Even those children with the poorest prognosis for reading success (inner-city children from schools whose reading achievement norms were catastrophically below national norms) acquired logographies with little difficulty. A logographic script taught by Gleitman and Rozin (1973a) was based on pictorial representations; more impressive, a script taught by Rozin, Poritsky, and Sotsky (1971) used Chinese characters with English translations; three examples of their sentences are shown in Figure 6.2. Children who had failed to acquire reading skills in first and second grades learned to recognize 30 characters in this script and read the

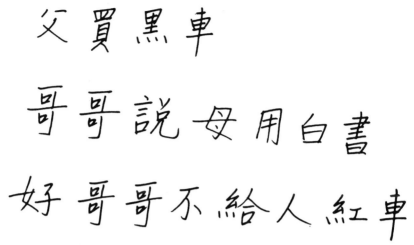

Figure 6.2. A few sentences in modern Chinese, with English interpretations.

Failing learners of an alphabet were taught to read Chinese characters, but with English interpretation. Samples are shown above. Reading across from left to right, these sentences can be translated as: *top*—father buys (a) black car; *middle*—older-brother says mother uses (the) white book; *bottom*—good older-brother (would) not give (the) man (a) red car. Note the approximately one-to-one mapping of English words to unitary Chinese characters (words in the translation that are not directly represented in the Chinese characters are included in parentheses). (From Rozin, P., Poritsky, S., and Sotsky, R., American children with reading problems can easily learn to read English represented by Chinese characters, *Science*, 1971, **171**, 1264–1267, Fig. 2. Copyright 1971 by the American Association for the Advancement of Science.)

materials with fair to adequate comprehension in from 5 to 8 hours of instruction.

The picture-based logography of Gleitman and Rozin was next expanded into a syllabary. See Figure 6.3 for samples of this script. Each item in the script represented a single syllable. Some of these were based on the logography; for example, an element such as *can* now represented the noun *can*, the auxiliary *can*, and the first syllable in *candy*. Some syllables had no word basis, such as the *dy* syllable which appears in *candy*. The children were taught both the syllabic elements and a convention for combining them. After 5–7 hours of instruction with 22 syllables and 16 polysyllabic words containing these, 5 inner-city kindergartners were able to identify *new* polysyllabic words (that they had not been taught, but which were in their oral vocabularies) in the syllabic notation (Gleitman and Rozin, 1973a).

A much more extensive syllabic script was acquired during the first year of schooling by inner-city 6-year-olds taught in a normal classroom setting by their own teachers. Figure 6.4 shows a page from an intermediate-level reader used in this project. Adequate fluency was achieved in this notation; but during this same time, neither these children nor a matched

Figure 6.3.   Samples of writing from a syllabary script used by Gleitman and Rozin for initial reading instruction.

Pictorial clues were used, as shown above, to help the children identify the syllable units. Boxes, lines, or dots were used to supply syllable segment boundaries. In some versions of this curriculum, boundary and picture clues were dropped out later in the instruction period. After 5–7 hours of instruction with 22 syllables and 16 polysyllabic words containing these, 5 inner-city kindergartners were able adequately to identify *new* polysyllabic words (that they had not been taught, but were in their oral vocabularies) in the syllabic notations. [From Gleitman, L., and Rozin, P., Teaching reading by use of a syllabary, *Reading Research Quarterly*, 1973, 8(No. 4), p. 471, Fig. 4.]

group of control children, learning to read by traditional means, adequately acquired the phonemic concepts of an alphabet (Rozin and Gleitman, 1977).

Summarizing, the logography was easier to acquire than the syllabary, which is based on the phonological properties of words. But the syllabary is a gross, molar representation of phonology. It was easier to acquire than the more analytic phonemic (alphabetic) script. Thus the population with poor reading prognosis differed from successful readers most in acquiring the phonemic concepts of an alphabet, and least in acquiring the ideas behind a logography: Phonology, not meaning, is at the crux of the early reading problem. The essential difficulty for poor readers seems to be in accessing their own phonological machinery. They have the requisite phonological organization in their heads; their problem is how to get to it.

Our supposition, then, is that unsuccessful beginning readers are generally characterizable as those who fail to acquire the alphabetic insight and thus read logographically. It is striking that failing readers are not people who literally can read nothing. They can read many hundreds of words but (as this is often put) they stop learning at about the "fourth grade level" of reading achievement. This level involves reading with

Figure 6.4. A page from an intermediate-level reader in the syllabary curriculum for reading acquisition.

This kind of writing was used by classroom teachers as a preliminary instructional device, in a number of Philadelphia-area kindergartens and first grades. Adequate fluency was achieved with this notation in from one to nine months, depending on the population of learners. About 70 syllabic elements are used in this version of the *Syllabary* reading curriculum. In the example here, some pictorial clues have been dropped out of the notation: the word *sand* was initially introduced with a pictorial hint (a sand bucket), but by this point in instruction is recognized from the letter array alone. From Rozin, P. and Gleitman, L. R. The structure and acquisition of reading II: The reading process and the acquisition of the alphabetic principle. In A. S. Reber and D. Scarborough (Eds.), *Toward a psychology of reading.* © 1977, L. Erlbaum Associates, Fig. 6, p. 120.] Hillsdale, N.J.

comprehension a couple of thousand (at most) simple words, in context. It is of some interest that normal readers of logographic scripts (Chinese readers) acquire a recognition vocabulary of only a few thousand items (Leong, 1973), this number apparently representing a limit on rote acquisition of arbitrary visual displays. Similarly, most deaf readers of English script (who are clearly denied the phonological route to reading acquisition) learn to read very slowly and generally do not attain as high a level of skill as hearing individuals (Furth, 1966; Gibson, Shurcliff, and Yonas, 1970). Gleitman and Rozin concluded that the failing American reader has learned a logography, not an alphabet.

2. ARE THE METALINGUISTIC FUNCTIONS
RELATED TO LANGUAGE USE AND LEARNING?

We have speculated elsewhere (Gleitman, Gleitman, and Shipley, 1972) that the metalinguistic function may be a single example of a more general metacognitive organization in humans. That is, a variety of cognitive processes seem themselves to be the objects of higher-order cognitive processes in the same domain—as if the homunculus perceived the operation of a lower-order system. Examples of metacognition in memory would be recollection (when we know that we remember) and intentional learning (when we know we must store the material for longer retrieval). On this view, there need be no formal resemblance between metacognition and the cognitive processes it sometimes guides and organizes. Rather, one might expect to find resemblances among the higher-order processes themselves, a general executive function which may take on aspects of what is sometimes called "the self." Thus language-judgment functions, in particular, could be orthogonal to language functions. One need have no disposition to think about language in order to use it appropriately.

The recent literature in psycholinguistics largely supports this interpretation. A wide variety of experiments effectively demonstrate that the structural relationships among sentences described in generative grammars (derived from the data of *judgments*) are not the same relationships required to describe language information-handling in real time (for which the data are *speech* and *comprehension* measures; for discussion see Bever, 1970; Fodor, Bever, and Garrett, 1974). As we mentioned in introductory comments, some have concluded from such facts that grammatical descriptions lack psychological reality. But it seems more realistic to conclude only that their relevance is not to speech and comprehension directly. Rather, grammars reflect the judgmental ("metalinguistic") aspects of language knowledge more directly than they do knowledge of language itself. Whatever resemblance exists between language processing strategies and grammars may derive from the fact that the human builds his grammar out of his observation of regularities in his own speech and comprehension. Whatever differences exist between these organizations may derive from the fact that the "executive" thinking capacities have properties of their own, which enter into the form of the grammars they construct.

Although we have argued that the metafunctions, if they exist, need not enter into the deployment of the cognitive processes they subserve, sometimes they may. Though one often remembers without awareness that one is remembering, more self-conscious activities are possible, and seem to be implicated in the structure of findings in memory experiments. For example, it is apparently possible to report what is in one's memory store ("yes, I'll recognize it if you mention it") without being able to retrieve the information (Hart, 1967). Furthermore, adults perform better on intentional memory tasks than on incidental memory tasks, presumably because they can willfully institute such strategies as rehearsal in aid of the memory functions when the task demands this. Analogously, metalinguistic functions may enter into speech and comprehension on those occasions when one wishes to pun or orate, or to read or write poetry; that is, when language manipulations are part of the definition of the task.

Could the metalinguistic functions enter into the process of learning a first language? The studies we have cited would argue not, for the language functions seem developmentally to precede the metalanguage functions, with only some rare exceptions. The children we studied judged sentences for syntactic form only some years after they used these forms correctly; they organized speech-sounds phonologically years before they could bring this organization (or a related one) to bear on the problem of understanding alphabets. There are some similar findings for other putative metafunctions. For example, unless specially instructed to rehearse, young children do no better in intentional learning tasks than they do in incidental learning tasks (Yendovitskaya, 1971). Perhaps this is because they have no functioning "metamemory" that spontaneously institutes the appropriate strategies available to memory.

Summarizing, we take the evidence to suggest that judgmental functions in language are separate from the language functions both on descriptive grounds (the data of linguistic judgments do not organize the findings for speech and comprehension in real time) and on developmental grounds (the presumed metafunctions are developmentally late to appear).

Some arguments can be made in favor of a more intimate connection between language and metalanguage, although these are perhaps not logically compelling. Some parallels exist between the development and use of restricted language-specific syntactic devices and the development and deployment of metalinguistic skills, as we have defined these. That is, certain elaborate inflectional devices appear only under special linguistic–cultural circumstances (present in creoles but not in pidgins, Sankoff and Laberge, 1973; present in speech but not in early writing systems, Gelb, 1952), are late to develop in the history of the individual (Slobin, 1973), and show extensive individual variation in rate of development, owing to environmental effects (Newport, Gleitman, and Gleitman, 1977) and, possibly, capacity differences (Lenneberg, 1967). The same is true for the metalinguistic functions which show extensive variability (Gleitman and Gleitman, 1970) and environmental sensitivity (reading disabilities of the sort we have described are largely isolated within restricted socioeconomic groups). Approximately these same aspects of language are those which seem to make trouble for the judgment-giver (he has more difficulty making syntactic judgments than semantic judgments; etc.).

3. SUMMARY AND DISCLAIMERS

We suppose that individual differences in language behavior occur more severely at the judgmental level than at the speech and comprehension level. We have invoked such ill-defined notions as "metalinguistic awareness" and "accessibility" to describe such findings. That is, we claim the differences in tacit knowledge are small in comparison to differences in the ability to make such knowledge explicit. We have some evidence that suggests greatest judgmental difficulty with least processed linguistic representations. However, our descriptions of these matters are at present merely metaphorical and not a little fuzzy. But the facts of individual language difference suggest that we will have to look seriously at the problem of "conscious knowledge."

ACKNOWLEDGMENTS

We wish to express our great intellectual debt to two colleagues whose collaboration with us is directly responsible for many of the ideas expressed in this paper. Many of the positions taken were developed in a collaboration with Paul Rozin, in the context of studies on the acquisition of reading (Gleitman and Rozin, 1973a, 1973b, 1977; and Rozin and Gleitman, 1974, 1977; see Section 1.3 of the present paper for summary discussion). A rather different physiological approach to the questions of *accessibility* and *metacognition* appeared in Rozin (1976) where many of our findings on reading are also discussed. Other contributions to the ideas discussed here come out of our collaboration with Elizabeth Shipley on topics in child language learning (Shipley, Smith, and Gleitman, 1969; Gleitman, Gleitman, and Shipley, 1972). The work described in this chapter was funded by Grant #5 R01 MH 23505 from the National Institutes of Health and The William T. Carter Foundation, whose support we gratefully acknowledge.

REFERENCES

Baron, J. The word-superiority effect. In W. K. Estes (Ed.) *Handbook of learning and cognitive processes*. Hillsdale, New Jersey: Erlbaum. In press.

Bever, T. G. The cognitive basis for linguistic structures. In J. R. Hayes (Ed.), *Cognition and the development of language*. New York: Wiley, 1970.

Blank, M. Cognitive processes in auditory discrimination in normal and retarded readers. *Child Development*, 1968, **39**, 1091–1101.

Bloomfield, L. *Language*. New York: Henry Holt, 1933.

Bolinger, D. L. and Gerstman, L. J. Disjuncture as a cue to constructs. *Journal of the Acoustical Society of America*, 1957, **29**, 778.

Bransford, J. D. and Franks, J. J. The abstraction of linguistic ideas. *Cognitive Psychology,* 1971, **2,** 331–350.

Brown, R. *A first language: The early stages.* Cambridge, Massachusetts: Harvard University Press, 1973.

Brown, R. and Hanlon, C. Derivational complexity and order of acquisition in child speech. In J. R. Hayes (Ed.), *Cognition and the development of language.* New York: Wiley, 1970.

Calfee, R. C., Lindamood, P., and Lindamood, C. Acoustic–phonetic skills and reading— kindergarten through twelfth grade. *Journal of Educational Psychology,* 1973, **64,** 293– 298.

Cutting, J. E. and Rosner, B. S. Categories and boundaries in speech and music. *Perception and Psychophysics,* 1974, **16,** 564–570.

Downing, J. (Ed.), *Comparative reading: Cross-national studies of behavior and processes in reading and writing.* New York: Macmillan, 1973.

Downing, J. and Oliver, P. The child's conception of "a word." *Reading Research Quarterly,* 1973–74, **9,** 568–582.

Eimas, P. D., Siqueland, E. R., Jusczyk, P., and Vigorito, J. Speech perception in infants. *Science,* 1971, **171,** 303–306.

Elkonin, D. B. USSR. Trans. by R. Raeder and J. Downing. In J. Downing (Ed.), Comparative reading: *Cross-national studies of behavior and processes in reading and writing.* New York: Macmillan, 1973.

Feldman, H., Goldin-Meadow, S. and Gleitman, L. Beyond Herodotus: The creation of language by linguistically deprived deaf children. In A. Lock (Ed.), *Action, gesture and symbol: The emergence of language.* New York: Academic Press, 1978.

Fillenbaum, S. Memory for gist: Some relevant variables. *Language and Speech,* 1966, **9,** 217–227.

Firth, U. *Components of reading disability.* Unpublished Doctoral dissertation, University of New South Wales, Kensington, N.S.W., Australia, 1972.

Fodor, J. A., Bever, T. G., and Garrett, M. F. *The psychology of language: An introduction to psycholinguistics and generative grammar.* New York: McGraw Hill, 1974.

Fodor, J. A. and Garrett, M. F. Some reflections on competence and performance. In Lyons, J. and Wales, R. S. (Eds.), *Psycholinguistic papers.* Edinburgh: Edinburgh Univ. Press, 1966.

Fowles, B. and Glanz, E. Competence and talent in verbal riddle comprehension. *Journal of Child Language,* 1977, **4,** 433–452.

Furth, H. G. *Thinking without language: Psychological implications of deafness.* New York: Free Press, 1966.

Geer, S. E., Gleitman, H., and Gleitman, L. Paraphrasing and remembering compound words. *Journal of Verbal Learning and Verbal Behavior,* 1972, **11,** 348–355.

Gelb, I. J. *A study of writing: The foundations of grammatology.* Chicago: University of Chicago Press, 1952.

Gibson, E. J., Shurcliff, A., and Yonas, A. Utilization of spelling patterns by deaf and hearing subjects. In H. Levin and J. P. Williams (Eds.), *Basic studies on reading.* New York: Basic Books, 1970.

Gleitman, L. R. and Gleitman, H. *Phrase and paraphrase.* New York: W. W. Norton and Co., 1970.

Gleitman, L. R., Gleitman, H., and Shipley, E. The emergence of the child as grammarian. *Cognition,* 1972, **1,** 137–164.

Gleitman, L. R. and Rozin, P. Teaching reading by use of a syllabary. *Reading Research Quarterly,* 1973a, **8,** 447–483.

Gleitman, L. R., and Rozin, P. Phoenician go home? (A response to Goodman). *Reading Research Quarterly,* 1973b, **8,** 494–501.

Gleitman, L. R. and Rozin, P. The structure and acquisition of reading I: Relations between orthographies and the structure of language. In A. S. Reber and D. Scarborough (Eds.), *Toward a psychology of reading*. Hillsdale, New Jersey, Erlbaum, 1977.

Hart, J. T. Memory and the memory-monitoring process. *Journal of Verbal Learning and Verbal Behavior*, 1967, **6**, 385–391.

Herodotus. *The Persian Wars*, c. 460 B.C., Rawlinson, G. (Tr.) New York: Random House, 1942.

Hirsh-Pasek, K., Gleitman, L. R., and Gleitman, H. What did the brain say to the mind? In A. Sinclair, R. Jarvella, and W. J. M. Levelt (Eds.), *The Child's Conception of Language*. Berlin, Heidelberg, New York: Springer-Verlag, 1978.

Holden, M. H., and MacGinitie, W. H. Children's conceptions of word boundaries in speech and print. *Journal of Educational Psychology*, 1972, **63**, 551–557.

Jeffery, L. H. *The local scripts of archaic Greece*. Oxford: Clarendon Press, 1961.

Kessel, F. S. The role of syntax in the child's comprehension from ages six to twelve. *Monographs of the Society for Research in Child Development*, 1970, **35**(6).

Kuhl, P. K. and Miller, J. D. Speech perception by the chinchilla: Voiced–voiceless distinction in alveolar plosive consonants. *Science*, 1975, **190**, 69–72.

Labov, W. Locating the frontier between social and psychological factors in linguistic variation. This volume.

Lackner, J. R. A developmental study of language behavior in retarded children. In D. M. Morehead and A. E. Morehead (Eds.), *Normal and deficient child language*. Baltimore: University Park Press, 1976.

Lenneberg, E. H. *Biological foundations of language*. New York: Wiley, 1967.

Leong, C. K. Hong Kong. In J. Downing (Ed.), *Comparative reading: Cross-national studies of behavior and processes in reading and writing*. New York: Macmillan, 1973.

Levin, H., and Kaplan, E. L. Grammatical structure and reading. In H. Levin and J. P. Williams (Eds.), *Basic studies on reading*. New York: Basic Books, 1970.

Liberman, I. Y., Shankweiler, D., Fischer, F. W. and Carter, B. Explicit syllable and phoneme segmentation in the young child. *Journal of Experimental Child Psychology*, 1974, **18**, 201–212.

Liberman, I. Y., Shankweiler, D., Liberman, A. M., Fowler, C., and Fischer, F. W. Phonetic segmentation and recoding in the beginning reader. In A. S. Reber and D. Scarborough, (Eds.), *Toward a psychology of reading*. Hillsdale, New Jersey: Lawrence Erlbaum Associates, 1977.

Morehead, D. M. and Ingram, D. The development of base syntax in normal and linguistically deviant children. In D. M. Morehead and A. E. Morehead (Eds.), *Normal and deficient child language*. Baltimore: University Park Press, 1976.

Newport, E. L. and Ashbrook, E. Development of semantic–syntactic relations in the acquisition of American Sign Language. Manuscript, University of California at San Diego, 1977.

Newport, E., Gleitman, H. and Gleitman, L. R. Mother, I'd rather do it myself: Some effects and non-effects of maternal speech style. In C. E. Snow and C. A. Ferguson (Eds.), *Talking to children: Language input and acquisition*. Cambridge, England: Cambridge University Press, 1977.

Nida, E. A. *Morphology: The descriptive analysis of words*. Second ed. Ann Arbor, Michigan: University of Michigan Press, 1949.

Read, C. Pre-school children's knowledge of English phonology. *Harvard Educational Review*, 1971, **41**, 1–34.

Rosner, J. *The development and validation of an individualized perceptual skills curriculum*. Learning Research and Development Center, University of Pittsburgh. Publication 1972/7. 1972.

Rosner, J. Auditory analysis training with prereaders. *The Reading Teacher*, 1974, **27,** 379–384.

Rosner, J., and Simon, D. P. *The auditory analysis test: An initial report.* Learning Research and Development Center, University of Pittsburgh, Publication 1971/3, 1971.

Ross, J. R. Where's English? This volume.

Rozin, P. The evolution of intelligence and access to the cognitive unconscious. In J. Sprague and A. N. Epstein (Eds.), *Progress in psychobiology and physiological psychology*, Vol. 6. New York: Academic Press, 1976.

Rozin, P. and Gleitman, L. R. The structure and acquisition of reading II: The reading process and the acquisition of the alphabetic principle. In A. S. Reber and D. Scarborough (Eds.), *Toward a psychology of reading.* Hillsdale, New Jersey: L. Erlbaum Associates, 1977.

Rozin, P., Poritsky, S., and Sotsky, R. American children with reading problems can easily learn to read English represented by Chinese characters, *Science*, 1971, **171,** 1264–1267.

Sachs, J. S. Recognition memory for syntactic and semantic aspects of connected discourse. *Perception and Psychophysics*, 1967, **2,** 437–442.

Sankoff, G. and Laberge, S. On the acquisition of native speakers by a language. *Kivung,* 1973, **6**(1), 32–47.

Shatz, M. Semantic and syntactic factors in children's judgment of sentences. Unpublished manuscript, University of Pennsylvania, 1972.

Shipley, E. F., Smith, C. S. and Gleitman, L. R. A study in the acquisition of language: Free responses to commands. *Language*, 1969, **45,** 322–343.

Shultz, T. and Pilon, R. Development of the ability to detect linguistic ambiguity. *Child Development*, 1973, **44,** 728–733.

Singer, H. IQ is and is not related to reading. In S. Wanat (Ed.), *Intelligence and reading.* Newark, Delaware: International Reading Association, 1974.

Slobin, D. Cognitive prerequisites for the development of grammar. In C. A. Ferguson and D. I. Slobin (Eds.), *Studies of Child Language Development.* New York: Holt, Rinehart and Winston, 1973.

Slobin, D. I. The more it changes . . . on understanding language by watching it move through time. In *Papers and Reports on Child Language Development*, No. 10. Department of Linguistics, Stanford University, Sept. 1975.

Smith, J. A. The relationship between phonemic sensitivity and the effectiveness of phonemic retrieval cues in preliterate children. Unpublished Doctoral dissertation. University of Pennsylvania, 1974.

Thorndike, W. E. Reading as reasoning: A study of mistakes in paragraph reading. *Journal of Educational Psychology*, 1971, **8,** 323–332. (Also in *Reading Research Quarterly*, 1970–1971, **6,** 425–434.)

Wepman, J. M. *Wepman auditory discrimination test.* Chicago: Language Research Associates, 1958.

Yendovitskaya, T. V. Development of memory. In A. V. Zaporozhets and D. B. Elkonin (Eds.), *The psychology of preschool children.* Cambridge, Massachusetts: M.I.T. Press, 1971.

7

Where's English?

JOHN ROBERT ROSS

1. BACKGROUND

Chomsky's original conception of a language (cf. Chomsky 1957) was that it was a set of strings of elements (for example, strings of words, morphemes, phonemes, or phonetic segments). Membership in the set was believed to be easy to determine: Grammatical sentences would be read and reacted to normally, while ungrammatical ones would be read with a special "list" intonation, and would elicit bizarreness reactions. A famous pair of examples from Chomsky is *Colorless green ideas sleep furiously* and *Furiously sleep ideas green colorless.* Chomsky held the first of these to be fully grammatical, though semantically anomalous, while claiming that the second, which is the same as the first except that the word order is reversed, was not only semantically anomalous, but also syntactically ill-formed.

As Chomsky's theory became more refined, the original assumption

127

Individual Differences in Language Ability and
Language Behavior

Copyright © 1979 by Academic Press, Inc.
All rights of reproduction in any form reserved.
ISBN 0-12-255950-9

that it was the job of the grammar to separate the set of all possible strings of elements into only two sets—a set of fully grammatical sentences, and a set of non-sentences—was modified, and various schemes were devised for assigning degrees of grammaticality to some of the non-sentences, by comparing them to the set of sentences along various axes. I will not review these proposals here.

What was not realized for many years was the staggering extent of interspeaker variation on any given set of sentences. It was apparently believed that if one took a set of sentences and elicited judgments about them from some group of speakers, these speakers would agree among themselves as to the degrees of grammaticality of the test sentences. Occasionally, one found asides to the effect that "one dialect," or more accurately, "some speakers," liked (or disliked) one test sentence more than the rest of the subjects did, but for a long time, syntacticians were content to proceed on the assumption that this was a rare phenomenon, and could be disregarded, as a first approximation.

After all, it may have been felt, since all these subjects are unquestionably English (Turkish, Mohawk, etc.) speakers, and do not report that they are speakers of different geographical dialects, they have to accept and reject the same sets of sentences, don't they? Otherwise, what could it mean to say "Those people speak the same language"?

It is precisely this question that I hope to cast some light on in the course of this chapter. For somewhere around the mid 1960s, it began to seem to many scholars that the working assumption described above—that interspeaker variation could be disregarded—was too rough to proceed on further. If a teacher of a syntax class, in attempting to find out what "the facts" are for some range of sentences, asks those attending the class to vote on three sentences, the only votes being "yes" or "no", a typical voting pattern is 22–8 for the first sentence, 11–19 for the second, and 5–25 for the third. And it is rarely the case that the 3 successive groups of "yes" voters are neatly arranged in subsets—that is, that the 11 "yes" votes for the second sentence are among the 22 "yes" votes for the first sentence, or that the 5 yesses for the third sentence are a subset of the 11 for the second. Rather, if the sentences are at all complex, more controversial, say, than *Please pass the olive oil* or *The cat is on the mat*, to take two (presumably) universally acceptable strings, or *Boys yours this of and Carl or* or *Dopes I around cats these each*, to take two from the other end, the classroom voters will not align themselves into neat blocs.

I take it that this is a result that is hard to believe, for if it were easy to believe, it wouldn't have escaped notice in so many syntax classes. Syntax teachers, I imagine, wanted their job to be easier than it is, and did not call attention to the non-overlappingness of the successive votes for a number of years.

But the past decade has seen many more careful studies of syntactic variation than I can review here. A good starting place for readers interested in entering The Swamp is Carden's pithy and excellent review (Carden, 1976), written by someone whose first field of study— quantifiers—permitted no easy simplifications of the quilted array of dialects that present themselves in this area.

I will comment on only one previous study, which makes a point that is basic for understanding the complexities of variation in syntax.

In Hindle and Sag (1975), the distribution of the emergent "positive" *anymore* is studied. Speakers were asked to judge the following sentences, in which *anymore* can be roughly paraphrased as "nowadays." (*op. cit.* p. 92)

(1)　　a. *We don't eat fish anymore.*
　　　　b. *Do you eat fish anymore?*
　　　　c. *We're reluctant to eat fish anymore.*
　　　　d. *I doubt that John eats fish anymore.*
　　　　e. *It's really hard for us to eat fish anymore.*
　　　　f. *I'm afraid to go out at night anymore.*
　　　　g. *It's impossible for John to eat fish anymore.*
　　　　h. *Fish is all we eat anymore.*
　　　　i. *It's amazing that John eats fish anymore.*
　　　　j. *We hate to eat fish anymore.*
　　　　k. *They've scared us out of eating fish anymore.*
　　　　l. *It's dangerous to eat fish anymore.*
　　　m. *All we eat anymore is fish.*
　　　　n. *Any neighborhood is dangerous to walk in anymore.*
　　　　o. *We've stopped eating fish anymore.*
　　　　p. *All we eat is fish anymore.*
　　　　q. *We only eat fish anymore.*
　　　　r. *We eat a lot of fish anymore.*
　　　　s. *Anymore, we eat a lot of fish.*
　　　　t. *Anymore, I never go to the movies.*
　　　　u. *Anymore, we eat fish.*
　　　　v. *We eat fish anymore.*

Hindle and Sag had abandoned the first assumption discussed above, which we might dub Hypothesis I.

(2)　Hypothesis I:　*For a given set of sentences, all speakers will agree on their grammaticality. English is that set of sentences which all speakers agree is grammatical.*

There is, of course, such a set, but most syntacticians would refuse to limit their investigations to it—it is too "small." Hindle and Sag, therefore, were interested in studying a less restrictive theory as to the nature of English (or any other natural language). For reference, let us call this view Hypothesis II.

(3) HYPOTHESIS II: *The "small" set of Hypothesis I above constitutes the core of English. There is a monolinear continuum of acceptability, shared by all speakers, leading away from the core. Speakers are free to pick points anywhere along this continuum to fix the "edges" of their English. Speakers are consistently either liberal or conservative, their liberality being indexed by their distance from the core.*

If Hypothesis II were true, any group of speakers, when presented with the *anymore* sentences in (1), might disagree on their absolute rankings of sentences, but would agree relatively. That is, it would be possible to set up a partially ordered hierarchy of the sentences in (1) so that it would never be the case that one speaker would judge one sentence better than another, while a second speaker would have the opposite preference.

Unfortunately, this last contingency is just what turned out to be the case. Hindle and Sag found that no single invariant ordering of all the sentences in (1) was possible.

They did find, however, that there were subhierarchies contained within (1). These are shown in (4)–(6) (cf. Hindle and Sag (*op. cit.*), p. 100, 101, and 107, resp.)

(4) a. *We're reluctant to eat fish anymore.*
     b. *I'm afraid to go out at night anymore.*
     c. *We hate to eat fish anymore.*
     d. *They've scared us out of eating fish anymore.*
     e. *We've stopped eating fish anymore.*

(5) a. *Fish is all we eat anymore.*
     b. *All we eat anymore is fish.*
     c. *All we eat is fish anymore.*

(6) a. *It's really hard for us to eat fish anymore.*
     b. *It's impossible for John to eat fish anymore.*
     c. *It's amazing that John eats fish anymore.*
     d. *It's dangerous to eat fish anymore.*
     e. *Any neighborhood is dangerous to walk in anymore.*

For all the speakers they interviewed, it was the case that accepting a lower sentence in any of these three lists implied accepting any higher sentence *within the same list.* However, there were no implications that obtained between lists.

It seems, then, that we must retreat from Hypothesis II to the weaker Hypothesis III.

(7) HYPOTHESIS III: *The single continuum of Hypothesis II must be replaced by an indeterminate number of continua, each leading away from the core in orthogonally different directions. Speakers are free to pick different points on different continua. There are implicational laws regarding each one of these in isolation: A speaker who accepts a sentence at distance x from the core along any continuum must accept any more central string **on the same continuum**. No such implications are known to hold between continua.*

2. THE EXPERIMENT

Given Hypothesis III as a baseline, then, let us ask the following question: Do speakers of English know "where" the core is? That is, since the indeterminate number of ordered continua of Hypothesis III form a space, do speakers know their location in this space? If a positive *anymore*-user accepts (5c), does (s)he realize that this is more "liberal," so to speak, than speakers who only accept (5a) and (5b), or only (5a)? Conversely, does someone who accepts only (5a) realize that (s)he is more "conservative" than speakers who accept more of the sentences in (5)?

A second issue, possibly unrelated, which I wished to gather information on, was the problem of confidence. Subjectively, I have often noted that my judgements about sentences vary from cases in which I can assess a sentence as being either a 1 or a 4 without (much) hesitation or uncertainty, to other cases in which I am very dubious about the accuracy and repeatability of my assessments. I wanted, therefore, to study how judgements of confidence would interact with those of liberality and those of grammaticality.

To attempt to answer these questions, I elicited judgements from a small group of speakers, gathered at a seaside location which shall remain nameless. The questionnaire that I used, slightly rearranged for greater clarity, and minus some typos, appears in the Appendix. In the time between the initial elicitation and now, I also subjected various (former?) friends to this questionnaire. The results, in which the names of the respondents are partially cloaked in the anonymity of initials, are given in (8).

(8)

Subject	Rating	The doctor is sure	Under no circumstances	Talked about	We don't believe	The fact θ	The idea θ	He touch	Nobody is here S_1 S_2	All the further	Nobody S_1, is here S_2	Writable down	And
SG	L – 2.83	2 + L	1 + M	1 + L	2 + L	2 + L	3 + L	1 + L	2 + L	4 + [L]	3 + L	4 + M	3 + L
JR	L – 2.42	1 + M	1 + L	1 0 L	3 0 C	3 + M	2 0 L	1 – L	1 + M	3 + M	2 0 L	2 0 L	4 + M
JS	L – 2.33	1 + M	2 + L	1 + M	1 + M	1 + M	1 + M	1 + M	3 + L	2 0 L	2 0 L	2 + L	1 0 L
MD	L – 2.25	1 – L	1 + L	2 / L	1 + M	3 + M	3 0 M	3 0 M	3 – M	3 + M	3 0 M	4 0 M	3 + M
WL	M – 2.08	1 + M	1 + M	2 + /	2 0 M	2 + C	2 0 M	3 0 M	2 + M	2 – M	2 0 M	3 0 L	4 + M
DK	C – 2.00	1 + M	1 + M	1 0 M	1 0 M	2 + /	1 0 M	1 + M	3 0 C	1 0 M	3 + M	2 + M	1 + L
CF	M – 1.91	1 + M	1 + M	2 + M	1 0 M	1 / M	1 + M	2 – C	2 0 M	2 – L	3 0 C	2 + L	4 + M
CJF	M – 1.83	1 + M	1 + M	1 + M	1 + M	1 + M	1 + M	2 + M	1 + M	2 + C	3 + M	2 + C	4 + M
PMP	C – 1.75	1 + M	1 + M	1 + M	1 + M	1 + M	1 + M	1 + M	1 + M		2 + C	4 + M	4 + M
PF	L – 2.25	1 + M	1 + M	1 + M	1 + M	1 + M	1 + M	2 + M	1 + L	4 – M	2 + L	2.5 – M	3 0 L
LF	M – 2.00	1 + M	1 – M	1 + M	1 + M	2 + C	2 + M	1 + M	2 + M	2 + M	1 + L	2 + M	4 + M
JG	C – 1.75	1 + [C]	1 + M	3 + C	3 + M	2 + M	3 0 L	3 + M	4 + C	3 + C	4 + M	4 + M	4 + M
UQ	C? – 1.64	1 + M	1 0 L	3 0 /	1 + M	3 0 M	3 0 M	2 + C	2 0 L	3 + /	3 + C	4 /	4 + M
MB		1 + /	2 0 /	2 0 /	1 + /	1 0 /		3 /	3 0 /	4 –	4 + /	3 + /	4 + /
EL		1 + /	3 – /	2 0 /	1 + /	2 + /	3 /	3 /			4 +	3 /	3 – /
RD	L – 2.42	1 + L	1 + L	1 + L	3 + C	1.5 + M	1 + L	2 + M	2 + L	3 + C	2 + L	1.5 + L	1.5 + M
RE	L(Sp) / C(W) – 2.42	1 + L	2 0 L	2 0 L	3 0 M	2 0 L	2 + L	2 0 M	3 + M	3 + L	4 + C	3 + L	4 + C
HG	L / M – 2.25	1 + M	1 + L		1 0 M	2 + L	2 0 C	3 0 L	3 – L	3 0 L	3 + C	3 0 C	3 + L
JK	L(somewhat) – 2.25	2 0 M	2 + M	[4] 0 L	2 + M	1 + L	2 0 M	3 + C	3 + L	3 + M	3 + L	3 + L	4 + M
CH	C – 2.17	1 0 L	1 + M	2 + M	1 + L	2 0 L	3 + C	2 + L	3 + M	3 + C	3 + L	4 + [L]	3 + C
MY	L – 2.08	1 + L	1 + L	2 + C	1 + L	2 + M	2 + L	2 0 M	3 0 M	2 + M	3 0 M	4 + C	2 0 C
HW	/ – 2.00	1 + M	1 + M	2 0 M	4 0 C	1 0 L	1 0 M	1 + L	2 0 M	3 + M	3 + M	3 + M	4 + M
JL	C – 1.92	1 + M	1 + M	2 0 C	2 0 C	2 + C	2 + C	3 + C	3 + C	3 + C	3 + C	3 + M	3 + M
JC	C – 1.50	1 + M	1 + M	1 + M	1 + M	1 + M	1 + M	3 + C	3 + C	3 + M	3 + C	4 + C	4 + M
HJ	C – 1.50	1 + M	2 + C	2 + C	1 0 M	2 + C	2 + C	3 + M	3 + C	2 + C	2 + C	3 + C	3 + M
DS	C – 1.42	1 + M	1 + M	2 0 M	1 + C	3 + C	2 0 C	1 + C	4 + C	2 + C	2 + C	4 + C	4 + C
KP	C – 1.42	1 + M	2 + M	1 + M	3 + C	1 + /	2 0 C	3 0 C	4 + C	3 +	3 +	3 0 M	3 + C
AG	L? – 1.25	1 + /	1 + /	2 0 C	2 0 /	1 +	2 0 C	3 0 C	3 /			3 0 C	2 0 L
TG	L – 2.27	1 + M	1 + M	2 0 M	2 0 M	3 + M	2 0 L	1 + [C]	4 – C	4 + [L]	3 /	3 – L	4 + [L]
IJ	C – 1.67	1 + M	1 + M	2 0 C	1 + M	2 0 C	2 + M	4 + M	3 + C	4 + M	3 + C	4 + M	4 + M

132

(9)

	Rating	2a + b − c − 2d	Confidence	a − b − c	Liberality
Core 10. *The doctor is sure*	28/2/0/0	+58	27/2/1	+24(90%)	6/20/1
1. *under no circumstances*	24/5/1/0	+52	25/3/2	+20(83%)	7/19/1
8. *talked about*	13/14/2/1	+36	19/10/0	+9(66%)	6/15/7
3. *We don't believe*	18/6/5/1	+35	20/10/0	+10(67%)	3/19/5
4. *the fact Ø*	11/14/5/0	+31	23/6/0	+17(79%)	6/13/7
12. *the idea Ø*	7/15/8/0	+21	16/13/0	+3(59%)	7/15/6
6. *he touch*	11/8/10/1	+18	22/5/2	+15(76%)	6/13/9
9. *Nobody is here* $S_1 S_2$	4/8/14/4	− 6	19/7/3	+9(66%)	6/10/11
7. *All the further*	1/11/12/6	−11	23/3/3	+17(79%)	6/14/8
2. *Nobody* S_1 *is here* S_2	1/7/18/4	−17	23/6/0	+17(79%)	8/8/10
13. *writable down*	1/6/13/10	−25	20/6/2	+12(71%)	9/11/7
Fringe 5. *and*	3/2/8/17	−34	25/4/1	+20(84%)	7/17/4

The sentences are arranged in the matrix from left to right in order of decreasing average grammaticality. I have repeated this listing from the top down in (9), where the number preceding each sentence corresponds to its number on the questionnaire.

In the second column of (9) is indicated the number of 1s, 2s, 3s, and 4s that each sentence received from all 30 subjects. Thus the indication "18/6/5/1" in the fourth line of (9) indicates that the third sentence of the questionnaire, *We don't believe the claim that Jimson ever had any money,* was given eighteen 1s, six 2s, five 3s, and one 4. In order to rank the sentences, the formula in the third column was used, where a–d designate the number of 1s, 2s, 3s, and 4s. Thus for the third sentence, a = 18, b = 6, c = 5, and d = 1, yielding a rating 2(18) + 6 − 5 − 2(1) = 35.

The fourth column of (9) gives the sum of the confidence scores, with the first number giving the number of 'pretty sure' votes, the second giving the number of 'middling' votes and the third giving the number of 'pretty unsure' votes.

The fifth column of (9) gives two indices of overall confidence. The first is a simple subtraction of the middlings or pretty unsures from the number of pretty sures, and the parenthesized percentage to its right gives the ratio of 'pretty sure' judgements to all judgements, for a given sentence. Thus the ratio of 'pretty sure' respondents for the sixth questionnaire sentence, *I urge that anything he touch be burned,* is 22/29, or 76%.

The notation used in this matrix is as follows. In each cell of the matrix, there will usually be 3 symbols: a number, from 1 to 4, giving the perceived degree of acceptability,[1] a "+," a "0," or a "−," corresponding to the degree of confidence [pretty sure, middling, and pretty unsure, respectively], and one of L, M, or C, designating "liberal," "middle of the road," and "conservative," respectively. Some answers did not include indications of confidence or liberality; in such cases, I have written"/."

[1] In some cases, respondents used intermediate values of grammaticality, namely 1.5, and 2.5. For the purposes of this study, I have simplified by scoring both of these as 2s.

Finally, the rightmost column of (9) gives the total numbers of liberal/ middle of the road/conservative responses for each of the tested sentences.

Returning again to the matrix in (8), I hope the rationale for ordering the columns has become clear.[2] Let us turn now to the ordering of the rows.

First of all, I have drawn three lines between the top 15 and the bottom 15 rows, to separate linguists from normal people. There are, as will become clear, significant differences between these two subgroups.[3] Second, I have divided, by means of heavy lines, each of these two subgroups up into native speakers of American English and non-native speakers.[4]

Thus the four groups are: 9 native linguists, 6 non-native linguists, 13 native normals, and 2 foreign normals.

Following each person's initials appears a capital L, M, or C, which indicates whether the person described himself or herself as basically liberal, middle of the road, or conservative.

Following this is a decimal which represents an index of liberality. This is arrived at by the formula shown in (10),

$$(10) \qquad \frac{3a + 2b + c}{N}$$

where a,b, and c are the number of Ls, Ms and Cs that an informant has marked on the questionnaire. For example, since the liberality score of CF is 2/6/3, the index computation is as shown in (11).

$$(11) \qquad \frac{3(2) + 2(6) + 1(3)}{11} = \frac{6 + 12 + 3}{11} = \frac{21}{11} = 1.91$$

To give some intuitive idea of what this index means, supposing that some subject had answered a test with 3 questions and had judged one response liberal, one middle-of-the-road, and one conservative. In such a case, the index would yield 2.00, as shown in (12).

[2] I have omitted from discussion the results of the eleventh questionnaire sentence, where some additional questions, of a semantic kind, were asked, because the variation among the respondents was so overwhelming as to defy analysis. As far as I have been able to ascertain, almost all speakers liked at least one version of one of the sentences, but all three meanings were ascribed to them—50%, approximately, were for meaning (i), with the other 50% splitting more or less evenly between meanings (ii) and (iii). With the exception of one pair of informants, whose answers were the same, and of one trio, whose answers were also identical among themselves, no others of the 24 respondents gave the same judgements.

[3] In some cases; my decision as to whom to call a linguist may have been erroneous, in one way or the other. Please do not be offended if you are a linguist and have been called a normal speaker, or *vice versa*. Whatever errors I have made here simply reflect my insufficient familiarity with the work of my informants. I would never knowingly accuse someone of being normal (or a linguist).

[4] The same apologies as in Footnote 3 apply here.

(12)
$$\frac{3(1) + 2(1) + 1(1)}{3} = \frac{6}{3} = 2.00$$

If the subject had given 2 liberal responses, and one conservative one, the index would be 2.33, as shown in (13).

(13)
$$\frac{3(2) + 2(0) + 1(1)}{3} = \frac{7}{3} = 2.33$$

And if the subject had given two conservative responses, and one liberal one, the index would be 1.67, as shown in (14)

(14)
$$\frac{3(1) + 2(0) + 1(2)}{3} = 1.67$$

Thus indices of above 2 indicate a predominance of liberal responses, while indices below 2 indicate a predominance of conservative responses.

A final note about (8): In 7 instances, I have enclosed an L or a C in a box, which is an indication that I believe that the respondent has made a confused response. A score of 1 and C, for example, would mean "I rate this sentence perfect, but I am conservative, and most people rate it even more highly." Similarly, 4 and L would mean "while I find this string hopeless, impossible to understand, and word-salad, I am much more liberal than most of my fellow speakers of English, who find it even worse."

Such judgements were probably in error, and it is reassuring to note that with the exception of TG, who has four such uninterpretable judgements, the other 3 cases are few and far between. This suggests that most informants have probably been able to at least understand the task involved in assigning Ls, Ms, and Cs. Whether or not they have been able to carry out this task is a different story, to which I will return below.

3. THE RESULTS

Clearly (I would imagine), English does not exist independently of those who speak it. If, as Hypothesis III claims, a natural language is an n-space, defined by an indeterminate number of axes radiating outward from a core, then these axes are defined on the basis of the implicationally arranged responses of speakers, who are the points of the n-space. Thus the space and the people in it define each other, and it is hard to talk about either in isolation.

Nonetheless, we must begin somewhere, whether it be with chicken or with egg, so let me fairly arbitrarily pick the sentences to talk about first.

3.1. The Sentences

3.1.1. The Geography of Grammaticality

There are three reasons to see the sentences as falling into 3 broad groups: *a core*, represented by the leftmost two or three (or possibly four) columns of (8); *a fringe*, represented by the rightmost two, or possibly three, columns; and *a bog*, between the core and the fringe. The three reasons are confidence, variation, and lack of conservatism.

In each of these areas, we find that though the bog, the area receiving 2s and 3s, on the average, lies by grading *between* the core and the fringe, the bog does not intervene between them with respect to the three parameters of confidence, variation and lack of conservatism. For them, the ordering is not core-bog-fringe, but rather core-fringe-bog.

Let us look at the reasons in turn. Taking confidence first, we see that the topmost sentence in (9), Sentence 10, has the highest confidence rating—90%, followed by the lowest sentence, Sentence 5, at 84%, with the second core sentence, Sentence 1, being in third position with 83%. I would be happy if I could report a monotonic decline to the nadir of the bog, Sentence 12, at 59%, followed by a monotonic climb in confidence as one proceeds towards the fringe. However, the facts don't seem to be that way: There are lots of hills and valleys *en route*.

Let us turn next to variability. If there were total agreement on any sentence, all 30 informants would have given it a 1, or a 3, or whatever. Sentence 10 comes closest to this ideal, with Sentence 1 close behind. In other words, there is very little variation on the grading for the core: English speakers know a good sentence when they hear one.

But let us ask what a maximally disagreeing set of judgements would look like. It is easy to conceive of the result: Each grade would have an equal number of adherents, namely 7.5. Such a sentence would receive 7.5 1s, 7.5 2s, 7.5 3s, and 7.5 4s. No sentence attains this ideal (I had no half-informants among the test subjects in any case), but Sentence 6 comes closest, possibly, to it.

As a way of getting a handle on disagreement, consider the following measure: In the ideal case, any two adjoining grades (i.e., 1s and 2s, or 2s and 3s, or 3s and 4s) would receive 7.5 + 7.5 = 15 adherents. So *the lowest sums of adjoining grades* should be looked at, for each sentence. This I have done in (15).

Here again, we see the core with the lowest sum, that is, least variation, the fringe with the next largest amount of variation, and a more or less monotonic rise towards the center of the bog, and a monotonic fall towards the fringe.

If we take the sums of *any* 2 grades, not requiring that they be adjacent, the results are similar: cf. (16).

This latter measure is the one we are looking for, for the maximum

(15)	Sentence	Grade profile	Lowest adjoining grades	Sum
10.	*doctor*	28/2/0/0	0 + 0	0
1.	*circumstances*	24/5/1/0	1 + 0	1
8.	*talked*	13/14/2/1	2 + 1	3
3.	*believe*	18/6/5/1	5 + 1	6
4.	*fact*	11/14/5/0	5 + 0	5
12.	*idea*	7/15/8/0	8 + 0	8
6.	*he touch*	11/8/10/1	10 + 1	11
9.	*here* S_1 S_2	4/8/14/4	4 + 8	12
7.	*further*	1/11/12/6	1 + 11	12
2.	*here* S_2	1/7/18/4	1 + 7	8
13.	*writable*	1/6/13/10	1 + 6	7
5.	*and*	3/2/8/17	3 + 2	5

(16)	Sentence	Two lowest numbers of grades	Sum
10.	*doctor*	0 + 0 =	0
1.	*circumstances*	1 + 0 =	1
8.	*talked*	2 + 1 =	3
3.	*believe*	5 + 1 =	6
4.	*fact*	5 + 0 =	5
12.	*idea*	7 + 0 =	7
6.	*he touch*	8 + 1 =	9
9.	*here* S_1S_2	4 + 4 =	8
7.	*further*	1 + 6 =	7
2.	*here* S_2	1 + 4 =	5
13.	*writable*	1 + 6 =	7
5.	*and*	3 + 2 =	5

possible sum that the two lowest numbers could attain would be 15—that would be in the case of 7.5 7.5 7.5 7.5. So as the sum rises in (16), the amount of disagreement also rises, reaching a peak for sentence 6, the center of the bog. And again the sum is smallest at the core, intermediate at the fringe, and largest in the bog.

One other point remains to be made with respect to the distribution of the grades, an observation which is in a way the opposite of the distribution of variation among the sentences of the sample. Notice how the grades *clump*, that is, how it is almost always the case that the two most frequently assigned grades for a given sentence are adjacent. This can be seen in (17), where for each sentence, the two most frequent grades are in boldface type. The percentages under the slash marks indicate the proportion of the grades that is accounted for by the sum of the two numbers on both sides of the slash. Thus the notation

13/ 14 / 2 / 1
90%53%10%

after sentence 8 in (17) indicates that $13+14=27$ is 90% of the 30 grades given, that $14+2=16$ is 53%, and that $2+1=3$ is 10%. Thus another way to see how variation increases in the bog is to observe how the highest percentage we find under any slash mark decreases, towards a theoretical minimum of 50%, towards the middle of (17).

(17)

Sentence	Grade profile
10. *doctor*	**28** / **2** / 0 / 0 100% 7% 0%
1. *circumstances*	**24** / **5** / 1 / 0 97% 20% 3%
8. *talked*	**13** / **14** / 2 / 1 90% 53% 10%
3. *believe*	**18** / **6** / 5/ 1 80% 37% 20%
4. *fact*	**11** / **14** / 5 / 0 83% 63% 16%
12. *idea*	7 / **15** / 8 / 0 74% 77% 27%
6. *he touch*	**11** / 8 / **10** / 1 64% 60% 37%
9. *here* $S_1 S_2$	4 / 8 / **14** / 4 40% 70% 60%
7. *further*	1 / **11** / **12** / 6 40% 77% 60%
2. *here* S_2	1 / 7 / **18** / 4 27% 83% 74%
13. *writable*	1 / 6 / **13** / **10** 23% 63% 77%
5. *and*	3 / 2 / 8 / **17** 16% 67% 83%

What interests me about the general adjacency of boldface numbers in the grade profiles of (17) is that there is only one (weak) counterexample to it—Sentence 6. I would have expected to see profiles like 15/0/0/15 (or in general, A/0/0/B, where $A+B=30$) showing up—these would be examples of dialect differences. I had thought that Sentence 7 would turn out to be a sentence that was either known to a respondent or hopeless, but this was not the case, as the 1/11/12/6 profile shows. Possibly a better example would be the Boston (and elsewhere?)-ese Invisible Negative, as seen in (18a)–(18c), which mean the same thing as (19a)–(19c), respectively.

(18) a. *You make good pizza, and so don't Ed's folks.*
      b. *Fred's working right now, and so is Jane.*
      c. *You could have helped me, and so couldn't he.*

(19) a. *You make good pizza, and so do Ed's folks.*
      b. *Fred's working right now, and so is Jane.*
      c. *You could have helped me, and so could he.*

These sentences usually occasion (sometimes polite) disbelief when they are mentioned to linguist acquaintances, and their meaning is mysterious to anyone who doesn't know the rule. Maybe this would be a true case of A/0/0/B [or A/0/B/0, or (less likely) 0/A/0/B]. At any rate, other sets of sentences should be tested, to find out whether the general adjacency of most frequent guesses which we observe in (17) is only due to a skew in the sentences that I chose to test, or whether it is in fact generally true, for any set of sentences. If it were to be true, the consequences for our understanding of the nature of speech communities would doubtless be profound, but unguessable at present. We had better speculate about that bridge when we get to it.

To recapitulate somewhat, for I have discursed, we have seen above how the ordering core-fringe-bog seems to be forced upon us by two factors: confidence, to some extent, and variability, to a greater extent. Let us now turn to the third factor, lack of conservatism.

As can be seen in the liberality column of (9), the "C" judgements (the numbers to the right of the second slash) start with a low of 1 in the core, rise (not quite monotonically) to a high of 11, in Sentence 9, and sink again (pretty close to monotonically) to 4 at the fringe. We of course expect there to be fewer Cs in the core than on the fringe (because of the uninterpretability of "1C" judgements, which was noted above), and we expect fewer Ls on the fringe than in the core (because of the uninterpretability of "4L" judgements). But note that a subject could easily give Sentence 10, the best sentence in (9), a "2," "3," or "4," and also, correctly perceiving himself or herself to be more conservative, a "C." Similarly for "1L," "2L," or "3L" judgements on the fringe. But note the asymmetry here between L and C judgements: At the core, there are 6 Ls for Sentence 10, and 7 for Sentence 1; at the fringe, there are 7 Ls for Sentence 5. The number of L judgements stays between 6 and 7 for most of the sentences checked—a strange result, in my opinion, but one which may not be statistically significant.

I have summarized the discussion above in the table in (20)

(20)   The Regions of English

		The Core	The Bog	The Fringe
a.	Average grammaticality	Highest	Medium	Lowest
b.	Confidence	Highest	Lowest	Medium
c.	Variation between speakers	Lowest	Highest	Medium
d.	Incidence of conservative judgements	Lowest	Highest	Medium

I have no explanation for the contiguity of core and fringe that we 'have seen. It is reminiscent, however, of a commonly observed tendency, for a number of psychological tasks, for the extremes of a continuum to be more salient than the middle. For instance, if a subject is asked to repeat a sufficiently long sequence of numbers, the memory will be best at the beginning of the sequence, next best at the end, and worst in the middle. Similarly, in Brown and McNeill (1966), subjects who had a word "on the tip of their tongue(s)" were studied, to see what phonetic properties of the word in question were known (beginning sound, number of syllables, etc.). It was again found that the memory was most accurate for the beginning of a word, next best for the end, and worst for the middle. To quote from George Miller a *bon mot* that describes this general state of affairs,

(21)   *The mind sags in the middle.*

Since it is unclear to me how to go about proving that (20) should be subsumed under (21), I must leave this issue unresolved for the moment.

3.1.2. Covariations

The next area that I wish to report on I know so little about that I might best pass over it in silence, were it not for its importance. I refer to the issue of covariation: How do the three factors of grammaticality, confidence and liberality correlate?

Though my ignorance of statistics is almost total, I do know that there are statistical measures of correlatedness. Unfortunately, I do not know how to apply them, and I have not been able to work with a statistical informant. Thus I will be using home-brew indices, groping for ways to indicate covariation. My hope is that if any of the correlations I have come across in this pilot study prove to be interesting, future studies, based on less haphazardly arrived at data, and treated with less statistical naiveté, can provide them with a solid statistical footing.

With this caveat, I will describe the procedure I followed to try to come to grips with the interactions of these three variables. First, I wanted to find the average distribution of the four indices of grammaticality, 1–4 (which I will sometimes refer to as grades), over all speakers. This distribution, broken down by groups, appears in the matrix in (22), where each cell gives the total number of occurrences of one grade for some group of subjects, with a percentage figure to its right giving the proportion of the total number of grades given by this group that the number of grades represents.

(22)   The Distribution of Grammaticality Judgements

	1s	2s	3s	4s	Total number of grades
Linguistics					
Native	46 (43%)	32 (30%)	20 (19%)	10 (9%)	108
Foreign	23 (32%)	17 (24%)	19 (26%)	13 (18%)	72
Total linguists	69 (38%)	49 (27%)	39 (22%)	23 (13%)	180
Normals					
Native	44 (28%)	47 (30%)	52 (33%)	13 (8%)	156
Foreign	6 (25%)	5 (21%)	5 (21%)	8 (33%)	24
Total normals	50 (28%)	52 (29%)	57 (32%)	21 (12%)	180
Total all	119 (33%)	101 (28%)	96 (27%)	44 (12%)	360

In (23) and (24), I have given the same breakdown for the variables of confidence and liberality, respectively.

(23)   The Distribution of Confidence Judgements

	Pretty sure ("+")	Middling ("0")	Pretty unsure ("−")	Blank ("/")	Total
Linguists					
Native	77 (73%)	23 (22%)	6 (6%)	2	108
Foreign	49 (73%)	13 (19%)	5 (7%)	5	72
Total linguists	126 (73%)	36 (21%)	11 (6%)	7	180
Normals					
Native	120 (77%)	34 (22%)	1 (1%)	1	156
Foreign	16 (70%)	5 (22%)	2 (9%)	1	24
Total normals	136 (76%)	39 (22%)	3 (2%)	2	180
Total all	262 (75%)	75 (21%)	14 (4%)	9	360

(24)   The Distribution of Liberality Judgements

	Liberal ("L")	Middle of the road ("M")	Conservative ("C")	Blanks	Total
Linguists					
Native	28 (26%)	69 (64%)	10 (9%)	1	108
Foreign	6 (13%)	31 (66%)	10 (21%)	25	72
Total linguists	34 (22%)	100 (65%)	20 (13%)	26	180
Normals					
Native	38 (25%)	62 (41%)	50 (33%)	6	156
Foreign	5 (22%)	12 (52%)	6 (26%)	1	24
Total normals	43 (25%)	74 (53%)	56 (23%)	7	180
Total all	77 (24%)	174 (53%)	76 (23%)	33	360

I now focus on the following type of questions. Given that the overall distribution of grades is 33% | 28% | 27% | 12%, as we see in (21), is this distribution changed when we look only at sentences which received "L" judgements? Or "M" judgements? Or "C", or "+" or any other judgements we may wish to specify?

The answer to the questions involving liberality I have given in (25).

(25)		Number of	Distribution of grades 1s 2s 3s 4s		
	a.	L judgements = 77	27 /27 /18 / 5 35%/35%/23%/ 6%		= 77
			$\lor$ $\land$		
		Overall distribution of grades:	33%/28%/27%/12%		
	b.	M judgements = 174	81 /39 /31 /23 47%/22%/18%/13%		= 174
			$\lor$ $\land$ $\land$		
		Overall distribution of grades:	33%/28%/27%/12%		
	c.	C judgements = 76	2 /30 /34 /10 3% 39% 45%13%		= 76
			$\land$ $\lor$ $\lor$		
		Overall distribution of grades:	33%/28%/27%/12%		

In other words, the greatest difference between the overall grade distribution and the grade distribution among L-judged sentences is that the number of 4s is halved, from 12% overall to 6% with L, a result which we expect, given the abovementioned uninterpretability of "4L" judgements. The next greatest difference when we restrict our attention to L-judged sentences is the 35% versus 28% contrast in the distribution of 2s. For each comparison, I have indicated the greatest percent change with a doubled and rotated inequality sign, "$\land$" or "$\lor$", and the next greatest with a single inequality sign, sometimes citing two, if they seem large.

Since the proportion of 2s increases with Ls, I will say that L *works for* 2; since the proportion of 4s decreases, I will say the L *works against* 4. And since the increase from 28% to 35% for 2s is an increase of 25%, while the decrease of 12% to 6% is a decrease of 50%, I will use these latter two percentages as an index of the amount of "work" that L does for/against 2. In (26), then, we see a reduced version of (25), with indications of the major influences of liberality on grades.

In (27) and (28), which parallel (25) and (26), I have tabulated the influence of confidence on grammaticality.

In the next two tables, I have charted the influence of liberality on confidence.

Before attempting to summarize the data below, we must, it seems to me, ask the reverse questions. That is, while we have seen, in (25a), that there are more 2s (and fewer 4s) among Ls than in the whole population, is

(26) The Influence of Liberality on Grammaticality

a.	i.	L *works for*	2	↑ 25%	(28% versus 35%)
	ii.	L *works against*	4	↓ 50%	(12% versus 6%)
b.	i.	M *works for*	1	↑ 40%	(33% versus 47%)
	ii.	M *works against*	3	↓ 33%	(27% versus 18%)
	iii.	M *also works against*	2	↓ 21%	(28% versus 22%)
c.	i.	C *works for*	3	↑ 66%	(27% versus 45%)
	ii.	C *also works for*	2	↑ 39%	(28% versus 39%)
	iii.	C *works against*	1	↓ 91%	(33% versus 3%)

(27)

Number of	Distribution of grades 1s 2s 3s 4s	
a. + judgements = 262	102 /60 /63 /37 39%/23%/24%/14% ⩔ ⩓	= 262
Overall distribution of grades	33%/28%/27%/12%	
b. 0 judgements = 75	13 /36 /23 / 3 17%/48%/31%/ 4% ⩓ ⩔ ⩓	= 75
Overall distribution of grades	33%/28%/27%/12%	
c. − judgements = 14	3 / 4 / 5 / 2 21%/29%/36%/14% ⩓ ⩔	= 14
Overall distribution of grades	33%/28%/27%/12%	

(28) The Influence of Confidence on Grammaticality

a.	i.	+ *works for*	1	↑ 18%	(33% versus 39%)
	ii.	+ *works against*	2	↓ 18%	(28% versus 23%)
b.	i.	0 *works for*	2	↑ 71%	(28% versus 48%)
	ii.	0 *works against*	4	↓ 66%	(12% versus 4%)
	iii.	0 *also works against*	1	↓ 48%	(33% versus 17%)
c.	i.	− *works for*	3	↑ 33%	(27% versus 36%)
	ii.	− *works against*	1	↓ 36%	(33% versus 21%)

it also true that among all 2s, there are more Ls? And that among all 4s, there are fewer Ls? That is, do L and 2 covary positively, and L and 4 negatively?

The last six tables, (25)–(30), investigated the influence in one direction; the next six contain corresponding information on the opposite implications.

In order to show the focus of the interaction of liberality and grammaticality, I have collapsed all of the influences shown in (26) and (32) in (37); braces group paired influences, and the sectioning into (37a)–(37c) groups all L interactions, then all M ones, then all C ones.

(29)

		Distribution of confidence judgements	
Number of		+'s 0's −'s	
a.	L judgements = 77	50 /22 / 5 64%/29%/ 6% ∧ ∨ ⩔	= 77
	Overall distribution of +/0/−	75%/21%/ 4%	
b.	M judgements = 174	143 /26 / 5 82%/15%/ 3% ∨ ⩕ ∧	= 174
	Overall distribution of +/0/−	75%/21%/ 4%	
c.	C judgements: 76	56 /18 / 2 74%/24%/ 3% ∨ ⩕	= 76
	Overall distribution of +/0/−	75%/ 21% 4%	

(30)   The Influence of Liberality on Confidence

a.	i.	L *works for*	−	↑	50% (4% versus 6%)
	ii.	L *also works for*	0	↑	38% (21% versus 29%)
	iii.	L *works against*	+	↓	15% (75% versus 64%)
b.	i.	M *works for*	+	↑	9% (75% versus 82%)
	ii.	M *works against*	0	↓	29% (21% versus 15%)
	iii.	M *also works against*	−	↓	25% (4% versus 3%)
c.	i.	C *works for*	0	↑	14% (21% versus 24%)
	ii.	C *works against*	−	↓	25% (4% versus 3%)

(31)

		Distribution of liberality judgements		
Number of		L / M / C		Blank
a.	1s = 119	27 /81 / 2 25%/74%/ 2% ∨ ⩕		9 = 119
	Overall distribution of L/M/C	24%/53%/23%		
b.	2s = 101	27 /39 /30 28%/41%/ 31% ∧ ⩔		5 = 101
	Overall distribution of L/M/C	24%/53%/23%		
c.	3s = 96	18 /31 /34 22%/37%/41% ∧ ⩔		13 = 96
	Overall distribution of L/M/C	24%/53%/23%		
d.	4s = 44	4 /25 / 9 11%/66%/24% ⩕ ∨		6 = 44
	Overall distribution of L/M/C	24%/53%/23%		

(32) The Influence of Grammaticality on Liberality

a.	i.	1 *works for*	M	↑	41% (53% versus 74%)
	ii.	1 *works against*	C	↓	91% (23% versus 2%)
b.	i.	2 *works for*	C	↑	34% (23% versus 31%)
	ii.	2 *works against*	M	↓	23% (53% versus 41%)
c.	i.	3 *works for*	C	↑	78% (23% versus 41%)
	ii.	3 *works against*	M	↓	30% (53% versus 37%)
d.	i.	4 *works for*	L	↑	25% (53% versus 66%)
	ii.	4 *works against*	M	↓	54% (24% versus 11%)

(33)

	Number of	Distribution of confidence judgements			Blank
		+	/0	/−	
a.	1s = 119	102	/13	/ 3	1 = 119
		86%/	11%/	3%	
		∨	∧	∧	
	Overall distribution of +/0/−	75%/	21%/	4%	
b.	2s = 101	60	/36	/ 4	1 = 101
		60%/	36%/	4%	
		∧	∨		
	Overall distribution of +/0/−	75%/	21%/	4%	
c.	3s = 96	64	/22	/ 5	5 = 96
		70%/	24%/	5%	
		∧	∨	∨	
	Overall distribution of +/0/−	75%/	21%/	4%	
d.	4s = 44	37	/ 3	/ 2	2 = 44
		88%/	7%/	5%	
		∨	∧	∨	
	Overall distribution of +/0/−	75%/	21%/	4%	

(34) The influence of Grammaticality on confidence

a.	i.	1 *works for*	+	↑	15% (75% versus 86%)
	ii.	1 *works against*	0	↓	48% (21% versus 11%)
	iii.	1 *also works against*	−	↓	25% (4% versus 3%)
b.	i.	2 *works for*	0	↑	71% (21% versus 36%)
	ii.	2 *works against*	+	↓	20% (75% versus 60%)
c.	i.	3 *works for*	−	↑	25% (4% versus 5%)
	ii.	3 *also works for*	0	↑	14% (21% versus 24%)
	iii.	3 *works against*	+	↓	7% (75% versus 70%)
d.	i.	4 *works for*	−	↑	25% (4% versus 5%)
	ii.	4 *also works for*	+	↑	17% (75% versus 88%)
	iii.	4 *works against*	0	↓	67% (21% versus 7%)

(35)

	Number of	Distribution of liberality judgements	
		L / M /C	Blank
a.	+ judgements = 262	49 /143 /55	15 = 262
		20%/58%/22%/	
		∧ ∨	
	Overall distribution of L/M/C	24%/53%/23%	
b.	0 judgements = 75	22 /26 /19	8 = 75
		33%/39%/28%	
		∨ ∧ ∨	
	Overall distribution of L/M/C	24%/53%/23%	
c.	− judgements = 14	5 / 5 / 2	2 = 14
		42%/42%/ 17%	
		∨ ∧ ∧	
	Overall distribution of L/M/C	24%/53%/23%	

(36)   The Influence of Confidence on Liberality

a.	i.	+ *works for*	M	↑ 9%	(53% versus 58%)
	ii.	+ *works against*	L	↓ 17%	(24% versus 20%)
b.	i.	0 *works for*	L	↑ 38%	(24% versus 33%)
	ii.	0 *also works for*	C	↑ 22%	(23% versus 28%)
	iii.	0 *works against*	M	↓ 26%	(53% versus 39%)
c.	i.	− *works for*	L	↑ 75%	(24% versus 42%)
	ii.	− *works against*	M	↓ 26%	(53% versus 42%)
	iii.	− *also works against*	C	↓ 26%	(23% versus 17%)

(37)   The Interaction of Liberality and Grammaticality

		For		Against	
a.		L 2 ↑ 25%		L 4 ↓ 50%	
				4 L ↓ 54%	
b.	i.	M 1 ↑ 40%		M 3 ↓ 33%	
		1 M ↑ 41%		3 C ↓ 30%	
	ii.	4 M ↑ 25%		M 2 ↓ 21%	
				2 M ↓ 23%	
c.	i	C 3 ↑ 66%		C 1 ↓ 91%	
		3 C ↑ 78%		1 C ↓ 91%	
	ii.	C 2 ↑ 39%			
		2 C ↑ 34%			

   In (38) and (39) appear tables like (37) which show how confidence and grammaticality interact, and how liberality and confidence interact, respectively.

(38)
The Interaction of Confidence and Grammaticality

	For			Against		
a.	$\begin{cases}+ & 1 & \uparrow\ 18\% \\ 1 & + & \uparrow\ 15\%\end{cases}$			$\begin{cases}+ & 2 & \downarrow\ 18\% \\ 2 & + & \downarrow\ 20\%\end{cases}$		
	4 + ↑ 17%			3 + ↓ 7%		
b.	$\begin{cases}0 & 2 & \uparrow\ 71\% \\ 2 & 0 & \uparrow\ 71\%\end{cases}$			$\begin{cases}4 & 0 & \downarrow\ 66\% \\ 0 & 4 & \downarrow\ 67\%\end{cases}$		
	3 0 ↑ 14%			$\begin{cases}1 & 0 & \downarrow\ 48\% \\ 0 & 1 & \downarrow\ 48\%\end{cases}$		
c.	$\begin{cases}- & 3 & \uparrow\ 33\% \\ 3 & - & \uparrow\ 25\%\end{cases}$			$\begin{cases}1 & - & \downarrow\ 36\% \\ - & 1 & \downarrow\ 25\%\end{cases}$		
	4 − ↑ 25%					

(39)
The Interaction of Liberality and Confidence

	For			Against		
a.	$\begin{cases}L & - & \uparrow 50\% \\ - & L & \uparrow 75\%\end{cases}$			$\begin{cases}L & + & \downarrow 15\% \\ + & L & \downarrow 17\%\end{cases}$		
	$\begin{cases}L & 0 & \uparrow 38\% \\ 0 & L & \uparrow 38\%\end{cases}$					
b.	$\begin{cases}M & + & \uparrow\ 9\% \\ + & M & \uparrow\ 9\%\end{cases}$			$\begin{cases}M & 0 & \downarrow 29\% \\ 0 & M & \downarrow 26\%\end{cases}$		
				$\begin{cases}M & - & \downarrow 25\% \\ - & M & \downarrow 26\%\end{cases}$		
c.	$\begin{cases}C & 0 & \uparrow 14\% \\ 0 & C & \uparrow 22\%\end{cases}$			$\begin{cases}C & - & \downarrow 25\% \\ - & C & \downarrow 26\%\end{cases}$		

Finally, since it is still somewhat difficult to see the main outlines of (37)–(39), I have condensed these three into a single table, (40), in which only the stronger interactions are highlighted. To estimate the strength of a pair of interactions, I have given the average percentage to the right of each (unordered) pair in (40). Thus, since we see from (37c-i) that C works for 3 (↑ 66%), and also that 3 works for C (↑ 78%), in (40a), to the right of C,3 we find the average of 66% and 78%, namely 72%.

I have included in (40) two types of interactions: *strong* (average percentage > 35%), and *medium* (average percentage > 26%). The latter types are boxed, in (40). The two thresholds of 35% and 26% were chosen impressionistically, with an eye towards making (40) as perspicuous as possible.

(40)   The Strongest Interactions among Liberality,
                        Confidence and Grammaticality

		For		Against	
a.	i.	{ C, 3 } ↑ 72%	{ L, 4 } ↓ 52%
	ii.	{ M, 1 } ↑ 40.5%	{ C, 1 } ↓ 91%
	iii.		{ M, 3 } ↓ 31.5%
b.	i.	{ 0, 2 } ↑ 71%	{ 0, 4 } ↓ 66.5%
	ii.		{ 0, 1 } ↓ 48%
	iii.	{ −, 3 } ↑ 29%	{ −, 1 } ↓ 29.5%
c.	i.	{ L, − } ↑ 62.5%	
	ii.	{ L, 0 } ↑ 38%	
	iii.		{ M, 0 } ↓ 27.5%
	iv.		{ M, − } ↓ 26.5%

We have finally boiled down the data to a point where it seems possible to begin to interpret some of these patterns.

First of all, we expect the strong negative interaction in (40a-ii) between C and 1: As I have noted above, in Section 2, "1C" judgements are uninterpretable. We expect also that, since "4L" judgements are equally uninterpretable, there should be a negative correlation between L and 4, as we indeed find in (40a-i). The difference in size between these two negative interactions is surprising, to be sure: We would expect to find, with "perfect" informants, no cases of either "1C" or "4L" judgements. We note from (8) that one informant, TG, has contributed more of these uninterpretable judgements than all other speakers combined; if we disregard these four cases, we find in the rest of (8) 2 cases of 4L, and one of 1C, a difference that is probably due to chance.

The rest of the interactions in (40a) are harder to explain. It is, to be sure, understandable that C and 3 should work for each other, but why don't C and 4 also do so? And if C works for 3, why shouldn't we find L, the opposite of C, correlating with 2, which could be called "the opposite grade" from 3? In fact, there are no interactions between 2 and any liberality indicator, a puzzling fact, since such interactions do exist for all the other grades.

A related asymmetry is the fact that L turns up in only one interaction in (40a), while C and M turn up in two each (though one of the M ones is only of medium strength).

The correlation of 1 and M is interesting: One is tempted to say "speakers only tend to feel 'middle of the road' in the core." But this would be an incorrect interpretation of (40a-ii), which only means that speakers tend to feel "middle of the road" for *their* core, that is, when they rate a sentence perfect. The medium-strength negative correlation [in (40a-iii)] between M and 3 is puzzling: Why should speakers feel less "middle of the road" when they give a sentence a 3 than when they give it a 2 or a 4?

Turning now to the interactions in (40b), the negative correlations between 0 and 4 and between 0 and 1 are doubtless related (indirectly) to the facts summarized in (20b) above: Confidence is highest at the core, lowest in the bog. But it remains mysterious why the interactions between 0 and grades are stronger than those between − and grades. And why should 0 work so strongly for 2, and not at all for 3?

A final question about confidence: Why is there no strong correlation between + and 1? To press this last point further, why are there no correlations at all between − and any grade or any liberality score, for that matter? Is this related to the absence of correlation between L and grades that was noted above? That is, since L and + are both "positive," in some sense, does this impede correlations for some reason?

Passing on to (40c), the strong correlations are easy to interpret: The more liberally one judges a sentence, the less sure one is of one's judgement. The absence of a similar correlation for C and uncertainty suggests that speakers are aware of the existence of a core, a "region" of English in which the judgements of all speakers will be more in agreement than elsewhere, a region whose typical judgement is "1+M," the most frequent judgement in all of (8).

To sum up, some of the correlations that I have teased out of (8) seem to be related to the "geography" of English, to be in general agreement with the core-bog-fringe partitioning summed up in (20). However, many asymmetries have turned up, and if these should turn out to be statistically significant, they will require hypotheses of a presently unexplored sort for their unravelment.

3.2. The Subjects

3.2.0.

In this section, I will begin with the lengthy task of describing the differences that appear between groups of speakers. Since there are 15 linguists and 15 normals, this bifurcation will yield the best-supported conclusions. The native–foreign split is 22–8, which may be enough for statistical significance, but in the main, I will be concerned with differences that occur between linguists and normals.

I will attempt to document the four differences in (41), which I hope will turn out to be statistically significant.

(41)   *As opposed to linguists,*
    a.   *Normals are less unsure.*
    b.   *Normals are more conservative.*
    c.   *Normals are tougher graders.*
    d.   *Normals make fewer distinctions between levels of grammaticality.*

A tabulation of the voting patterns of all the subjects appears in (42).

(42)

Liberality		Liberality Index	Confidence	+ a − b − c	Grading Profiile	Grade Index 4a + 3b + 2c + d
SG	10/2/0	2.83 L	12/0/0	+12	3/4/3/2	32
JR	6/5/1	2.42 L	6/5/1	0	5/3/3/1	36
JS	4/8/0	2.33 L	9/3/0	+6	8/4/0/0	44
MD	3/9/0	2.25 L	8/3/1	+4	4/1/6/1	32
WL	2/10/0	2.08 M	4/5/2	−3	2/6/3/1	33
DK	1/10/1	2.00 C	11/1/0	+10	7/3/2/0	41
CF	2/6/3	1.91 M	4/5/2	−3	6/3/2/1	33
CJF	0/10/2	1.83 M	11/1/0	+10	5/4/1/2	37
PMP	0/9/3	1.75 C	12/0/0	+12	6/4/0/2	38
PF	3/9/0	2.25 L	9/1/2	+6	7/3/1/1	40
LF	1/10/1	2.00 M	11/0/1	+10	6/5/0/1	40
JG	1/7/4	1.75 C	11/1/0	+10	2/2/4/4	26
UQ	1/5/5	1.64 C?	7/4/0	+3	3/3/4/2	31
MB	——		7/5/0	+2	3/2/4/3	29
EL	——		4/2/2	0	2/2/6/2	28
RD	7/3/2	2.42 L	12/0/0	+12	4/6/2/0	38
RE	7/3/2	2.42 {L(Sp) / C(W)}	7/5/0	+2	1/5/4/2	29
HG	6/3/3	2.25 L/M	6/5/1	0	3/3/6/0	33
JK	4/7/1	2.25 L (somewhat)	10/2/0	+8	2/4/5/1	31
CH	6/2/4	2.17 C	10/2/0	+8	3/3/5/1	32
MY	4/5/3	2.08 L	8/4/0	+4	3/6/2/1	35
HW	1/10/1	2.00 /	10/2/0	+8	6/1/3/2	35
JL	2/7/3	1.92 C	7/5/0	+2	4/4/3/1	35
JC	0/6/6	1.50 C	12/0/0	+12	4/2/6/0	34
HJ	0/6/6	1.50 C	11/1/0	+10	5/1/5/1	34
DS	0/5/7	1.42 C	12/0/0	+12	2/5/2/3	30
KP	0/5/7	1.42 C	10/2/0	+8	4/3/4/1	34
AG	1/0/5	1.25 L?	5/6/0	−1	3/4/5/0	34
TG	5/4/2	2.27 L	6/3/2	+1	3/2/3/4	28
IJ	0/8/4	1.67 C	10/2/0	+8	2/3/2/4	25

Note first of all that there is good agreement between the self-descriptions by the subjects, as to whether they are L, M, or C in general, and their indices of liberality. With the exception, among the linguists, of DK, whose index would put him among the self-styled Ms, but who styles himself a C, and among the normals, of CH, whose index is that of a liberal, but who styles himself a conservative, and of AG, who has the most conservative of all indices, yet who styles himself a liberal—with these exceptions, each of the four subgroups of (42) shows non-overlapping areas of self-stylings of L, M, and C.

I find this non-overlappingness a healthy sign, an indication that speakers do have a general notion of their own liberality, for in most cases, the overall judgement was given some time after the test had been taken, and in no case did the speakers seem to be reviewing their judgements on just these 12 sentences. Only linguists described themselves as being general middle-of-the-roaders, a surprising result, in my view. Possibly HW, a normal, whose questionnaire was incomplete, would have described himself as being in general M, since all informants whose number of Ms exceeded the sum of their Ls and Cs by 8, as his does, called themselves Ms. But if subsequent research should lead to the conclusion that normals, in fact, do not generally call themselves Ms, this may be part of the wider phenomenon of categorylessness, which I will discuss below.

3.2.1. Confidence

As can be seen in (23), normals voted "+" slightly more often than linguists (75% versus 73%), but voted "−" only one-third as often as linguists (2% versus 6%). There are very few −s in the whole sample, but I suspect this trend would hold up with larger data bases. The conclusion seems to be that thinking about language makes one realize how little one knows about it, and shatters one's confidence in one's own judgement. Or, to put it in the pithier words of John Lawler,

(43)   *Doing syntax rots the brain.*

3.2.2. Conservativeness

As (24) shows, while linguists and normals are in rough agreement with respect to the percentage of liberal judgements, they differ with respect to middle-of-the-road judgements, which linguists show about 20% more of (65% versus 53%), and conservative judgements, which normals make almost twice as often as linguists (24% versus 13%).

In addition, if we inspect the liberality indices for the two groups, we see that the distribution of the Cs within subjects is different. There are 5 normals (JC, HJ, DS, KP and AG) whose indices are below the lowest index posted by a linguist, UQ's 1.64.

There is a further regularity among (almost) all subjects, a relation not visible in (40c).

(44)   *All self-styled conservatives (except two: UQ and JL) are highly confident; none shows any −'s.*

That is, 80% of the self-styled conservatives had far more +'s than 0s or −'s. The reverse implication, (45),

(45)   *All subjects who are highly confident style themselves as conservatives.*

has 3 exceptions: JK, whose confidence score is +8, and the two most firebrand radicals of the two groups, SG for the linguists, and RD for the normals. Is this an accident, or one of the many cases where "les extrèmes se touchent"? Without a larger sample, we can only guess.

3.2.3. Grade Inflation

This demon of academic life seems to have worked its tentacles even into the hallowed groves of grammaticality. We note from (22) that while linguists and normals used roughly the same number of 2s and 4s, the linguists used about 35% more 1s (38% versus 28%), and the normals used about 45% more 3s (57% versus 39%). That is, linguists tended to give sentences higher grades than normals.

The interested reader can verify that this is true not only globally, but also sentence by sentence in (8). For one sentence, *and,* the sum of linguist grades was equal to the sum of normal grades, and for 3 sentences—*circumstances, fact,* and *idea*—the linguists' sum was higher than the normals' sum (in the first 2 of these sentences, the difference between the sums was only one point). But for 8 of the 12 sentences, the linguists' sum was lower than the normals' sum.

Another way of seeing the average difference of grading patterns between groups of subjects is to convert the grading profile shown in (42) into a number, as shown in the rightmost column of (42), the Grade Index. This is computed from the Grading Profile by taking four times the number of 1s (a), adding to it three times the number of 2s (b), plus two times the number of 3s (c), plus one times the number of 4s (d). Thus this computation for SG yields $4(3) + 4(3) + 3(2) + 2 = 12 + 12 + 6 + 2 = 32$. The highest possible score, which is almost attained by JS, would be $4(12) + 4(0) + 4(0) + 0 = 48$; the lowest would be $0 + 2(0) + 3(0) + 12 = 12$.

The average values of the grade Index for various groupings of subjects are shown in (46).

(46)
    a. *Average for all subjects* (30):   33.6
        i. *All native speakers* (22):   34.8
       ii. *All foreign speakers* (8):   30.1

    b. *Average for all linguists* (15):   34.7
        i. *Native linguists* (9):   36.2
       ii. *Foreign linguists* (6):   32.3

    c. *Average for all normals* (15):   32.5
        i. *Native normals* (13):   33.4
       ii. *Foreign normals* (2):   28.1

These figures show a surprising degree of regularity, and seem to be derivable from the following general hypothesis:

(47) *The more "contact" with American English, the higher will be the Grade Index.*

This accounts for the difference between all natives and all foreign speakers [(46a-i) versus (46a-ii)], the difference between native and foreign linguists [(46b-i) versus (46b-ii)], and for the difference between native and foreign normals [(46c-i) versus (46c-ii)]. Furthermore, if we assume that for someone to think metalinguistically, the stock in trade of all linguists, increases that person's "contact" with their own language (or even with all languages?), (47) can suggest an explanation for why native linguists graded higher than native normals [(46b-i) versus (46c-i)], and why foreign linguists graded higher than foreign normals [(46b-ii) versus (46c-ii)].

It begins to become obvious that "contact" is not such a clear term as might have been thought (which is why I have been enclosing it in quotes), but if we can assume that the four groups shown in (48) decrease monotonically in contact, then their average grading indices match this sequence exactly.

(48)
a.	*Native linguists*	(36.2)	>
b.	*Native normals*	(33.4)	>
c.	*Foreign linguists*	(32.3)	>
d.	*Foreign normals*	(28.1)	>

A further prediction, looking within groups, is that among the foreign linguists, PF, LF and JG, who all live within English-speaking communities, should have higher grade indices than UQ, MB, and EL, who live in Germany. This prediction is borne out:

(49)
a.	*Average Grade Index for PF, LF and JG:*	35.3 >
b.	*Average Grade Index for UQ, MB and EL:*	29.3

Furthermore, it may be significant that within the subgroups of (49), UQ has had more contact with American English than MB and EL, because she has lived in the United States for more than a year, while MB and EL have never visited the US. UQ's index is the highest of these three.

Among the subgroup in (49a), we would expect LF to have the highest index, for only she presently lives in America. While her score is not higher than those of PF and JG, at least it is not lower than either of these.

The only counterexample I can see to (47) is the fact that IJ lives in America, while TG does not, despite the fact that their indices would indicate the opposite.

I am aware, of course, that these facts can only be taken as suggestions for further checking—the numbers of subjects involved are too small for significance.

One final, intriguing, possibility suggests itself. If (47) is taken literally, it should imply that grade indices will rise with age. Since no such hypothesis had ever occurred to me at the time I gathered the data, I did not gather age data. However, by a combination of guessing and prior acquaintanceship, I have tried to divide the two larger groups of subjects, native linguists (9) and native normals (13) into those under 35, and those over 35. There are three native linguists who I believe to be under 35 (namely SG, MD, and DK), and their average index is 35. The index of the six remaining native linguists is 36.8. Among native normals, the average index of the 6 (namely RD, CH, MY, JL, KP, and DS) who I believe to be under 35 is 34; that of the remaining 8 is 32.9. Disappointing, but it may be worthwhile to make a more detailed investigation in the future of a systematic correlation of age and grading.

3.2.4. Categorylessness

The last observation that I wish to make about the difference between linguists and normals is that the former seem to make fuller use of the four grades than the latter do. It would appear, if some informant returns a questionnaire which only uses grades 1, 2, and 4, that (s)he is fusing 2 categories (2 and 3? or 3 and 4?) to span the entire gamut of grammaticality. However, this may in fact be wrong—the informant may protest "I do make use of a category 3, but there were no examples of it among the test sentences."

I think the only way to decide this armchair dispute is to devise a sufficiently (whatever statistical sense can be made of this term) large test, so that we are sure, to reasonable confidence levels, that sentences of all grammatical types will appear on the test.

Pending the resolution of this possibly quite complex task of sampling, we should more correctly speak of "apparent categorylessness," but I will leave off the adjective, and hope that no confusion will be caused by this decision.

Before we look at the actual grading profiles, I want to suggest that we might distinguish between "having n categories" and "having n categories weakly." That is, we would all agree, I think, that an informant whose grading profile was 3/3/3/3 was fully using all four grades, and that one whose profile was 3/3/0/6 was categoryless. But what of a profile like 3/3/1/5? That is, cases where a category is used just once. Can we call this partial, or near, category loss? Of course, the same questions of data skew arise as we have discussed for category loss, but I will even-handedly disregard them in both instances.

The facts are these: There are somewhat more linguists who use a category at least twice than there are normals who do. The figures appear in (50).

(50)   a.   *Number of linguists who make "full use" of* 1–4:   5 (33%)

       b.   *Number of normals who do:*   3 (23%)

(51)

Types of Categorylessness by Group

	Number of grades used					
Subjects	(A) All four grades used at least twice	(B) Three grades used at least twice, one used once	(C) Only three grades, all used at least twice	(D) Two grades used only once, two used at least twice	(E) One grade used at least twice	(F) Only two grades used
Linguists Native	1 (SG)	2(DK_4, PMP_3)	4(JR_4, WL_4, CF_4, CJF_3)	1($MD_{2,4}$) 1($PF_{3,4}$)	1($LF_{4,3}$)	1($JS_{3,4}$)
Foreign	4 (JG, UQ, MB, EL)					
Normals Native	1 (DS)	4(RD_4, HG_4, AG_4, JC_4)	7(RE_1, JK_4, CH_4, MY_4, HW_2, JL_4, KP_4)	1($HJ_{2,4}$)		
Foreign	2 (TG, IJ)					

When we look at the issue of partial category loss (or use), the facts are less clear. Possibly the table in (51) will help to display the data. When subscripts follow a subjects' initials, they indicate which grades are absent, or are present only once.

Surveying the subscripts, we see that it is predominantly the grade 4 that is omitted entirely (in Column C, 83% of the cases of one grade missing were 4s), or used only partially (in Column B, 73% of the "weak" grades were 4, and in all cases in which more than one grade is weak or missing, 4 is one of the two grades). 3 seems to be the next most frequently un(der)used grade, then 2, then 1. This overall asymmetry between 1 and 4 I have no explanation for.

In (50), I compared the 5 linguists who use all grades fully with the 3 normals who do, noting a small percentual difference, quite possibly a non-significant one. A much more revealing comparison, however, is that between natives and foreign speakers:

(52)   *Number of subjects using all four grades at least twice:*

Natives (22)		
Linguists	1	(11%)
Normals	1	(8%)
Total	2	(9%)
Foreigners (8)		
Linguists	4	(66%)
Normals	2	(100%)
Total	6	(75%)

The obvious conclusion—that foreign speakers use the grades more fully than do natives—is given further support by the observation that among the foreign linguists, we see that the three German linguists (UQ, MB, and EL) have no category loss, while 2 of the English-speaking foreigners (PF and LF) do.

3.3. Summary

To sum up the most important points of the discussion in Sections 3.1 and 3.2, the sentences of a language seem to be viewed by speakers as falling into three groups: a core, a bog, and a fringe. Turning to the speakers, there are fairly clear differences between linguists and normals (the latter view themselves as more conservative than the former, and the latter reject more sentences, and with greater confidence, than the former do). There are also differences between native and foreign speakers, with the latter tending to reject more sentences than the former do, and also tending strongly to make fuller use of all four grades than the former do.

4. DOWNSHOT AND UPSHOT

What conclusions can be drawn from the investigations? First, let me say what can't be.

I have tried to say above, in many ways, that this research should be looked at as only a pilot study, but perhaps this point cannot be overemphasized enough. If I had the experiment to do over again, I would try to plug the following leaks:

1. I would get more speakers, enough in each group so that the variables of linguist versus normal, and native versus foreign could be studied satisfactorily. Also, I would gather data about the ages of the subjects, to check out the possibility that grade inflation might be a function of age.

2. I would include some simpler sentences, which hopefully all speakers could agree to judge as 1s—garden variety examples like *The carafe is on the giraffe* or *This furnace heats well*—as well as some more clearly hopeless strings, like *Than is* or *Either as Zonk along*, to try to rule out the possibility that there is no adequate baseline.

3. I would use sentences that differed minimally from one another in structure, or sentences whose implicational relationships had been established in previous studies, such as the hierarchically arranged sentences in (4)–(6). The present study suffers greatly from the sentences being such a motley gang.

4. I would replace the L/M/C task by another. I would instruct speakers to (try to) give two grades to each example—their grade and that grade that they believe most people would assign to it, if it was higher or lower than their grade. This would automatically prevent such confusions as the uninterpretable "1C" or "4L" judgements that I have pointed out above, and in addition, it would lay to rest a nagging suspicion I have that many "1L" or "4C" judgements (and both types occur rather frequently) do not mean what I asked the respondents to mean with them. For instance, "1L" is supposed to mean, "I give this sentence a top grade—it's perfect for me, but most people rate it lower." But when I see such judgements on core sentences, or "4C" judgements on the fringe, I fear that the respondent is meaning "This sentence is fine (alternately wretched) for me. By the way, I'm in general pretty liberal (alternately conservative)." I may be wrong here, but I cannot tell with the L/M/C way of posing the question.

I hope that this last change in the form of the question would yield data which would bear on one of the original questions that I asked myself at the outset: Namely, do speakers know that their judgements are in agreement with or in disagreement with those of most speakers? Do they know

which way to the core? As things stand, I have not been able to find any
evidence that they do.

What conclusions can be drawn?

One of some interest is that probably no one in the world has the same
set of judgements for any large set of sentences. This can be seen in (53)
below, in which I have constructed a decision tree for the matrix in (8),
using only grades—confidence and liberality judgements have been
excluded.

(53)

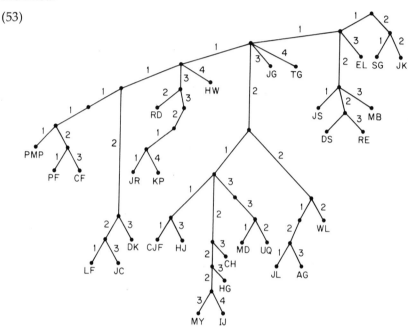

The notation used in this tree is the following: The topmost node
represents the grade given by a speaker for the most popular sentence in
(8), *doctor*. Most respondents gave the grade 1, so to "find" them in the
tree, we follow the leftmost branch, labeled "1." The two speakers who
rated this sentence 2 are found by following the rightmost branch, labeled
"2," which descends from the topmost node.

The next node below the topmost one shows, similarly, how the speakers rated the second most popular sentence, *circumstances*. Each speaker's
gradings are followed to uniqueness. That is, there is only one speaker
(JK) who gave "best" two sentences the grade of 2, so the branch representing his decisions stops after two sentences. Similarly, only one
speaker (EL) voted 1 on *doctor* and 3 on *circumstances*, so here again the
branch stops after the top two sentences. However, both DS and RE gave
identical grades to the first three sentences, namely 1-2-2, so their

branches are pursued until the fourth sentence, where they differ, thus ending the need to continue to check their responses.

The longest shared branches are those which terminate in the following three groupings: {MY, IJ}, {JR, KP}, and {PF, CF}. Each member of these pairs of speakers voted the same as the other member of that pair for the first 7 sentences, then differed. So seven sentences are enough here to show all 30 subjects to be responding differently. Logically, of course, three sentences would have been enough, since with four grades to choose from, there are 4×4×4 = 64 different ways of voting on the first three sentences.

It might be thought that the reason for all this variation is that speakers were asked to respond to too fine a category grid—that had they been asked to vote just "yes" or "no," things would have been neater.

Not much neater, I don't think. The subjects were not asked, but maybe we can estimate what their votings might have looked like by eliminating the middle grades in favor of the extremes, that is, by lumping 2s and 1s together as "yesses" (i.e., 1s), and 3s and 4s as "noes" (i.e., 4s). The results of such lumping appear in (54).

(54)

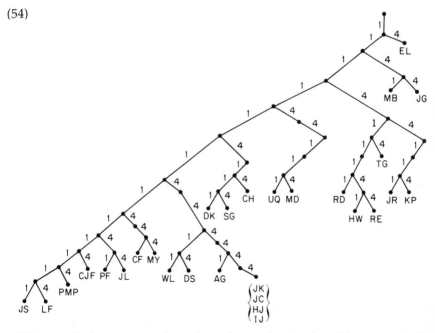

Here we find some grouping of speakers—the bracketed foursome in the middle of (54) are not distinct from one another in terms of our yes–no simulation. But all of the other 28 subjects are distinct, and it is pretty clear to me that as this foursome is asked a few more sentences in the (huge)

mid area, between humdrum (*My feet itch*) and salad (*Itch feet my*), they too will part company.

So where *is* English? If we restrict our attention to the native American subjects, and exclude those among that group who spoke a clearly identifiable regional dialect, we are left with a large group, a solid majority of the native American group, who would all describe themselves as "speaking the same way." The differences uncovered by this questionnaire do not rise to the conscious level, and rarely make trouble [although this can happen, if no surrounding context can be leaned on to find out what (55) means].

(55)   *When you're writing checks, remember that we barely have $500 in our account.*

Retesting the subjects would doubtless show that the judgements recorded in (8) are as unreliable as those in the other studies that Carden reported on (Carden, 1976). It is certainly possible that repeated retesting, of this and other groups, would gradually lead to a set of clear, reliable data for these sentences which showed much less intersubject variation. That would certainly be nice.

But I confess that I am doubtful. The view of a language that seems most plausible to me is that the sentences of a language are points in an n-space, for some value of n certainly in the hundreds, probably in the thousands. The axes of this space are made up of such implicationally ordered sequences as those exemplified in (4)–(6) above. An idiolect is a vector in this n-space, giving at least the threshold values between grammaticality and ungrammaticality for every axis. I say "at least" here, because it seems more than likely that it will also be necessary to specify, for each axis and for each speaker, *how fast* the sentences along it proceed from grammaticality to ungrammaticality, as the threshold value (area?) is approached and left behind. And each speaker's vector, or path, through the space will, I expect, be as individual as his or her face—a linguistic fingerprint.

I should perhaps mention that the full picture will probably be orders of magnitude more complex than the above suggests. For we have been talking only about the grammaticality n-space—there may be other n-spaces pertaining to judgements of formality, of clarity, of slanginess, of floweriness, of sentences that one would use in speech but not in writing, of sentences with the opposite preference, of sentences that one would not use, but would accept. . . . And we do not know to what extent the hierarchies that define these many spaces remain constant under change of space. In the worst case, then, a speaker's competence would have to be represented by a set of vectors, one for each space. But could it be that the centers of all spaces coincide? Could it be that the core of the grammatical space is also the least formal, most clear, least slangy, least flowery, etc. of all sets of sentences? An intriguing possibility.

And if such attributes of judgements as confidence and liberality can be shown to have value in studying the grammaticality space, it is plausible to assume that this will also hold true for many of the other spaces.

It is to be hoped that improved methodologies will reveal that speakers know where they are in each space, which way the center is. Further studies may try to ascertain whether the correlation of grade inflation with "contact" with a language (in all ill-defined sense) is true only of the grammaticality space or is more generally valid.

The present study, a nudge at the lid on Pandora's Box, can only serve to provide a glimpse of how vast and little-understood a structure a human language is.

ACKNOWLEDGMENTS

This work was supported in part by a grant from the National Institute of Mental Health (Grant number MH 13390-12) and by a fellowship from the John Simon Guggeheim Memorial Foundation, which support I gratefully acknowledge.

I have been thinking (ineffectually) about grammaticality for about 15 years now, an interest that may have its roots in Zellig Harris's routinely distinguishing between 4 or 5 levels of grammaticality in his work on English. This framework gave me a space to think in; I've been roaming around in that space ever since.

More recently, my views have been shaped by the powerful work of Derek Bickerton, Guy Carden, Donald Hindle, Bill Labov, Terry Moore, and Ivan Sag; and John Schumann, more of all of whose insights, and in some cases advice and criticism, of this paper, and the thinking out of which it has grown, would have been better, had I made fuller use of.

Without the help of the 29 friends whose initials appear in the leftmost column of (8), of course, there would have been no data for me to cudgel my brains out on. So for their time and patience, and for these facts, which have taught me a lot, I thank them most sincerely.

I'd also like to thank Ed Walker for doing his best to raise a corner of the curtain of darkness which shields the laws of statistics from my comprehension.

Many errors remain, of course; just as the Navajo weavers purposely make one error in a rug, to let the soul out, so I cannily craft errors into all of my papers.

Lastly but not leastly, my thanks to Chuck Fillmore and Bill Wang for putting together a great conference at a seaside location which shall remain nameless, and to them and Dan Kempler for endless patience.

APPENDIX

Please rate the following sentences as to their grammaticality, using the following numerical prefixes:

1. The sentence sounds perfect. You would use it without hesitation.
2. The sentence is less than perfect—something in it just doesn't feel comfortable. Maybe lots of people could say it, but you never feel quite comfortable with it.
3. Worse than 2, but not completely impossible. Maybe somebody might use the sentence, but certainly not you. The sentence is almost beyond hope.
4. The sentence is absolutely out. Impossible to understand, nobody would say it. Un-English.

Place one number in the dash provided at the end of each sentence.

In addition, try to indicate how confident you are of your judgement [Example: I *think* the following sentence is OK (rates a 1) but I'm not sure: *I have scant reason to complain.* I don't think it's ungrammatical—it's just that I'm not sure of my judgement.] After each sentence, please indicate your confidence by circling the appropriate word: *Pretty sure/ Middling/ Pretty unsure*

Finally, one sometimes feels that one's own feelings about a sentence are unrepresentative. Some sentences which I accept many people reject: [an example of this: *We fear that these points the teacher may not cover in depth*], but the opposite happens also [for instance, in *Mildred depends on Sheila, and Sheila (on) Michael,* most people I have asked can omit the *on* before *Michael*: I can't]. Thus in this last case, I am *conservative* with respect to most speakers; in the former case, I am *liberal*. In case you feel that your reaction to any of the sentences below is either liberal or conservative, please indicate this by circling the appropriate word. Otherwise, circle *middle of the road.*

1. Under no circumstances would I accept that offer._____
    Pretty sure/ Middling/ Pretty unsure   Liberal/Middle of the road/Conservative

2. Nobody who I get along with is here who I want to talk to._____
    Pretty sure/ Middling/ Pretty unsure   Liberal/Middle of the road/Conservative

3. We don't believe the claim that Jimson ever had any money._____
    Pretty sure/Middling/ Pretty unsure   Liberal/Middle of the road/Conservative

4. The fact he wasn't in the store shouldn't be forgotten._____
    Pretty sure/ Middling/ Pretty unsure   Liberal/Middle of the road/Conservative

5. What will the grandfather clock stand between the bed and?_____
    Pretty sure/ Middling/ Pretty unsure   Liberal/Middle of the road/Conservative

6. I urge that anything he touch be burned._____
    Pretty sure/ Middling/ Pretty unsure   Liberal/Middle of the road/Conservative

7. All the further we got was to Sudbury._____
    Pretty sure/ Middling/ Pretty unsure   Liberal/Middle of the road/Conservative

8. That is a frequently talked about proposal._____
    Pretty sure/ Middling/ Pretty unsure   Liberal/Middle of the road/Conservative

9. Nobody is here who I get along with who I want to talk to._____
    Pretty sure/ Middling/ Pretty unsure   Liberal/Middle of the road/Conservative

10. The doctor is sure that there will be no problems._____
    Pretty sure/ Middling/ Pretty unsure   Liberal/Middle of the road/Conservative

11. a. We ⎰ have barely ⎱ $500 in our account._____ Pretty sure/ Middling/ Pretty unsure
       ⎱ barely have ⎰   _____Pretty sure/ Middling/ Pretty unsure

    b. We have ⎧ scarcely $500 ⎫ in our account.____ Pretty sure/Middling/ Pretty unsure
               ⎨ scarcely have ⎬   _____ Pretty sure/ Middling
               ⎩ $500   ⎭   Pretty unsure

What do these sentences, if grammatical for you, mean? Check once—after (i), (ii), or (iii)—and indicate

(i)   We have a little more than $500 [say $501 or $502]_____Liberal/Middle of the road/Conservative

(ii) We have a little less than $500 [say $499 or $498]_____Liberal/Middle of the road/ Conservative

(iii) We have around $500 [say $500 give or take $5]_____Liberal/Middle of the road/ Conservative

12. The idea he wasn't in the store is preposterous._____
    Pretty sure/ Middling/ Pretty unsure   Liberal/Middle of the road/Conservative

13. Such formulas should be writable down._____
    Pretty sure/ Middling/ Pretty unsure   Liberal/Middle of the road/Conservative

    Finally, would you feel that you are in general, not only with respect to these
    sentences, basically liberal, middle of the road, or conservative?

REFERENCES

Bickerton, D. *Dynamics of a creole system*. Cambridge, England: Cambridge University Press,
    1975.
Brown, R. and McNeill, D. The tip of the tongue phenomenon. *Journal of Verbal Learning and
    Verbal Behavior*, 1966, 5, 325–337.
Carden, G. Syntactic and semantic data: Replication results. *Language and Society*, Vol. 5. Pp.
    99–104.
Chomsky, N. *Syntactic structures*, s'Gravenhage, Holland: Mouton and Co., 1957.
Coleman, L. Why the only interesting syntactic dialects are the uninteresting ones. In C.
    Corum, T. C. Smith-Stark, and A. Weiser (Eds.), *Papers from the ninth Regional Meeting
    of the Chicago Linguistic Society*, Chicago, Illinois: Chicago Linguistic Society, 1973, pp.
    78–88.
Hindle, D. and Sag, I. Some more on *anymore*. In R. Fasold and R. Shuy (Eds.), *Analyzing
    Variation in Language. Papers from the Second Colloquium on New Ways of Analyzing
    Variation*. Washington, D.C.: Georgetown University Press, 1975.
Moore, T. Judgments and stars: Preferences and daggers. Unpublished   multilith, Cam-
    bridge University, Cambridge, England, 1973.
Schumann, J. H. The implications of pidginization and creolization for the study of adult
    second language acquisition. In J. H. Schumann and N. Stenson (Eds.), *New Frontiers in
    Second Language Learning*. Rowley, Massachusetts: Newbury House Publishers, 1974.
Spencer, N. Differences between linguists and non-linguists in intuitions of
    grammaticality–acceptability. *Journal of Psycholinguistic Research*, 2, 83–98.

III

ACQUISITION

8

Profile Analysis of
Language Disability

DAVID CRYSTAL AND PAUL FLETCHER

This chapter outlines the motivation and general characteristics of the notion of *Profiles* of grammatical ability, for use in the assessment and remediation of language disorders. A full rationale and detailed illustration of the procedure is given in Crystal, Fletcher, and Garman (1976). The topic seems appropriate for the present volume, as its focus is very much on patterns of *individual* disability. Although we would like to make generalizations about disability, and contribute to diagnosis, at present we do not think that sufficient empirical work has been done to enable us to provide a coherent linguistic account of the major clinical syndromes, or a set of criteria which would lead to more precise definitions of terms used in this field. We have begun to make suggestions in this area now, but the bulk of our work in recent years has been to identify the linguistic characteristics of an individual patient's disability, and to suggest guidelines for individual therapy. Our aims, in the first instance, are pragmatic—to make a useful contribution to ongoing therapy. We wish to look, in as much detail

167

Individual Differences in Language Ability and
Language Behavior

Copyright © 1979 by Academic Press, Inc.
All rights of reproduction in any form reserved.
ISBN 0-12-255950-9

as possible, at samples of language behavior, in order to define immediate and long-term teaching goals, and then to explore the several different routes a therapist can take in order to arrive at one of these goals. In due course we hope, by examining several cases of successful and unsuccessful therapy, to develop some kind of explanatory account of the nature of linguistic intervention, and thus, ultimately, to contribute to a theory of language disability.

Our initial motivation, then, was to establish criteria for evaluation. What would count as a "useful contribution"? Such criteria, of course, must come from the professions involved (therapist, remedial teacher, etc.) and not from the linguist directly—though he will necessarily have to interpret these criteria in terms of his own framework of reference. Our interpretation of the clinical literature suggests that, to be justified, a linguistic approach must be able to contribute to both of the main areas of clinical inquiry: *assessment* (in its broadest sense, to include screening and diagnosis) and *remediation*. Its role must be judged, first, by the extent to which it provides the teacher or therapist (T, hereafter) with insight into the character of a patient's or pupil's (P, hereafter) disability, or of a disorder seen as a general type. By "insight" here, we mean two things: (a) the observations made by the linguist were not being made by Ts working within traditional paradigms of inquiry (or which could not have been made thereby, due to their limited range); (b) the observations are productive, that is, they suggest patterns of assessment (by demonstrating the *systematic* nature of the data of disability, in given instances) and patterns of remediation (by making *predictions* concerning progress, motivating "What to teach next?" and indicating specific strategies of T–P interaction, such as the type of stimulus sentence to use).

Second, the role of linguistics must be judged by the extent to which it can introduce an element of conscious control into a clinical situation. This point, of course, applies to any technique of intervention, and indeed to the entire concept of speech therapy. The aim of the exercise is not solely to obtain progress in P, but to be sure that the progress obtained was due to the intervention of T, using the training which qualified T as a therapist in the first place, and thus be able to explain the basis of any improvement or deterioration. It is a commonplace that many Ps can improve given plenty of sympathy from relatives and a rich language environment. To what extent is improvement facilitated by therapeutic intervention? Sometimes it is possible to say with confidence that the therapy "caused" the progress, especially when a rapid change in language ability is produced after a long period of stability or regression. It is even sometimes possible to arrange for comparative studies using control groups, though here the methodological and ethical problems are well known. But on the whole, verification of the efficacy of most therapeutic strategies is lacking, in scientifically convincing terms. If linguistic techniques are to be valuable, then, they should be able to introduce a greater measure of control over the nature of T–P interaction, thus helping to build up the professional confidence that clinical language work badly needs. There is no attempt here to suggest how far these techniques can help in achieving such a goal. By themselves they are not enough, as so many of the variables are nonlinguistic in character. But it should be possible to show a *relative* gain in control, compared with current practice; and it is just such an increased awareness of the linguistic variables involved affecting assessment and remediation that linguistics, in our view, aims to provide, and by which it should be judged.

It will be evident from this orientation that we feel the linguistic study of language disability to be still at an empirical and methodological stage. We are as anxious as anyone to see theoretical progress being made, to see the development of consistent, comprehensive, and formally based diagnostic classification, and to relate the findings of language pathology to the study of language behavior in general. But such progress is not going to be made until far more patients have been studied in linguistic depth from several linguistic points of view than has yet happened. Case studies abound, but the differences in theory and methodology used (e.g., sampling procedures, choice of linguistic model) make comparison of results extremely difficult. What is needed is the large-scale analysis of patient language, using a standardized procedure, and a sufficiently sophisticated linguistic framework to be able to cope with the range of patterns that are found. In our case, we focused our attention on the possibility of developing such a framework for grammatical analysis, an area which has, on the whole, received little systematic investigation by clinicians, and where there was a great deal of accumulated wisdom already available in general linguistics and psycholinguistics to indicate what could and should be done. The framework which was ultimately established came to be known as LARSP, the Language Assessment Remediation and Screening Procedure, and this has now been used routinely in several centers in Britain for some time. The salient characteristics of LARSP are threefold: descriptive, developmental, and interactional. (See the Appendix at the end of this chapter for a sample chart.)

DESCRIPTIVE

The descriptive framework is a simplified version of the grammatical approach found in Quirk *et al.* (1972), and is, in principle, capable of handling the whole range of adult syntactic structures in English. Four levels of grammatical organization are recognized in this model: simple sentence (or clause), phrase, word, and sentence (clause) connectivity. At each level, there is a classification of the main structures operating in

English. At the level of the clause, all utterances are analyzed into combinations of Subject, Verb, Object, Complement or Adverbial, for example, SVO (*John kicked the ball*), VOA (*Kick the ball quickly*), etc. At the level of the phrase, the range of expansions that may occur at each element of clause structure is given, for example, Determiner + Noun, Adjective + Noun, Preposition + Determiner + Noun. At the level of the word, the set of inflectional morphemes is given −*ing*, −*ed*, etc. Under the heading of connectivity, we give the set of devices that build up complex structures—the main means of coordination and subordination.

In addition, two functional distinctions are introduced: (*a*) the traditional classification of sentence types into statement, question, command, and exclamatory (≠"exclamation") is made; (*b*) a distinction between major sentence types (as given above) and minor sentence types (grammatically unanalyzable or nonproductive patterns, for example, responses such as *yes−no* and stereotyped phrases such as *How's tricks?*).

Finally, measures of sentence length (in terms of institutionalized words) and interaction (number of sentences per conversational turn) are given, to assist the comparison of our results with those for whom assessment in terms of length is a primary factor.

DEVELOPMENTAL

A synthesis of the descriptive findings of the language acquisition literature provides a postulated set of age-related stages of syntactic development. Ages are averages, which will ultimately need to be refined with reference to socioeconomic, sex, and other well-known variables. Seven stages are recognized:

Stage I	(0:9–1:6)	Single-element sentences, for example, N (*daddy*), V (*gone*)
Stage II	(1:6–2:0)	Two-element clauses, for example, SV (*daddy gone*), VO (*kick ball*), PrepN (*in box*), Det N (*that ball*).
Stage III	(2:0–2:6)	Three-element clauses, for example, SVO (*daddy kick ball*)
Stage IV	(2:6–3:0)	Four-(or more) element clauses, for example, SVOA (*daddy kick ball hard*)
Stage V	(3:0–3:6)	Clause sequence and connectivity, for example, coordination (*daddy gone in the garden and him hurt his knee*)
Stage VI	(3:6–4:6)	Completion of grammatical "systems": elimination of local child forms, for example, in the pronoun system (*he* for

<table>
<tr><td></td><td></td><td>him above), and the addition of further members of a system, for example, pre-determiners in the NP (all, both, etc.).</td></tr>
<tr><td>Stage VII</td><td>(4:6–?)</td><td>Other structures, for example, sentence connectivity using adverbials (actually, frankly), emphatic word order variation (it was X that Y, etc.).</td></tr>
</table>

No attempt is made to explain these stages in nonlinguistic terms (for instance, whether the basis of development between Stages I and IV is best seen in terms of the child's increasing ability in memory, cognitive processing, auditory attention, or whatever). The developmental framework is simply being used as a yardstick against which individual variation can be plotted. At each Stage on the profile chart, the most commonly noted structures are given, those not receiving separate mention being subsumed under the label "Other." Any P who idiosyncratically used a structure not on the chart with particular frequency could of course have this counted separately, by adding a category to the chart in an ad hoc way. The pragmatic validity of the selection of structures represented lies in the fact that, having now analyzed several hundred Ps in these terms, there have been few occasions when this ad hoc procedure has proved necessary. Putting this another way, the more we would find ourselves having to put structures under the Other heading, the less useful our procedure would become (see following).

INTERACTIONAL

P's sentences are classified into whether they are spontaneous or response. Under the latter heading, a primary classification is made of T's stimulus sentences into whether they are questions or not, and the type of P's responses is analyzed into full, elliptical, zero, and so on. It is plainly of importance that T should know the vagaries of P's response patterns, in order to focus his attention on possible weaknesses in his stimulus or reinforcement language.

The aim of the LARSP procedure is to provide a profile of language use in samples of data obtained from P. We operate with 30-min samples of unstructured interaction between P and an adult (usually a therapist or teacher) in carrying out a full assessment (30 min being the average time of a clinical session, in our experience), though this depends to some extent on the nature of the inquiry. (LARSP has also been used on written samples, e.g., in deaf education; on samples of signing—where the signing system reflects linguistic structure, as in the Paget-Gorman Sign System; and in routine screening contexts, samples have been

as short as 5–10 min.) All the structures found in the sample are analyzed using the above descriptive framework and transferred onto
the profile chart, thus producing a set of raw figures across the range of
structures represented. No attempt is made to turn these figures into a
single "score" (a procedure which we find of little value, in view of the
range of variables involved), or to think solely in terms of percentages (in
view of the small totals often found). The aim is to search for general
patterns of distribution—a balanced use of structures at a given level, an
imbalance (e.g., many phrase structures compared with few or no clause
ones), a mismatch between structural use and chronological age (the
traditional notion of "delay"), and so on. Various examples of profiles are given in the Appendix: It is their interpretation that we now
turn to.

PROFILES AND LANGUAGE DISABILITY

Perhaps the most striking feature of language disability, particularly to
the linguist encountering the field for the first time, is its heterogeneity.[1]
Occasionally, a specific feature of a child's linguistic behavior can be tied
to some underlying condition: There are syndromes which have recognizable and relatively predictable effects, like deafness or cerebral palsy.
More commonly, however, the effects of a particular syndrome (like
Down's—see following) on language performance are more diffuse and
unpredictable. And in very many cases where children are referred to
speech clinics, their linguistic abnormality has no obvious organic basis.
Nevertheless, there are limits to the variability among subjects, provided
that a measure of performance at a suitable level of generality is selected.
The more detailed an analysis is, in syntactic terms, obviously the more
differences can arise. The level of detail of the LARSP profile is intended to
allow the assessment of individual differences within categories which
will admit the recognition of patterns among subjects. The long-term aim
of a research strategy based on this procedure is to determine such linguistic patterns as there are, and correlate them with external variables: physiological, psychological, social, and educational. At the present early stage,
however, we are at the point of looking for patterns that emerge from
profile assessments of a number of individual cases. For the most part, the
patterns we are looking for are in production, and it is in the study of
disorders of production that we envisage a syntactic procedure of this kind
being most useful. In principle, of course, the procedure can also be used

---

[1]Our comments on language disability are limited here to children. Profiles have however
been used with adult language disability. See in particular Chapter 8 of Crystal, Fletcher and
Garman (1976).

to isolate patterns which may be causing comprehension difficulties, or to structure and grade sentence patterns for comprehension work.

The most obvious feature to emerge from the cases we have looked at so far is language delay. The provision of a developmental scale correlated with age[2] allows a straightforward assessment of immature language, whenever a sample of a subject's structures is seen to be characteristic of much younger children. Profile 1 serves as a good example of this, for a child in the earliest stage of language development.

PROFILE 1: HUGH

This shows the analysis of a sample of language from a boy of 3:4, normal in all other respects, whose language consisted of single-element utterances only, as this sample shows: (T stands for Therapist here; P for Patient).

T:	*shall we 'make her sít/ or lìe/*	
P:	*dòwn/---*	
T:	*Húgh/-*	
P:	*dòwn* [ɲi]/ *dòwn/.*	
T:	*yes what's thàt for/--*	5
P:	*gìrl* [ɲi]/	
T:	*the gìrl/-.*	
P:	**yès/*	
T:	**is she 'going to sít/ or lìe/*	
P:	*lìe*	10
T:	*hḿ/*	
P:	*lìe/*	
T:	*lìe/*	
P:	*yès/--*	
T:	*thère/.'what a'bout gràndpa/.I mean dàddy/*	15
	is 'he 'going to sìt/ or lìe/--	

[2]There are, of course, difficulties with correlating scales of language development with age estimates, as anyone familiar with Roger Brown's work knows. Even with Brown's data, though, it is striking that two out of his three subjects perform very closely in terms of age (cf. Limber, 1973, who reports in a sample of 12 children, a partitioning into one group which shows very little individual variation in development, and another more unpredictable group. See also Ramer (1976) concerning distinct styles or strategies of language acquisition.). In addition, large sample studies of phonological acquisition (e.g., Templin, 1957; Olmsted, 1971) have not found individual age variation in relation to patterns of development impossible to handle. We are therefore assuming that large sample syntax studies (e.g., Wells, 1974) will enable us to eventually predict within a small range the kind of syntax one might expect from children of particular ages. The figures used currently on the chart are best estimates, based on information available, and therefore likely to be superseded or at least revised.

P: *sīt/*

T: *sìt*

P: *yès/---*

T: *ôo/.I've 'bent his 'legs the 'wrong wày/* (laughs)   20
     'what's he dòing/--
     he's sìtting/.
     'what about Mûmmy/
     is 'she going to sít/ or lìe/-

P: *sīt*   25

(Transcriptional conventions are as follows, tone-unit boundaries: /; nuclear tones: ` , ´ , ¯ , ˇ , i.e., falling, rising, level, and
falling-rising, respectively; pause distinctions: - is used if the
pause length is comparable to a pulse of a speaker's rhythm; . if it
is short relative to this; and --, --- are used for relatively longer
pauses; stressed syllable: ' precedes; * before a part of an utterance indicates that it was spoken simultaneously with another
utterance.)

As well as a summary of the child's production, the profile also provides,
via the interactional information at the top of the chart, data on stimuli to
which the child is not responding. For example, the Hugh profile shows
(in the Ø category under *Abnormal* response) that the child did not respond
to 25% of the questions asked him. Checking back to the transcript
revealed that in a number of cases it was questions of the *What's he doing*
type which were not responded to (see line 21 preceding). These questions
require a verb in any appropriate response, and this inability to supply
verbs when they are not directly modeled for him fits in with the remain-
der of the child's language behavior at this point in his development. He
only produces utterances which are verbs, or verblike, when the therapist
models them for him (cf. lines 9 and 10, 16, and 17 preceding). Information
derived from the top of the profile chart, together with details from the
original transcript, is a useful complement to the assessment of production
data, and may of course be essential if the right decisions are to be made
about remediation. In this case the therapist ensured that the child could
use verbs spontaneously before trying to teach Stage II clause structures
like SV and VO.

    Once a child's language is even slightly more advanced than single-
word utterances, it is unusual to find cases of 'pure' delay—an even
distribution of structures across the chart. It is more common to find a
sample showing up on the profile with *structural gaps*, either in terms of (a)'
sentence function; or (b) within one of the sentence structure levels. It is
not uncommon to find language-delayed children not asking questions,
for example, perhaps because the roles adopted in a clinical setting en-

courage the child to answer questions, but not to learn how to ask them. This limitation would need identifying for remediation. Recognition of sentence structural gaps is facilitated by the clause–phrase–word level division. On this basis we can potentially identify four salient patterns:

1. Phrase structure imbalance—a tendency to develop phrase structure without clause structure (this is the most common of these patterns for our cases, and is illustrated below by the Peter profile). A comparable phenomenon within a transformational grammatical framework is reported by Morehead (1972) who points to a tendency for his subjects to expand phrase structure before clause structure in the early stages).

2. Clause structure imbalance—a spread down the chart to Stage III or IV of clause structures, without parallel phrase structure differentiation. There is often a one-to-one relationship between elements of clause and elements of phrase structure, for example, *man make boat, they got lorry.* Hierarchical organization within elements of clause structure is minimal. Lackner's (1976) report on research with mentally retarded children gives some evidence of this for his subjects; older children tended to elaborate phrase structure (noun and verb phrases) whereas the younger ones did not. There is some indication in the cases we have seen that noun phrases and verb phrases (in the sense of modals or auxiliaries plus main verb) have to be regarded as separate problems.

3. Poor word-level development, in comparison to clause- and phrase-level. This is only apparent if clause and phrase-level development reaches into Stages III and IV, and is reflected in an absence of inflections in obligatory contexts. Among other investigators, Johnston and Schery (1976) report a similar finding: For their sample of "atypical" children, there was a similar order of acquisition of inflectional morphemes to that reported by Brown (1973) for normals, but acquisition was delayed.

4. Strong word-level development, with very few structures at all at phrase- and clause-level. This has been noted by a number of investigators working with educationally subnormal children (e.g., Newfield and Schlanger, 1968; see also Dever, 1972). Morehead and Ingram (1973) suggest that inflections, being more obvious features of surface structure, are easier for children whose general rate of learning is slow.

PROFILE 2: PETER

Pattern (1)—phrase structure imbalance— is found among language-delayed children somewhat more advanced than Hugh, and shows up as the production of some isolated words, a few phrase types, with a lack of any coherent relationships among them, an absence of clause patterns,

and a high proportion of *Ambiguous* cases.[3] The basis for the (partial) Peter
profile is utterances like this:

cár/	on bùs/
lórry/	clèaning/
across chàir/	blue pàint/
dàddy/	and the mán/
in bòx/	big pàrcel/
trèes/	mé/
bùshes/	nò/
ègg.box/	daddy màn/

The child was 4:6 at the time when the assessment was made. There is
very little clause structure evident, and clearly any remediation in a case
like this will concentrate on clause-level structural types. Individual problems can of course arise even when the subject falls within a general
pattern of assessment and it will perhaps be informative to look briefly at
the early course of Peter's remediation. In this instance the first verb-
based structures modeled for the child following initial assessment were
verb + object. When the child had to use these structures himself to
describe pictures, he often inserted *of* between verb and object:

> *jumping of* [əv] *fence*
> *eating of orange*
> *climbing of ladder*

The reason for these deviant structures[4] was not immediately clear. It is
true that prior to the LARSP assessment his therapist had worked on
prepositions with him. Possibly, therefore, he supposed that nouns in
construction were to be preceded by **some** element, and used *of* for the
purpose, so that structures like *eating of orange* were idiosyncratic syntactic blends. This would not explain, however, why he did produce, in the
same session as the deviant structures, normal verb + object sentences. Or
why, in a subsequent session, he used *girl of riding of horse*. It is possible
that *of* was being used variably at any point in sentence structure where a
grammatical word could appear (or had appeared in sentences of this type
modeled for him). An alternative explanation hinges on the relationship
between the structures he was learning and the pictures that were normally used as a stimulus for these structures. He may in certain cases have

---

[3]*Ambiguous* is the category used under Section A of the chart for utterances which could
receive two or more equally plausible syntactic interpretations. An example would be
Bloom's *mommy sock* example without the contextual clues to help decide whether it is a
Subject–Object clause type, or a Noun–Noun phrase type (Bloom, 1970).

[4]Deviant in the sense that this is not an acceptable adult structure for verb + object, or part
of the expected grammatical development of normal children (see Crystal, Fletcher, and
Garman, 1976, pp. 28–29).

had word-finding difficulties, or have been unsure of what he was describing, and used *of* as a gap-filler. One example of ambiguity in a picture
which caused him difficulty was when he used *cutting of water* to describe
a man sawing a log. In the picture, however, the log had a blue wavy line
underneath it, which could have been the reason for the structural uncertainty signaled by *of*. Subsequent therapy concentrated on (*a*) modeling
SV and VO structures using the same verbs in both cases, from the set that
conveniently function with or without a direct object in English, like *eat,
drink, paint,* to reduce at least one aspect of the structural uncertainty; and
(*b*) to model appropriate uses of *of,* in phrases like *cup of tea, in front of.*
Over a number of sessions, these tactics succeeded in eliminating *of* from
the inappropriate places in structure that it had been used in.

This brief excursion away from assessment into Peter's remedial history
underlines the ever-present possibility of quite idiosyncratic problems
that can arise with language-delayed children who may conform to a
common assessment pattern, and illustrates the care that has to be taken
not only with the form of syntactic structures selected for remediation, but
also the relation between the content of the models used and the actions or
pictures which are chosen to exemplify them. After a decade of concentration on syntax in child language research, more recent work has emphasized that the child is not simply learning the rules of grammar, but
rather learning how to mean; or, in case the emphasis on meaning is
interpreted as an argument for ignoring syntax, it is perhaps better to say
that the child is learning how to match surface structures he hears to states
of affairs he apprehends. While LARSP is conceived of in terms of syntax
both because this is an aspect of language development that we can
describe, and also because it appears to be the locus of a high proportion
of language disabilities, remediation cannot neglect the meanings that
syntactic structures express, and that may be a source of confusion to the
child.

PROFILES 3, 4, AND 5: DIFFICULTIES WITH
COMPLEX SENTENCES

A recurrent problem in our data, for children somewhat more advanced
than Peter, but still apparently lagging behind their peers, turns out on
closer examination to be an inability to combine simple sentences into
complex structures, which shows up on the profile as an absence of
structures at Stage V, even though up to that point there is clause, phrase
and word-level development, as in the following examples from a boy of
8:0.

'my 'rabbit 'nearly did dìed/
'then the 'guinea-pigs did nòt 'nearly 'died/
and 'I did stròke it/
'us 'play with the fòotball 'game
'you 'hold thìs one/
'then I 'put some 'sticks on the hòle/
we thròwed the 'stones/
'I make a 'bow àrrow/

In this case there are clause structures up to Stage IV, as well as comparable phrase structures, and a reasonable integration of phrase with clause structure. Nevertheless, the child does not use coordinate or subordinate structures, some of which we know the normal child is developing from 3:0 onward (cf. Limber, 1973). Sometimes in cases like this, the child may string a number of sentences together, but there will be little linguistic or logical connectivity between them. This area of difficulty is also referred to by Menyuk (1975), who claims that conjunction and embedding cause particular difficulty for children she calls aphasic.

Profiles 3 and 4 show two Down's Syndrome children (from Owen, 1976). The obvious linguistic difference between them, clearly shown by the profiles, is that DSA can use complex structures, whereas DSB, for the most part, cannot, even though he can use clause and phrase structures up to the end of Stage IV. The children are both 12-years old. Of course, DSA is still not using the language of a normal 12-year old, but at least she has begun to link sentences using the conventional syntactic devices. Most of her complex structures are coordinate, though she does use some relative clauses (relativizing objects only—cf. Limber, 1976). These profiles are included here not only because they demonstrate how a detailed syntactic analysis can isolate this specific structural problem, but also because of the interest that has been shown in the linguistic characteristics of this syndrome. The examples in fact seem to contradict Lenneberg's assertion (1967, p. 311) that for DS children "chronological age is a much better predictor for language development than computed IQs." These subjects were roughly the same age, but the most recent IQ estimates were: DSA, IQ 56; DSB, IQ 40.

It is of course not only some DS children for whom the transition to complex structures appears to be difficult. Profile 5 represents Sarah, a child of 5:8 who was thought to be a victim of rubella, and who had also come to a halt, as far as syntagmatic organization was concerned, at Stage IV. As with DSB, there is considerable expressive output, much of it spontaneous[5] but only simple sentence structures. Like DSB also, a number of the utterances consist of only single elements (if we compare

---

[5]The definition of *spontaneous* here (see Section C at the top of the profile) is an utterance which is **not** an immediate response to a question or some other linguistic stimulus.

the proportion of single element utterances in Profiles 4 and 5 with the proportion in Profile 3, we might suspect that the restriction to simple sentences is accompanied by a more general immaturity). Unlike DSB, many of Sarah's utterances are unanalyzable because they cannot be understood. Again, unlike DSB, her sentences lack complex verb phrases— she does not use auxiliaries. Within what seems to be a general pattern there will, as we have already seen, be individual differences which may have considerable bearing on the kind of remediation attempted (and may also cause a particular pattern hypothesis to be revised or abandoned). Some of the relevant information on individuals will be extralinguistic, and will depend on other aspects of the child's cognitive abilities: Sarah, for example, showed little coordination to begin with of language and action patterns. When asked *show me the X and the Y*, she was likely to point to X, and then to Y, but while pointing give the names of the objects in the order Y and X. Remediation was concerned not simply with her learning of devices for connecting simple sentences into longer structures, but also with the matching of actions appropriately to the parts of the coordinated structures.

PROFILES EXTENDED

These examples of the application of a syntactic profile based on normal language development to the area of language disability demonstrate, in our view, the effectiveness of the notion both for isolating individual differences and for generating interesting hypotheses concerning patterns of disability. We should like now to briefly consider the question of how far the notion of a profile can be extended.

In principle, the profile idea is applicable to any area of linguistic inquiry, given the existence of relevant descriptive and developmental information. One could, for instance, think in terms of phonological profiles; and within this, in terms of profiles for segmental as opposed to nonsegmental phonology; and within this, profiles for the acquisition of specific systems, for example, vowels, fricatives. In the present case, LARSP pays particular attention to structures at early developmental levels (for obvious pragmatic reasons). The further down the chart one proceeds, the less specific is the information given. At Stage VI, for example, all the chart tells you about pronouns, for instance, is the total number of "errors" made (which can be compared with the total number of pronouns used, given at Stage III). But there is then nothing to stop the analyst extending the notion of profile to pronouns as such, and constructing, on the basis of the available language acquisition research, a developmental profile of pronominal usage. And the same applies to any of the other categories on the chart. The profile chart is a first approximation only. Any of the structures listed may need to be more closely scrutinized in order to provide a specific remediation procedure. Apart from anything else, one will always need to look at some of the high-scoring structures to see whether there might not be semantic reasons for the apparent ability, for example, a child who is "good" at colors may produce a high score in the Adjectival boxes, but the restricted semantic range of the items used would have to be borne in mind in evaluating his command of that syntactic category.

Could the profile idea be extended beyond the field of language disability? In principle, yes—though not this particular profile. LARSP was constructed to try to meet a very specific aim. The particular selection and ordering of structures arrived at, and the general level of abstraction provided, stemmed from a consideration of the range and frequency of the speech patterns impressionistically noted in our early encounters with language disordered patients. In a sense, all the profile chart is is a systematization of these first impressions. Before it could be extended, then, a corresponding preliminary inquiry would have to be made, to see whether other dimensions, not needed in the context of language disorders, would need to be introduced. For example, if the notion of profile was extended to the field of foreign language teaching, one would immediately have to introduce a dimension to cope with the problems of L2 interference. Moreover, the closer one came to the study of normal language use in adults, the more modifications would need to be introduced. This can be seen clearly if one tries to use the present profile for the analysis of normal adult language. In the Appendix, we give a profile of one speaker engaging in a 30-min conversation (Profile 6). The most noticeable characteristic is perhaps the high proportion of totals under the various Other categories—a clear example of the limitation of the profile referred to earlier. To make the profile idea work well in such contexts, one would have to think again about how the data should be organized. There is presumably some limit on the amount of detail that can be introduced into a description before the perceptibility of the profile becomes obscured. At some point, to preserve the identity of a profile, a greater degree of hierarchic organization would have to be introduced. On the other hand, the more abstract the categories in a profile, the less informative the profile becomes. One needs profiles that are in a reasonably close relationship to the data, if they are to generate interesting hypotheses. This can be seen in a field such as authorship identification, or in stylistic analyses in general, where several hundred variables are involved. It is perfectly possible—indeed, desirable—to develop more well-balanced accounts of an author's use of structures, to avoid the word–phrase bias in traditional accounts of style. But to make this good, one would have to pay particular attention to clause and sentence structure and sequence, and here any inventory of possible effects would run into several hundreds. Obviously some grouping of these effects is necessary, but the more one sets up higher-order categories, the less discriminating analyses become. Perhaps there is some optimum balance between generality and detail which will most satisfactorily discriminate the main possibilities of authorial style; but the stylistic literature is nowhere near identifying what this might be.

In short, the idea of profile analysis, itself nothing new, could be profitably extended to other areas of inquiry. It provides an example of a methodology which raises interesting theoretical questions, for example, what are the most salient criteria of linguistic identity. It is for this reason that we felt a report on our work in the restricted field of language disorders might be of general interest.

APPENDIX

Profile 1

A	**Unanalysed**						**Problematic**			
	1 Unintelligible **35**	2 Symbolic Noise		3 Deviant			1 Incomplete		2 Ambiguous **8**	

B Responses

Stimulus Type		Totals	Repet-itions	Elliptical Major 1	2	3	4	Full Major	Minor	Struc-tural	Ø	Prob-lems
200	Questions	**117**	**2**	**48**					**69**		**51**	
21	Others	**10**	**1**	**2**					**8**			

(Normal Response spans Repetitions through Minor; Abnormal spans Structural, Ø, Problems)

C Spontaneous Others

Stage I (0;9–1;6) — Sentence Type

Minor **77** Social **77** Stereotypes Problems

Major **50** Sentence Structure

Excl.	Comm.	Quest.		Statement
		'V'	'Q'	'V' **5** 'N' **36** Other **9** Problems

		Conn.	Clause			Phrase		Word

Stage II (1;6–2;0)

V X	Q X		SV	V C/O	DN	VV		-ing
			S C/O	A X	Adj N	V part		
			Neg X	Other	NN	Int X		pl
					PrN	Other		

Stage III (2;0–2;6)

V X Y		X + S:NP	X + V:VP	X + C/O:NP	X + A:AP	-ed
	Q X Y	SVC/O	VC/OA	D Adj N	Cop	-en
let X Y	VS	SVA	VO_dO_i	Adj Adj N	Aux	
		Neg X Y	Other	Pr DN	Pron **4**	3s
do X Y				N Adj N	Other	gen

Stage IV (2;6–3;0)

		XY + S:NP	XY + V:VP	XY + C/O:NP	XY + A:AP	n't
S	QVS	SVC/OA	AAXY	N Pr NP	Neg V	
	QXYZ	SVO_dO_i	Other	Pr D Adj N	Neg X	'cop
				cX	2 Aux	'aux
				XcX	Other	

Stage V (3;0–3;6)

		and	Coord. 1 1+	Postmod. 1 clause 1+	-est
how	tag	c	Subord. 1 1+		-er
		s	Clause: S	Postmod. 1+ phrase	
what		Other	Clause: C/O		-ly
			Comparative		

Stage VI (3;6–4;6)

(+)			(−)		
NP	VP	Clause	NP	VP	Clause
Initiator	Complex	Passive	Pron Adj seq	Modal	Concord
Coord		Complement	Det N irreg	Tense	A position
				V irreg	W order

Other Other

Stage VII (4;6 +)

Discourse	Syntactic Comprehension
A Connectivity it	
Comment Clause there	Style
Emphatic Order Other	

Total No. Sentences **127**	Mean No. Sentences Per Turn **0·54**	Mean Sentence Length **1·0**

© D. Crystal, P. Fletcher, M. Garman, 1975 University of Reading

Profile 2

<table>
<tr><td>A</td><td colspan="3">Unanalysed</td><td colspan="2">Problematic</td></tr>
<tr><td></td><td>1 Unintelligible</td><td>2 Symbolic Noise</td><td>3 Deviant</td><td>1 Incomplete</td><td>2 Ambiguous</td></tr>
</table>

<table>
<tr><td>B</td><td colspan="2">Responses</td><td></td><td colspan="5">Normal Response</td><td colspan="2">Abnormal</td><td></td></tr>
<tr><td></td><td colspan="2"></td><td rowspan="2">Totals</td><td rowspan="2">Repet-itions</td><td colspan="4">Elliptical Major</td><td rowspan="2">Full Major</td><td rowspan="2">Minor</td><td rowspan="2">Struc-tural</td><td rowspan="2">∅</td><td rowspan="2">Prob-lems</td></tr>
<tr><td></td><td colspan="2">Stimulus Type</td><td>1</td><td>2</td><td>3</td><td>4</td></tr>
<tr><td></td><td></td><td>Questions</td><td></td><td></td><td></td><td></td><td></td><td></td><td></td><td></td><td></td><td></td><td></td></tr>
<tr><td></td><td></td><td>Others</td><td></td><td></td><td></td><td></td><td></td><td></td><td></td><td></td><td></td><td></td><td></td></tr>
</table>

<table>
<tr><td>C</td><td colspan="3">Spontaneous</td><td colspan="2">Others</td></tr>
</table>

Stage I (0;9–1;6) — Sentence Type	**Minor**			*Social* **35**	*Stereotypes* **4**	*Problems*
	Major				Sentence Structure	
	Excl.	*Comm.*	*Quest.*		*Statement*	
		·V·	·Q·	·V· **1** ·N· **16**	Other **12**	Problems

Stage		Conn.	Clause		Phrase		Word
Stage II (1;6–2;0)	V X Q X		SV	V C/O	DN **5**	VV	-ing **1**
			S C/O **2**	A X	Adj N **3**	V part	pl **4**
			Neg X	Other	NN **7**	Int X	-ed
					PrN **1**	Other **8**	
Stage III (2;0–2;6)	V X Y		X · S:NP	X · V:VP	X · C/O:NP	X · A:AP	-en
	Q X Y		SVC:O	VC/OA	D Adj N **1**	Cop	
	let X Y VS		SVA	VOdOi	Adj Adj N **2**	Aux	3s
	do X Y		Neg X Y	Other	Pr DN **2**	Pron **8**	gen
					N Adj N	Other	
Stage IV (2;6–3;0)			X Y · S:NP	X Y · V:VP	X Y · C/O:NP	X Y · A:AP	n't
	S QVS		SVC/OA	AA X Y	N Pr NP	Neg V	'cop
	Q X Y Z		SVOiOi	Other	Pr D Adj N	Neg X	'aux
					c X	2 Aux	
					X c X **1**	Other	
Stage V (3;0–3;6)	how	tag	and	Coord. **1**	**1** ·	Postmod. **1** clause	**1** ·	-est
			c	Subord. **1**	**1** ·			-er
	what		s	Clause: S		Postmod. **1** · phrase		-ly
			Other	Clause: C/O				
				Comparative				

	(+)			(−)		
	NP	*VP*	*Clause*	*NP*	*VP*	*Clause*
Stage VI (3;6–4;6)	Initiator	Complex	Passive	Pron	Adj seq	Modal	Concord
	Coord		Complement	Det	N irreg	Tense	A position
						V irreg	W order
	Other			Other		

	Discourse		*Syntactic Comprehension*	
Stage VII (4;6+)	A Connectivity	*it*		
	Comment Clause	*there*	*Style*	
	Emphatic Order	Other		

Total No. Sentences **94**	Mean No. Sentences Per Turn	Mean Sentence Length

© D. Crystal, P. Fletcher, M. Garman, 1975 University of Reading

Profile 3

A **Unanalysed**

1 Unintelligible **6** 2 Symbolic Noise 3 Deviant

Problematic

1 Incomplete **6** 2 Ambiguous **3**

B **Responses**

Stimulus Type		Totals	Repetitions	Elliptical Major 1	2	3	4	Full Major	Minor	Structural	Ø	Problems
169	Questions	**151**	**1**	**17**	**12**			**51**	**62**	**6**	**12**	**2**
88	Others	**72**		**13**	**1**			**26**	**31**		**15**	**1**

(Normal Response — Elliptical Major / Full Major / Minor; Abnormal — Structural / Ø; Problems)

C **Spontaneous** **90** **3** **2** Others

Minor 127   Social **118**   Stereotypes **9**   Problems **14**

Major   Sentence Structure

Sentence Type

Stage I (0;9–1;6)

	Excl.	Comm.	Quest.	Statement
		'V' **1**	'Q'	'V' **8** 'N' **11** Other **10** Problems

Stage II (1;6–2;0)

Conn.	Clause			Phrase		Word
	VX	QX	SV **19**	V C/O **13**	DN **101**	VV **4**	-ing **20**
2			S C/O **6**	AX **2**	Adj N **19**	V part **16**	pl **35**
			Neg X **1**	Other **5**	NN **2**	Int X **2**	-ed **37**
					PrN **23**	Other	

Stage III (2;0–2;6)

X · S:NP **11**	X · V:VP **17**	X · C/O:NP **10**	X · A:AP	
VXY **2**	QXY **1**	SVC:O **131**	VC/OA **4**	D Adj N **12**	Cop **10**	-en **9**
let XY	VS **1**	SVA **50**	VO$_d$O$_i$	Adj Adj N	Aux **40**	3s **13**
do XY		Neg XY	Other	Pr DN **23**	Pron **181**	gen **5**
				N Adj N	Other **1**	

Stage IV (2;6–3;0)

XY · S:NP **18**	XY · V:VP **21**	XY · C/O:NP	XY · A:AP **7**	
· S	QVS	SVC/OA **28**	AAXY **2**	N Pr NP	Neg V **13**	n't **16**
	QXYZ	SVO$_i$O$_i$ **1**	Other	Pr D Adj N	Neg X	'cop **48**
				cX	2 Aux **2**	'aux **28**
				XcX **12**	Other	-est

Stage V (3;0–3;6)

		and **25**	Coord. 1 **22** 1+ **9**	Postmod. 1 clause	1+	-er
how	tag	c	Subord. 1 **9** 1+ **2**			
		s **11**	Clause: S	Postmod. 1+ **4** phrase		-ly **5**
what		Other **13**	Clause: C/O **1**			
			Comparative			

Stage VI (3;6–4;6)

(+)			(−)		
NP	VP	Clause	NP	VP	Clause
Initiator **7**	Complex	Passive	Pron **7** Adj seq	Modal **5**	Concord **30**
Coord **9**		Complement	Det **5** N irreg **1**	Tense **22**	A position **4**
				V irreg **4**	W order **1**
Other			Other		

Stage VII (4;6+)

Discourse		Syntactic Comprehension
A Connectivity it **4**		**6**
Comment Clause **1** there **1**		Style
Emphatic Order Other		

Total No. Sentences **319**	Mean No. Sentences Per Turn **1.3**	Mean Sentence Length **4.8**

© D. Crystal, P. Fletcher, M. Garman, 1975 University of Reading

Profile 4

A

Unanalysed			Problematic	
1 Unintelligible **11**	2 Symbolic Noise **16**	3 Deviant **2**	1 Incomplete **5**	2 Ambiguous **4**

B Responses

Stimulus Type	Totals	Repet-itions	Elliptical Major 1	2	3	4	Full Major	Minor	Struc-tural	Ø	Prob-lems
158 Questions	**136**	**5**	**42**	**18**	**5**		**5**	**41**	**4**	**19**	**16**
135 Others	**96**	**6**	**23**	**12**	**1**		**8**	**43**		**34**	**4**

C Spontaneous

Spontaneous	**7**	**22**	Others	**112**

Minor **142**   Social **113**   Stereotypes **4**   Problems **25**

Sentence Type — Major

Stage I (0;9–1;6)

Excl.	Comm.	Quest.	Statement				
1	'V' **2**	'Q' **2**	'V' **13**	'N' **61**	Other **20**	Problems	

Stage II (1;6–2;0)

		Conn.	Clause			Phrase		Word
VX **6**	QX **13**		SV **11**	VC/O **14**	DN **29**	VV **1**		-ing **11**
			S C/O **1**	AX **6**	Adj N **8**	V part **8**		pl **19**
			Neg X **3**	Other **1**	NN	Int X **1**		-ed
					PrN **1**	Other **1**		

Stage III (2;0–2;6)

			Clause		Phrase		Word
VXY **3**	QXY **4**	X · S:NP	X · V:VP **12**	X · C/O:NP **7**	X · A:AP **2**		-en
let XY	VS **1**	SVC/O **32**	VC/OA **2**	D Adj N **3**	Cop **23**		3s
do XY		SVA **1**	VO_dO_i	Adj Adj N	Aux **12**		gen
		Neg XY	Other **5**	Pr DN **2**	Pron **16**		
				N Adj N	Other		

Stage IV (2;6–3;0)

			Clause		Phrase		Word
· S	QVS	XY · S:NP **2**	XY · V:VP **1**	XY · C/O:NP **1**	XY · A:AP		n't **10**
	QXYZ	SVC/OA	AAXY	N Pr NP **1**	Neg V **13**		'cop **20**
		SVO_dO_i	Other	Pr D Adj N	Neg X		'aux **3**
				cX	2 Aux		-est **1**
				XcX	Other		-er **1**

Stage V (3;0–3;6)

how	tag	and **2**	Coord. 1 **2**	1 ·	Postmod. 1 clause	1 ·	-ly
what		c	Subord. 1	1 ·			
		s	Clause: S				
		Other	Clause: C/O	Postmod. 1 phrase			
			Comparative				

Stage VI (3;6–4;6)

(+)			(−)		
NP	VP	Clause	NP	VP	Clause
Initiator **4**	Complex	Passive	Pron	Adj seq	Modal	Concord
Coord		Complement	Det	N irreg	Tense	A position
					V irreg	W order
Other			Other		

Stage VII (4;6+)

Discourse		Syntactic Comprehension
A Connectivity	it **3**	
Comment Clause **2**	there	Style
Emphatic Order	Other **1**	

Total No. Sentences **374**	Mean No. Sentences Per Turn **1.24**	Mean Sentence Length **2.2**

© D. Crystal, P. Fletcher, M. Garman, 1975 University of Reading

Profile 5

© D. Crystal, P. Fletcher, M. Garman, 1975 University of Reading

A Unanalysed

1 Unintelligible **88** 2 Symbolic Noise **1** 3 Deviant **1**

Problematic

1 Incomplete **1** 2 Ambiguous **14**

B Responses

Stimulus Type	Totals	Repet-itions	Elliptical Major 1	2	3	4	Full Major	Minor	Struc-tural	Ø	Prob-lems
14 Questions	**12**		**6**	**1**	**1**			**2**		**2**	**2**
64 Others	**50**	**4**	**13**	**6**	**5**			**11**			**15**

C Spontaneous **138** | **7** | **80** | Others **58**

Minor			Social **14**		Stereotypes **1**		Problems

Sentence Type

Stage I (0;9–1;6)

Major — Sentence Structure

Excl.	Comm.	Quest.	Statement
	·V· **5**	·Q· **1**	·V· **4** ·N· **68** Other **13** Problems **1**

Stage II (1;6–2;0)

	Conn.	Clause	Phrase	Word
V X		SV **6** V C/O **9**	DN **21** VV	-ing **2**
Q X		S C/O AX **2**	Adj N **11** V part **12**	pl **20**
		Neg X **3** Other	NN **14** Int X **1**	-ed **1**
			PrN **4** Other **2**	

Stage III (2;0–2;6)

V X Y		X · S:NP **2** X · V:VP **3** X · C/O:NP **4** X · A:AP **1**		-en **1**
	Q X Y	SVC O **16** VC/OA **2**	D Adj N **1** Cop **13**	3s **1**
let X Y VS		SVA **2** VOdOi	Adj Adj N Aux	
do X Y		Neg X Y Other	Pr DN **2** Pron **4**	gen
			N Adj N Other **1**	

Stage IV (2;6–3;0)

· S	QVS	X Y · S:NP X Y · V:VP **1** X Y · C O:NP **2** X Y · A:AP **2**		**34**
	Q X Y Z	SVC/OA AA X Y	N Pr NP Neg V **1**	n't **1**
		SVO_dO_i Other	Pr D Adj N Neg X	·cop
			cX **2** 2 Aux	**11**
			XcX **1** Other	·aux

Stage V (3;0–3;6)

		and	Coord. **1** **1** ·	Postmod. **1** clause **1** ·	-est
how	tag	c	Subord. **1** **1** ·		-er
		s	Clause: S	Postmod. **1** · phrase	
what	Other		Clause: C/O		-ly
			Comparative		

Stage VI (3;6–4;6)

(+)			(−)		
NP	VP	Clause	NP	VP	Clause
Initiator	Complex	Passive	Pron **4** Adj seq	Modal	Concord **1**
Coord		Complement	Det N irreg **1**	Tense	A position
				V irreg **1**	W order **5**
Other		Other **Intonation 4**			

Stage VII (4;6+)

Discourse	Syntactic Comprehension
A Connectivity **0**	
Comment Clause there **2**	Style
Emphatic Order Other	

Total No. Sentences **304**	Mean No. Sentences Per Turn **3·9**	Mean Sentence Length **1·6**

© D. Crystal, P. Fletcher, M. Garman, 1975 University of Reading

Profile 6

A	**Unanalysed**				**Problematic**	
	1 Unintelligible **3**	2 Symbolic Noise	3 Deviant		1 Incomplete **36**	2 Ambiguous

<table>
<tr><td rowspan="4">B</td><td colspan="2">Responses</td><td></td><td></td><td colspan="4">Normal Response</td><td colspan="2">Abnormal</td><td></td></tr>
<tr><td colspan="2" rowspan="3">Stimulus Type</td><td rowspan="3">Totals</td><td rowspan="3">Repet-itions</td><td colspan="4">Elliptical Major</td><td rowspan="2">Full
Major</td><td rowspan="2">Minor</td><td rowspan="2">Struc-
tural</td><td rowspan="2">Ø</td><td rowspan="2">Prob-lems</td></tr>
<tr><td>1</td><td>2</td><td>3</td><td>4</td></tr>
<tr></tr>
<tr><td colspan="2" align="center">**17** Questions</td><td>**17**</td><td></td><td>**1**</td><td>**1**</td><td></td><td></td><td>**6**</td><td>**9**</td><td></td><td></td><td></td></tr>
<tr><td colspan="2" align="center">**40** Others</td><td>**40**</td><td></td><td>**1**</td><td></td><td></td><td></td><td>**12**</td><td>**37**</td><td></td><td></td><td></td></tr>
</table>

C	Spontaneous **264**		**4**	Others **260**	

	Minor **96**			Social **96**	Stereotypes		Problems

Major 235

		Excl.	Comm.	Quest.		Statement		

Stage I (0;9-1;6)								

			·V·	·Q·	·V·	·N·	Other	Problems

Sentence Structure

Sentence Type

Stage II (1;6-2;0)					Conn.	Clause				Phrase		Word

Stage II (1;6-2;0):
- V X, Q X
- SV **36**, VC/O **15**, DN **69**, VV
- S C/O, AX **3**, Adj N **16**, V part **41**
- Neg X, Other **7**, NN **3**, Int X **3**
- PrN **24**, Other **42**
- Word: -ing **42**, pl **101**

Stage III (2;0-2;6):
- V X Y, Q X Y **1**
- let X Y, VS **9**
- do X Y
- X · S:NP **10**, X · V:VP **7**, X · C/O:NP **15**, X · A:AP
- SVC/O **98**, VC/OA **12**, D Adj N **31**, Cop **48**
- SVA **27**, VO_dO_i **1**, Adj Adj N, Aux **105**
- Neg X Y, Other, Pr DN **26**, Pron **270**
- N Adj N **6**, Other **28**
- Word: -ed **123**, -en **24**, 3s **120**, gen **6**

Stage IV (2;6-3;0):
- · S, QVS
- QXYZ
- XY · S:NP **41**, XY · V:VP **31**, XY · C/O:NP **33**, XY · A:AP **12**
- SVC/OA **78**, AAXY **34**, N Pr NP **12**, Neg V **6**
- SVO_dO_i **3**, Other **31**, Pr D Adj N **12**, Neg X
- cX, 2 Aux
- XcX **3**, Other **67**
- Word: n't **76**, 'cop **14**, 'aux

Stage V (3;0-3;6):
- how
- what
- tag **3**
- and **14**, c **4**, s **44**, Other
- Coord. 1 **10**, 1 · **8**
- Subord. 1 **16**, 1 · **18**
- Clause: S **3**
- Clause: C/O **21**
- Comparative
- Postmod. 1 **22** clause, 1 ·
- Postmod. 1 · phrase
- Word: -est, -er, -ly

	(+)				(−)		
	NP	VP	Clause		NP	VP	Clause

Stage VI (3;6-4;6):
- Initiator **14**, Complex **57**, Passive **18**, Pron, Adj seq, Modal, Concord
- Coord **6**, Complement **7**, Det, N irreg, Tense, A position
- V irreg, W order
- Other | Other

	Discourse		Syntactic Comprehension

Stage VII (4;6+):
- A Connectivity **12**, it **48**
- Comment Clause **60**, there **15**
- Emphatic Order **16**, Other
- Style

Total No. Sentences **321**	Mean No. Sentences Per Turn **4.2**	Mean Sentence Length **8.0**

© D. Crystal, P. Fletcher, M. Garman, 1975 University of Reading

REFERENCES

Bloom, L. *Language Development: form and function in emerging grammar.* Cambridge, Massachusetts: M.I.T. Press, 1970.

Brown, R. *A first language.* London: George Allen and Unwin, 1973.

Crystal, D., Fletcher, P., and Garman, M. *The grammatical analysis of language disability: a procedure for assessment and remediation.* London: Edward Arnold, 1976.

Dever, R. A comparison of the results of a revised version of Berko's test of morphology with the free speech of mentally retarded children. *Journal of Speech and Hearing Research,* 1972, *15,* 169–238.

Johnston, J. and Schery, T., The use of grammatical morphemes by children with communication disorders. In D. M. Morehead and A. E. Morehead (Eds.), *Normal and deficient child language.* Baltimore: University Park Press, 1976.

Lackner, J. A developmental study of language behavior in retarded children. In D. M. Morehead and A. E. Morehead (Eds.), *Normal and deficient child language.* Baltimore: University Park Press, 1976.

Lenneberg, D. *Biological foundations of language.* New York: John Wiley and Sons, 1967.

Limber, J. The genesis of complex sentences. In T. E. Moore (Ed.), *Cognitive development and the acquisition of language.* New York: Academic Press, 1973.

Limber, J. Unravelling competence, performance and pragmatics in the speech of young children. *Journal of Child Language,* 1976, *3,* 309–318.

Menyuk, P. Children with language problems: What's the problem? In Daniel P. Dato (Ed.), *Georgetown University Round Table on Languages and Linguistics,* Washington, D.C.: Georgetown University Press, 1975.

Morehead, D. M. Early grammatical and semantic relations: some implications for a general representation deficit in linguistically deviant children. Stanford University: Committee on Linguistics, *Papers and Reports on Child Language Development,* 1972, *4,* 1–12.

Morehead, D. M. and Ingram, D. The development of base syntax in normal and linguistically deviant children. *Journal of Speech and Hearing Research,* 1973, *16,* 330–352.

Newfield, M. U. and Schlanger, B. B. The acquisition of English morphology by normal and educable mentally retarded children. *Journal of Speech and Hearing Research,* 1968, *11,* 693–706.

Olmsted, D. *Out of the mouth of babes.* The Hague: Mouton, 1971.

Owen, P. Some aspects of the linguistic development of severely subnormal children with Down's Syndrome. Unpublished dissertation, Polytechnic of Central London.

Quirk, R., Greenbaum, S., Leech, G. and Svartvik, J. *A grammar of contemporary English.* London: Longman, 1972.

Ramer, A. L. Syntactic styles in emerging language. *Journal of Child Language,* 1976, *3,* 49–32.

Templin, M. *Certain language skills in children: their development and interrelationships.* Institute of Child Welfare Monograph 26. Minneapolis: University of Minnesota Press, 1957.

Wells, G. Language development in preschool children. *Journal of Child Language,* 1974, *1,* 158–162.

9

Phonology as an Individual Access System: Some Data from Language Acquisition

CHARLES A. FERGUSON

1. INDIVIDUAL DIFFERENCES IN PHONOLOGY

Systematic similarities and differences in human language behavior may be explored on at least three linguistically relevant levels: universals, particular languages or language varieties, and individuals. In other words, we may look for characteristics of human language which are—or tend to be—present in all human behavior, or we may try to characterize particular varieties of human language to discover in principle how they may differ from one another, or we may characterize the language of individual human beings to discover in principle how individuals differ and how these differences are related to the similarities and differences at the other levels. This crude division of all linguistics into three parts would have to be elaborated to include varying notions of language universals, design features, metatheory and the like and to include the study of structural and functional variation within language varieties and be-

Individual Differences in Language Ability and Language Behavior

Copyright © 1979 by Academic Press, Inc.
All rights of reproduction in any form reserved.
ISBN 0-12-255950-9

tween them, synchronically and diachronically. It will, however, serve to indicate the level which this paper explores—that of individual differences and their place in the whole scheme of things. Elsewhere (e.g., Ferguson, 1975) I have made programmatic statements about the importance of linguistic analyses of individuals and the contribution of individual language profiles, but here I attempt a small exploratory study in phonology, adducing principally data from children's acquisition of the phonology of their mother tongue, with the intention of contributing to our understanding of phonological organization and phonological processes, not just in child language development but in general.

The range of individual variation in phonology first impressed me in 1965 during a seminar in child language at the University of Washington. The members of the seminar decided to design a research project on the acquisition of certain types of "irregular" plurals in American English, extending the findings of Jean Berko Gleason's classic "wugs" study (Berko, 1958). The problem we wanted to investigate was the acquisition of those English noun plurals in which the final voiceless fricative /Θ, f, s/ of the singular appears as the corresponding voiced fricative /ð, v, z/ in the plural, along with the appropriate allomorph of the plural ending /s, z, əz/ respectively, for example, *path, paths, leaf, leaves, house, houses,* as opposed to the "regular" *myth, reef, noose* in which the voiceless fricative appears also in the plural. We had made considerable progress in delimiting the population of school children to be studied, concocting appropriate elicitation sentences, composing instructions for the experimenter, and the like, when we decided to check out the exact extent of the phenomenon in the adult target language, to see just what the children were supposed to be acquiring. It was disconcerting to discover that no two of the dozen native speakers of American English in the seminar had the same lexical incidence of the voicing rule and that even the rule itself did not seem to be uniformly present. One person had *NO* instances of *th* or *s* voicing in her speech and only a few examples of $f \rightarrow v$. The group as a whole showed striking variability in the *rf* words (e.g., *dwarf, scarf, wharf*), which not only had "free variation" in some individuals' plurals but also had in some instances some specialized meanings or connotations for the *f* and *v* plurals of the same singular. There were surprising mismatches between spelling and pronunciation, for example, *roof, roofs* pronounced /ruwf, ruwvz/, *hoof, hooves* pronounced /huf, huwvz/. Also, the incidence of the voicing rule in noun plurals showed poor correlation lexically with the same rule in making denominative verbs [e.g., *wreath, wreathe; grief, grieve; house(n), house(v)*]; and in the latter there was also individual variation, although not as much as in the noun plurals.

The variation in the voicing rule in American English, which is substantial but inadequately described in grammars of English (cf. Jespersen, 1942, Part VI, pp. 258–264; Quirk, Greenbaum, Leech, Svartvik, 1972, pp.

176–177; Long, 1961, pp. 204–205)[1] is principally of the kind which reflects broad patterns of regional and social variation by virtue of the geographically and socially mobile personal life histories of the informants. Current studies of the dialectal kind of individual variation as in the work of Labov and his associates (e. g., Payne, 1975), are done primarily in order to gain understanding of the processes of language change. Payne's study followed individuals of a number of families who had moved into a town in the metropolitan area of Philadelphia from New York City and elsewhere, and investigated in particular the distribution of "short *a*" sounds in their speech as their phonologies gradually adjusted to the Philadelphia pattern. Although some kinds of change were common to all speakers, and there were interesting regularities in the processes of change, no two individuals arrived at exactly the same distribution of sounds. Studies of the same kind of data could also be done to investigate individual differences as such, so that instead of a focus on the distribution of particular traits over social classes, styles of speech, or regional provenience and on language change, the focus could be on individuals' clusters of traits and the nature of individual differences.

Some individual differences in phonology, however, are not of the dialectal type but are more clearly idiosyncratic and have such sources as accidents of language input, anatomical and physiological characteristics, different learning strategies and phonological hypotheses, or personality characteristics. Three types will be identified here: phonetic variants, lexical exceptions, and phonological deviance.

Examples of individual *phonetic variants* are plentiful in American English. A common one is the range of pronunciation of /l/. The allophonic differences which depend on position in the syllable and the quality of the following vowel (e.g., extremes of *lee* and *hall*) are widespread and well known (cf. Jones, 1956) though even in these there are regional differences (e.g., the *l* of *million* may be either "clear" or dark" depending on the area) and social differences (e.g., the highly labialized velar *l* of much "Black English"). What is not mentioned in the phonetics textbooks is the quite common "abnormal" dark *l* pronunciation (sometimes flapped or "snapped") in positions where the clear *l* is expected.[2] This kind of individual variation does not seem regional or social but yet it must somehow be part

[1]This voicing phenomenon resulted from sound changes in Middle English and ever since that time it has been the arena of conflicting tendencies to generalize the voicing and to generalize the "regular" plural. The fluctuation seems likely to last for centuries.

[2]It is possible that the sporadic individual extension of the velar *l* is part of a long term change of all *l*s to velar pronunciation or vocalization to *w* or *u*, but it is difficult to investigate this without extensive data. In this question, as in most questions of language change in the United States, we are severely handicapped by having no accepted base line data for comparison. One of the most serious desiderata in the study of dialect variation and language change is the availability of comparable samples of data at regular time intervals.

of English phonology since this pronunciation of *l* is quite rare in most other European languages. This kind of phenomenon raises the interesting question of the kinds of "speech defects" or deviant pronunciations (lisping, lalling, etc.) which occur and are recognized in different languages. It seems likely that such variants are in some sense part of the total phonological framework of each language variety, since otherwise the same defects should occur approximately equally in all languages in which the target sound occurs.

Lexical exceptions, that is, particular words in which otherwise general allophonic or morphophonemic rules do not apply, are frequently discussed in the phonological literature, but similar exceptions in the speech of individuals which are not shared by other speakers of the language are usually ignored or excluded from discussion. For example, most phonologists would disregard the exceptional pronunciation of *giddy* by a speaker of American English I knew. She pronounced the first vowel of the word higher than the vowel of *biddy* but monophthongally and shorter than the vowel of *beady.* This special pronunciation, which seemed invariable for that word, might be called "expressive" since she regularly used the word as a slightly pejorative adjective referring to human beings, and I never had the chance to elicit it as an ordinary nonexpressive adjective. A better example may be another speaker's pronunciation of *lemme* (*let me*) with /e/ although his /e/ and /i/ elsewhere were neutralized before nasals to an intermediate vowel nearer to /i/ (Harrell, 1961). The source of the exception in this case seems clear, namely, the original (or underlying) /t/ which disappeared without the neutralization process affecting the preceding /e/, but the incidence of the exception does not seem regional or social.

One obvious kind of individual difference in phonology is that of so-called "functional articulatory disorders," cases where the patient has no apparent organic defects in the vocal tract but has a markedly *deviant phonology.* At long last linguists are beginning to do serious phonological analyses of such cases, and we now have a book (Ingram, 1976) which reviews this literature and offers phonological analysis as a tool for the speech clinician. Deviant phonologies typically show (*a*) normal phonological processes in operation at a later period than usual; (*b*) phonological developments out of phase with one another in comparison with normal patterns of development; and (*c*) phonological processes which are rare or nonexistent in normal development. Each deviant phonology is, of course, unique, although similarities between cases are apparent, but such deviant phonologies may be regarded as merely extreme cases of the general phenomenon that every individual's phonology, deviant or normal, is unique.

The position I am assuming in this paper is that every user of a language variety develops over time his own inventory of phonetic elements, the phonological organization of them, and a set of processes applied to them, and this phonological development begins at or before birth and continues until death. Taking this position for phonology is just recognizing for phonology what is universally acknowledged for lexicon (every individual's stock of vocabulary is unique) and occasionally recognized for syntax (e.g., Carden, 1970).[3]

Another perspective on individual differences in phonology is offered by Sapir's generally forgotten paper (Sapir, 1927) in which he points out that idiosyncratic characteristics of a person's speech may reflect or give clues to characteristics of personality. While acknowledging biological and cultural sources and limits of this kind of variation, Sapir focused on the direct language–personality relationships, "there are *individual* variations of sound which are highly important and which in many cases have a symptomatic value for the study of personality [Sapir, 1927, p. 901]." Very few linguists or psychologists have followed the leads given in this paper of Sapir's. Apart from Newman's description of the language and personality characteristics of one adolescent boy (Newman, 1941), the literature in this field has paid almost no attention to linguistic characteristics, relying instead on measures of voice quality, listeners' judgments of speakers' personalities, and other aspects of speech which are at most marginally or indirectly linguistic. The analysis of all these forms of individual differences in adult phonologies is a difficult and uncharted field, requiring techniques of informant elicitation and experimental verification which are yet to be devised. One small study is under way (Ferguson, in progress), but a great deal of work is required before such analysis can become routinized and reliable. In the meantime one profitable field of investigation is phonological development in childhood, which is currently being studied in a number of places. Much individual variation in early childhood seems to bear little relation to variation in later childhood let alone in adult phonology (cf. comments in Farwell, 1976, p. 103), but study of the phenomenon does seem promising both for prognosis of the child's development and for understanding of the basic processes of phonology (Ferguson, 1976, Section 3.3).

2. INDIVIDUAL DIFFERENCES IN CHILD PHONOLOGIES

The bulk of linguistically oriented research on child phonology since Jakobson's *Kindersprache* (Jakobson, 1968) has been more concerned with discovering a universal order of phonological development than with the

---

[3]Cazden (1967) attempted to discuss individual differences in relation to a Chomskyan model of language, but this early effort was not followed up.

identification of individual differences. Recently, however, a number of studies have called attention to individual differences (e.g., Ferguson, Peizer, and Weeks 1973; Stoel, 1974; Ferguson and Farwell, 1975; Farwell, 1976; Straight, 1976b; Priestly, 1977), and at least one paper has attempted to resolve the paradox of universal order *and* individual differences (Solberg, 1976).

One kind of individual variation in phonological development is the apparent chance following of *alternate paths* or routes in the acquisition of particular sounds. For example, Stoel (1974) found that young children acquiring Spanish as their mother tongue typically master the pronunciation of intervocalic /r, ř, l, ð/ one of two ways. Either they (*a*) pronounce the two rs/ð/ and /l/ all as a lateral for a long period, perhaps a year, after which a single r phone is acquired for /r, ř/ but not for the others, followed shortly thereafter by the acquisition of two distinct rs; or (*b*) pronounce the two rs and /ð/ as some sort of *d* or *r* phone for a long period, after which a single *r* phone is acquired for /r, ř/ but not for /ð/, and finally two distinct rs appear. Another example is given by Ingram, (1975) in his discussion of alternative "substitution paths" which children may follow in acquiring the fricatives of English. He claims that there is an invariant order of types of substitutions in the development of fricatives (deletion, stop, sonorant, affricate, fricative) although not all stages may occur in a given case. Along with this invariant order, however, the existence of the two interacting processes of voicing and fronting and the fact that each fricative tends to develop more or less independently allow for a great array of possible routes or substitution paths, well illustrated by the 15 normal children whose phonological data he examined.

This kind of individual difference in phonological development is certainly worth exploring, particularly for what it may show about phonological structure in general, for example, the nature of distinctive features, the role of marking, and the like. Individual differences of this kind in patterns of acquisition have already led Stephen Straight, in his monograph on the acquisition of Yucatec (Straight, 1976b), to take the position that there is "quite consistent phonetic patterning within the speech of each child which is often strictly idiosyncratic [p. 21]" and even that "more than one possible set of distinctive feature definitions may emerge in different children [p. 41]."

Of greater interest for our purposes here, however, are some striking individual strategies in phonology acquisition. The term "strategy" has been used in a variety of meanings. A strategy may be a universal, presumably innate, means which children have at their disposal for processing language input and discovering its structure (e.g., Bever, 1970; Slobin, 1973) or it may be one of a closed set of alternative ways of coping with language learning (e.g., Nelson, 1973). Here I use it in the same sense indicated by Farwell (1976): "ways in which a child takes an active organizational role in determining the structure of his language [p. 2]" which are not necessarily either universal or modal types of exclusive alternatives.

One common type of phonological strategy is what may be called *preference strategies*, that is, the favoring or disfavoring (avoidance) of a particular sound or class of sounds. Thus one child may produce many words (and many instances of the same word) containing a particular sound in the adult mode. For example, one of the seven children studied by Farwell used a number of words in her early vocabulary which in the adult models contained mid to back fricatives and affricates which she pronounced in that phonetic range. Among her first 50 words were *see, fish, shoes, cereal, cheese, eyes, ice and juice*. She pronounced these words with fricatives or affricates and seemed to like to play with these words and say them often. This preference strategy was especially interesting when compared with the child's very limited inventory of sounds at the time (Farwell, 1976). Another of the Farwell subjects said no fricative words at all for 2 months. For another 2 months he produced only one fricative word with regularity. Then suddenly he began to acquire fricative words and within a month over 50% of his vocabulary contained fricatives, in a few cases even adding fricatives to words which did not have them.

Such periods of "favorite sounds" or avoidance have been attested for various sounds and sometimes are related to other aspects of the child's phonology. For example, a child may avoid adult *p*-words at a time when he is apparently trying to sort out the *p–b* voicing distribution, or his preference for velars may extend to velar harmony in which nonvelar stops in the same word are assimilated to velars (Ferguson and Farwell, 1975). In any such case such individual strategies are striking and offer an important qualification to the model of a universal route to the mastery of phonology.[4] As has been suggested elsewhere (Ferguson and Farwell, 1975), individual adult phonologies also exhibit preferences and avoidances, which can be illustrated anecdotally or intuitively but have not yet been studied systematically.

Another kind of strategy is the individual's effort to bring all words of certain structural characteristics into a favorite word shape. A *word-shaping strategy* typically reduces the phonetic or structural complexity of a whole word in a way which goes beyond segmental sound substitutions and assimilations. The most common type of word-shaping strategy is reduplication, which is so widely attested it is tempting to consider it a wired-in universal (cf. Jakobson, 1960), and some theories of phonological development give it a large place (e.g. Moskowitz, 1973). In fact, however, it is very variable in detail, and in particular it shows great variability in

----

[4]Celce-Murcia (1977) gives an interesting example of phonological avoidance in a bilingual child who in a number of instances seemed to use only the easier to pronounce of French-English pairs of equivalent semantic value.

type and frequency from one child to another. While some children have only a few examples derived from baby talk input, others make reduplication a major strategy in phonological development (Ferguson, Peizer, and Weeks, 1973). An extreme example of idiosyncratic use of reduplication is the child reported in Kunsmann (1976) who, for over three months, regularly expressed negation by reduplicating the second syllable to two-syllable words (e.g., *wati* 'water', *watiti* 'no water') and by similar reshaping of other words (e.g. *up* 'up' *upapa* 'not up, down'). A less widespread but well attested word-shaping strategy is the use of a device for reducing polysyllabic words which consists typically of repeating the salient syllable (or contructing a basic syllable from salient features) of the whole word and then adding a stock element, often a syllable, to represent the rest of the word. The most detailed description of a strategy of this kind appears in Priestly (1977). In this case the child regularly constructed a word shape (C)V́jVC from words of two or more syllables (e.g., *basket* → [bájak], *candle* → [kájal], *elephant* → [éjat]). Cf. Ferguson (1976) for discussion of "unique reduction devices" of this general type.

Some individual differences in phonological development may be attributed to the much more general notion of *learning styles*. In many cases it is possible to give an overall characterization of the way a child goes about acquiring phonology and to compare such a characterization or "learning style" with styles of other children. Such phonological learning styles may be related to nonphonological or even nonlinguistic developmental characteristics of the child.

On the basis of a few longitudinal studies of phonological development it is possible to identify several typical learning styles. One familiar type is the cautious system-builder. This kind of child constructs a tight phonological system into which he fits his vocabulary; he acquires new vocabulary slowly and does not attempt a new word unless it is within or just outside his current system. He has strong phonetic and structural constraints on his words and very few exceptions or marginal cases. His development is characterized by a gradual, orderly relaxation of the constraints, so that the word shapes gradually become more diversified as the phonology expands. Such a child is typically cautious and systematic in other aspects of development. For example, he may be less likely to produce semantic overgeneralizations and less likely to imitate adults' utterances than children of a different learning style (Macken 1976). Examples of children in the literature include Hildegard (English and German, Leopold, 1939–1949), "J" (Spanish, Macken, 1976), and Virve (Estonian, Vihman, 1977).

The opposite learning style is imitative, attempts new words beyond current capabilities, and shows a loose and variable phonological organization; there may be a considerable gap in phonetic accuracy between immediate mimicry and spontaneous speech. Examples of such children include "Si" (Spanish, Macken, 1976) and Hildegard's sister Carla (English and German, Leopold, 1939–1949). Many children can be assigned to one or the other of these two types or placed on a scale along this dimension. Of the five children acquiring Spanish as their mother tongue who were studied by the Stanford Child Phonology Project, four fit into this framework, ranging from J at one end to Si at the other (one nearer to J, the other nearer to Si). Some children do not seem to fit this scheme, however, and follow different learning styles; for example, one of the Stanford Spanish-learning children ("R") was different from the others. Leslie (Ferguson, Peizer, and Weeks, 1973; Weeks, 1974) also had a different learning style. She had difficulty with many aspects of phonology and, in spite of excellent comprehension and fluency in speech, her phonology lagged for a long period during which much of her speech was unintelligible. She drilled herself on particular problem words and as she began to learn to read she apparently sometimes improved her pronunciation from the spelling.[5] The identification and description of common learning styles in phonological development and the study of their correlation with other developmental characteristics belongs high on the agenda of research in developmental psycholinguistics.

Analogs to these individual strategies and learning styles exist in adult phonologies but are less evident simply because so much of the speaker's phonology is stabilized. Several contexts are likely places to observe such analogs, for example, when a person learns to say a new word or proper name, learns to pronounce a foreign language, engages in language play, or adjusts to a new dialect. The foreign language teacher is familiar with students who mimic much better or about as well as they pronounce spontaneously, students whose pronunciation improves gradually or rapidly, students for whom certain sound sequences or sound alternations are tied to particular lexical items versus those who generalize easily. It seems likely, though I know of no evidence for or against it, that some of the same strategies and learning styles shown by a child in acquiring his mother tongue remain available and preferred for that child later on, when as an adult he acquires additions and changes in his phonological repertoire. By the same token, if an individual's phonology at any point in his lifetime represents the accumulated effects of individual processes of acquisition, then THE phonology of a language variety—the normal object

---

[5]In the current Stanford study of children's voice onset time characteristics in acquiring English, Spanish, and Cantonese, preliminary analysis of the English data shows that three out of the four children acquired distinctive VOT values for voiced and voiceless initial stops at a very early age whereas the fourth one, who seemed normal in language development, acquired it much later (Macken and Barton, 1977).

of phonologists' study—is a composite of individual phonologies in which the shared structure inevitably has indeterminacies, fuzzy boundaries, and both dialectal and idiosyncratic variation. Which is to say that phonology is like syntax, lexicon, and all the rest of human language.

3. TOWARD A MODEL OF PHONOLOGY

Phonologists' analyses of particular languages and also phonological theory in general have been getting more sophisticated, more complex, and more highly formalized. The perennial question of what it is that phonologists are describing is correspondingly more urgent. What is the relationship between the phonologists' accounts and overt human behavior, human mental processes, and the processes of social interaction? Adequate answers to these questions would constitute a whole model of phonology, which I cannot provide. Some indications can be given, however, carrying forward some of the points made in Ferguson and Farwell (1975) and Ferguson (1976). These are offered in the form of six assumptions relevant to the topic of individual differences in phonology.

1.   Human beings have the capacity to hear and reproduce word-length stretches of speech, associate them with a semantic value, function, or occasion of use, and remember them. This can be done with a new expression in one's own language, an item in an unknown language, or a stretch of synthetic nonsense syllables. Such stretches can be held in auditory exactness in one's short-term memory and can also be put in the "permanent" memory, that is, be entered into one's lexicon. Some animals can do some of these things. Dogs can apparently perceive, assign some kind of meaning, and remember items, although with limitations on phonetic accuracy and number of items stored. Mynah birds can hear, remember, and reproduce items without the assignment of meaning in the same sense. The full set of processes is characteristically human.

2.   Processing speech in this way presents the individual with problems. Some things are harder to hear correctly than others, some are harder to assign meaning to, to remember, or to produce.

3.   The human organism is an active hypothesizer and problem solver, and in particular, children acquiring their mother tongue keep trying to organize the sound–meaning pairings in ways which will make them easier to perceive and recognize, easier to call up for use, and easier to produce. Part of this effort yields phonological organization. The phonology is "recreated by each child on the basis of the speech data it hears [Kiparsky 1968, p. 175]."

4.   Lexical items extracted from the speech data are stored in a complex network of representations which are accessible in many ways (e.g., by

synonyms, rhymes, collocates, syllable structure), some of which depend primarily on phonetic shape. It is the child's attempts to improve his phonetically based means of access which create his phonological organization. The child's phonological accessing systems for perception and production are relatively independent (Ferguson 1976, Straight 1976a), but as he grows older the connections between these two become stronger and denser, and by virtue of morphological alternations, paradigms, spelling, etc., his phonological organization includes deeper, more abstract relations. His means of access become correspondingly more varied and many "shortcuts" become available. There is no reason to assume a unique lexical representation for each word or morpheme (Hudson, 1976).

5. The phonetic facts of a language are so complex and have so many local autonomies (e.g., subsystems, lexical exceptions, dialect and register variation) that alternative analyses of the same data (by child or linguist) are highly probable. Physiological (both perceptual and articulatory), cognitive, and social constraints common to human beings and to the human condition will tend to cause congruence between the phonological systems of individuals learning the same language, but the constraints will also allow considerable individual variation.

6. The phonologists' primary goals are to identify the universal human constraints on the use of sounds in language and to characterize the sound systems shared by particular speech communities and their changes through time, but another productive line of research—relevant for the same goals and for others—is to write individual phonological profiles, that is, to characterize the phonological organization of particular individuals.

ACKNOWLEDGMENTS

Some of the work on this chapter was done as part of the Stanford Child Phonology Project, supported by the National Science Foundation, Grant BNS 76-08968.

REFERENCES

Berko, J. The child's learning of English morphology. *Word,* 1958, *14,* 150–177.
Bever, T. G. The cognitive basis for linguistic structures. In J. R. Hayes (Ed.), *Cognition and the development of language.* New York: Wiley, 1970.
Carden, G. A note on conflicting idiolects. *Linguistic Inquiry,* 1970, *1,* 281–290.
Cazden, C. On individual differences in language competence and performance. *Journal of Special Education,* 1967, *1,* 135–150.
Celce-Murcia, M. Phonological tactics in vocabulary acquisition: A case study of two-year-old English-French bilinguals. *Working Papers on Bilingualism,* 1977, *13,* 27–41.
Farwell, C. B. Some strategies in the early production of fricatives. *Papers and Reports on Child Language Development,* 1976, *12,* 97–104.

Ferguson, C. A. Applications of linguistics. In R. Austerlitz (Ed.), *The scope of American linguistics*. Lisse, Belgium: de Ridder, 1975.

Ferguson, C. A. Learning to pronounce: the earliest stages of phonological development and the child. *Papers and Reports on Child Language Development*, 1976, *11*, 1–27.

Ferguson, C. A. Vowel contrasts before *r* in American English: A study of individual differences in perception and production. In progress.

Ferguson, C. A., and Farwell, C. B. Words and sounds: Early acquisition. *Language*, 1975, *51*, 419–439.

Ferguson, C. A., Peizer, D. B., and Weeks, T. E. Model-and-replica phonological grammar of a child's first words. *Lingua*, 1973, *31*, 35–65.

Harrell, R. S. A linguistic anomaly. *General Linguistics*, 1961, *5*, 37–38.

Hudson, R. A. Lexical insertion in a transformational grammar. *Foundations of Language*, 1976, *14*, 89–107.

Ingram, D. The production of word initial fricatives and affricates by normal and linguistically deviant children. In A. Caramazza and E. Zurif (Eds.) *The acquisition and breakdown of language: Parallels and divergences*. Baltimore: John Hopkins University Press, 1975.

Ingram, D. Phonological disability in children. *Studies in Language Disabilities and Remediation*, 1976, *2*.

Jakobson, R. Why 'mama' and 'papa'? In B. Kaplan (Ed.), *Perspectives in psychological theory*. New York: International Universities Press, 1960.

Jakobson, J. *Child language, aphasia and phonological universals*. The Hague: Mouton, 1968. (Originally published as *Kindersprache, Aphasie und allgemeine Lautgesetze*, 1941.)

Jespersen, J. O. *A modern English grammar on historical principles. Part IV Morphology*. Heidelberg, Winter, 1942.

Jones, D. *An outline of English phonetics*. Eighth edition. Cambridge: Heffer, 1956, 173–178.

Kiparsky, P. Linguistic universals and linguistic change. In E. Bach and R. T. Harms (Eds.), *Universals in linguistic theory*. New York: Holt, Rinehart, and Winston, 1968.

Kunsman, P. Reduplication as a strategy for language acquisition. Paper presented at the summer meeting of the Linguistic Society of America, Oswego, New York, 1976.

Leopold, W. F. *Speech development of a bilingual child: A linguist's record*. 4 Volumes. Evanston, Illinois: Northwestern University Press, 1939–1949.

Long, R. B. *The sentence and its parts*. Chicago: University of Chicago Press, 1961.

Macken, M. A. Permitted complexity in phonological development: One child's acquisition of Spanish consonants. *Papers and Reports on Child Language Development*, 1976, *11*, 28–60.

Macken, M. A., and Barton, D. The acquisition of the voicing contrast in English: VOT data for four children. *Journal of Child Language*. Forthcoming.

Moskowitz, A. I. The acquisition of phonology and syntax: a preliminary study. In Hintikka *et al.*, (Eds.), *Approaches to natural language*. Dordrecht, Netherlands: Reidel, 1973. Pp. 48–84.

Nelson, K. Structure and strategy in learning to talk. *Social Research in Child Development Monograph*, 1973, *38*, Chicago: University of Chicago Press.

Newman, S. S. Behavior patterns in linguistic structure: A case study. In L. Spier *et al.*, (Eds.), *Language, culture and personality*. Menasha, Wisconsin: Sapir Memorial Publishing Fund, 1941. Pp. 94–106.

Payne, A. The re-organization of linguistic rules: A preliminary report. *Pennsylvania Working Papers on Linguistic Change and Variation*, 1975, *1*.

Priestly, T. M. S. One idiosyncratic strategy in the acquisition of phonology. *Journal of Child Language*, 1977, *4*, 45–65.

Quirk, R., Greenbaum, S., Leech, G., and Svartvik, J. *A grammar of contemporary English*. London: Longmans, 1972. Pp. 176–177.

Sapir, E. Speech as a personality trait. *American Journal of Sociology*, 1927, *32*, 892–905.

Slobin, D. I. Cognitive prerequisites for the development of grammar. In C. A. Ferguson, and D. I. Slobin (Eds.), *Studies of child language development*. New York: Holt Rinehart and Winston, 1973. Pp. 175–208.

Solberg, M. E. Developing phonological systems: Nomogenesis or individual strategies? Paper read at the summer meeting of the Linguistics Society of America, Oswego, New York, 1976.

Stoel, C. M. The acquisition of liquids in Spanish. Unpublished doctoral dissertation, Stanford University, 1974.

Straight, N. S. Comprehension versus production in linguistic theory. *Foundations of Language*, 1976a, *14*, 525–540.

Straight, N. S. *The acquisition of Mayan phonology: Variation in Yucatec child language*. New York: Garland, 1976b.

Vihman, M. M. From pre-speech to speech: Early phonology. *Papers and Reports on Child Language Development*, 1977, *12*, 230–243.

Weeks, T. E. *The slow speech development of a bright child*. Lexington, Massachusetts: Lexington Books, D. C. Heath, 1974.

10

Individual Differences in Second Language Acquisition

LILY WONG FILLMORE

There is some difference of opinion concerning the role of individual differences in second language acquisition. One view is that individual variation is an all-important factor—one which differentiates the process of second language acquisition from that of first language acquisition. This position has been widely held by investigators who are interested in the acquisition process principally as it occurs in adolescents or adults learning foreign languages in formal classroom settings. In such settings, it is apparent that individuals vary greatly in the ease and success with which they are able to handle the learning of new languages, and hence, it is argued that second language learning must therefore be different from first language learning. Whereas first language acquisition is quite uniform across populations in terms of developmental scheduling, the strategies used to achieve it, and the control over the language which is ultimately achieved, there is considerable variation among individuals in the ability to acquire second languages. Some individuals seem to acquire

Individual Differences in Language Ability and Language Behavior

Copyright © 1979 by Academic Press, Inc.
All rights of reproduction in any form reserved.
ISBN 0-12-255950-9

languages after the first with ease, and they manage to achieve a degree of mastery over the new languages comparable to the control they have over their first language in a relatively short time. Others find it quite difficult to learn later languages, to learn them as well as the first, or to do so at all without a great deal of conscious effort. Much of the research activities on second language acquisition until recently was aimed at finding explanations for this apparent variability. The favored explanations have centered on variations in learner characteristics such as motivation, attitudes, and language learning aptitude; and the research linking these characteristics to variation in language learning ability has been carried out largely on late adolescent and adult students of foreign languages with formal tests of achievement used as criterion measures. The investigations of Wallace Lambert and R. C. Gardner on the role of attitudes and motivations (Lambert et al., 1962; Gardner and Lambert, 1972) and those of John Carroll (1963) on language learning aptitude have been particularly important in this regard.

The second and opposing view is that individual variation plays no greater a role in the acquisition of second languages than it does in the learning of first languages—that is to say, its role, if any, is trivial. This position is taken by more recent investigators who have been looking at the acquisition of second languages by relatively young children in naturalistic settings where the language is not taught explicitly. The goal of these investigators is to demonstrate that the same processes which account for the learning of first languages are also responsible for the learning of later ones. Thus they look for evidence of acquisitional procedures and developmental schedules which resemble those found in first language learning, and they attempt to infer the existence of the same uniformity in acquisition that has been claimed in first language learning. Any evidence of individual variation among second language learners tends to get overlooked—partly because of the orientation of these investigators, and partly because much of their research has been carried out as single-subject case studies which attempt to map the developmental course of second language acquisition in individuals (e.g., Huang, 1971; Hakuta, 1974; and Milon, 1974), or as cross-sectional studies of a relatively large number of subjects tested on a one-shot basis, which attempt to establish statistical evidence of uniformity in the developmental sequence of a small number of specific grammatical items or processes (e.g., Dulay and Burt, 1974; Chun and Politzer, 1975; and Fathman, 1975).

In the case of the cross-sectional studies, the objective is to establish norms, and therefore, the statistical measures typically used are those which are not especially sensitive to variation: What variation there is manages to get lost with little difficulty in the statistical manipulations. The single-case studies, of course, do not yield any evidence of variation, since in order to show variation, there must be comparison—and in such studies, there is nothing to compare. Nor have attempts to compare findings across studies been especially fruitful since, in general, such studies tend to be noncomparable with respect to their subjects (in age, first language background, or circumstances under which the second language was being learned), the type of data used, the way they were collected, and the methods used to analyze the data.

And so it is that the issue of individual variation is rarely discussed in studies of childhood second language acquisition, this despite the fact that even the most casual observations of the language performance of any group of children in the process of learning a second language naturalistically or otherwise would reveal considerable variation in the rate and ease at which they are managing the learning of it, and in how well they are able to use the language they are learning. But because researchers are more interested in discovering what is universal about the acquisition process than in knowing whether the process might vary in individuals, the question is never discussed, or even raised.

In my own research on second language acquisition (Fillmore, 1976), I was not looking for individual differences either, but the research design I used would not permit me to ignore evidence of variation, as I might have been able to do had I limited myself to a sane single-subject case study or a tidy cross-sectional study. Instead, I did a longitudinal study of five subjects, tracking their second language development (English) for the period of one school year. But while the comparisons of the speech development of the five children during that year would have yielded evidence of variation, comparisons alone would not have revealed the factors which produced that variation, nor the manner in which those factors managed to affect the language learning of each child. This was done by another fortuitous aspect of the research design: I paired the five subjects who were Spanish-speakers with five English-speaking friends for observations. The five subjects and their friends shared no common language at first, and my purpose in observing the children in pairs was to discover what social processes might be involved when children who need to learn a new language come into contact with those from whom they are to learn it—but with whom they can not communicate easily. A language can be learned only if there is input of the proper sort—for the child second language learner, this is language as it is used in social situations which make sense, and in which the learner is himself involved. To get this kind of input, the typical second language learner must play an active role in inviting interaction from the speakers of the language, and in maintaining contact once it is established. Since all of this must be managed at a time when the learner cannot communicate with those from whom he is to learn the language, he needs some very special social skills. These social issues were at least as important as the cognitive issues I hoped to examine, and I wanted to discover what sorts of strategies the children would need to apply in order to handle the problem of making social contact. Thus I observed the subjects, not as they responded to me in elicitation sessions, but as they interacted and played with age-mates. It was in the course of these play sessions that the children revealed the impressive ways in which they were individuals, and which specific characteristics affected the way they approached the task of learning a second language.

Each of the five pairs of children—a Spanish-speaker and his or her English-speaking friend—was observed at play one hour each week in a playroom which was stocked with school materials and toys. These play sessions were audiorecorded, and written records were also kept of the children's interaction during these sessions. The audiotapes were all transcribed, and in all, there were 106 hours of transcribed conversations which served as the data for this study. The five Spanish-speaking subjects were all newly arrived from Mexico, and spoke no English at the beginning of the study period. All five were the children of farmworkers, and their parents planned to stay in the area where there was promise of year-around work. There were three boys and two girls: The youngest was Nora who was 5:7 and in kindergarten; Ana who was 6:5, Alej who was 6:9, and Juan who was 7:3 were all in the first grade; Jesus at 6:11 was in the second grade. Juan and Jesus had each had a year of school in Mexico before coming to California, but for the others, the study year was the first year of school. Two of the boys, Juan and Alej, were in the same class, but otherwise, the children were in different classrooms. None of the children received any formal language instruction during the study year. The source of their learning was the language used by their teachers and classmates.

Each of the English-speaking friends was close in age to the subject with whom he or she was paired, and attended the same classrooms as the subject. All but one were "anglos." The one exception was Juan's friend, Carlos. Carlos was a Mexican-American bilingual child, and he represented the only departure from the original plan of pairing the subjects with English monolingual friends. The reason for the departure was that Juan refused to have anything to do with English-speakers, and would only play silently beside the ones I attempted to pair him with for the purposes of the study. Carlos was Juan's own choice—and I thought it only fair that he should have a self-selected friend as the others did, especially after a month and a half of no success in trying to match him up with an English-speaker. Otherwise, the friends were self-selected, and while the study had the effect of prolonging friendships which might have been more temporary, the friendships between the Spanish and English-speakers were genuine enough, and reflected the social life of the children outside the Playroom during the school day and year.

The criteria for selecting the Spanish-speaking subjects were several—besides having an anglophone friend with whom he or she could be paired for the study, each had the following characteristics as far as could be determined through observations and without tests: (*a*) a reasonably outgoing personality; (*b*) normal first language development and fairly clear articulation; (*c*) normal intellect (i.e., was reasonably alert); and (*d*) parents who were willing to give assurances that they intended to stay in the community for at least the year. The object was to select five children who were as "ordinary" as possible, so that their second language might be offered as representative of other children their age, and from a similar linguistic and cultural background. I expected that the second language development of the five would be fairly uniform after 9 months of exposure to the new language as it was used in the classroom and in the playground by their teachers and classmates. But the results were quite different.

By the end of 3 months of observations, it became quite clear that there would be enormous differences among the five children in what they would achieve during the study year. In fact, after just 3 months of exposure, one child, Nora, had already learned more—or at least she was producing better-formed and more varied sentences—than two of the others, Juan and Jesus, would be able to manage by the end of the study period. And by the end of the study period, Nora herself was speaking English as well as her friends who came from bilingual homes, and very nearly as well as her English monolingual friends. In order to achieve the same degree of proficiency, the others in the study would need at least another year of exposure, and at the rate that Juan and Jesus were progressing, even two. This was the principal manifestation of individual differences in the data. It showed up in the records of the children's speech performance as differences in ease and rate of development rather than in acquisitional procedures—but these differences were related to the children's cognitive approaches to the learning task in interesting ways. In fact, the individual differences found among the five learners in this study had to do with the way in which the cognitive and social factors of language acquisition interact together. But before this can be described or shown, I will need to discuss what I found about the cognitive and social problems in second language learning, and of the strategies the children employed in dealing with these problems.

COGNITIVE AND SOCIAL STRATEGIES IN SECOND LANGUAGE LEARNING

The cognitive problem facing the second language learners is an immense one—he has everything to learn about the language, and little to work with, save a general awareness of how languages function, based on his first language experience. Thus he must approach this task with some strategies in hand. For starters, however, the first strategies that occur to him for dealing with language learning have nothing to do with learning a language. It is safe to say that none of the five children in this study approached the task as if they knew that is what they were doing. Instead, they seemed more aware of the problem of establishing social relations with the children who spoke that language. As pointed out earlier, language cannot be learned without input, and to get input of the right sort, the learner needs exposure to the language as it is used in social situations which involve him. To get into these social situations in the first place, and to establish a relationship with the speakers of the language so they are willing to provide the necessary input to him, the learner needs some special social strategies. And since all of this is to be accomplished at a time when he has little or no language in common with these people, the learner has a very sticky and circular problem on his hand. So the social problem in second language learning reduces to two major issues: How to get along for a while without a common language, and how to get your friends to want to help you learn theirs.

The cognitive problems are much more complex: Before the structures of the new language can be learned, the learner needs first to comprehend them. Second, he needs somehow to gain entry into the language, and then to figure out how the pieces of it fit together. Furthermore, he has somehow to develop fluency in the language, and to ferret out its structural details, so that his version of it matches the one spoken by the people around him. But while the children were quite aware of the social problems facing them, they appeared quite unconcerned about the cognitive ones. Perhaps they understood the social issues better, since the social ones had more direct relevance to them. They never seemed particularly motivated to learn the new language as they were to get along with the people who spoke it. Juan was the exception in this regard; he was not interested in associating with the English speakers, and the result was that he learned less than any of the others during the study year. But it was not for lack of interest in the learning of the new language, nor for want of trying: He frequently asked how one said this or that in English, repeated things he heard people saying, and he seemed to try hard to remember what he learned. But he truly did not care much to socialize with the people who spoke the language, and hence, he had little reason to use what he was learning. The other four children were far more interested in making friends than they were in learning any language, and they learned considerably more than Juan during the year.

To deal with the task of learning a language which they were largely unconcerned about learning, the children had to have some rather special cognitive and social strategies. The strategies which were revealed through the interactional and linguistic records of the children are summarized in Table 10.1. These strategies are phrased as maxims that the

TABLE 10.1
Cognitive and Social Strategies

Social strategies	Cognitive strategies
S-1: Join a group and act as if you understand what's going on, even if you don't.	C-1: Assume that what people are saying is directly relevant to the situation at hand, or to what they or you are experiencing. Metastrategy: Guess!
S-2: Give the impression—with a few well-chosen words—that you can speak the language.	C-2: Get some expressions you understand, and start talking.
	C-3: Look for recurring parts in the formulas you know.
S-3: Count on your friends for help.	C-4: Make the most of what you've got.
	C-5: Work on big things first; save the details for later.

children might have formulated for themselves, following the convention used by Slobin in discussing the operational principles of children in first language acquisition (1973). The cognitive and social strategies are presented together because it is difficult to separate them. They are presented this way to show how the social strategies relate to the cognitive ones, and in a way that might be taken as providing the motivation for several of the most important cognitive strategies.

The first social strategy is one which gets the learner into a position in which he is able to learn the language:

S-1: *Join a group and act as if you understand what's going on, even if you don't.*

Ordinarily, it is up to the learner to invite interaction. He is the "outsider" and he must somehow give the impression that he is worth talking to before the speakers are willing to have him join the group. The way the learner does this is to behave as if he understands, although obviously in the early stages of language learning, he will understand little. This means that he must pay attention to what is going on, and guess at what people are saying on the basis of contextual information.

This strategy worked because it had an important effect on the friends of the learners. The learners behaved as if they understood what was going on; the friends, believing that the learners understood them, included them in their conversations. Nevertheless, while the English-speaking friends believed that the learners understood English, they also recognized that their comprehension was limited, perhaps in the way one understands that the comprehension of younger or less experienced people is likely to be limited, and they therefore modified their language use accordingly. The crucial factor was this: Because the friends believed that the learners could understand them, and that communication between them was possible, they included them in activities and conversations, and this allowed the learners to assume roles in social situations and activities that made sense to them, and gave them an opportunity to observe and acquire the kind of language children use in these activities, despite their initial inability to speak or understand the language.

This, then, is the motivation for applying the first of the cognitive strategies:

C-1:   *Assume that what people are saying is directly relevant to the situation at hand, or to what they or you are experiencing. Metastrategy: GUESS!*

The first social strategy constitutes the learner's motivation for making the effort to figure out what is being said; its related cognitive strategy (C-1) constitutes the plan that enables the learner to begin comprehending the language used around him—the necessary first step in language learning. The use of situational information for speech interpretation is a very important strategy, one which the learners provided ample evidence of using. An obvious kind of language use in the classroom which lends itself to easy interpretation is the use of speech routines such as *It's time to clean-up now. Who's buying lunch in the cafeteria today? Let's line up for recess. Let's see which table can sit-up the straightest!* Such utterances through repeated or routine use quickly become associated with their related activities, and thus, can be readily interpreted and comprehended. However, the great majority of utterances produced in a day in the classroom or playground are not routine, but are situationally anchored nevertheless, whether they are formulaic or propositional. By paying close attention to what is going on when they are spoken, the learner can interpret with fair accuracy what is being said. Of course, not every instance of language use lends itself to interpretation this way, and there were many times, obviously, when the children did not know what was going on. Still, the daily experience of a child in the classroom and in the playground contains ample occasions when the situation provides the means for figuring out rather easily what people must be saying.

The second social strategy has to do with maintaining social contact once it has been established:

S-2:   *Give the impression—with a few well-chosen words—that you can speak the language.*

If the desire to join a social group whose language the learner does not speak is the social motivation for using contextual information to figure out what people are saying, then the desire to maintain contact and to sustain social relations with members of the group is the motivation to begin using the language. The learner cannot continue for long his charade of "knowing" the language without giving evidence of being able to speak it as well. What he must do is to acquire some language which will give the impression of ability to speak it, so that his friends will keep trying to communicate with him. This is accomplished through the use of the second cognitive strategy which gives the learner the needed entry into the new language:

C-2 *Get some expressions you understand, and start talking.*

The children in this study applied strategy C-2 by picking up formulaic expressions—expressions which were acquired and used as unanalyzed wholes. This strategy is extremely important since it allows the learner to use and become familiar with the language long before he knows anything about its structure, and before he can create any sentences in the language himself. There was a striking similarity among the five subjects in the acquisition and use of formulaic expressions.

All five quickly acquired repertories of expressions which they knew how to use more or less appropriately, and put them to immediate and frequent use. The phrases they learned were those they found most useful—expressions which helped them to appear to know what was going on (e.g., *Oh yeah? Hey, what's going on here? So what? No fighting, now.*), to participate in games and play activities (e.g., *You wanna play? It's my turn. Me first. No fair!*), and to request information, confirmation, and clarification from their friends (e.g., *How do you do this? What's happening? Is this one all right? What did you say?* and *I don't understand.*). The following are just a few of the typical formulas found in the spontaneous speech records of the children:

Lookit.	*I wanna play.*	*Liar, panzón fire.*
Wait a minute.	*Do you wanna play?*	*It's time to clean up.*
Lemme see.	*Whaddya wanna do?*	*OK, you be the X,*
Gimme.	*I gotta hurry up.*	*I'll be the Y.*
Let's go.	*I get 2 turns.*	*I tell you what to do.*
I don't care.	*Whose turn is it?*	*Shaddup your mouth.*
I dunno.	*You have to do it this way.*	*Beat it.*
You know what?	*I'm gonna tell on you.*	*Knock it off.*

This kind of language was extremely important, because it permitted the learners to continue participating in activities which provided contexts for the learning of new material. This new material was learnable and memorable by virtue of being embedded in current, interest-holding activities over which the learners had already acquired some mastery, and from which they had already received social rewards. Without doubt, the process would have been far less successful if the children had been only passive observers, rather than active participants. In order to make the progress they did, they needed to be in a position to discover under what pragmatic conditions particular utterances could appropriately be uttered, and they needed to be able to test their conclusions by using these utterances and getting feedback from their interlocutors to confirm whether they had guessed rightly or not. A good part of learning a language involves this kind of feedback. If the learner is not trying out his newly acquired language, he is not in a position to distinguish right guesses from wrong ones and thus discover what he needs to learn.

Other researchers (such as Huang, 1971; Hakuta, 1976) have observed the use of such language in second language learners. Huang has suggested that imitation may be a secondary strategy for language acquisition which is used in conjunction with the primary one of "rule formation" and acquisition. The point which has been missed so far is that the strategy of acquiring formulaic speech is central to the learning of language: Indeed, it is this step that puts the learner in a position to perform the analysis which is necessary for language learning. Formulaic speech in this study turned out to be important not only because it permitted the children to begin speaking the language long before they knew how it was structured, but also because the formulas the children learned and used constituted the linguistic material on which a large part of the analytical activities involved in language learning could be carried out. These formulas were generally expressions which were highly situational in use, and could be learned and used with the learner knowing nothing about their internal structures. In general, they were used as invariant forms, and the children had a fairly good idea of the appropriateness conditions for their use. Once in the learner's speech repertory, they became familiar, and therefore could be compared with other utterances in the repertory as well as with those produced by other speakers. Their function in the language learning process, then, is not only social, but cognitive too, since they provided the data on which the children were to perform their analytical activities in figuring out the structure of the language.

This, then, is the third cognitive strategy:

C-3:   *Look for recurring parts in the formulas you know.*

There are two ways in which the learner begins to analyze the formulaic expressions in his repertory. The first involves noticing how parts of expressions used by others vary in accordance with changes in the speech situation in which they occur. The second involves noticing which parts of these formulaic expressions are like parts of other utterances the learner knows or hears, or noticing variations of these utterances in the speech of others. For example, Nora had in her speech repertory two related formulas: *I wanna play wi' dese* and *I don' wanna do dese.* No doubt the similarity of these expressions allowed her to discover that the constituents following *wanna* were interchangeable, and that she could also say *I don' wanna play wi' dese* and *I wanna do dese.* As soon as she realized that these phrases were interchangeable, she was on her way to discovering that similar phrases could be inserted. At that point, these formulas became formulaic frames with analyzed slots: *I wanna X/X=VP* and *I don' wanna X/X=VP*, that is, where other verb phrases (VP) can be inserted into the slot represented by X.

Through a gradual process of figuring out which parts of the formulas in their speech repertories could be varied, the children were able to free the constituents in many of them to become units in productive constructions. In the above formulas, the phrase *play wi' X/X=NP* became a formulaic verb phrase unit which could be used in the verb phrase slot of other frames such as *Le's X/X=VP* (e.g., *Le's play wi' that one*) and in productive constructions as well: *She's play wi' dese.* Thus the analytical process carried out on formulas yielded formulaic frames with abstract slots representing constituent types which could substitute in them, and it also freed constituent parts of the formula to function in other constructions either as formulaic units or as wholly analyzed items. Finally, when all of the constituents of the formula have become freed from the original construction, what the learner has left is an abstract structure consisting of a pattern or rules by which he can construct like utterances.

The formula-based analytical process just outlined was repeated in case after case of the children's spontaneous data. A particularly clear example of it can be seen in the evolution of a formula in Nora's speech record, *How do you do dese?* Table 10.2 summarizes the developmental course of this expression over time, as it evolved from a wholly unanalyzed formula into a productive construction.

Nora first acquired this useful question during the second quarter of the study year which is designated Time 2 on the table, and she used it frequently, but only in the form, *How do you do dese?* Early in the next quarter, Time 3, she began appending noun phrases or preposition phrases to the formula: *How do you do dese X/X=NP, PP.* At this point the phrase itself was as yet unanalyzed, but was nevertheless being treated as a sentence frame with a noun phrase (NP) or a preposition phrase (PP) slot appended to it:

> *How do you do dese September por mañana?*
> *How do you do dese flower power?*
> *How do you do dese little tortillas?*
> *How do you do dese in English?*

Soon afterwards, the constituent following *you* became analyzed when Nora realized that she could substitute other verb phrases in that slot: *How do you X/X=VP.* With this frame, she produced questions such as

> *How do you like to be a cookie cutter?*
> *How do you make the flower?*
> *How do you gonna make dese?*

TABLE 10.2
How do you do dese?—from Formula to Productive Speech (Nora)

Structure	Examples
Time 2	
Wh[F]: *How do you do dese?*	*How do you do dese?*
Time 3–4	

Wh[Fx]¹: *How do you do dese (X)/*
    $X = NP,PP$
	How do you do dese?
	How do you do dese September
	  por mañana?
	How do you do dese flower power?
	How do you do dese little tortillas?
	How do you do dese in English?

Wh[Fx]²: *How do you* ⎱
    How did you ⎰ $X/X = VP$
	How do you make a little gallenas?
	  (= ballenas)
	How do you like to be a cookie cutter? (= How
	  would you . . .)
	How do you like to be a shrarks?
	How do you make the flower?
	How do you gonna make dese?
	How do you gonna do dese in English?
	How did you make it?
	How did you lost it?

Time 4	

Wh[Fx]³: *How do* ⎱
    How does ⎬ $X/X = Clause$
    How did ⎰
	How do cut it?
	How do make it?
	How does this color is?
	How did dese work? (= How does this work?)

Wh[S]: *HOW is freed, preposed*	*Because when I call him, how I put the number?* *(= How will I dial his number?)* *How you make it?* *How will take off paste?*

A second version of this formulaic frame was acquired, perhaps based directly on questions produced by others: *How did you X/X = VP*. With it she produced questions of the following sort:

> *How did you lost it?*
> *How did you make it?*

Nora was able to pick up variant forms rather quickly, and once she had some version of an expression in her speech repertory she would manage to find several others like it. In the fourth quarter (Time 4), the formulaic frame showed signs of further analysis—this time up to the auxiliary *do:*

> *How do* ⎱
> *How did* ⎰ $X/X = Clause$

This frame took a clause in the analyzed slot, and the frame itself might have been regarded as a question-word unit which could be preposed to a clause to be questioned:

> *How did dese work?*
> *How do cut it?*
> *How does this color is?*

In the final step, the question word was freed completely, and was used as a question word like the others in Nora's repertory of wh-forms, which could be used productively according to her current tactics for producing questions. These tactics included the selection of *how* as a manner adverb, and the positioning of interrogative words in front of the clause, but did not yet include *do* insertion or auxiliary inversion, as we see in the following:

> *Because when I call him, how I put the number?*
> *How you make it?*
> *How will take off paste?*

Thus we see the formulaic question *How do you do dese?* becoming increasingly analyzed until only the question word remains. At that point, *how* questions were productive, but they lacked the detailed refinements which required further analysis. Having the auxiliary *do* in the formulaic frames and recognizing that it usually followed the question word directly would surely aid the learner in figuring out the rules which take care of those details, but at the point where the study ended, there was no evidence that these final steps in the analysis were being taken. Looking at this data without the time periods specified, we might have guessed that the developmental course went the opposite direction—from the less well-formed versions to the well-formed ones at the top. Indeed, this would have been the case if the acquisitional procedure had been a gradual sorting out of the rules whereby the learner was able to structure the utterances herself. Instead, the procedure was one which might be described as "speak now, learn later."

Eventually, through the use of these analytical procedures, the learner is freed from his dependence on strictly formulaic speech. For a long while, however, much of his speech will consist of formulas or be constructed of formulaic units according to rules which are being derived through the analytical procedures described above.

The fourth cognitive strategy is one which permits the learner to develop fluency in the new language, and it is also related to the second social strategy (S-2):

C-4: *Make the most of what you've got.*

There was, in the speech records of the children, much evidence of application of the strategy of making the greatest use of whatever is already known. During the acquisition period, the children's repertories of forms and structures were limited. Their communicative needs far exceeded their current knowledge of the language. One way in which the children were affected by this discrepancy between what they wanted to say and their ability to say it was that they tended to limit what they talked about. However, if they had in their speech repertories expressions which could somehow be stretched to perform the communicative functions they had in mind, they were very likely to use them. Evidence of their following this strategy can be seen in the numerous instances of semantic extension found in the speech records. Ana, for example, used the phrase *putting in a hat* to locate objects on surfaces, as *in X is on Y.* Juan used the word *sangwish* to refer to food in general. Alej used the phrase *no good* as the adjective *dead*, and *gotcha* as the verb *kill* (e.g., *Bang, dese one no good*, i.e., *This one is dead*; and *Hey look, you gotcha one cowboy*, i.e., *You've killed one cowboy*). Similarly, he used the question formulas *Wha' happen?* and *Wha'sa matter?* to perform a variety of interrogative functions—in fact, almost anything he wanted to ask.

Other evidence of this strategy is found in the children's inclination to make frequent and overly generous use of forms they had, sometimes appropriately, and sometimes not. Thus, as we can see in the following text, when Nora acquired the form *anyway*, she attempted to use it in as many sentences as she possibly could:

> (We were drawing pictures—Nora was working on a fish, and Heidi a flower:)
>
> Nora: *Anyway I making a fitching.*
> Observer: *A what?*
> Nora: *Anyway a fitching.*
> Observer: *Are you?*
> Nora: (Looking over at Heidi's flower)
> *Yeah, I making a flower.*
> Heidi: *I'm making a flower power.*
> Nora: *How do you make a flower power?*
> Heidi: (Looks at Nora's picture which is clearly a fish)
> *That's not a flower.*
> Nora: *Yeah it is.*
> Heidi: *What is that anyway?*
> Nora: *Anyway a flower. That what is that anyway.*
> Heidi: *That sure doesn't look like a flower to me.*
> Nora: *But to me it looks like a flower, and to you, don't looks a flower, and to me, yeah! And you're a cookie cutter, and how do you like to be a cookie cutter? How do you like to be a cookie cutter? (Sings) How do you like to be a cookie cutter?*
> (Observational Records: March 16)

The strategy of making the most out of whatever has been learned has important consequences for the development of language. Nora's practice with adverb forms such as *anyway* established a slot within the sentence structure for them, and allowed her to notice and quickly acquire a large variety of similar forms. The other payoff is in the development of fluency. If the learner were to stop speaking each time he realized he did not have the appropriate word to insert in his sentence, rather than to take the most appropriate form in his repertory and let it substitute for the item he did not have, he would be far less fluent. This is especially clear in sentences such as Alej's *You gotcha one cowboy* where the formula *gotcha* as in *I gotcha!* is pressed into service as the verb *kill* which he apparently did not have or could not remember, and in sentences of his such as *C'mon me you house* where *c'mon* functions as the verb *come*.

This latter sentence of Alej's illustrates another way in which the learners tried to make the most of what they had. In the early acquisition period, they were all handicapped by having no easy way to structure sentences to express themselves propositionally. Until they learned how sentences were put together in the new language, either they were limited to what they could say with formulas, or they had to devise some sort of temporary makeshift pattern. Each of the children devised some idiosyncratic patterns for creating sentences using the speech units they had in their repertories. While these did not constitute major devices among their sentence producing tactics, still, they served a useful function. The goal, of course, was to communicate—and they had to do the best they could with what they had. Thus Alej devised a pattern with a pronominal noun phrase representing either a subject or indirect object preceded by a predicate which was generally a formulaic unit of one kind or another, as in *C'mon me you house* (=*I'll come to your house*), *C'mon me the shoe* (=*Won't you give me the shoes?*), and *What time you my house?* (=*What time are you coming to my house?*). Similarly, Ana produced sentences during Times 1 and 2 by stringing formulaic and lexical units together: *My sister—uh— come out—uh—dese—la quebró—dese*, and *Broke it—and my mother—said no—and my brother broke it*.

By making the best use of what they had, the children managed to get by quite nicely in English long before they actually knew very much. From the beginning, all of them tried to make the most of the English they knew. Juan, of course, said little or nothing in those early periods, since he did not care to communicate with the English-speakers with whom he had originally been paired. Still, what little he had to say to them, he generally said in English. In fact, the children resorted to Spanish only when their English failed them completely, even though they were all aware that they were free to use Spanish if they chose.

The fifth cognitive strategy is one which the children appeared to follow in the scheduling of their analytical activities which led eventually to learning the language. The task of learning a language is an impressively big one—there is everything to learn, and all of it is required for the creation of even very simple utterances, it seems. But obviously, the learner cannot deal with everything at once, and hence he needs a strategy for deciding what to work on first, and what to save for later. The strategy they followed was one which permitted them to make maximal use of what they had at any given point during the period of acquisition:

C-5 *Work on big things: save the details for later.*

All of the learners followed the first part of this strategy—only two of them got to the second part by the end of the study year. They were apparently dealing with major constituents first, and leaving the grammatical details to be worked out later. In fitting the major constituents into their sentences, the children generally followed English word order which they had ample opportunity to become familiar with through the use of the many formulaic utterances in their speech repertoires. The process of gradual analysis by which parts of formulas become freed from their original frames yielded sentence patterns by which the learners could produce nonformulaic sentences. In the process, some of the grammatical morphemes and grammatical distinctions are unnoticed and lost. Therefore, when the learner begins producing his own constructions on the basis of the derived patterns, he does not include all of the details of the originals. We saw, for example, that Nora's productive *how* questions did not make use of the auxiliary *do,* although the original formula and all of her formulaic frames did. The function of the auxiliary in both questions and negatives was a detail that she would have to deal with later. This strategy makes a lot of sense considering what is involved in the task of learning a language. It would be an overwhelming task if one had to be concerned with all its aspects at once, and hence, it seems smart on the part of the learner to deal with the large problems first, and work on the details later. Once the learner has a basic grasp of the structural features of the language, he can focus better on the small ways in which his utterances differ from those produced by other speakers of the language. When that happens, he will be able to begin sorting out the detailed features.

The final strategy is a social one:

S-3:   *Count on your friends for help.*

The acquisition of language, perhaps more than any other kind of learning activity, requires the participation of at least two parties—the learner, and someone who speaks the language already. Without the help and cooperation of friends, the children in the study would have learned little. The children's friends helped in many ways. First of all, there was their belief that the learners were capable of learning the language, and that they would succeed in learning it. There were numerous expressions

of this belief, such as in the following conversation with Nora and a friend
of hers a few weeks after the school year began:

Observer:	*¿Quieres hablar por el micrófono?*
	(=*Do you want to say something for the microphone?*)
Nora:	*Sí. ¿Qúe digo?* (=*Sure. What shall I say?*)
Observer:	*Di, "hello".*
Heidi:	*She can't. She can't talk English.*
Observer:	*Oh, she can repeat. Say "hello".*
Nora:	*No puedo. No puedo hablar en inglés.*
	(*=I can't speak English*)
Observer:	*Entonces, contéstame: ¿Cómo te llamas?*
	(*In that case, answer me: What is your name?*)
Nora:	*Nora.*
Heidi:	*But she can say things like "Me don't speak English" and all that.*
Observer:	*Who taught her that?*
Heidi:	*I don't know. She just learned. She just caught up with us, I guess.*

(Observational Records, September 25)

Such expressions of faith proved to be more than mere goodwill: The
friends acted on their belief. Because they believed that the learners could
learn, the friends talked and interacted with them in ways that guaranteed
that they would. They used gestures to aid in communication, but they
did not limit their communication efforts to nonverbal modes. They simplified their speech, but in ways that aided learning rather than distorted
the input that the children received. Most important, the friends included
the learners in their activities, and it was in the context of these activities
and relationships that the learners were able to get the exposure they
needed to the new language in use.

Yet another way in which the cooperation of the friends was important
was that they provided the learners with needed encouragement. From the
beginning of the study year, the friends nearly always tried to make the
most of the learners' efforts at speaking the language by figuring out what
they were trying to say. The friends sometimes had to ask the learners
what they meant, or to ask them to repeat something, in order to confirm
their guesses. There were few genuine communication failures, however,
since the friends were making use of contextual information to figure out
what the learners were saying, and this contextual information was always
relevant since the learners tended to limit their speech efforts to comments
related to the activities at hand. It is a sign of their mutual success that the
learners and their friends managed to get along well in endless hours of
play throughout the school year.

The most vital kind of help friends gave the learners in this study was in the linguistic input they provided for the language learning effort. The language the friends used in playing with the learners can best be characterized as natural: Although there were simplification, careful contextualization, and repetitiveness, the language was, above all, very similar to the language children ordinarily use in playing with one another. It is not until it is examined closely and compared with the language spoken to others that the modifications the children made are revealed. One of the ways that the children modified their language use in talking to the learners had to do with limiting their speech topics to the activities at hand. In general, the friends tended to avoid talking to the learners about displaced events or topics. They discussed such matters with me from time to time, but it was clear that the speech effort was directed at me alone, and not at the learner.

SOURCES OF INDIVIDUAL DIFFERENCES IN SECOND LANGUAGE LEARNING

The individual differences found in the learning of a second language by the five children in this study had to do with the nature of the task, the sets of strategies they needed to apply in dealing with it, and the way certain personal characteristics such as language habits, motivations, social needs and habitual approaches to problems affected the way they attacked it. They differed greatly in such characteristics, and in the course of the study year, it became quite apparent that it was the interaction of all these factors that produced the observed differences in the rate at which they learned the new language. One of the most critical ways in which they differed was in having the social skills required to make use of the social strategies which have been discussed. Before the learner could be in a position to exercise the cognitive strategies which would ultimately result in language learning, he needed to be in social contact with the speakers of the new language, but to do that, he needed some very special social skills.

This discussion of individual differences will focus on the ways the children differed in their approach to second language learning. It should be stated at the outset that these remarks are based strictly on the observations made during the study year, and that no independent measures of intelligence, personality or language aptitude were administered to verify or support the comments which are made here. The children were not formally tested in these areas because none of the standard measures seemed appropriate for their age. Furthermore, the language they spoke was different from the one in which most tests have been prepared, and they came from a culture substantially different from that of the populations on which these tests have been normed.

With that caveat aside, it should be said that observational data of the sort gathered in this study can provide better insights into what children are like than any tests that might have been given. Children, when they are tested, sometimes behave in ways that they believe will please the tester, rather than as they might normally. Observations of naturalistic behavior over an extended period of time are, for this reason, more accurate, since "model behavior" is not likely to be sustained for long. Since play is the most natural medium of expression for children, much can be learned if they are observed at play over a period of time, as these children were. The children were observed at weekly intervals for the period of a school year as they interacted with friends. Over the course of the year, they revealed the impressive extent to which they differed in their feelings, attitudes, interests, and customary approaches to problems. By way of discussing these differences, I will review some of the observations made in the course of examining the children's speech records. Since Nora was the most successful learner, she will serve as the basis for comparison in much of this discussion.

The secret of Nora's spectacular success as a language learner can be found in the special combination of interests, inclinations, skills, temperament, needs, and motivations that comprised her personality. It seems that she was inclined to do just those things that promote language acquisition. She was strongly motivated to be associated with the English-speaking children in her classroom, and she sought them out to play with to an extent that none of the other children in the study did. In nearly all of the observations of her outside of the playroom in the first three periods of the study—whether in the classroom, cafeteria, or playground—she was with English-monolingual children. Since one-half of her classmates were Spanish-speakers (some monolingual like herself, others bilingual), it was more than a coincidence that she was seldom observed with these children with whom she might have interacted more easily. In fact, by the end of the study year, she was clearly identifying herself more as an English than as a Spanish-speaker. Note for example, her desire to exchange her name for a more English-sounding one in the following excerpt from an observational record:

> (Beginning of the session. As usual, the girls are asked to record
> their names on the tape-recorder:)
> Observer: *Wait—say your name first.*
> Nora: *Uh—*
> Observer: *You forgot?*
> Nora: *N—un—*
> Observer: *What's your name?*

Nora:	*Nora.* (English Pronunciation—[noɹə])
Observer:	*Nora?*
Nelia:	*Nora!* (Spanish pronunciation—[noɾa])
Nora:	*Nora!* (English)
Observer:	*Oh!*
Nelia:	*Nora.* (Spanish)
Observer:	*'Scuse me, Nora.* (English)
Nora:	*No—no, but my, my, but my mother tomorrow she's gonna give me another name, Lora.*
Observer:	*What? Lora? Is that what your mother's gonna do, Nora?*
Nora:	*Um-hum. Lora.*
Observer:	*OK, so you wanna be—*
Nora:	*Lora, Lora, not Nora* (Spanish). *Teacher, teacher, but, but, you can call me, uh, by now, Orla.*

(Observational Records, May 23)

In contrast to Nora on this score, Juan avoided English-speakers almost altogether and was apparently uncomfortable around them. He preferred the company of those with whom he could communicate freely, and so he played only with other Spanish speakers or with bilingual children. The others—Alej, Jesus, and Ana—played with English speakers, but not exclusively. Alej and his friend, Kevin, played together a great deal, but usually with a larger group of boys. Most of the boys were bilingual, and in their games, both English and Spanish were spoken. Thus Alej was perhaps exposed to more Spanish than English. Kevin, his English-speaking friend, was unusual in this respect: He was the only one of the four English-speaking children in the study who associated almost exclusively with Spanish-speaking children. Jesus's friend Matthew was not ordinarily included in the games and activities of Jesus's principal group of playmates, who were all bilingual. Matthew was something of an "outsider": Jesus played with him from time to time in the playground, but Jesus's friends did not. When they played, Jesus's friends used both English and Spanish, but most of them were more inclined to speak English than Spanish. Jesus used what English he had, but mostly he spoke Spanish. Ana did not belong to any group at all. While she did not always get along well with Margot, her English speaking friend, still they seemed to be best friends, and either she played with Margot, in which case she used English, or she tagged along after her older sister, who spoke only Spanish.

And so only Nora put herself in a position to receive maximum exposure to the new language. Ana was in a somewhat similar position since, aside from her sister, she did not play with Spanish-speaking children at school.

The difference between Nora and Ana was that where Nora had many friends, Ana had only Margot. And while Ana and Margot played together, they did not talk much. Furthermore, Ana played only with her siblings (who were Spanish-monolinguals) at home; whereas in addition to her brothers and sisters, Nora played with Heidi, who lived on the same block as she did. Thus Ana had far less exposure to English than Nora, both during and after school.

Another way in which Nora differed from the other children in the study was in her choice of play activities. Where the others—especially the boys—usually were involved in super-macho games that required little real talk, such as baseball, kickball, and marbles, Nora preferred activities that depended on verbalization. Her favorite ones involved dramatic play, and it was in the context of such games that she learned and was able to put to use the language she was picking up from her friends. She engaged in these play activities not only in the playroom but on the playground and in the classroom as well. And from her reports, this was how she and Heidi played together after school. Nora's interest in such games reflected her overall concern for social relations—the sort of dramatic play she and her friends customarily engaged in involved the taking of roles and the working out of relationships. They pretended to be teachers and students, mothers, fathers, and babies, doctors and nurses, and boyfriends and girlfriends. They conjured up problems and situations, all of which needed to be talked out, argued over, and resolved. These dramatic play situations were rather tame in comparison with Nora's real-life involvement with her friends. She had a tendency to develop intense relationships with her friends. Because of that, she was, once she had adequate command of the new language, constantly embroiled in one controversy after another, all of which required a great deal of verbal activity. In fact she wore out three friends during the study period. At 6 years of age, she was capable of becoming angry enough at her playmates to declare that she would have nothing more to do with them and actually follow through on her threat. Such was the fate of Heidi who from October to mid-March was her closest friend, of Nelia who was her friend from mid-March to May, and finally of Magda who was on her way out of Nora's circle of friends when the study year came to a close.

While the peer group was important to the other children, none seemed as caught up in its concerns as Nora. Ana, in fact, seemed to prefer the company of adults. When Margot was not around, she was at her sparkly best. Then she did not have to compete with Margot for my attention and she had an undivided audience for her stories and proposals. Both Nora and Ana had a great need to talk, but they were differently motivated. Nora's need stemmed from the more basic one of wanting to belong to the peer group; and communication was essential to the maintenance of relationships within it. Ana was less concerned with maintaining relationships with her age-mates than she was with communicating her problems and needs to adults. These were not matters she could share with friends her own age, and it is doubtful that she ever attempted to do so with Margot, since Margot was not particularly receptive or sympathetic to Ana's problems. Instead, she spent a lot of time talking with her teacher, who spoke only English, with the teacher's assistant, who spoke Spanish, and with me. Often on the days when I was at the school, Ana would visit me during recess and during the lunch hour just to talk. Of the two children, Nora's motivation for talking was the more profitable one for language learning purposes, since it placed her in precisely those situations in which the language spoken was most useful as input. Ana's adult friends could hardly have provided her with enough input of the right sort.

The other children were communicative, but they managed to suppress their need to communicate until they were with people with whom they could talk freely. With their English-speaking friends, the boys were able to limit themselves almost exclusively to talk which had to do with the activities they were engaged in at the moment. This, of course, was fine during the early stages of acquisition, but to go beyond the early stages they needed the opportunity of hearing and attempting to use more diversified language. Even in Spanish, the boys tended not to engage in conversations as such. Of the three, only Jesus did—but not frequently. The others were satisfied most of the time to limit their verbalizations, in English and in Spanish, to comments, responses, and sound effects which carried little informational weight. In general, Juan, Alej, and Jesus were more inhibited about using their new language than Nora and Ana were. Juan was the most cautious of all and rarely said anything in English unless he was quite sure of himself. Alej was less cautious, but still he sometimes mumbled what he had to say as if he was embarrassed or not sure of himself. Jesus gave the impression of having a great deal of confidence in what he was saying, but he seldom tried to communicate much in English beyond what he could say with formulas. Otherwise, he used Spanish or kept his thoughts to himself.

In contrast, Nora was quite uninhibited in her attempts at speaking the new language. After the first 2 months, she was able to get by almost exclusively with English, and from the first she was far more concerned with communication than with form. She used what she knew to say what she needed to say, and she usually made good enough sense. Ana, too, was quite uninhibited about using her new language, although she was somewhat more conscious of her limitations than Nora. Still, Ana was not particularly worried about how she sounded when she was speaking English. Both Nora and Ana were inclined to be experimental and playful in their efforts to speak English. Both engaged in syntactic play—a practice which resulted in the development of fluency and control over grammatical structures. Jesus, too, engaged in verbal play, but his was of a different sort. Where Nora and Ana took patterns and varied them by changing the words, Jesus took phrases and sang them repeatedly but with little variation. Compare, for example, Nora's syntactic play in

> *She said me that it wa' not too raining by she house.*
> *She said it wa' not too raining by she house.*
> *She said she not raining by she house.*

with Jesus's in

> *Somebody dance, somebody dance, somebody da, da, da!*
> *Somebody dance, dumbody dance, dumbody da, da, da!*

Nora's syntactic play is experimental in a way that is likely to result in better grammatical control, where Jesus's is not. He saw the possibility of playing with sounds, but apparently not with structures as Nora did. The syntactic play that Nora and Ana engaged in was indicative of their attention to structural matters. Nora was especially quick in figuring out which parts of the expressions in her repertory of formulas could be varied, and in analyzing them. Similarly, Ana could extrapolate patterns from the sentences she had in her repertory and produce endless variations on them, as she often did when she pretended to read from books. Consider the patterning, for example, which is apparent in these ersatz story-telling sentences:

> *She, the cat, she, what is this? A waterfly, ah, the cat she was playing with the waterfry—and the, the blue cat. What is this? Espider! spider, espider! espider and the cat, one day she was crying—the—what is this? What is this color? Black color—she was—what is—play wi' ji—What is dese color? 'Rown! 'Rown, 'rown cat. She wit' the laller. She run an' run an' run an' the res'—and the, what is this? What is this? A peeg? Pig! What is she doing? The dog, I can't do it. The dogs, she was playing. An' the dog she was playing with the, wi'—wit' da shoes. It's funny, huh? Doaks—she was playing in the grass—sapi! Eswans, she was playing in the water.*

(Observational Records, March 27)

Nora's rapid analysis of formulas had a correlate in her disposition to figure out how toys, games, and gadgets were put together, and how they worked. She was constantly playing with things and taking them apart, and her doing so with linguistic structures was consistent with her overall approach to whatever she came across. Jesus, by contrast, was uninclined to disassemble his structures. In fact, he tended to maintain his expressions in the forms in which they were learned. While he (as did the others) eventually analyzed some of these formulaic expressions to get frames which could be used productively, still no one was as fast at doing this as Nora. Jesus's rigidity in dealing with linguistic structures was reflected in his general approach to new ideas. Once he thought he knew something, he found it difficult to change his mind. At least, he seldom admitted he was wrong, and it usually took an enormous amount of evidence to convince him that he was. For example, when he decided that *fitch* was the English word for *pigeon*, no amount of argument could convince him that he was wrong. Jesus liked to be right, and once he decided on any issue, he tended to protect his decision against change or modification. This was not a particularly profitable trait to have while learning a new language, since inflexibility can reduce the ability to see structural patterns and possibilities. There is no reason at all to believe that Jesus was less able to analyze than Nora or Ana—but his inclination to be inflexible in approaching new ideas and evidence slowed down his performance in those analytical activities which were essential to the language learning process.

Jesus, the audio records showed, was one of the best of the five children at mimicry. He had a talent for remembering and precisely reproducing formulaic expressions that he heard. Furthermore, he had a talent for recognizing and picking up memorable and useful expressions. But these abilities alone were insufficient for rapid progress in learning the new language. Alej was much poorer in these areas: He had difficulty remembering how expressions in the new language sounded, and an enormous difficulty reproducing them. He often garbled what he was saying so badly that it was nearly impossible to understand him. But despite his imprecision in hearing and reproducing sounds, he made greater actual progress than either Jesus or Juan did. Like Jesus, Juan was fairly good at remembering and reproducing utterances, but he did not make much use of these skills. Alej, on the other hand, made good and immediate use of whatever he learned and looked for ways to vary the expressions he had in his repertory. Thus he was able to make fairly rapid progress in learning the new language, and if he did not sound very authentically English-speaking, still he was able to express himself quite adequately by the end of the school year.

Juan had a one-step-at-a-time approach to language learning: That is, he tended to work on one kind of construction at a time, and seldom used anything until he was quite certain of its use. This is in sharp contrast to Nora's habit of putting whatever she learned to immediate use. Where Juan worked on one problem at a time and did not attempt to use what he was learning until he had most of the details worked out, Nora tended to work whatever she picked up into as many sentences as she could as a way of figuring out the potential uses of the new form. She learned to use vocatives, temporal adverbs, and tags by way of overusing them when they were first acquired. Juan's approach, of course, was much safer. He seldom said what he had not intended to say, as Nora sometimes did. However, his method was also much slower: He did not get the chance to say a fraction of what Nora was able to say—even if she was wrong now and then.

SUMMARY

In summary, the individual differences among the five children in the study had to do with the interaction between the nature of the task of learning a new language, the strategies that needed to be applied to the task, and the personal characteristics of the individuals involved. The children, it seems, were more or less equally endowed with the intellectual capacity to learn a new language—after all, they had already acquired one with comparable facility—but they were differently disposed to take the necessary steps to insure the learning of the second. Nora was particularly motivated by the desire to be a part of the social group that spoke the new language, and thus she sought out the company of the children she wanted to be with. At the other extreme, Juan avoided contact with people who did not speak his language. Thus Nora was in a position to learn the new language where Juan was not. That difference presumably had nothing to do with intellectual or cognitive capacity. It was solely a matter of social preference, and perhaps of social confidence as well. Furthermore, Nora and Ana tended to be playful and experimental with language, while Jesus was rather rigid and inflexible. Again, Nora's and Ana's proclivity permitted them to discover the structural possibilities in the new language, where Jesus was pretty much limited to the phrases he had in his repertory for much longer. Yet, the fact that Jesus did not analyze his expressions quickly and play with them cannot be taken as evidence that he was unable to do so. He eventually did analyze some of his expressions and was able to use the structures productively. It was not that he could not see the structural possibilities of the expressions in his repertory; he just was not looking for them.

To learn a language rapidly, it is perhaps most necessary to identify with the people who speak it, as Nora did. She not only wanted to be around English speakers, she wanted to be *like* them, and, therefore, she adopted their way of talking. The desire to be like the speakers of the new language was the motivation Nora needed to modify and adjust her speech according to their norms. By actively working to sound like them, she eventually was able to achieve just that goal. This, apparently, was not something the other children were as willing to do. While most of them were cordial and sociable with English speakers, no one else identified with them to the extent that Nora did, at least during the study year. The others will surely learn the language just as well as Nora did, even it it takes several years longer. One can hope that all five will maintain their individual identities while doing so.

REFERENCES

Carroll, J. B. Research on teaching foreign languages. In N. L. Gage (Ed.), *Handbook of research in teaching.* Chicago: Rand-McNally, 1963. Pp. 1060–1100.

Chun, J. A. and Politzer, R. L. A study of language acquisition in two bilingual schools. Final project report, School of Education, Stanford University, 1975.

Dulay, H. C. and Burt, M. K. Natural sequences in child second language acquisition. *Language Learning,* 1974, *24,* 37–54.

Fathman, A. K. Language background, age, and the acquisition of English structures. In M. K. Burt and H. C. Dulay (Eds.), *New directions in second language learning, teaching and bilingual education.* Washington, D. C.: TESOL, 1975. Pp. 33–43.

Fillmore, L. W. The second time around: Cognitive and social strategies in second language acquisition. Unpublished Doctoral dissertation, Stanford University, 1976.

Gardner, R. C. and Lambert, W. E. *Attitudes and motivations in second language learning.* Rowley, Massachusetts: Newbury House, 1972.

Hakuta, K. A case study of a Japanese child learning English as a second language. *Language Learning,* 1976, *26,* 321–351.

Huang, J. A Chinese child's acquisition of English syntax. Unpublished Master's thesis, UCLA, 1971.

Lambert, W. E., Gardner, R. C., Barik, H. C., and Turnstall, K. Attitudinal and cognitive aspects of intensive study of a second language. *Journal of Abnormal and Social Psychology,* 1962, *66,* 358–368.

Milon, J. P. The development of negation in English by a second language learner. TESOL QUARTERLY, 1974, *7,* 137–144.

Slobin, D. I. Cognitive prerequisites for the development of grammar. In C. A. Ferguson and D. I. Slobin, (Ed.), *Studies of child language development.* New York: Holt, Rinehart, and Winston, 1973.

11

Individual Variation in Some Phonetic Aspects of Language Acquisition

JOHN H. V. GILBERT

INTRODUCTION

Theoretical problems associated with individual differences have for long been a focus of psychology. Recently, these problems have received closer scrutiny from investigators concerned with both perceptual and productive aspects of speech processes. Any cursory review of experimental results reveals the large inter- and intrasubject variability which exists for all manner of experiments; no where is this more so than in those conducted with children as subjects. Quite often, measures of central tendency tend to mask out "grubby data" which is euphemized as "individual differences." The variability that exists both within individual talker results and across a group of talkers engaged in the same speaking activity has led to the frustration of attempts to develop a comprehensive and generally acceptable theory which might, for example, specify the prosodic features of speech and their acoustic correlates.

229

Individual Differences in Language Ability and Language Behavior

Copyright © 1979 by Academic Press, Inc.
All rights of reproduction in any form reserved.
ISBN 0-12-255950-9

In this chapter I shall attempt to focus on individual variation in some phonetically related aspects of language acquisition with the intention, if not the realization, of further elucidating some corners of the perception–production ontogeny. That is, what evidence exists that the child perceives speech in terms of the adult system but that phonological patterns parallel the development of what MacNeilage (1970) has called "an internalized space coordinate system."

APOLOGIA

A discussion of this nature makes certain assumptions of its readers. The first is that it is somewhat redundant to talk of individual differences, since we know they exist. What is of interest is not the differences per se, but rather the sizes they can assume for a given individual on a given task. The second assumption concerns a faith in experimental paradigms and the observation that perhaps one experimental method may not give the whole answer. Pisoni's (1975) experiment on the categorical perception of vowels is a nice case in point. The third assumption is that we recognize the power (or lack of power) of central tendency statistics to adequately describe the complex of speech behavior.

In order to handle these caveats with some integrity I propose to examine some factors which affect the developing child to create *similar* conditions of development and then to examine some manifestations arising as a result of these conditions, yet which give rise to individual variation.

ASPECTS OF PERCEPTION

A year following his classical experiments with Nicely (Miller and Nicely, 1955), George Miller wrote:

> The psychological space that we discover with auditory recognition tasks is quite small; it seems likely that the sounds of speech fill a large portion of it and that we could not greatly increase the number of phonemes we use without running serious risks of perceptual confusion. [Miller, 1956, p. 355].

Even within the limited set of phonemes available to him, the child must experience such perceptual confusion. The one problem involved in interpreting child data is to determine whether one is examining the transducing capability of the auditory mechanism (a task usually undertaken in auditory psychophysics) or whether the perceptual results represent some linguistic capability.

Auditory Aspects

Related perhaps to experiments with chinchillas conducted by Kuhl and Miller (1975), we have recently seen the emergence of interest in the investigation of human hearing from an evolutionary and biogenetics standpoint, investigations which demonstrate that the human auditory apparatus has a different resolving power than does that of the higher primates. Stebbins (1973) has shown that monkeys can resolve a difference of about 7 Hz at 1 kHz, which increases to about 50 Hz at 8 kHz, whereas for man, Showers and Biddulph (1931) showed much smaller values, being about 3 and 20 Hz respectively. Man's ability to discriminate intensity also appears better than that of the monkey, Riesz (1928) having shown a resolving capability of .5 dB for man and 60 dB SL, whereas at the same intensity levels, the monkey can resolve differences down to 1.5 dB. These differences in response to primary psychoacoustical attributes of auditory signals should be compared with the *similarity* in results on categorical discrimination tasks performed by infants, monkeys, and chinchillas (Eimas, 1974; Sinnott *et al.*, 1976; Kuhl and Miller, 1975). Cutting and Dorman (1976) have recently shown, for example, that the inability to detect intensity differences carried on the formant transitions of stop consonants is a *psychoacoustic* rather than a *phonetic* effect. Thus we might, with justification, expect the child's peripheral transducing system (complete and ready for action at birth) to perform the same analysis on auditory signals as would the cochlea of a fully grown adult. It is of interest to consider (in the light of the HAS—high amplitude sucking—literature) just whether difference limens (DLs) for frequency, intensity, and duration would be the same for young children as they are for adults. The nearest experiment I have been able to find which might answer this tantalizing question, was reported by Bond and Stevens (1969). They tested children at 5 years of age to determine whether they could perform cross-modal matching between two sense continua—a light and a 500 Hz tone. The tone was presented at eight different levels from 40 to 110 dB. Not only were the children able to perform that task well, but the individual variability of response was small—on the same order as that of adults. In their discussion of this experiment, Bond and Stevens suggest that "the strength of our sensory impressions depends on the transducer properties of the sense organs and that the eyes and ears of children perform like those of adults [p. 339].

Certainly the hearing threshold curves obtained for 4-and 5-year-olds would tend to confirm this suggestion. The auditory–phonetic transformation in the maturing child cannot simply be explained away in terms of a linguistic–nonlinguistic discontinuity, since there are by now, multiple experiments which suggest otherwise for adults (see, for example, Blechner, Day, and Cutting, 1976). There appears to be only one other paper which relates directly to auditory psychoacoustic information in the DL mode. In a recent paper, Eguchi (1976) examined DLs for formant frequencies in children aged 7–15 years and showed a learning curve reaching adult values around the twelfth year. What is of interest in this paper is the very large variability in Δ F/F for both F_1 and F_2 between the ages of 7–9. Whether this variability is a function of the auditory or phonetic aspects of the sounds with which Eguchi's subjects were presented, *or* whether the results represent task difficulty (Eguchi used an ABX paradigm) *or* whether the ISI (interstimulus interval) affected response times, is difficult to disambiguate. In a recent paper (Gilbert, 1976b) we have shown, for example, very clear identification and discrimination of vowels at 2.5 years of age; these results, admittedly in a different mode, are difficult to reconcile with Eguchi's data. We suggest that interstimulus interval might cause difficulties in such a task since Tallal (1976) has recently reported that for nonverbal auditory signals the ability to respond correctly to a two-tone task is better when the ISI is long (947–4062 msec), than when it is short (8–305 msec). Eguchi's test items would have fallen within the second category.

In sum, it would appear appropriate to conclude that at least the transducing mechanism for linguistic and nonlinguistic auditory signals is set for the *perceptual* process immediately following birth. In this, the auditory components of language give an obvious and overwhelming advantage to the perception of speech, and thus the development of "the psychological space" for "auditory recognition." There is, perhaps, some tenuous parallel and corroboratory evidence to be found in left hemisphere functioning; particularly EEG data (Molfese, 1976); dichotic listening results (Gilbert and Climan, 1974; Ingram, 1975) and recent reports on language acquisition following hemidecortication (Dennis and Whitaker, 1976).

Although one might suggest that there is relative invariance in the signal proceeding past the peripheral auditory analyzer, obviously at some level the signal must undergo a "physical–psychological transformation" (Fry, 1956). What I should like to suggest is, that for the child learning language, conditions are opportune for the transformation and subsequent erection of "psychological space" for the sounds of speech, which occurs quickly and allows the trailing production system to make for more efficient acoustic–articulatory matches than would be possible if both systems developed along the same time course. To clarify this point I should now like to turn to the available physiological evidence.

Physiological Aspects

If we accept the relative invariance of the acoustic signal being transduced from the periphery and the development of some multidimensional space for multidimensional speech signals, then it is perhaps in the effecting of some linguistic response (measured in different parameters) that individual differences will become most interesting as indicators of rule development. Since fundamental frequency (F_0), formant frequencies (F_2, F_3, etc.), duration (in msec) and intensity (in dB) carry the *information* intended by a central processor, then we might expect to find some regularity in their variability as they are manipulated to achieve adult forms of speech signals. Physiologically, with respect to the adult, the child as speaker is at some considerable disadvantage. It is this disadvantage which tends to confound phonological realizations of speech sounds.

In his seminal paper on motor control of serial ordering of speech, MacNeilage (1970) neatly encapsulated the problem as I have tried to elaborate it. He wrote: "How do articulators always come as close to reaching the same position as they do? [p. 183]". He went on to conclude that the speech production process is not an inefficient response to invariant central signals but rather that it represents an elegantly controlled variability of response to the demand for a relatively constant end. A question subsidiary to my initial one, but directly related, then, is whether the *variability* as we see in child speech production remains constant for one child across time, while the central tendency measure (whether for F_0, FF, dB, or msec) moves to some adult value, which itself will show a similar degree of variability *or* whether the variability *decreases* with the same movement to adult values. Kent (1976), for example, in discussing the data of Tingley and Allen (1974) has suggested that 5-year-old children have learned strategies for the preprogramming of motor control, even though the precision of motor control continuously improves for a period of at least 4 more years. I shall return to this point later.

At the risk of opening the continuity–discontinuity debate concerning the onset of speech, I should like, in fact, to contribute to its final demise. An examination of data relating to wakefulness (Sostek, Anders, and Sostek, 1976) the growth of the larynx (Noback, 1923) breathing mechanisms (Lieberman *et al.*, 1967) lead to a *continuity* conclusion concerning data on various forms of infant cry. Acknowledging the difficulties inherent in acoustical analyses of "sounds" produced during the first year (e.g., formant–harmonic interaction, Fant, 1968), it is of interest to observe the shaping of vocal behavior which appears to take place. In an early investigation conducted by Fairbanks (1942), the hunger wails of an infant between 0–9 months were observed to shift up to 22 tones, with the lowest frequency observed being 63 Hz and the highest being 2631 Hz, that is, a fairly respectable bass climbing more than 3 octaves above middle C.

Since a natural assumption would be that the size of the larynx would, in fact, limit vocal output in some way, then at first sight these findings are surprising. As the sleep:wakefulness ratio decreases, it is not surprising to find that the expiratory cry decreases (Preston, 1975), so that as Stark and her coworkers are beginning to show (Stark, Rose, and McLaren, 1975; Stark, 1976) the discomfort and vegetative sounds produced by infants differ from one another in important segmental and suprasegmental features. For instance, the cry and discomfort sounds recorded in their studies contained less consonant-like elements than did vegetative sounds. These consonant-like elements were mostly liquids and nasals. On the other hand, discomfort and vegetative sounds resembled each other more closely in suprasegmental than in segmental features. Stark (1976) has suggested that what one is seeing is a recombination of earlier sounds during the process of cooing. Thus this incorporation of one kind of activity of the vocal tract into another gives a new series of combinations of features which are in fact moving in the direction of the child's language environment. Such a suggestion is not implausible. In an interesting article on front cavity resonance, Kuhn (1975) has pointed out an interesting relationship between the fundamental resonance of the front cavity and perceived place of articulation. He points out that this relationship would tend to arise to the extent that speech requires significant constriction of the vocal tract, as may be the case for consonants generally, and also for many vowels. Day and Wood (1972) in this context, have proposed that the perceptual processes for place of articulation and for vowels, are strongly interdependent. Kuhn concludes that such constriction contributes to the solution of the problem of deriving an articulatory description from the acoustics of speech. Such a notion would, in fact, lend credence to the suggestions of Stark *et al.* (1975) that the first sounds in the infant repertoire to be considered as having some resemblance to speech do in fact have their antecedants in earlier vocal behaviors, those of crying and vegetative activity of the vocal tract. To such behavior must be added the elaborations of gaze, visual contact, and caretaker input.

If, given an acceptance of its variability, one accepts the notion of continuity, then a view of the acquisition process can in fact *accept* the variability as representing a normal course of events. For example, Zlatin (1974) has made measurements of the duration and fundamental frequency associated with the production of 'agua' in children between 5 and 14 weeks of age. The duration of utterances produced on a single breath group ranged from 325 to 1897 msec, the average being about 900 msec. One of her subjects primarily produced utterances in which there were two vocalic peaks whereas her two other subjects produced an equal number of two and three peak patterns. The range of F_0 she reports coincides fairly well with that reported by Fairbanks. It is of interest to note that despite the variation in output an average value per syllable would be not much greater than for the same syllable, produced by an adult speaker with a much larger respiratory mechanism. Reports of babbling (Cruttendon, 1970; Huber, 1970) appear to lend support to the emerging syllable. Oller (1974), for instance, indicates that babbling does appear to be governed by restrictions of the human phonological capacity and that it is possible to make quite accurate predictions on the nature of the most commonly reported substitutions and deletions which occur in meaningful speech.

Although, as might be expected, the development of fundamental frequency (and therefore formant frequencies) develop in accordance with the physiological growth of the child (Eguchi and Hirsh, 1969; Gilbert, 1970a, 1973), it is not as yet clear how or to what extent the actual maturation of these parameters is linked to their control through the perceptual process. Eguchi and Hirsh (1969) have shown that the greatest change in *mean* values of these parameters occurs between ages 3 and 6, that is, during the period of most rapid growth in head size but that after this time the process slows down. They point out that the change in precision or reproducibility of certain aspects of speech sounds, that is, F_1 and F_2 of vowels and one temporal aspect of the transition from a plosive consonant to the following vowel or semivowel proved of some interest since both formants showed a decrease in variability on successive repetitions of the experimental task (repeating two sentences) although there were differences among the individual vowels in absolute values. Lindblom (1972) pointed out, however, that a hypothetical curve relating the error of formant frequency estimation to the fundamental frequency is similar in form to the age-dependent standard deviation curve presented by Eguchi and Hirsh. As indicated earlier, what this means is that measurement error might prove a significant part in variability data obtained from spectrographic measurements of children's speech. Whether children do not move their tongues to exactly the same position for a particular vowel as do adults, is a moot point. The answer to the question will probably arise from direct physiological measurements. Our own data (Gilbert, 1970a) comparing delayed language users and normal language users of preschool age on measures of F_2, support a physiological, as opposed to a linguistic, interpretation of F_2 development.

Despite the considerable amount of data relating to the acquisition of phonemes, there is virtually no data on, for instance, the spectral characteristics of stops and fricatives of the kind presented by Zue (1976), so that development indicators are lacking for such parameters as formant transitions. Spectral analyses of burst noise and fricatives as the CV emerges (See Branigan, 1976 for a discussion of the CV issue), along the lines of analyses conducted by Stark, might provide interesting insights into this issue since analysis of adult productions of /s/, for example, are believed to involve a more complex act on the part of the articulators. A more detailed spectral analysis of fricatives might lend some insight to the significant difficulties children experience in the discrimination learning of fricatives (Gilbert, 1976a). One study by Dalston (1975) shows that for /w/,

/r/, and /l/ produced by adults and children 3–4 years of age, shows that formant frequency patterns, plotted as the F_3/F_1 ratio as a function of the F_2/F_1 ratio, for these sounds are larger and more overlapping for children than for adults; the variance was particularly marked. Dalston noted that children produced these three sounds with distinctive differences in formant frequency origins, durations of steady state portions and the rate of formant movement, all recognizable attributes of early studies of /b, d, g/ (Lieberman et al., 1967). In view of the acoustic theory of speech production (Fant, 1960), these differences are not too surprising since differences in vocal tract length would contribute largely to their appearance. Nonetheless the results are of interest since they demonstrate that although at this age the children were producing tokens of /w, r, and l/ acceptable to adult judges, their production mechanisms (as exemplified in the acoustic signal) is still, as it were, hunting to achieve some adult system of values.

Time taken to produce a speech event (e.g., a syllable) and the intrinsic time of a speech sound have received considerable attention in experiments and in a developmental analysis contribute to our understanding of how the articulators always come close to reaching the same position as they do. In their study, Eguchi and Hirsh (1969) demonstrated that the explosion of a stop consonant is followed by a time interval before the following voiced sound, which interval shows great variability decreasing over time until adult values are achieved around 8 years of age. Their observations were corroborated and extended (for a small sample of children) by Kewley-Port and Preston (1974) who reported that when words beginning with /d/ and /t/ were first observed (about 2 years of age for their subject E4) the characteristics of their VOT distributions remained constant until at least 4.5 years CA. In a report to appear (Gilbert, 1977) we show for a group of six children at 3 years of age that values for /d/ clearly achieve the short voicing lag category of adults, reported by Lisker and Abramson (1964, 1970, 1971), whereas values for /t/ are much more widely dispersed than adult values for /t/ although falling within the category *long voicing lag*. Whether or not short voicing lag stops are indicating less complex articulations for the infant to control successfully than the articulations necessary for long voicing lags, remains an hypothesis to be tested. What is apparent is that the variability of VOT would appear to decrease over time to some adult value (which itself shows variability) although tokens with quite disparate VOTs are still identified as belonging to the same phoneme class when produced by children.

An experiment in the perception of VOT conducted by Winterkorn, MacNeilage, and Preston (1967) tends to confirm the perception over production aspects of VOT. Employing a group of 3-year-old children as subjects, the authors showed that children at this age are capable of discriminating one of a pair of alveolar stop consonantal stimuli as /da/ or

/ta/ in precisely the same fashion as adult listeners. Needless-to-say, a more detailed account of the development of VOT across age and within the same subjects is necessary to our understanding of the role of this particular process in developing articulatory capacity underlying language usage; that is, many languages have, in fact, evolved category boundaries at similar values on the VOT continuum. Parenthetically, it should be noted that VOT values in speech would seem to be at least partly attributable to contextual dependencies that are both regular and lawful (Klatt, 1975). It would be of interest to know at what ages such regularities occur, since this would provide further opportunity to perhaps use a single acoustic dimension in the description of phonetic development. By analogy it is also possible that such contextual dependencies may help to explain part of the variability that has been observed in the developmental studies cited above.

The final parameter underlying phonetic development to which references should be made, is that of segment duration. The *possibility* that speech is isochronous has intrigued a number of researchers for a long time. Lenneberg (1967) proposed one-sixth of a second as being the time unit in the programming of motor speech patterns, a figure which was later roundly demolished by Ohala (1975). It would, however, be of interest to determine whether the appearance of phonological rules is reflected in some preplanned motor behavior, evidenced in the temporal structure of utterances, that is, whether the development of "the specification of targets in an internalized space coordinate system [MacNeilage, 1970, p. 189]" complement the development of phonological rules. Some very preliminary data of our own (Gilbert and Johnson, 1976) lend credence to this possibility. In an experiment on the temporal and segmental structure of polysyllabic English words containing the syllable C/jul/ (e.g., pediculous) we suggested: (*a*) that in order to meet certain phonological conditions syllable duration undergoes modification to adult duration values; and (*b*) that the achievement of such values is accompanied by some quasi-systematic alteration in phonological rules. In a second experiment (Gilbert and Purves, 1976) we show that cluster duration shows a plateauing at 5–7 years of age, climbs to different values by 9 years, and ultimately reaches adult value at 11 years. In this final respect, our data confirm those of Tingley and Allen (1974), although we do not yet believe that for our 5-year-olds that motor patterns for speech are preplanned rather than feedback controlled. Until more is known about ways of controlling speaking rate in statistical evaluation of durational information, conclusions can only be tentative. Hawkins (1976) has suggested two strategies to account specifically for some aspects of the increasing organization of speech timing in clusters. They are (*a*) "concurrent planning" implying a gradual refinement and increasing precision of performance; and (*b*) "replanning" implying uneven development of segments within a cluster due to the breaking down of a complex sequence into a series of shorter, less complex ones as an intermediate stage in the acquisition of fully integrated execution (Hawkins, 1976, p. 452). One study (Gallagher and Shriner, 1975) which found that, in normal 3-year-old children, inconsistent production of /s/ and /z/ was found to be related to motor frequency constraints, is seen as further support for Hawkin's "concurrent planning" view, and is paralleled in perception by an analysis of discrimination among a group of English consonants by 3-year-olds, which showed that the discrimination errors were similar to those of adults, except that the children produced more of them (Graham and House, 1970). In any event, a better understanding of timing characteristics will have to await some more explicit recognition of the role of the syllable in the onset of speech production, particularly the imposition of timing control over small groups of continuous segments, where it is known that the exact nature of timing control varies as a function of stress.

CONCLUSION

In such a brief review it is impossible to do justice to the many varied studies which contribute to an understanding of phonetic factors in the development of speech and language. To return to my original hypothesis: "The child perceives speech in terms of the adult system, but his production is affected by motor difficulties," I would suggest that the bulk of existing evidence would support such a view. It is apparent that *reliable* control over the coordination of articulatory movements may not emerge until 11 years of age. It is also apparent (*a*) that the motor acts of speech continue to be perfected even after adults judge the child's repertoire of phonemes to be complete; and (*b*) that phonetic judgements on the part of adult listeners give the lie to only gross aspects of the development of speech and are almost totally insensitive to some of the parameters I have mentioned above. What is also clear is that individual child speakers may vary considerably in the strategies they use, while still achieving their goals of communication. As concerns an answer to a secondary question raised earlier in this chapter, that is, whether the degree of variability actually *decreases* or remains the same over time, I propose that present evidence is equivocal. Some experiments appear to show a decrease, others do not. Without a close comparison of both individual and group data of children and adults, on the same task, a confident answer is not possible.

In conclusion, it would appear that if we are to add anything of value to already existing phonological descriptions of the language acquisition process, it will require painstaking and arduous physical measurements of perceptual and articulatory activity, in both the acoustic and aerodynamic domains, in a group of willing children across time. Only by performing such measurements will we better be able to understand and interpret the variability which is present in the process.

ACKNOWLEDGMENTS

Preparation of this chapter was supported by grant MT-4217 from the Medical Research Council of Canada. In gratitude for his constant support and continued encouragement, this chapter is dedicated to the memory of Professor Sydney Israels, Head of the Department of Pediatrics at the University of British Columbia who died July 1978.

REFERENCES

Blechner, M. J., Day, R. S., and Cutting, J. E. Processing two dimensions of nonspeech stimuli: The auditory phonetic distinction reconsidered. *Journal of Experimental Psychology: Human Perception and Performance,* 1976, 2, 257–266.

Bond, B. and Stevens, S. S. Cross-modality matching of brightness to loudness by 5-year olds. *Perception and Psychophysics,* 1969, 6, 337–339.

Branigan, G. Syllabic structure and the acquisition of consonants: The great conspiracy in word formation. *Journal of Psycho. Ling. Res.,* 1976, 5, 117–133.

Cruttendon, A. A phonetic study of babbling. *British Journal of Dis. Comm.,* 1970, 5, 110–117.

Cutting, J. E. and Dorman, M. F. Discrimination of intensity differences carried on formant-transitions varying in extent and duration. *Perception and Psychophysics,* 1976, 20, 101–107.

Dalston, R. M. Acoustic characteristics of English /w, r, l/ spoken correctly by young children and adults. *Journal of the Acoustical Society of America,* 1975, 57, 462–469.

Day, R. S. and Wood, C. C. Mutual interference between two linguistic dimensions of the same stimuli. Haskins Labs, SR 29/30 69–74, 1972.

Dennis, M. and Whitaker, H. A. Language acquisition following hemidecortication: Linguistic superiority of the left over the right hemisphere. *Brain and Language,* 1976, 3, 404–433.

Eguchi, S. and Hirsh, I. J. Development of speech sounds in children. *Acta Oto-laryngologica,* 1969, Supplement 257.

Eguchi, S. Difference limens for the formant frequencies: Normal adult values and their development in children. *Journal of the American Audiology Society,* 1976, 1, 145–149.

Eimas, P. Linguistic processing of speech by young infants. In R. Schuefelbusch and L. Lloyd (Eds.), *Language perspectives–acquisition, retardation and intervention.* Baltimore: University Park Press, 1974. Pp. 55–73.

Fairbanks, G. An acoustical study of the pitch of infant hunger wails. *Child Development,* 1942, 13, 117–232.

Fant, G. Analysis and synthesis of speech processes. In B. Malmberg (Ed.), *Manual of phonetics.* Amsterdam: North Holland, 1968. Pp. 173–227.

Fant, G. *Acoustic theory of speech production.* The Hague: Mouton, 1960.

Fry, D. B. Perception and Recognition in Speech. In *For Roman Jakobson.* The Hague: Mouton, 1956.

Gallagher, T. M. and Shriner, T. H. Articulation inconsistencies in the speech of normal children. *Journal of Speech and Hearing Research,* 1975, 18, 168–175.

Gilbert, J. H. V. Formant concentration positions in the speech of children at two levels of linguistic development, *Journal of the Acoustical Society of America*, 1970a, *48*, 1404–1406.

Gilbert, J. H. V. Vowel productions and identification by normal and language delayed children. *Journal of Experimental Child Psychology*, 1970b, *9*, 12–19.

Gilbert, J. H. V. Acoustical features of children's vowel sounds: Development by chronological age *vs*. bone age. *Language and Speech*, 1973, *16*, 218–223.

Gilbert, J. H. V. and Climan, I. Dichotic studies in 2 and 3 year olds: A preliminary report. *Proceedings of the Speech Communications Seminar*, 1974, Stockholm: Alqvist and Wiksell, 70–75.

Gilbert, J. H. V. Discrimination learning of stops and fricatives in CVC syllables, by five-year-olds. *Canadian Journal of Linguistics*, 1976a.

Gilbert, J. H. V. The identification of four vowels by children at 3 years CA as indicator of perceptual processing. In S. Segalowitz and F. Gruber (Eds.), *Language development and neurological theory*. New York: Academic Press 1976b.

Gilbert, J. H. V. and Johnson, C. E. The "Ambliance" phenomenon: Some observations concerning temporal and sequential constraints on six year olds phonological productions. *Papers and Reports on Child Language Development*, November, 1976.

Gilbert, J. H. V. and Purves, B. A. Temporal constraints on consonant clusters in child speech production. Supplement *Journal of Child Language*, 4, 417–432. 1976.

Gilbert, J. H. V. A voice onset time analysis of apical stop production in 3-year-olds. *Journal of Child Language*, 1977, *4*, 103–110.

Graham, L. A. and House, A. S. Phonological oppositions in children: A perceptual study. *Journal of the Acoustical Society of America*. 1970, *49*, 559–566.

Hawkins, C. A. The developing organization of speech production in children: Evidence from consonant clusters. Unpublished Doctoral dissertation, Cambridge University, 1976.

Huber, H. A preliminary comparison of English and Yucatee infant vocalizations at nine months. *Papers from the fifth regional meeting Chicago Linguistic Society*, 1970. Pp. 114–119.

Ingram, D. Cerebral speech lateralization in young children. *Neuropsychologia*, 1975, *13*, 103–106.

Kent, R. D. Anatomical and neuromuscular maturation of the speech mechanism: Evidence from acoustic studies. *Journal of Speech and Hearing Research*, 1976, *19*, 321–447.

Kewley-Port, D. and Preston, M. S. Early apical stop production: A voice onset time analysis. *Journal of Phonetics*, 1974, *2*, 195–210.

Klatt, D. H. Voice onset time, frication and aspiration in word-initial consonant clusters. *Journal of Speech and Hearing Research*, 1975, *18*, 686–706.

Kuhl, P. K. and Miller, J. D. Speech perception by the chinchilla: The voiced voiceless distinction in alveolar plosive consonants. *Science*, 1975, *190*, 69–72.

Kuhn, G. M. On the front cavity resonance and its possible role in speech perception. *Journal of the Acoustical Society of America*, 1975, *58*, 428–433.

Lenneberg, E. H. *Biological foundations of language*, New York: Wiley, 1967.

Lieberman, A. M., Cooper, F. S., Shankweiler, D. S., and Studdert-Kennedy, M. Perception of Speech Code, *Psychological Review*, 1967, *74*, 431–461.

Lieberman, P. On the Evolution of Language, *Cognition*, 1973, *2*, 59–94.

Lindblom, B. Comments on "Development of speech sounds in children," by S. Eguchi and I. J. Hirsh. In G. Fant (Ed.), *International Symposium on Speech Communication Ability and Profound Deafness*. Washington D.C.: Volta Bureau, 1972. Pp. 159–162.

Lisker, L. and Abramson, A. S. A cross-language study of voicing in initial stops: Acoustical measurements. *Word*, 1964, *20*, 384–422.

Lisker, L. and Abramson, A. S. The voicing dimension: some experiments in comparative phonetics. *Proceedings of the Sixth International Congress of Phonetic Sciences of Prague*, Prague: Academia, 1970, 563–567.

Lisker, L. and Abramson, A. S. Distinctive features and laryngeal control. *Language*, 1971, *47*, 767–785.

MacNeilage, P. F. Motor control of serial ordering of speech. *Psychological Review*, 1970, *77*, 182–196.

Miller, G. M. and Nicely P. E. An analysis of perceptual confusions among some English consonants, *Journal of the Acoustical Society of America*, 1955, *27*, 338–352.

Miller, G. A. The Perception of Speech. In *For Roman Jakobson*. The Hague: Mouton, 1956.

Molfese, D. L. Auditory evoked potential differences in infants and children. Paper presented at the *Conference on Sign Language and Neurolinguistics*, Rochester, New York, September 24–26, 1976.

Noback, G. J. The developmental topography of the larynx, trachea and lungs in fetus, newborn, infant and child. *American Journal Dis. Child*, 1923, *26*, 515–533.

Ohala, J. J. The temporal regulation of speech. In G. Fant and M. A. A. Tatham (Eds.), *Auditory analysis and perception of speech*. London: Academic Press, 1975. Pp. 431–454.

Oller, D. K., Wieman, L. A., Doyle, W. J., and Ross, C. Child speech babbling and phonological universals. Unpublished manuscript, 1974.

Pisoni, D. Auditory short term memory and vowel perception. *Memory and Cognition*, 1975, *5*, 7–18.

Preston, R. Infant cry sound: developmental features. *Journal of the Acoustical Society of America*. 1975, *57*, 1186–1191.

Riesz, R. R. Differential intensity sensitivity of the ear for pure tones, *Physiological Review*, 1928, *31*, 867–875.

Showers, E. B., and Biddulph, R. Differential pitch sensitivity of the ear. *Journal of the Acoustical Society of America*, 1931, *3*, 275–287.

Sinnott, J. M., Beecher, M. D., Moody, D. B., and Stebbins, W. C. Speech sound discrimination by monkeys and humans, *Journal of the Acoustical Society of America*, 1976, *60*, 687–695.

Sostek, A. M., Anders, T. F., and Sostek, A. J. Diurnal rhythms in 2- and 8-week old infants: Sleep waking organization as a function of age and stress. *Psychosomatic Medicine*, 1976, *38*, 250–256.

Stark, R. E., Rose, S. N., and McLaren, M. Features of infant sounds the first eight weeks of life. *Journal of Child Language*, 1975, *2*, 205–221.

Stark, R. E. Features of infant sounds: The emergence of cooing. *Journal of the Acoustical Society of America*, 1976, *59*, Supplement 1, 556.

Stebbins, W. C. Hearing of old world monkeys (cercopithecine). *American Journal of Physical Anthropology*, 1973, *38*, 357–364.

Tallal, P. Rapid auditory processing in normal and disordered language development. *Journal of Speech and Hearing Research*, 1974, *19*, 186–194.

Tingley, B. M., and Allen, G. D. Development of speech timing control in children. *Child Development*, 1975, *46*, 186–194.

Winterkorn, J. M. S., MacNeilage, P. F., and Preston, M. S. Perception of voiced and voiceless stop consonants in 3-year-old children. Haskins Labs, SR-11, 1967, 41–45.

Zlatin, M. A. Variations on a theme-/agəvəl. *Purdue University Contributed Papers in Speech Language and Hearing*, 4, Fall, 1974, 104–121.

Zue, V. W. Spectral characteristics of English stops in pre-stressed position. Paper presented at the Ninety-first Meeting of the Acoustical Society of America, April, 1976.

IV

Neurolinguistics

12

Individual Variations in the Perception of Dichotic Chords

ROBERT EFRON

Psychophysicists are often dismayed when they find large differences in the behavior of different subjects on a particular perceptual task. This distress is aggravated when, as is usually the case for such tasks, there is also a large intrasubject test–retest variability. The reason for this frustration is not obscure: Psychophysicists are paid to discover the "laws" of perception—principles applicable to all subjects—and the occurrence of individual differences and large test–retest variances not only makes it very difficult to discriminate the perceptual laws from the individual "noise" but also makes it difficult to earn a living.

The perceptual phenomenon I will describe has been particularly frustrating since it represents the unusual case where intersubject variability is very large, but intrasubject variability is virtually absent. It turns out that the "laws" which govern this perceptual process may be very simple but can account nevertheless for this unusual combination of variances.

The discovery and the subsequent analysis of the phenomena to be

245

*Individual Differences in Language Ability and
Language Behavior*

Copyright © 1979 by Academic Press, Inc.
All rights of reproduction in any form reserved.
ISBN 0-12-255950-9

described has been a collaborative effort of E.W. Yund and myself and, in the past few years, of P.L. Divenyi, M. Dennis, D.C. Tanis and J.E. Bogen. A series of reports (Divenyi, Efron, and Yund, 1977; Efron and Yund, 1974, 1975a, 1975b, 1976a, 1976b, 1977; Efron, Tanis, and Yund, 1977; Efron, Bogen, and Yund, 1977; Efron, Dennis, Bogen, and Yund, 1977; Yund, Efron, and Divenyi, 1979) have been published which describe in detail various aspects of phenomena: This article merely represents an overview and an attempt to relate this auditory perceptual phenomenon to the more general subject of this volume.

To set the context for this discussion, imagine that two keys on a piano are struck simultaneously. What is heard is a two-tone chord in which both pitch components are readily identified. If both keys are struck equally forcibly, the two tones will be heard with equal salience. That is to say, the two pitch components of the mixture (chord) will be equally loud. However, if one of the keys is struck with slightly less force, making that tone only 2–3 dB less intense than the other, the salience of that tone in the pitch mixture will be detectably diminished. Expressed in the turgid language of psychophysics, this experiment can be summarized by saying that the relative salience of the two pitch components of a monaural chord is *intensity dependent*.

When Yund and I performed the same experiment dichotically, one tone to each ear via earphones, we were startled to discover that the perception of dichotic chords differed radically from that of monaural chords: The relative salience of the two pitch components of dichotic chords is *intensity independent*. That is to say, the relative salience of the two pitch components of a dichotic chord does not change as a function of the relative intensity of the two tones. Now what is astonishing about this finding is the size of the intensity-independent effect: One tone can be as much as 45 dB *less* intense than the other, and the relative salience of the pitch of this less intense tone is exactly the same as when it is 45 dB *more* intense than the other. In sum, the relative salience of the two pitch components of a dichotic chord is intensity independent over a range of interaural intensity differences which can be as large as ± 45 dB.

It should be emphasized at this point that the dichotic chords which display the phenomenon of intensity independence are composed of two tones whose frequencies differ by not much more than 6–8%. The sound image of such chords is "compact," and is perceptually located in the midline (when the two tones are of equal intensity). With two tones having this frequency separation, the subject cannot say which tone is presented to which ear. However, as the frequency difference increases above 8–10%, the perceptual experience of the chords changes: The sound image becomes less compact and ultimately splits, enabling the subject to report which ear has received the higher (or lower) frequency tone. As the frequency difference is increased from 1% to 10% the range of interaural intensity differences over which the relative salience of the pitch components is invariant also becomes less marked, until the phenomenon of intensity independence disappears entirely.

We will return somewhat later to a more extended discussion of dichotic chords (and other stimuli) whose components have major differences in the frequency domain, but first I will describe another unexpected property of dichotic chords composed of tones having small frequency differences.

If the two tones of such a dichotic chord are presented at equal intensity, the relative salience of the two pitch components is *rarely* perceived to be equal. For one-half the normal population, the pitch of the tone presented to the right ear is distinctly more salient in the chord; for the other half of the population the left ear tone is more salient. We have called this an "ear dominance" for pitch. And this is where the individual differences come in: Different normal subjects vary from being very strongly right-ear dominant, to being weakly right-ear dominant, to having no readily detectable ear dominance, to being weakly left-ear dominant and finally to having a strong left-ear dominance. Thus a complete spectrum of ear dominance exists in a population of subjects with normal hearing. One critical point must be stressed: Whatever may be the relative salience of the two pitch components when they are presented at equal intensity (to any one subject), this same relative salience remains unchanged despite huge changes in the relative intensity of the two tones. In sum, it is the phenomenon of ear dominance which *primarily* determines the relative salience of the two pitch components—the phenomenon of intensity independence merely causes whatever asymmetry which is present to remain unchanged by large interaural intensity differences.

Experiments have shown that the phenomenon of ear dominance is unaffected by (a) the duration of the tones; and (b) the rise–decay times of the tones. The only stimulus parameters which affect ear dominance are the frequency and to a lesser extent, the intensity of the tones. While some subjects are right or left ear dominant regardless of the frequencies (or intensities) used, other subjects are right ear dominant at some frequencies (and intensities) and left ear dominant for others.

Unlike the well-known slight ear dominance which is seen with the use of dichotic speech signals, the ear dominance we are discussing today does not correlate with the subject's handedness, nor does it correlate with the ear advantage in listening to dichotic speech sounds—the correlation coefficient between the two tasks was -0.08. Speakers of tonal languages and professional musicians showed the same distribution of ear dominance as did other English speakers. Even commisurotomized subjects— all of whom display a strong right ear dominance with dichotic speech sounds—had the same distribution of ear dominance for dichotic chords as was seen in normal subjects. It was only when we studied patients with complete hemispherectomy that we found some consistent results with respect to ear dominance. For these subjects, the ear contralateral to the remaining hemisphere is always the dominant one—and it is always strongly dominant. In sum, except for subjects with an absent hemisphere, the phenomenon of ear dominance is idiosyncratic and unpredictable.

In contrast to the "nonlawful" nature of ear dominance, the phenomenon of intensity independence is highly regular and predictable for *all* subjects. In a series of experiments we have found that *range* of interaural intensity differences over which the relative salience of the two pitch components of the chord is *constant* is increased in all subjects by (*a*) decreasing the frequency difference between the two tones of the chord; (*b*) increasing the sound pressure level at which the experiments are performed; (*c*) decreasing the duration of the tones; (*d*) increasing the signal-to-noise ratio in the dominant ear; and (*e*) decreasing the bone conducted energy from one earphone to the opposite ear (by the use of insertion earphones).

This highly regular, and now predictable, behavior of the phenomenon of intensity independence spurred us to develop a model of the auditory system's processing of pitch information. This model, which will be described below, "explains" why the relative salience of the pitch mixture of monaural chords is intensity dependent and why the pitch mixture of dichotic chords is intensity independent. It also accounts for the effects on the range of intensity independence of each of the parametric changes which have just been described. Although the model was primarily intended to account for the phenomenon of intensity independence (which is a right–left *symmetrical* function), it contains several opportunities for an asymmetry to occur which could result in the phenomenon of ear dominance.

The model is based on three generally accepted properties of the auditory system:

1. That energy delivered to one ear crosses the head, by bone conduction, to stimulate the contralateral ear with approximately a 50 dB attenuation.
2. That the energy received by the ear at one frequency spreads to excite channels that are optimally sensitive to nearby frequencies. That is to say, the tuning curves in the cochlea are not infinitely sharp.
3. That the response of a monaural frequency channel is a compressive function of the amount of energy exciting that channel. We assume that the response of the monaural frequency channels is approximately logarithmic—merely a restatement of the Weber-Fechner law of the intensity–response function.

The model makes only one novel, but hardly a sophisticated, assumption: That the responses of corresponding monaural channels are simply added to produce the binaural pitch mixture. That is to say, the response of the 1000 Hz channel from the left ear is simply added, at a central location, to the response of the 1000 Hz channel from the right ear. The conceptual heart of the model thus lies not in the assumptions per se, but in the *order* in which these processes occur: It is assumed that the log compression must occur before the binaural addition.

With these assumptions, coupled with reasonable estimates for the shape of the tuning curve and the intensity–response function, the model displays the phenomenon of intensity-independence. It also accounts for the effects on the range of intensity-independence of all the parameters we have studied, and "explains" why intensity-independence occurs only for dichotic chords having relatively small frequency differences.

As I have pointed out, the model was not primarily intended to account for the phenomenon of ear dominance. However, minor modifications of the model's parameters can give rise to ear dominance as well—and two of these predictions have already been verified. These and other successful predictions of the model encourage us to believe that we now understand, at least to a first order level, how the wide individual variations in the perception of dichotic chords—variations which seemed incomprehensible to us only 4 years ago—can now be reduced to a small set of lawful relations involving the mechanisms by which the pitch information from the two ears is combined. (For a detailed exposition of the model, the reader is referred to Yund and Efron, 1977).

Our goal for the future is to discover how this mechanism (which combines pitch information from the two ears) processes signals other than pure tones and, in particular, how speech signals from the two ears might interact. Using the same paradigm employed for dichotic chords we presented two computer synthesized speech sounds to the two ears (Divenyi and Efron, 1979): If a subject is right (or left) ear dominant for pure tones, his ear dominance is largely unchanged for vowel sounds. This appears to be true regardless of whether the vowels differ in only one formant or several—a result which appears to differ from that obtained by Shankweiler and Studdert-Kennedy (1967) who have reported that there is little or no ear dominance for steady state vowel sounds. It is of interest to note that subjects also retain their ear dominance for dichotically presented stop consonant–vowel sounds that differ in the feature of *place of articulation*. However, subjects with left-ear dominance for pure tones become right-ear dominant for dichotically presented stop consonant–vowel sounds that differ in the feature of *voicing* where the critical information which distinguishes the two stimuli lies in the temporal domain. The change of ear dominance from left to right for the feature of voicing thus suggests that the feature of speech sounds related primarily to temporal organization is processed better by the right ear (by the left hemisphere?).

One key question remains: Is there any biological role for the phenomenon of intensity-independence and ear dominance? Such a question is particularly germane since a dichotic chord (or a dichotic speech signal) appears to be a totally artificial stimulus which never occurs in nature.

We think that the answer to this question may be quite simple: Dichotic chords are *not* as artificial a stimulus as they at first appear to be. Consider the phenomenon of binaural diplacusis: People who have this "syndrome"—and we all do to a greater or lesser degree—report that a pure tone of a given frequency has a higher (or lower) pitch when heard with one ear than it has when heard with the other. For such an individual, therefore, a single pure tone presented from a source in front of him will actually be perceived as a dichotic chord: That is to say, he will hear two different pitches in the two ears. Now, if he did *not* have the property of intensity independence of dichotic chords, the pitch of this tone would vary as a function of the position in space of the source: As the source moved to his left, increasing the intensity to the left ear and decreasing the intensity to the right ear, the pitch heard by the left ear would increase in salience, and the source's overall pitch would change. Conversely, when the source moved to his right side, it would sound more like the different pitch heard by his right ear. Without intensity independence, then, the pitch of the pure tone would change as a function of the spatial localization of the source. In brief, without intensity independence the pitch of the tone would lose its perceptual constancy. The property of intensity independence provides a compensation for our binaural diplacusis provided it is not excessive. It keeps the pitch mixture constant despite large changes in interaural intensity differences. With some degree of binaural diplacusis, but without the property of intensity independence, the auditory perceptual world would alter as we turned our head. Further, it is the very existence of the phenomenon of intensity independence which accounts for the fact that we are never even *aware* of our own diplacusis. It is somewhat analogous to the blind spot in vision of which we are never spontaneously aware. Like the blind spot, this may be the reason it took so long before it was discovered.

Although some appreciable degree of binaural diplacusis may be compensated for by the phenomenon of intensity independence, I doubt that it was for this particular advantage that the binaural system evolved in the way it did. If the model we have proposed is correct, the property of intensity-independence emerges merely as an incidental consequence of the fact that the compressive energy-to-neural transformation in each ear occurs *prior* to the central combination of the neural messages from the two ears.

While the phenomenon of intensity-independence does appear to have some biological utility (survival value), we are still at a loss to discover any advantage which is to be gained from the phenomenon of ear dominance. Our hunch here is that ear dominance emerges as an indirect consequence—perhaps an epiphenomenon—of some other aspect of auditory pitch processing: The essentially bell-shaped distribution of the direction and magnitude of ear dominance in the normal population suggests that there is no particular biological advantage to either. However, the fact previously mentioned, that hemispherectomy is associated with a strong dominance (of the ear contralateral to the existing hemisphere) does suggest that some cortical factor influences the way the pitch information from the two ears is "weighted." Why the cortex should be involved in such a regulatory process remains to be discovered.

REFERENCES

Divenyi, P. L., Efron, R., and Yund, E. W. Ear dominance in dichotic chords and ear superiority in frequency discrimination. *Journal of the Acoustical Society of America,* 1977, *62,* 624–632.

Divenyi, P. and Efron, R. Spectral vs. temporal features in dichotic listening. In press, *Brain and Language,* 1979.

Efron, R. Dichotic competition of simultaneous tone bursts of different frequency, duration and loudness. In M. D. Sullivan (Ed.), *Central Auditory Processing Disorders.* University of Nebraska Medical Center, Omaha, 1975.

Efron, R., Bogen, J. E., and Yund, E. W. Perception of dichotic chords by normal and commissurotomized human subjects. *Cortex,* 1977, *13,* 137–149.

Efron, R., Dennis, M., Bogen, J. E., and Yund, E. W. The perception of dichotic chords by hemispherectomized subjects. *Brain and Language,* 1977, *4,* 537–549.

Efron, R., Tanis, D. C., and Yund, E. W. Effects of signal intensity and noise on the pitch mixture of dichotic chords. *Journal of the Acoustical Society of America,* 1977, *62,* 618–623.

Efron, R., and Yund, E. W. Dichotic competition of simultaneous tone bursts of different frequency: I. Dissociation of pitch from lateralization and loudness. *Neuropsychologia,* 1974, *12,* 249–256.

Efron, R., and Yund, E. W. Dichotic competition of simultaneous tone bursts of different frequency: III. The effect of stimulus parameters on suppression and ear dominance functions. *Neuropsychologia,* 1975b, *13,* 151–161.

Efron, R., and Yund, E. W. Ear dominance and intensity independence in the perception of dichotic chords. *Journal of the Acoustical Society of America,* 1976b, *59,* 889–898.

Shankweiler, D., and Studdert-Kennedy, M. Identification of consonants and vowels presented to left and right ears, *Quarterly Journal of Experimental Psychology,* 1967, *19,* 59–63.

Yund, E. W., and Efron, R. Dichotic competition of simultaneous tone bursts of different frequency: II. Suppression and ear dominance functions. *Neuropsychologia,* 1975a, *13,* 137–150.

Yund, E. W. and Efron, R. Dichotic competition of simultaneous tone bursts of different frequency: IV. Correlation with dichotic competition of speech signals. *Brain and Language,* 1976a, *3,* 246–254.

Yund, E. W., and Efron, R. A model for the relative salience of the pitch of pure tones
    presented dichotically. *Journal of the Acoustical Society of America,* 1977, *62,* 607–617.
Yund, E. W., Efron, R., and Divenyi, P. L. The effect of bone conduction on the intensity
    independence of dichotic chords. *Journal of the Acoustical Society of America,* 1979, *65,*
    259–261.

13

Effect of Aphasia on
the Retrieval of Lexicon
and Syntax

HAROLD GOODGLASS

Injury to the lateral convexity of the left cerebral hemisphere in man almost always produces a disturbance of language. In many instances, to be sure, the damage is widespread and the resulting incapacity is so indifferently distributed and severe across all modalities of input and output that the analysis of component deficits is not too rewarding. However, in a large number of cases we find dramatic dissociations in which some linguistic components are impaired while others are suprisingly intact. A number of different configurations have been recognized as repeatedly observable as correlates of circumscribed lesions in particular parts of the language zone. These phenomena have recently attracted the attention of linguists, who have been lured from pure linguistics to the specialty of neurolinguistics.

In this paper I will discuss some of the problems in the understanding of selective disorders of syntax, commonly referred to as "agrammatism" and selective disorders of lexical retrieval, which is referred to as "anomia."

Individual Differences in Language Ability and
Language Behavior

Copyright © 1979 by Academic Press, Inc.
All rights of reproduction in any form reserved.
ISBN 0-12-255950-9

These deficits, like others in aphasia, are not absolute. The memories of the deficient operations have not been excised; they are usually recoverable with certain facilitating cues or, sporadically, on repeated testing. Moreover, as a patient makes some recovery, performances once unavailable again appear. These observations have led some writers, such as Weigl and Bierwisch (1970) Bliss, Tikofsky, and Guilford (1976), to state that aphasics have intact linguistic competence and are deficient only in performance. Indeed the deficits seen in aphasia put the concept of "competence" to a severe test. Having examined the phenomena of agrammatism and anomia in their ordinary clinical guise and under experimental conditions in this paper, I would hope that we can draw some conclusions for ourselves as to the usefulness of the construct of competence in aphasia.

AGRAMMATISM

Lesions of the anterior portion of the speech zone, compromising Broca's area and the region surrounding it, usually produce a severe impoverishment of speech output in which the most distinctive features are awkwardness of articulation and reduction of syntax to the simplest utterances—in severe cases to holophrastic sentences, much like those of 2-year-old children. Because of the effort required in finding words and articulating them, it appeared to some writers that agrammatism was merely the by-product of an economy of effort. The patient confined his production to the key words needed to convey his message—the substantives and principal verbs—giving rise to the so-called telegraphic style. However, it takes very little probing of the abilities of an agrammatic patient to demonstrate that his loss of access to grammatical structures goes far beyond an economy of effort. For example, these patients are unable to duplicate the inverted word order of a Yes–No question such as, *Is the door open?* when asked to repeat it. The most likely repetition is, *Door is open.*

From a descriptive standpoint, we notice a dropping out of grammatical morphemes of all types, both free and bound. Verbs generally appear in uninflected form, although some patients have a predilection for the present progressive or the -ing form without the auxiliary form of *to be*, regardless of the tense implied by the message. However, agrammatism involves a deeper disturbance than the omission of morphemes. The syntactic relationships of subordination are most severely affected but so are relationships indicating modification, agreement and government. Indeed some patients recover access to a considerable vocabulary of nouns and verbs, but from the point of view of syntactic structure their sentences have been described as a "word heap." Luria (1970) points out that the severe agrammatic seems to nominalize all his concepts—even action concepts. When the patient says, *Yesterday, birthday party, eat, lots of food, eat,* he is probably using the verb in its infinitive form as a noun. In languages which have an inflection indicating the infinitive, the use of the infinitive in such utterances by agrammatics is unambiguous.

Given that the aphasic with agrammatism has undergone some basic changes in his approach to syntax, is it possible that he develops an internally consistent grammar, based on a more primitive rule system than that of standard English? If this is the case, one would expect to find changes in decoding which paralleled those observed in speech output. Indeed my colleague, Edgar Zurif, and his co-workers (Zurif and Caramazza, 1976) find that Broca's aphasics ignore the articles and perform randomly when the distinction between two minimally differing sentences hinges on a purely grammatical element. Their apparently excellent auditory comprehension was found to depend on the semantic decoding of contentives, reliance on simple word order strategies, and knowledge of the real world. However I do not believe that Zurif's data represent proof of a one-to-one correspondence between the expressive features of a-grammatics and the sentence comprehension process of these patients.

Perhaps the strongest arguments favoring the view of a self-consistent, reduced grammar come from the examination of the speech of the most severely impaired agrammatics. Rosemary Myerson and I (Myerson and Goodglass, 1972) approached a corpus of speech from such a patient much as Roger Brown approached that of Adam, Eve, and Sarah. The resulting summary of this patient's syntax is stunningly simple:

1. A sentence may consist of either a noun phrase *or* a verb phrase, optionally followed by an adverb, or an adverb alone.
2. A sentence might be modified for Emphasis, Negation, or Question.
3. A VP consisted of the verb stem plus an optional ING plus an optional particle. An example of maximum expansion of the VP is "falling down." Alternatively, VP may consist of predicate adjective without a copula.
4. An ADV may consist of an adverb of time or place or both. Adverbs of place are realized only as place names, without preposition. Adverbs of time may consist of a measure expression, like 4 *years,* optionally followed by an adverb like *ago.*
5. A NP consists of a noun optionally preceded by a cardinal number. Nouns are appropriately pluralized after a number.
6. There are no prepositions or articles; no combinations of adjective with noun or verb with adverb. Since there are no copulas, it is uncertain whether the ING form of the verb is a truncated present progressive or a nominalized verb.
7. The Question is realized only by "intonation" and Emphasis is

realized by intonation and/or by multiple repetitions. Negation is realized by the word No, either preposed or appended to the sentence.

8. Up to two sentences may be joined by AND.

With this simple assemblage, one can generate all the possible utterances consistent with this patient's grammar. An actual sample of this patient's free conversation is transcribed as follows:

> Yes ... ah ... Monday ... er ... Dad and Peter H. ... (His own name), and Dad ... er ... hospital ... and ah ... Wednesday. ... Wednesday, nine o'clock ... and oh ... Thursday ... ten o'clock, ah doctors ... two ... an' doctors ... and er ... teeth ... yah.

However, subsequent study of agrammatic patients suggests that the idea of a self-consistent reduced grammar resulting from aphasia is an artifact of the extreme limitation of this patient's repertory. With somewhat more recovery, a different picture emerges.

I should note that the exploration of syntactic competence is full of methodological traps. Ideally, one would like to work from free conversation. However, free conversation rarely produces questions or commands, and, generally speaking, samples those constructions which the patient prefers, leaving us in the dark as to whether he could use other constructions if the structure of the situation demanded them. Repetition provides a means of constraining the patient to precisely those constructions one wishes to sample, but has the serious defect that many subjects are extraordinarily facilitated by repetition. Only in a fraction of subjects does the repetition technique reflect fairly the pattern of the patients' spontaneous grammatical use.

In an effort to find a compromise task, Jean Berko Gleason and I, with our collaborators, Mary Hyde, Eugene Green, and Nancy Ackerman, devised a Story Completion Test (Gleason et al., 1976)—a series of brief situational anecdotes leading to a final sentence whose form and content were strongly constrained by the preceding story, and which the patient was required to supply. Fourteen syntactical problems were posed, from intransitive and transitive imperatives through comparatives, passives to embedded verb complement clauses and future tenses. By repeating the test five times with each of eight agrammatic subjects of varying severity, we were able to derive a rough hierarchy of difficulty, observe some consistent principles relating to agrammatism, but above all, to evaluate the question of consistency of performance.

To briefly summarize our findings: First, the four easiest constructions were the intransitive and transitive imperative, cardinal number plus noun, and a single adjective plus a noun. The three hardest were the future, two adjectives plus noun, and embedded clause. The middle range included declaratives, comparative constructions, WH and Yes–No questions, and passives. Confirming repeated earlier observations, we found that unstressed functors in sentence initial position were much more frequently omitted than stressed functors (such as WH interrogatives) or than the identical unstressed term in medial position. We have interpreted this observation, in the past, as a product of the agrammatics' orientation towards an emphatic, information carrying word, which helps him overcome a raised threshold for initiating an utterance. All of our patients, but most conspicuously the severe agrammatics, displayed compensatory devices which placed a stressed word in the first position where normal controls used an unstressed functor. These included a predilection for using an initial vocative in direct discourse, and the habitual use of an opening noun subject where a pronoun is normally expected.

From the point of view of the present discussion the most important observation concerns within-subject variability. Variability is noted both from trial to trial and in the struggle for self corrections within a single trial, since some patients made five or six stabs at a response, usually stopping at that which matched or most nearly matched the conventional. In the course of these efforts even the most severely aphasic often produced at least one response which was totally correct. When they failed, it was not always the same part of the target which was omitted. That is, in attempting to say, *The baby cries*, a patient might on one occasion say, *Baby cryin'*, on another occasion he might say, *Cries*, and on a third, *The baby cry*. These observations add up to the suggestion that the correct target is, somehow, available as a goal, even where the actual production is a single word. Both the notion of economy of effort and that of a self-consistent, simplified grammar must be discarded. Can we conclude, then, that the agrammatic has an intact syntactical competence but is only impaired in performance? We think not.

A reasonable analogy to the status of an aphasic's knowledge of his language is to compare it to a once-used path through a forest which is now overgrown, so that only traces of it remain. On any attempt to retrace this path, he may go astray at a different point, or with luck, retrace the original path. With practice or with recovery, it is the original path, rather than any other, which stands the greatest chance of being reestablished. In short, we argue that competence and performance, like storage and retrieval, are inextricably linked in brain damage.

The second aspect of this presentation concerns lexical retrieval. While virtually all aphasics have reduced access to their premorbid vocabulary, the clinical features of word-finding difficulty take so many different forms that one is led to believe that retrieval is a multistage process which may break down at different points. Motor aphasics often seem to have the acoustic structure of a word in mind as they approximate but do not succeed in articulating it. Often, hearing the initial syllable as a cue has a remarkably facilitating effect on production. Wernicke's aphasics often appear to suffer from a two-way dissociation between word and referent—neither able to grasp the semantic value of the word offered by the examiner, nor to retrieve the name in response to confrontation with an object. Instead, they have ready access to words which are off-target but which are in the same connotative field; they may produce these paraphasias without being aware of an error. Anomic aphasics have fluent command of English syntax but, like Wernicke aphasics, they cannot access the major contentive words in their message. Unlike the Wernicke aphasic, they usually recognize it when it is offered and rarely produce inadvertent errors.

One might infer from this account that word-finding difficulty may entail the complete dissociation between a motor–acoustic pattern and its referent; at another stage it may entail difficulty in retrieving the memory of the acoustic pattern; at still another it may entail difficulty only at the final stage of motor execution.

In order to submit this sort of model to experimental test, Edith Kaplan and I with two collaborators (Goodglass *et al.*, 1976) carried out a modified version of Brown and McNeill's tip-of-the-tongue experiment (1966). We reasoned that if a patient failed to retrieve a word as a result of failure only at the motor articulatory stage, he should have some knowledge of the initial sound and number of syllables in the target. Failure in selecting first letter and syllable count would be evidence of a breakdown prior to retrieval of the auditory pattern. Our subjects were 42 aphasics, distributed among 4 diagnostic subgroups whose naming behavior is clinically distinctive in different ways. These were Broca's aphasics ($N = 13$), Wernickes ($N = 8$), conduction aphasics ($N = 12$), and anomics ($N = 9$). They were first trained in the task of indicating on a prepared card the number of syllables from 1 to 5 on a series of introductory words. If this task was mastered, they were shown a series of 48 pictures whose names were of intermediate frequency, equally divided among 1, 2, 3, and a combined set of 4 and 5 syllables in length. If they failed to recall the name they were urged to guess the intial letter by pointing to an alphabet card and to indicate the number of syllables. One of our patient groups clearly outdid the rest. The conduction aphasics succeeded in indicating both syllable length and initial letter for 34% of their failures to name. Clinically, these patients often show, in their failures, a partial knowledge of the target word, but their efforts to name are spoiled by sound transpositions and intrusions of unwanted sounds. Wernicke and anomic aphasics identified acoustic elements of fewer than 10% of failed items—below chance for syllables, because they generally refused even to guess. It is important to note that the successful naming rate did not differ significantly between diagnostic groups. It appears then that for the anomics and Wernicke patients naming is an all or none process—either they associate directly to target or they have no partial recall of the word sound. Broca's aphasics were in an intermediate position and we cannot draw definite inference about their implicit word finding processes at this time.

A final word to tie lexical and syntactic retrieval problems together. In both of these domains there is some residual knowledge, even when aphasia prevents recovery of this knowledge. Partial knowledge is often sufficient for recognizing when an utterance—lexical or syntactic—sounds correct. Even a deteriorated template in memory is sufficient to make a judgment of match versus no match.

ACKNOWLEDGMENTS

Supported in part by the Medical Research Service of the Veterans Administration and by NIH Grants NS 07615 to Clark University and NS 06209 to Boston University.

REFERENCES

Bliss, L. S., Tikofsky, R. S., and Guilford, A. M. Aphasic sentence repetition behavior as a function of grammaticality. *Cortex*, 1976, *12*, 113–126.

Brown, R. W. and McNeill, D. The "tip-of-the-tongue" phenomenon. *Journal of Verbal Learning and Verbal Behavior*, 1966, *5*, 325–337.

Gleason, J. B., Goodglass, H., Ackerman, N., Green, E., and Hyde, M. R. Retrieval of syntax in Broca's Aphasia. *Brain and Language*, 1975, *2*, 451–471.

Goodglass, H., Kaplan, E., Weintraub, S., and Ackerman, N. The tip-of-the-tongue phenomenon in aphasia. *Cortex*, 1976, *12*, 145–153.

Luria, A. R. *Traumatic aphasia*. New York: Basic Books, 1970.

Myerson, R. and Goodglass, H. Transformational grammar of three aphasic patients. *Language and Speech*, 1972, *15*, 40–50.

Weigl, E. and Bierwisch, M. Neuropsychology and linguistics: Topics of common research. *Foundations of Language*, 1970, *6*, 1–18.

Zurif, E. B. and Caramazza, A. Psycholinguistic structures in aphasia, studies in syntax and semantics. In H. A. Whitaker and H. A. Whitaker (Eds.), *Studies in Neurolinguistics*. New York: Academic Press, 1976.

14

How Shall a Thingummy[1] Be Called?

CURTIS HARDYCK, HILARY NAYLOR,
AND REBECCA M. SMITH

A title such as the above requires at least one apology. However, it does no injustice to Roger Brown to remark that, in his 1958 paper, he was concerned with some general characteristics of how names are assigned to things and not with variations among individuals.

The ways in which individuals choose names for things and the extent to which individual differences are present in the use or nonuse of names seems a neglected area in psychological research. Studies of the processes of verbal control are plentiful, but emphasis is usually on experimental control of labeling versus nonlabeling. Subjects in experiments of this type are usually instructed to remember names through rote rehearsal, or to

---

[1]"Thingamajig, thingumabob, thingummy, etc. *n*. Used to indicate any item of which the speaker does not know or has momentarily forgotten the name especially used to ref. to any, usu. a small, new or unfamiliar device, mechanical part, gadget, tool or ornament; a thing." [Wentworth, H. and Flexner, S. B. (Eds.), *Dictionary of American Slang*, New York, Thomas Y. Crowell Co, 1960].

Individual Differences in Language Ability and Language Behavior

Copyright © 1979 by Academic Press, Inc.
All rights of reproduction in any form reserved.
ISBN 0-12-255950-9

"keep a visual image of the items" or some similar kind of instruction assumed to be effective in insuring that the subject does what is requested. There is an implicit assumption that the subject does as he is told and complies with the instructions to the best of his ability.

Certainly the systematic effects associated with instruction differences support this assumption. Since the usual goal is an examination of general laws of behavior, the extent to which variations exist among individuals is of only peripheral interest. Individual variations in approaches, strategies, styles, etc. are usually not assessed in these experiments or if assessed, not reported. This is understandable, if not ideal, since the views of subjects on their own performances are of unknown value, difficult to quantify, and, frequently hard to understand.

A lack of interest in individual differences seems to characterize much of the research on hemisphere lateralization of cognitive processes. This is somewhat surprising, since the consideration of individual differences is almost invariably a factor in the selection of subjects for visual field or dichotic listening experiments. Almost every published research report on hemisphere function differences reports the selection of subjects for the presence or absence of certain characteristics. In many studies, the selection process is exclusionary, designed to eliminate the left-handed, who tend to minimize hemisphere differences regardless of the stimuli used. In other studies, right- and left-handed subjects have been systematically selected and handedness (and associated differences in cerebral organization) included as an experimental variable. In recent work, family history of left-handedness has also been included as a subject selection factor since a number of studies have found (Hines and Satz, 1971; McKeever, VanDeventer, and Suberi, 1973; McKeever, Gill, and VanDeventer, 1975) the familial left-handed to show different patterns of response to hemisphere function tasks than the left-handed who are unitary in right-handed families.

However, when the classification variables are determined and the subject appropriately classified as right- or left-handed, positive or negative family history, etc., the examination of individual differences is usually halted. Perhaps the best example is offered by the apparent lack of concern with the interaction of verbal and visuo-spatial abilities. Many studies seem to experimentally treat these abilities as if no interactive processes were present, as though hemispheric interaction was similar to the commissurotomy patient. While it is not argued here that research workers in the field of lateralization of function hold such a view, the failure to consider such interactive possibilities does lead to such impressions.

There are numerous examples of this outlook, Rizzolati, Umilta, and Berlucchi (1971) measured reaction time to recognition of single human faces using four faces and 736 trials on 12 subjects. They found a consistent left visual field-right hemisphere (LVF–RH) superiority in reaction time. A similar result was reported by Geffen, Bradshaw, and Wallace (1971) in measuring reaction time for recognition of one out of four faces to a test face for 80 trials on 15 subjects. Bruce and Kinsbourne (1974) in a test of the Kinsbourne activation hypothesis (1970) found a left hemisphere superiority in memory for complex forms when a concurrent verbal load was carried in memory. An extension and replication of this work was carried out by Hellige and Cox (1976) who found left hemisphere superiority present only for an intermediate size verbal memory load. Subjects asked to retain 2–4 words in memory while performing a recognition memory task on complex visual forms achieved a superior left hemisphere performance as compared to the same recognition task when no verbal memory load was present. However, when the verbal memory load was increased to six words, form recognition accuracy in the left hemisphere decreased to a level below that of the zero memory load condition.

The intent is not to question the validity of this work, but to inquire after the unexplored possibilities. Did the subjects of Rizzolati et al. (1971) or of Geffen et al. (1971) assign names to these faces at any time through the long series of recognition trials? If this possibility was explored with the subjects, no mention of it appears in the published accounts. (The work to be reported here had its genesis, as far as can be ascertained, during a rereading of the Geffen et al. (1971) paper, specifically their phrase "human faces which are immediately recognizable, but difficult to encode verbally . . . [p. 416]" while thinking that one of the Identi-Kit faces used in their experiment had a superficial resemblance to Richard Nixon.)

Similar speculations can be developed for the Bruce and Kinsbourne (1974) and the Hellige and Cox (1976) studies. Given the nature of their tasks, the possibility exists that subjects may have tried to construct paired associate relationships between the figures and the terms to be remembered. Such a process seems unproductive, since the net effect might well be confusions on the next trial where the same figure appears with a different set of terms. Some systematic interviewing of the subjects might have clarified what is, at present, an intriguing but complex finding.

In the work reported here, we systematically examined the interaction of verbal and visuo-spatial processes in relation to hemisphere function differences. At the time this study was undertaken, we were in agreement with current interpretive models of the differential functioning of the right and left cerebral hemispheres. We assumed that in right-handed subjects with no family history of left-handedness, processing of nonverbal material such as abstract forms would be superior if done in the right hemisphere and that verbal processes such as the generation of a name for an abstract form would be superior if done in the left hemisphere. We also assumed that between hemisphere differences in these abilities would be less marked for the familial left-handed, since these individuals show consistently smaller between hemisphere differences in such tasks as visual discrimination (Bryden, 1965), recognition accuracy (Bryden, 1973) ear dominance in dichotic listening (Dee, 1971; Zurif and Bryden, 1969) and letter recognition (McKeever, Gill, and VanDeventer, 1975). The McKeever *et al.* study offers an excellent demonstration of the differences in cerebral organization associated with familial handedness. Their right-handed subjects showed a statistically significant advantage in vocal reaction time to letters projected to the left hemisphere as compared to the right (36.9 msec difference favoring the left hemisphere). Their left-handed subjects had a difference of only 13.6 msec favoring the left hemisphere. When the left-handed subjects were divided into familial and nonfamilial left-handed, the nonfamilial left-handed were found to have a significant left-hemisphere advantage (21.3 msec) while the familial left-handed had no left-hemisphere advantage at all (−0.57 msec). While the number of subjects in their study is quite small, the data are an impressive illustration of differences in cerebral organization associated with familial handedness. (For a more extensive review of this area, see Hardyck, 1977.)

We had several goals: We wished to examine the range of individual variation in the generating of names to our stimuli and to see if naming was of any advantage in recognition accuracy. We were interested in individual differences in recognition accuracy on interhemispheric tasks when compared to intrahemispheric tasks and in any relationships of naming to inter and intrahemispheric accuracy. Finally, we wished to examine differences in performance related to sex and handedness.

We made the following predictions for right-handed subjects with no family history of left-handedness:

1. Abstract forms shown initially in the left visual field–right hemisphere (LVH–RH) will be recognized more often on a second showing than forms shown in the right visual field–left hemisphere (RVF–LH).
2. Forms shown in the RVF–LH will be assigned names more frequently than forms shown in the LVF–RH.
3. Forms which are named will be recognized more frequently than unnamed forms when shown in the RVF–LH.
4. Forms that are named will be recognized more frequently in a visual field different from first showing than unnamed forms. The assumption is that a name added to the memory of the form will facilitate interhemispheric transfer and recognition in a different visual field.
5. Forms shown in a given visual field, named or unnamed, will be recognized more frequently if shown again in the same visual field, as compared to forms shown in the opposite visual field.
6. Reaction time to unnamed forms will be faster in the LVF–RH than in the RVF–LH.

7. Reaction time to named forms will be faster in the RVF–LH than in the LVF–RH.

We made the following predictions for our familial left-handed subjects (hereafter L+).

1. There will be no statistically significant hemisphere differences in reaction time or recognition accuracy for both named and unnamed forms.
2. L+ subjects will have higher recognition accuracy scores on inter-hemispheric judgments than will right-handed subjects with no family history of left-handedness (hereafter R−). The assumption here is that the bilaterality of cerebral organization characteristic of the L+ will facilitate interhemispheric recognition tasks.
3. The L+ subjects will respond more quickly to interhemispheric comparisons than the R−. The rationale for this prediction is the same as for (2) just preceding.

We did not attempt specific predictions for sex differences. Some studies (Harshman and Remington, 1976; McGlone, 1976; McGlone and Davidson, 1973; McGlone and Kertesz, 1973) would suggest that women, regardless of handedness, will show performance patterns similar to the left-handed, but we did not feel that the evidence was sufficient to generate specific predictions.

METHOD

Subjects

Subjects were 80 undergraduates who were paid $2.50 for participation in one experimental session. Prior to the experimental procedure, subjects completed a questionnaire on family history of left-handedness and a modified version of the Oldfield (1971) handedness inventory. An additional measure of handedness was obtained by having subjects trace the outline of an irregularly shaped figure in a border 2 mm wide. This task was done twice, once with each hand and errors (line crossovers) and time were recorded.

Materials

Stimuli were 96 drawings selected from the Welsh-Barron Figure Preference Inventory. The test was originally developed as an exploratory measure of creativity as related to an individual's preference for complex asymmetrical figures as compared to simple regular figures. The test consists of over 400 black and white line drawings.

From the full set of figures, five judges selected figures which they found difficult to name. Forty-eight figures judged as difficult to name were selected as the "difficult" set. For these figures, frequency of judgments of difficult ranged from 2 to 4. No figures were ever selected by all judges as being difficult to name. A corresponding set of "simple" figures were chosen by the reverse process, all judges finding them easy to name. As a post hoc check on the validity of the judgments, the set of 48 figures were later shown to a group of 24 undergraduates who were asked to rate them on a nameability scale ranging from 1 (easy) to 7 (difficult). The mean rating for the simple figures was 2.4 and for the difficult figures, 4.5. Figures so similar as to be easily confused were excluded. A typical simple (top) and difficult figure are shown in Figure 14.1.

Figures were reduced in size to 45 × 78 mm and mounted on 22.5 × 15.4 cm cards. When viewed in an Iconix 3-field tachistoscope, figures occupied 2.04° of vertical visual angle and 1.54° of horizontal angle. Stimuli were located at 2.5° of visual angle from the point of fixation and were shown at an illumination level of 9 fl.

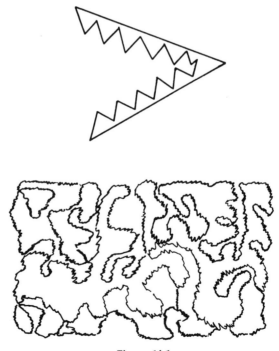

Figure 14.1.

Procedure

After completing the handedness testing, subjects were shown some sample figures (not used in the experiment). They were told that they would see a number of figures of this type, each for only 150 msec and that they were to try to remember as many as possible since they were later to identify previously seen figures from a larger set, each shown individually for 150 msec. A few preliminary trials with the sample figures were done to familiarize subjects with the tachistoscopic procedure.

At an alerting signal from the experimenter, the subject focused on a + in the center of the viewing field. When the subject indicated readiness, a stimulus figure was exposed for 150 msec. Forty-eight figures, 24 simple, and 24 difficult, were shown in right and left visual fields in random order and location. Figures were shown once, with no repetitions.

Immediately following the showing of the first set, the test series of figures were shown. Subjects responded by pressing one of two buttons to indicate whether the figure was new or had been seen previously. Subjects were told that position in the visual field was irrelevant and that they should respond as quickly as possible. The choice of right or left hand to indicate new or old stimuli was counterbalanced among subjects. Order of presentation was such that lag time was approximately equal for all previously seen figures in the first set.

A total of 96 figures were shown in the test series. Displays in visual fields were balanced equally among simple and difficult figures in the following placements:

1. Sameside (S): First and second displays of the figure were in the same visual field.
2. Crossover (C): The figure was shown in the visual field other than that of first display.
3. Both (B): The figure was shown in the exact center of the viewing area at the point of fixation, being visible in both visual fields.

Three measures were taken on each figure: The subject's judgment of "previously seen" or "new" was recorded, as was reaction time in milliseconds. After the tachistoscopic judgments were completed, the subject was given a booklet containing the 48 figures shown in the first part of the experiment and asked to write down any names or verbal labels that occurred to him on first seeing the figures. Subjects were cautioned against inventing new terms at this time and were asked to list only those names that had occurred (if any) when they had first seen the figures. Following this, the subject was interviewed for his reactions to the experiment and his opinions of the procedure.

RESULTS

Results are divided into three sections. First, a general summary of results over all subjects is given. An account of hemisphere function differences is then presented and the final section reviews individual differences in sex and handedness groups.

For All Subjects

Accuracy

Out of a total of 48 possible correct responses, the average number of correct responses for all subjects was 29.53, slightly over half that actually possible. Subjects were reasonably cautious in their judgments, the mean number of responses indicating previously seen figures being 49.41. Such a result is not significantly different from chance, although the later analysis indicates that selection was not on a chance basis.

The mean number of names assigned by subjects was 17.29. When this is divided into names given to simple and difficult forms, the respective means are 12.39 and 4.89, indicating that our initial judgments of naming difficulty were reasonably accurate. When responses are classified as to correct–incorrect and named–unnamed, the averages given in Table 14.1 are found.

Naming

The tendency to name figures, especially if they are in the simple category, is obvious. When formal tests are done on correct responses, the differences indicated in Table 14.1 are substantiated. A repeated measures analysis of variance indicated statistically significant effects for placement—sameside (S), crossover (C), or both (B)—$[F(2,152) = 25.66]$ and difficulty $[F(1,76) = 12.66]$.

TABLE 14.1
Average Correct and Incorrect Responses By Difficulty and Naming

		Simple	Difficult
Correct	Named	10.07	4.01
	Unnamed	5.54	9.90
Incorrect	Named	2.32	0.89
	Unnamed	6.06	9.19

Statistically significant interactions were found for placement by naming [$F(2,152) = 5.72$], difficulty by naming [$F(1,76) = 191.34$], and placement by difficulty by naming [$F(2,152) = 7.65$]. Figures are more often recognized when shown in the same visual field as first shown and more often recognized if simple.

If figures are shown in other than the S placement, they are more often recognized if simple and labeled. When examined over all subjects, simple figures shown in C and B placements were actually recognized slightly more often if labeled than figures in the S placement. This pattern is not present for unlabeled simple figures. A reverse effect is present for difficult figures, with unnamed figures being consistently recognized more frequently than named figures, regardless of placement. The relationships are illustrated in Figure 14.2.

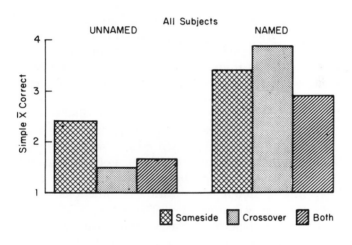

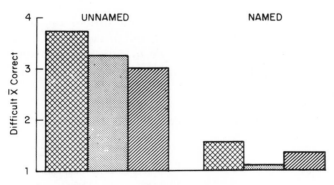

Figure 14.2.

Response Latency

A simpler set of results is found for reaction times. Mean reaction time over all subjects (correct responses only) was 1099 msec. When times are calculated separately for named and unnamed figures, the respective means are 977 and 1220 msec. Mean values for named–unnamed by simple–difficult classifications are given in Table 14.2.

An analysis of variance of reaction times revealed only one significant effect, that for naming. The generating of a name for a form, whether simple or difficult, significantly improves speed of recognition, independent of placement [$F(1,78) = 72.25$]. No other effects approached significance. Apart from the intrinsic interest of the findings, the result indicates that post hoc naming of figures was not a problem.

Visual Field–Hemisphere Effects

The analysis of visual field–hemisphere differences produced entirely negative results. A series of analyses in which different aspects of the data were examined in relation to visual field–hemisphere differences yielded a set of F statistics ranging from a low of .004 to a high of 3.37 ($df = 1,78$). This last value, which has an associated probability of .09, was obtained on an analysis of unnamed responses and indicates that subjects were more likely to remember unnamed figures if they first appeared in the RVF–LH. We are inclined to regard this as a chance deviation from a condition of zero difference rather than as a meaningful finding.

Of the seven predictions we made for hemisphere differences—predictions which seemed reasonable at the time and in general accord with current thinking about lateralization of functions in the cerebral hemispheres—not one was supported. There are no hemisphere differences present in these data. If we classify our accuracy scores by visual field–hemisphere of first showing, the mean accuracy scores shown in Table 14.3 result.

As can be seen in Table 14.3, hemisphere differences are trivial and about equally divided between expected and unexpected directions. If we do the comparison maximally favorable to detecting hemisphere differences and limit the analysis to sameside comparisons, we would expect to

TABLE 14.2
Average Reaction Times in Milliseconds By Naming and Difficulty

	Simple	Difficult
Named	1120	1154
Unnamed	1264	1312

TABLE 14.3
Average Correct for Hemisphere of First Showing By Naming and Difficulty

		Simple	Difficult	Total	
Right hemisphere	Named	5.27	1.92	6.88	
	Unnamed	2.58	4.81	8.04	14.59
Left hemisphere	Named	6.88	2.08	7.19	
	Unnamed	2.96	5.08	7.39	14.93

find a right hemisphere superiority for recognition of unnamed figures and a left hemisphere superiority for recognition of named figures. The mean accuracy scores for named and unnamed figures shown in the LVF–RH are 2.58 and 3.18. The corresponding values for the RVF–LH are 2.33 and 2.99.

Similar sets of near zero differences were found in the analysis of reaction times by visual field–hemisphere. Since there seems little point in elaborating on evidence for a null hypothesis, these results will not be presented.

Individual Differences

An examination of individual differences indicated several relationships of interest. Our analysis revealed a significant difference in accuracy for handedness groups [$F(1,76) = 4.69$] and differences on a borderline of significance for sex by placement [$F(2,152) = 2.65$, $p = .07$], difficulty by handedness [$F(1,76) = 2.69$, $p = .10$] and naming by difficulty by handedness [$F(1,76) = 2.65$, $p = .10$]. The left-handed subjects do slightly better on total accuracy, with a mean correct of 32.10 as compared to 28.00 for right-handed subjects. There were no differences between familial and nonfamilial left-handed as had been predicted. The effect found for sex by placement is primarily due to the slightly superior performance of women in the C and B placement conditions. The difficulty by handedness interaction is principally a function of the slightly superior performance of the left-handed on difficult figures. This also accounts for the naming by difficulty by handedness interaction because of a superior performance on named difficulty forms by the left-handed subjects. These results are shown in Figure 14.3.

Discussion

Probably the most surprising finding, at least to researchers interested in hemisphere function, is the complete lack of any sign of cerebral lateralization differences. Given the conditions of the experiment, cerebral lateralization differences should be present and in accord with the predic-

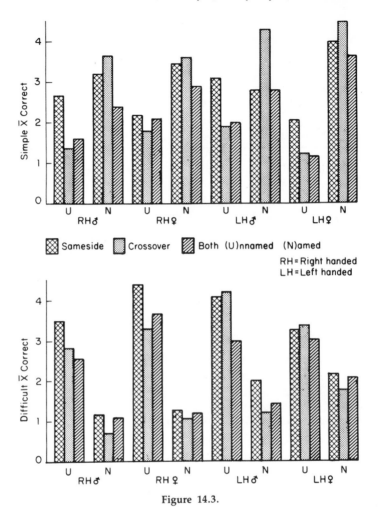

Figure 14.3.

tions. This finding was not as surprising to us as might be expected because of the results of other lateralization experiments completed while the work reported here was still in the data collection stage.

A series of visual half-field experiments just completed by Hardyck, Tzeng, and Wang (1978) on semantic judgments, using Chinese-English bilinguals as subjects, led to a conclusion that hemisphere differences will be found only under certain highly restricted conditions. In these experiments, fluent Chinese–English bilinguals made judgments of "same meaning" or "different meaning" to pairs of common nouns in Chinese and English shown in a single visual field for 150 msec. A unique advantage of this experiment on these subjects is that pattern matching cues are nonexistent—there are no structural similarities between the Chinese character for "hand" and the English word "hand," even though both are unambiguous common nouns and were so judged by the bilingual subjects. In two separate experiments, no hemisphere differences were present either for accuracy or reaction time. However, at the close of the second experiment, the subjects were asked to write down as many words as they could remember from the set shown (in either language). Analysis of this recall data revealed that subjects remembered significantly more terms originally shown in the RVF–LH, suggesting a memory advantage for the left hemisphere. In a third experiment, monolingual English-speaking subjects were shown Chinese-Chinese and English-English pairs within visual fields. No hemisphere differences in either accuracy or reaction time were found in judgments of same–different, regardless of language.

The three experiments just reviewed all had one common element—word pairs were shown once and never repeated. Under these conditions, even though the subject knows the type of judgment to be made, the information presented on each trial is new to him. To test the effect of new information, a fourth experiment was done using monolingual English-speaking subjects and three English-English and three Chinese-Chinese word pairs, presented randomly within visual fields for 200 trials. By the time 40 trials were completed, strong lateralization differences were present, with a strong RVF–LH advantage in reaction time to English and a less strong, but significant LVF–RH reaction time advantage for Chinese. These results suggest that cerebral lateralization effects are more a function of changes in task strategy by subjects than actual thinking differences.

Using these results as a guide, the lack of any hemisphere differences in the present recognition of figures experiment is exactly what should be expected. In this experiment, new information was provided on every trial in the first series and there was the possibility of new information on every trial in the recognition series. Under these conditions the lack of hemisphere differences is not surprising.

In this context, it should be noted that those experiments detecting significant hemisphere function differences (see Hardyck et al., 1978 for a review) report, almost exclusively, reaction time differences to a small number of stimuli over a large number of trials. By contrast, experiments reporting no lateralization effects have used roughly equal numbers of stimuli and trials. Such an interaction of results with experimental context suggests that lateralization differences—at least in the majority of experiments reported to date—reflect hemisphere differences in memory location rather than thinking or ongoing cognitive processing. Such a formulation is consistent with much of the published research on lateralization differences, and suggests that a subject, after completing a certain number of trials on a limited set of stimuli, changes strategy from an evaluative processing to a process that can best be described as a "table look-up." In such a process, the incoming information is limited to a set of n possibilities, all well known to the subject, and each having an appropriate and unvarying answer. Cerebral hemisphere differences in such experiments seem to be primarily an indication of where the reference table is stored, once it has firmly been committed to memory storage sufficient at least for the duration of the experiment. The use of previously "overlearned" items such as familiar words probably facilitates the process of constructing a table reference strategy, since no real encoding is needed. By contrast, a situation where new information is present on every trial, even if overlearning can be assumed, does not allow the construction of a table reference strategy. When the items are relatively unfamiliar, such as the figures used in the present study, it is necessary to encode the information, as well as to remember it well enough to differentiate it from other new information. The absence of any hemisphere differences in such a process suggests that this type of cognitive processing is relatively independent of hemisphere location.

The effects of naming can be summarized quickly. The present results are generally in accord with other results found in verbal coding experiments. Ellis (1973) has reviewed a number of studies using forced labeling and finds results similar to those reported here. There is, in general, a definite advantage to naming, whether forced or free, as in our study. However, it also appears that the facilitatory effect of naming interacts with the complexity of the figure—naming a simple figure seems to aid in remembering it, but naming a complex figure may actually hinder recognition. A possible explanation may be that naming a complex figure is not as helpful in differentiating it from other complex figures because of the difficulty in generating a discriminating label. For example, a common label for complex figures was "modern art," a label too general to be of much use in discriminating a particular complex figure from other complex figures.

The evidence for individual differences in the present study suggests that, even though lateralization effects are not present under conditions where new information is evaluated on every trial, differences in cerebral organization are present among our subjects. Our data suggest that our left-handed subjects are superior at providing verbal coding for difficult information and that this provides some advantages in later recognition. When this naming ability is examined in relation to the areas where it seems most useful—in correctly recognizing a form presented under conditions requiring interhemispheric transfer, it suggests that bilaterality of cerebral organization may have some unique advantages in allowing the linking of complex visuo-spatial information to verbal processes.

The bilateral cerebral organization characteristic of many left-handed is by now well recognized. The numerous clinical studies of lesion effects and the extensive number of behavioral studies of cerebral lateralization all suggest that the left-handed have a well developed bilateral organization, for both verbal and visuo-spatial processes. Although the present results, along with the bilingualism experiments, suggest that lateralization processes are primarily memory effects, the individual differences remain unaffected by this finding. A bilateral storage organization may have some unique advantages, especially in the area of verbal transformations of complex visuo-spatial material. While the superiority of recognition in the unnamed difficult category for all subjects suggests that some things are better left unsaid, the advantage of the left-handed in naming complex forms suggests that if you wish to know what to call a thingummy, it might be more efficient to ask someone who is left-handed.

ACKNOWLEDGMENTS

This work was supported by a grant from the Spencer Foundation.

REFERENCES

Brown, R. How shall a thing be called? *Psychological Review,* 1958, *65,* 14–21.

Bruce, R. and Kinsbourne, M. Orientational model of perceptual asymmetry. Paper presented at the 15th annual convention of the Psychonomic Society, Boston, November, 1974.

Bryden, M. P. Tachistoscopic recognition, handedness, and cerebral dominance. *Neuropsychologia,* 1965, *3,* 1–8.

Bryden, M. P. Perceptual asymmetry in vision: Relation to handedness, eyedness, and speech lateralization. *Cortex,* 1973, *9,* 419–435.

Dee, H. L. Auditory asymmetry and strength of manual preference. *Cortex,* 1971, *7,* 236–245.

Ellis, H. C. Stimulus encoding processes in human learning and memory. In G. Bower (Ed.), *The psychology of learning and motivation.* Vol. 7, New York: Academic Press, 1973.

Geffen, G., Bradshaw, J. L., and Wallace, G. Interhemispheric effects on reaction time to verbal and non-verbal stimuli. *Journal of Experimental Psychology,* 1972, *95,* 25–31.

Hardyck, C. A model of individual differences in hemispheric functioning. In H. Avakian-Whitaker and H. A. Whitaker (Eds.), *Studies in neurolinguistics.* Vol. 3, New York: Academic Press, 1977.

Hardyck, C., Tzeng, O. J. L., and Wang, W. S-Y. Lateralization of function and bilingual judgments: Is thinking lateralized? *Brain and Language,* 1978, *5,* 56–71.

Harshman, R. A. and Remington, R. Sex, Language and the Brain, Part I: A review of the literature on adult sex differences in lateralization. Mimeographed, Phonetics Laboratory, University of California, Los Angeles, 1976.

Hellige, J. B. and Cox, P. J. Effect of concurrent verbal memory on recognition of stimuli from the left and right visual fields. *Journal of Experimental Psychology: Human Perception and Performance,* 1976, *2,* 210–221.

Hines, D. and Satz, P. Superiority of right visual half-fields in right-handers for recall of digits presented at varying rates. *Neuropsychologia,* 1971, *9,* 21–25.

Kinsbourne, M. The cerebral basis of lateral asymmetries in attention. *Acta Psychologica,* 1970, *33,* 193–201.

McGlone, J. *Sex differences in functional brain asymmetry.* Research Bulletin #378, Department of Psychology, University of Western Ontario, London, Canada, 1976.

McGlone, J. and Davidson, W. The relation between cerebral speech laterality and spatial ability with special reference to sex and hand preference. *Neuropsychologia,* 1973, *11,* 105–113.

McGlone, J. and Kertesz, A. Sex differences in cerebral processing of visuospatial tasks. *Cortex,* 1973, *9,* 270–281.

McKeever, W. F., VanDeventer, A. D., and Suberi, M. Avowed, assessed, and familial handedness and differential hemispheric processing of brief sequential and non-sequential visual stimuli. *Neuropsychologia,* 1973, *11,* 235–238.

McKeever, W. F., Gill, K. M., and VanDeventer, A. D. Letter versus dot stimuli as tools for "splitting the normal brain with reaction time." *Quarterly Journal of Experimental Psychology,* 1975, *27,* 363–373.

Oldfield, R. C. The assessment and analysis of handedness: The Edinburgh Inventory. *Neuropsychologia,* 1971, *9,* 97–113.

Rizzolati, G., Umilta, C., and Berlucchi, G. Opposite superiorities of the right and left cerebral hemispheres in discriminative reaction time to physiognomical and alphabetical material. *Brain,* 1971, *94,* 431–442.

Zurif, E. B. and Bryden, M. P. Familial handedness and left–right differences in auditory and visual perception. *Neuropsychologia,* 1969, *7,* 179–187.

15

On the Evolution of Neurolinguistic Variability: Fossil Brains Speak

HARRY J. JERISON

Did the evolution of language depend on the evolution of an unusually large amount of brain tissue? The answer is certainly yes, and one can even argue that all of the encephalization of the human brain beyond the grade of other primates was related to the evolution of language (Jerison, 1976b). For this volume on variability in linguistic ability within *Homo sapiens* a second question should be asked: Is the variability in human brain size biologically unique, reflecting unique encephalization correlated with this unique behavior? The answer here is no, as we shall see, and the "no" seems unequivocal given the usual difficulties in asserting a negative.

Before reviewing the evidence let us consider what we should expect to find. That will depend on how we define encephalization, how we think of brain size as a measure, and how we think about morphological variations and their correlations with adaptive behavior. Encephalization can be defined as the residual of the regression of brain size on body size. [The

277

Individual Differences in Language Ability and
Language Behavior

Copyright © 1979 by Academic Press, Inc.
All rights of reproduction in any form reserved.
ISBN 0-12-255950-9

definition is presented because it is the one commonly used, whether recognized or not by those who have analyzed encephalization. It is possible to present a more substantial definition grounded in a theory of brain size (Jerison, 1977), but most people can agree on this empirical one. It amounts to the statement that there is an "expected" brain size defined by the regression, or allometric, brain:body equation, which tells us how much brain controls the body. The residual, or what is left over after the body-size component is taken care of, tells us how much brain is attributable to encephalization.] I think brain size is a fine measure, a kind of natural, biological, statistic that estimates many aspects of the brain's structure and organization. It tells us how densely nerve cells are packed, how extensively they arborize, how many times they make connections with one another, how much neocortex there is in the brain, how extensive the cortical surface is, how much DNA there is in the brain, what the ratio of neurons to glial cells is, and many other interesting things related to differences among species in their brains.

The correlation of morphology with adaptations, of structures with functions, is a tougher problem. In analysis above the species level, in which one compares different species with respect to a trait or set of traits, it seems clear that encephalization as measured by the encephalization quotient (measured brain size divided by "expected" brain size), by the "extra neurons index," and by several other indices does distinguish among species with respect to what might be labeled as competence or intelligence (Jerison, 1973, 1975). There is, furthermore, clear evidence of advances in grade with respect to encephalization when one compares classes of vertebrates and orders or even families of mammals (Jerison, 1973, 1976a). Attempts to extend this kind of analysis to individual differences within a species regularly fail, however, except for cases in which populations are given systematically different treatments such as environmental enrichment (Rosenzweig, Bennett, and Diamond, 1972) or deprivation (Winick, 1976).

The correlation between brain size and competence within the human species is small, if present at all. This statement is actually much harder to document than one may suspect. There is little really good evidence on it, and I make it on the basis of two analyses that I have performed, neither of which is published. The first is a review of Spitzka's (1907) data on the brains of "eminent" men. I could detect no correlation between brain size and eminence within that sample of over 100 postmortem measures. Similarly, in a review of data on cranial circumference and IQ (Robinow, 1968) I found no correlation when height was controlled by partial regression methods. But from the evidence on comparisons among populations, and from what is presently known about developmental neurobiology, one anticipates at least a small positive correlation within-species between brain size and competence. There must, of course, be some within-species correlation if the between-species effects are to be generated. And the size of the within-species correlation can be so low as to be missed entirely if samples are relatively small.

Given all of this, what should we expect to find in an analysis of the variability of brain size within-species? We expect, first, to discover that brain size is a fairly variable trait, notoriously so in *Homo sapiens* by popular belief. We all know the stories about Anatole France's 1000 g brain and Turgenev's 2000 g brain. These are approximately true, though an aging factor was probably present in Anatole France's case. On the whole we expect brain size to be less variable than body size in other species (Radinsky, 1967), but we have had no real idea how species should be compared with respect to variabilities when their average brain sizes differ by as much as they do. We also have little idea about how variable this measure was in the history of a species—how we compare with our ancestors—although there are now a fair amount of data available for us to inspect. I have published a summary of these (Jerison, 1975) and review them in Figure 15.1 (see p. 281).

There are enough data in the literature to enable one to analyze variability as a trait, and the usual measure for such an analysis is the coefficient of variation: the ratio of the standard deviation to the mean, stated as a percentage. I will review these data. Finally, since we are concerned with the evolution of variation I will emphasize the evidence of fossil brains—casts of the endocranial cavity or endocasts. This will tell us what we have, but we must still consider why we will get what we get.

How should variability in human brain size compare with that in other mammals? In mammals as a whole almost all of the variance in brain size is accounted for by a body size factor, and only about 10% can be attributed to encephalization. In humans the ratio is reversed with about 80% attributable to encephalization and only about 10% to body size. If the encephalization component in brain size is different in its within-species variability from the other component then we expect human brain size to be peculiar with respect to variability, though we have no idea in advance whether variability should be unusually high or low. If all of human encephalization is attributable to the evolution of language, and if linguistic ability is a peculiarly variable trait, we have a second source of potential peculiarity in variability. Here we anticipate more variability in the human brain than in other mammals. In arranging comparisons we should consider humans compared to other highly encephalized animals, in particular primates and fossil hominids. If part of the peculiarity in human variability is due merely to the fact of encephalization, then the other highly encephalized species should be like humans in this regard. We should examine the variability in brain size in negligibly encephalized species for a clue on the basic mammalian pattern from which encephalized species have departed. This is the "control" for encephalization.

MATERIALS AND METHODS

Data from all known fossil hominid endocasts prior to *H. sapiens* are summarized in Jerison (1975) and are reviewed here. In addition, a sample of about 2000 living human brains also reviewed in Jerison (1975) is reviewed for comparisons. A sample of 25 chimpanzee brains (Jerison 1976b) is analyzed, and a few cats and horses are tossed in to enrich the stew. Finally, new data on 20 individual primitive oreodons *Bathygenys reevesi* are presented (Wilson, 1971) for the first time. These mammals are from a family that has been extinct for many millions of years and represent a single population of over 100 individuals that lived in what is now the Big Bend country in Southern Texas. These small oreodons (about the size of house cats) lived 35 million years ago. The family of mammals of which they are members was unusually small-brained as a group. They are of the order Artiodactyla, even-toed hooved mammals that include today the deer, swine, cattle, sheep, camels, and so forth. They do not include horses, or rhinos. *Bathygenys* can be used to represent a primitive mammalian condition with respect to the diversity of brain size within-species.

Endocast volumes in ml are considered equivalent to brain weight in grams, and the two measures are presented together. With the exception of the oreodons I rely on reports in the literature for the weights and volumes. I measured the volumes of 20 endocasts of *B. reevesi* by water displacement. A full report on these data will be presented elsewhere. (It is presently in preparation for the *Pearce-Willards Series* of the Texas Memorial Museum, Austin, Texas.)

All of the analysis for this report is graphic, though some numerical analysis is included in the text. Graphs make the most dramatic picture of the regularities that can be demonstrated. Archival analyses including numerical measures will be presented elsewhere. The basic estimator will be the coefficient of variation, as described above, but a simple graphic transformation and analysis is used to enable one to evaluate that coefficient without using numbers. Since the method of analysis may be unfamiliar I will describe it in relation to Figure 15.1, which reviews the history of variability in the hominid brain. The description focuses on the data of *Homo habilis* because only five numbers are involved.

Note the habiline line in Figure 15.1 ("H"). It is based on five reconstructed endocasts with volumes of 593, 633, 652, 682, and 775 ml. I assume that these are from a population in which brain size (endocast volume) is

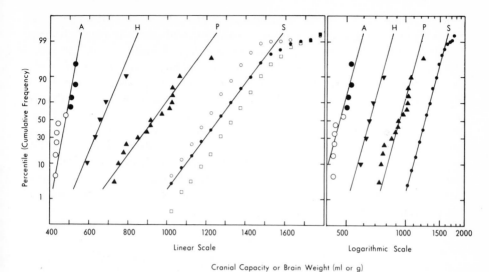

Figure 15.1. Evolution of cranial capacity (ml) in hominids. Data on *Homo sapiens* are brain weights (g), approximately 90% of cranial capacity. Labels are A: australopithecines (open circles are gracile, filled are robust); H: habilines including KNM–ER 1470 (top point); P: pithecanthropines; S: living sapiens (filled circles are total sample of 1898, open squares are subsample of 852 men, and open circles are subsample of 1046 women). The graphs are cumulative frequency distributions drawn on normal probability paper. When a measure of a population is Gaussian (normally distributed), its graph on such paper will be a straight line, the slope of which is proportional to the standard deviation with the mean at the fiftieth percentile. The use of such curves in this application is reviewed in Jerison (1973) under the heading "cumulative frequency." Data from Tobias (1975) on fossils and from Gjukic (1955) on *H. sapiens*. A comparable analysis (Jerison, 1973) has shown that Neandertals should not be distinguished from other *H. sapiens* with respect to cranial capacity. This figure summarizes the pattern of evolution of cranial capacity with respect to typical values and diversity. The approximately equal slopes on the logarithmic scale indicate that diversity has been proportional to average cranial capacity in these populations. (From Jerison (1975) © Annual Reviews, Inc. All rights reserved.)

normally distributed. In that case, assuming random sampling, the lowest value can represent the bottom 20% of the population, the next lowest represent the interval between the 20–40 percentiles in the population, and so forth. Graphing percentiles as a function of absolute volume should then yield an ogive, or cumulative normal frequency distribution. For convenience I assign each volume to the midpoint of the range of percentiles. Thus the five volumes correspond to the percentiles: 10, 30, 50, 70, 90. I now graph percentile as a function of volume, that is, a set of 5 points in a coordinate system with percentiles on the ordinate and absolute volume on the abcissa. I perform the graphing on "probability" paper, in which the ordinate is scaled to linearize the S-shaped curve that represents the integral of the normal probability density function. This paper can be imagined as stretching away from the fiftieth percentile to produce the kind of scale seen on the ordinate of Figure 15.1. On this scale the cumulative normal distribution, or Gaussian distribution, is a straight line the slope of which is proportional to the standard deviation. One can read the standard deviation from the difference between the mean (fiftieth percentile) of the normal probability curve and either the sixteenth or eighty-fourth percentile, since the interval $\pm 1\sigma$ includes about two-thirds of its central area. In the case of the habiline data it is apparent that the mean is about 670 ml and the standard deviation about 70 ml, giving a coefficient of variation of about 10%. On the right side of Figure 16.1 the same data were graphed using log cranial volume on the abcissa. This was done because when the coefficient of variation is constant—the standard deviation proportional to the mean—one gets a set of parallel lines on log-probability coordinates.

RESULTS

The earliest results that I obtained with this analysis were presented in Figure 15.1. It was clear, first, that the orientations (slopes) of the lines on the linear-probability coordinate system was shifting as one progressed from the australopithecine grade ("A") to the habiline grade ("H") to the pithecanthropine grade ("P") of *H. erectus*. As average brain size increased, its variability also increased. In terms of the passage of time the data of Figure 15.1 begin with the earliest measured hominid grade, that of the australopithecines, which may have been achieved more than 5.5 million years ago (the date of the earliest fossil, but prior to the oldest known endocast). There is an advance to the perhaps contemporaneous but one assumes later habiline grade of perhaps 3 million years ago, and then to the pithecanthropine grade about 1.0 to 1.5 million years ago. These are older dates than usually presented and represent the current (frequently unpublished) judgments of paleoanthropologists. The sapient grade represented by brains rather than endocasts is nevertheless also appropriate for endocasts. The fact that approximately parallel slopes work for the data of both *H. sapiens* and *H. erectus* on the linear scale is actually disconcerting. In terms of the introductory statements in this report this may signify a peculiarity in the variability measure within *H. sapiens*—less variability than one would anticipate from other data in that one expects increased variability as one goes to larger brains.

To consider this question the data were regraphed on log scales as shown on the right in Figures 15.1, with variability at about 10% of the mean—a fixed coefficient of variation of 10%. The lines were to be drawn parallel to one another, and one could judge visually whether it was reasonable to consider the coefficient or variation as fixed in these populations. It is clear that these are indeed reasonably considered to display the same coefficient of variation.

The question then arose whether this fixed value was characteristic only of the hominids, representing possible evolutionary trends toward some special adaptation (e.g., language). This should not produce quite the sort of thing shown in the log-probability graphs, since the "lower" grades would be expected to have much less specialized tissue in the brain for the encephalized adaptation than in the "more advanced" grades. In any event, it appeared that the picture in the hominids might not be peculiar to the hominids but might also occur in any highly encephalized primates.

As a control for this possibility I examined data on 25 chimpanzees, not differentiated by sex (Bauchot and Stephan, 1969). The criterion for including an animal was that it weigh at least 35 kg. The resulting sample was of 12 females with brain weights of from 275 to 379 g and body weights of from 36 to 44 kg, 11 males with brains from 326 to 444 g and bodies from 35 to 79 kg. Two animals unidentified by sex were included with brains of 379 and 363 g and bodies of 38 and 61 kg respectively. Data from these animals were graphed and added to the previous graph. They are shown as distributed about the chimpanzee ("C") line in Figure 15.2. The fit of a line parallel to that determined for the hominids and displaced to the left is striking. In Figure 15.2 the log-normal bell-shaped curves corresponding to the lines are drawn above the graph to illustrate the transformation involved in the log-probability graph. The use of the hominoid data in Figure 15.2 to consider Rubicon models of the evolution of language for decision-theory approaches is discussed in detail in Jerison (1976b).

We now have enough data to show that the fixed, or reasonably fixed, value of the variability of brain size in *H. sapiens* and our ancestors was predictable from the fact that all were highly encephalized species of primates. The issue was now: Is this unique to primates or does it also occur in other mammals? More—is it simply a property of brain as an organ of the body? If the latter is true we are also interested in how long it has been true, how long ago it appeared in mammalian evolution. There happened to be one fossil assemblage available for this issue, the 20 specimens of *B. reevesi* that I had been analyzing. Graphed on the same coordinate system as the primates, but with the abcissa extended to allow for the two orders of magnitude differences in absolute brain size, this assemblage was remarkable in showing exactly the same slope on log-probability coordinates as did the highly encephalized primates including humans. They cluster around the line labeled "B."

To allow one to see immediately the enormous difference in size between the primitive oreodon endocasts and those of living and fossil hominoids, the x-axis of the graph was extended somewhat (though the gap between 35 ml and 200 ml was left as a gap). Since *Bathygenys* was probably about the size of living domestic cats, it was a harmless exercise

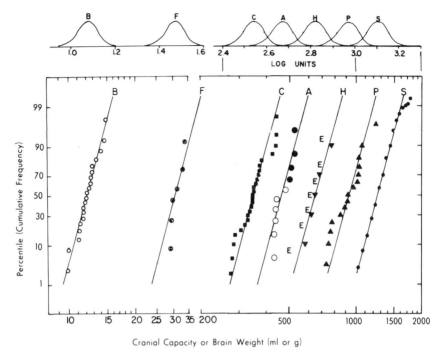

Figure 15.2. Cumulative frequency distributions of brain size or endocranial volumes for various mammalian species. This graph is the log-probability graph of Figure 15.1 to which new data are added and normal (bell-shaped) curves representing the first derivatives of the "sloping" lines are drawn above the graph proper. Species identified by letters are: *Bathygenys reevesi* (B), which was a fossil ungulate that lived in the Big Bend area of Texas some 35 million years ago; the domestic cat, *Felis domestica* (F); the chimpanzee (C); and the hominid species of Figure 15.1. The latter are the australopithecines (A), with robust species as the filled circles and gracile as the open circles; the habilines (H); the pithecanthropines (P); and the combined sample of about 2000 male and female *Homo sapiens*. Data on horses are represented by E (*Equus*) for each of seven individuals; they could obviously be fitted by a line slightly to the left and parallel to the habiline line.

to find some cat-data ("F") to add to the graph—these also served an aesthetic purpose in filling an otherwise disconcerting void on the graph paper, and a scientific purpose in demonstrating encephalization in living cats relative to a fairly typical species from the Lower Oligocene. The evidence for encephalization is from the fact that two species (*Bathygenys reevesi* and *Felis domestica*) of similar body size have characteristically different brain size. Regardless of how encephalization is measured, cats are relatively bigger-brained than the oreodons. On variability, the cat-data result in a calculated coefficient of variation of about 6%, although it is evident from the good fit of the line drawn with a slope of about 10% that either figure is reasonable. The last is a disconcerting fact that provides a nice caveat for the analysis. It would require a very unusual sample of brains or endocasts to be fitted inappropriately by the lines of Figure 15.2. But it is just such an unusual sample that one might have expected for that cerebrally odd population called *Homo sapiens,* which sport brains so big that they support the specialized neural systems of speech and language. Odd as we are cerebrally, we are not so odd that we shake the structure of Figure 15.2.

As yet another exercise, I added seven horses ("E") to the graph. Both the horses and the cats, incidentally, come from data published by Count (1947). The horses do give a coefficient of variation of 10%, even when calculated numerically. They were added to provide another mammalian sample, within the range of brain sizes of the highly encephalized hominoids but representing a species that, like the cat, is encephalized only to an average mammalian extent.

In essence, Figure 15.2 shows that mammalian species, past and present, are not to be differentiated with respect to the variability of brain size. In a sense, Figure 15.2 represents a scientific experiment. It was actually drawn, first, as the right-hand part of Figure 15.1 when the latter was first prepared. The chimpanzee data ("C") were added for the preparation of an illustration on the paleoneurology of language (Jerison, 1976b), but the chimpanzee line was drawn to be parallel to the sapient ("S") line. This same illustration was used as the base on which to place the additional points presented here on three more species of mammals. One might, therefore, think of Figure 15.2 as testing the hypothesis that the orientation (slope) of the line of the right-hand part of Figure 15.1 is constant— stating that hypothesis in suitable scientific terms (constant variability, or a 10% coefficient of variation). Figure 15.2 shows that the hypothesis is supported.

DISCUSSION

This "negative" result should be most illuminating for neurolinguistics and for the analysis of the variability of capacities for language. It is also interesting and important for the analysis of brain evolution and variability in brain structure and function. The demonstration is clearly that the variability of brain size, even when as notable as in *H. sapiens,* is actually a rather fixed evolutionary trait. It is proportional to mean brain size and is truly predictable. In more or less casual examination of data on insectivores and prosimians as presented by Bauchot and Stephan (1966) I have found the same value, a coefficient of variation of about 10%, and one can see this in the data on gibbons and other apes as presented by Tobias (1971) even where he has obviously combined groups from many sources with possible overlaps in descriptions and with possible multiple listing of some individual specimens.

The first conclusion, of course, is that at least as far as its structural basis goes human linguistic capacity should be considered as a normally variable trait or character. It is unfortunate that there is no measure of behavioral traits that can be carried across species in the way that morphological measures carry. If it were possible to perform the measurement, the present result indicates that unique as we are with respect to language we are doing no more than carrying out a normal biological adaptive behavior, with normal biological systems to support it. Language is unique, but it is as "unique" as other species-specific adaptations.

I should comment briefly on the comparative research on language in other primates, in particular in the great apes. It seems to me that these ape "languages" are considered in the same class as human language only at one's peril. They may be logically similar in many ways, just as many cognitive activities lead to logical analysis with similar logical systems whether they are cognitive activities of fish, rats, or people. If these are analyses by humans, we have a word for such logical systems: "languages". But the biological definition of language in humans is non-tautologically made if one includes the brain structures and brain functions in human language. In short, human language may be definable as behaviors controlled by the speech and language systems of the brain. The identification of these systems in the brain may require more of us as theoreticians and scientists, but that is another issue.

I note, second, that the least encephalized and most encephalized populations available to us showed essentially identical variations in brain size. This indicates that the brain is built up by systems in which the variability of the system is determined by the fact that it is brain tissue, not by the fact that it is encephalized or not encephalized. One can reasonably conjecture that this would also be true for the various more specifically identifiable systems in the brain such as visual or auditory cortex, cerebellum, or the speech and language systems. Their structural variability within a species is determined by the fact that they are brain tissues.

SUMMARY AND CONCLUSIONS

Variations in human brain size, supposedly enormous and too great to permit one to make any generalizations, turn out to be exactly what one expects of brains in mammals. To the extent that human brain size evolved to its present highly encephalized condition as a consequence or correlate of the evolution of language capabilities, one may put the causal arrow of variation in the opposite direction. One may consider the individual differences in human language abilities as representing the normal variability of a trait in a species under natural selection and not particularly unique, at least in that respect. Like all species-specific adaptations, human language is unique. But its variability is not.

REFERENCES

Bauchot, R., and Stephan, H. Données nouvelles sur l'encéphalisation des insectivores et des prosimiens. *Mammalia*, 1966, *30*, 160–196.
Bauchot, R., and Stephan, H. Encéphalisation et niveau evolutif chez les Simiens. *Mammalia*, 1969, *33*, 225–275.
Count, E. W. Brain and body weight in man: Their antecedents in growth and evolution. *Annals of the New York Academy of Science*, 1947, *46*, 993–1122.
Gjukic, M. Ein Beitrag zum Problem der Korrelation zwischen Hirngewicht and Körpergewicht. *Zeitschrift für Morphologie und Anthropologie*, 1955, *47*, 43–57.
Jerison, H. J. *Evolution of the brain and intelligence*. New York: Academic Press, 1973.
Jerison, H. J. Fossil evidence of the evolution of the human brain. *Annual Review of Anthropology*, 1975, *4*, 27–58.
Jerison, H. J. Paleoneurology and the evolution of mind. *Scientific American*, 1976a, *234*(1), 90–101.
Jerison, H. J. Discussion Paper: The paleoneurology of language. *Annals of the New York Academy of Sciences*, 1976b, *280*, 370–382.
Jerison, H. J. The theory of encephalization. *Annals of the New York Academy of Sciences*, 1977, *299*, 146–160.
Radinsky, L. B. Relative brain size: A new measure. *Science*, 1967, *155*, 836–838.
Robinow, M. The relationship of head circumference to height and weight in healthy and malnourished infants. Paper presented to the child development section of American Academy of Pediatrics, 1968.
Rosenzweig, R., Bennett, L., and Diamond, M. C. Brain changes in response to experience. *Scientific American*, 1972, *226*(2), 22–30.
Spitzka, E. A. A study of the brains of six eminent scientists and scholars belonging to the American Anthropometric Society, together with a description of the skull of Professor E. D. Cope. *Transactions of the American Philosophical Society*, 1907, *21*, 175–308.
Tobias, P. V. *The brain in hominid evolution*. New York: Columbia University Press, 1971.
Tobias, P. V. Brain evolution in the Hominoidea. In R. H. Tuttle (Ed.), *Primate functional morphology and evolution*. The Hague: Mouton, 1975, 353–392.
Wilson, J. A. *Early tertiary vertebrate faunas, Vieja Group. Trans-Pecos Texas: Agriochoeridae and Merycoidontidae*. Texas Memorial Museum (Austin), Bulletin 18, 1–83, 1971.
Winick, M. *Malnutrition and brain development*. New York: Oxford University Press, 1976.

16

Strategies of Linguistic Processing in Human Split-Brain Patients

LATERALIZATION AND LANGUAGE

In almost all species of mammals, the two cerebral hemispheres appear to be symmetric in function, or, if asymmetric, the asymmetries are of such a subtle nature that they are very difficult to reveal. Certainly in the phyletic series representative of man's evolutionary history, only our closest relatives, the great apes, appear likely to have laterally differentiated higher cognitive functions in the two hemispheres. Among chimpanzees (Yeni-Komshian and Benson, 1976) and orangutans (LeMay, 1976), neuroanatomical asymmetries have been observed that appear homologous with asymmetries in the human brain that are related to differential hemispheric function. In monkeys, however, these asymmetries are not observed (Yeni-Komshian and Benson, 1976), and a series of studies on split-brain and unilaterally lesioned monkeys failed to reveal

Individual Differences in Language Ability and
Language Behavior

Copyright © 1979 by Academic Press, Inc.
All rights of reproduction in any form reserved.
ISBN 0-12-255950-9

any evidence for functional lateralization (Hamilton, 1977; Warren and Nonneman, 1976).

In man, anatomical differences between the two sides of the brain have been seen in a variety of structures (Geschwind and Levitsky, 1968; Witelson and Pallie, 1973; LeMay and Culebras, 1972; Wada, Clarke, and Hamm, 1975; Rubens, 1977), and functional lateralization is profound and obvious (Broca, 1861; Wernicke, 1874; Hécaen, 1969; Sperry, Gazzaniga, and Bogen, 1969; Levy, Trevarthen, and Sperry, 1972; Sperry, 1974; Levy, 1974).

Following the report of Dax in 1836 (Dax, 1865) that the human left hemisphere was specialized for language, neurologists believed for the next 100 years that the left side of the brain was not only the language specialist, but was also dominant for thought and behavioral control, the right hemisphere being subordinate for all higher cognitive activity and containing no specialized functions of its own. Though evidence accumulated over the last 40 years has proved beyond question (see Bogen, 1969, for review) that each cerebral hemisphere is predominant and superior in different sets of functions, there is still controversy regarding the role of the right hemisphere in language, the majority of neurologists believing that it is not only mute, but also word deaf. This belief derives from the fact that certain unilateral lesions of the left hemisphere lead to total receptive aphasia, the patient behaving as if he had no understanding of words or speech.

Thus language is held to be unique to the left hemisphere, even to the extent that the right hemisphere is incompetent to derive meanings from words. If true, since other mammals, with the possible exception of apes, do not appear to have lateralized brains, an anatomical basis is provided for the contention that language is a uniquely human characteristic.

Until recently, psycholinguistic research, also, seemed to imply that the comprehension of spoken language was restricted to the human species. With the discovery that synthesized syllables having continuous changes in the characteristics of formant transitions were, nevertheless, categorically perceived by infants as belonging to one or another discontinuous phonemic dimension (Eimas et al., 1971), some investigators reached the conclusion that only people could understand words, because only people had categorical perceptions. Word perception was thought to depend on a phonetic analysis of inherent linguistic elements, and would be impossible without it. The categorical boundaries observed were taken to reflect specifically human neurological substrates of phonemic elements, substrates confined to the left hemisphere.

The proposed relationship between categorical perception, phonetic analysis, and word discrimination could not, however, be maintained when it was found that not only did monkeys (Morse, 1976) and chinchillas (Kuhl and Miller, 1974, 1975) manifest categorical perception, but also that synthesized violin notes were categorically perceived by people as being bowed or plucked though the acoustic dimensions of the synthesized notes were continuously varied (Cutting and Rosner, 1974; Jusczyk *et al.*, 1977). It may well be that a single psychophysical function can describe the relationship between all acoustic signals and their percepts, and that whether perception is categorical or continuous merely depends on the values of certain terms or factors in the function. The fact that no such function has yet been discovered may merely mean that it is complex.

LANGUAGE LIMITATIONS OF THE RIGHT HEMISPHERE

In any case, if subhuman animals are capable of discriminating human speech sounds, as the work with monkeys and chinchillas demonstrates (and as any dog owner can testify!), it would be quite remarkable if the human right hemisphere could not. Receptive aphasias, and particularly word deafness, following left hemisphere lesions are likely to be due to a loss of left hemisphere function *plus* disruption of right hemisphere activity via the corpus callosum, rather than to an inability of the normal right hemisphere to discriminate words.

The inability of animals and of the human right hemisphere to speak cannot be due either to an inability to discriminate words or to an inability to associate discriminated words with meaning. If a mammal can discriminate an acoustic signal, that signal can be associated with any meaning in the mammal's cognitive repertoire. Thus any semantic limitations of the right hemisphere would not be due to an associative deficit, but to constraints regarding the concepts that can be understood.

That such constraints exist, relative to the left hemisphere, seems apparent. Sperry, Gazzaniga, and Bogen (1969) reported that though the right hemisphere in split-brain patients could understand nouns and adjectives, it could not understand verbs. However, Levy (1970), using a different behavioral index of comprehension, showed that the right hemisphere *could* understand even written verbs, when the verbs were all concrete. More recently, Zaidel (1976a) has found that the word comprehension capacity of the right hemisphere on the Peabody Picture Vocabulary Test equals that of a normal 12-year-old child, but that it has little capacity to process sequential, semantically unconstrained information (Zaidel, 1975, 1977). A recent study by Day (1977) in normal people showed that the right hemisphere, though understanding concrete nouns (e.g, *horse*), could not understand abstract nouns (e.g., *faith*). It is as if meaning for the right hemisphere can only be derived for those concepts that are codeable in the form of some literal analogy with concrete objects or events in the real world. It appears that the more abstract is a concept, rule, or structure, that is, the more transformations that must be made from real events to the concept, the less likely is the right hemisphere to be able to acquire its meaning or to derive its implications.

The right hemisphere's difficulties with grammar are likely to be due to the complexity and abstraction of the transformational rules that must be acquired, rather than to a specific deficit confined to syntax per se. Even adult infantile hemiplegics, in whom the left hemisphere was dysfunctional from birth and who have undergone total left hemispherectomy, though capable of relatively normal speech and language comprehension, are quite limited in syntactical understanding. In the absence of semantic contraints, passive voice sentences are interpreted as if they were in the active voice (Dennis and Kohn, 1975). Indeed, it may well be that a correct interpretation of such semantically constrained passive voice sentences as, *The candy was eaten by the child*, depends, in these patients, on a simple extraction of the content words and a subsequent construction of the only possible meaning that could be attached to *candy*, *eat*, and *child*.

However, even if it were to be granted that the right hemisphere's cognitive organization is simply too limited with respect to certain abilities to understand abstract words, grammatical rules, and any but the simplest syntactical forms, the fact that it can comprehend *some* words and *some* sentences, and yet cannot speak (except in cases of early infantile injury to the left hemisphere), suggests that the language of the left hemisphere is fundamentally different from that of the right. Language comprehension by the left hemisphere may utilize processes also important in language generation, while language comprehension by the right may depend on more general processes that are applied to nonlinguistic signals also. It is being suggested that at least some of the components of left hemisphere language *are* species specific and are qualitatively different from strategies used by the right hemisphere or by apes or other animals for language comprehension and nonvocal communication, and that it is these unique strategies and operations that are normally necessary to permit the generation of speech itself.

WHAT IS MEANT BY LANGUAGE?

The current arguments regarding whether apes do or do not have language are all centered on the question of what constitutes the necessary and sufficient conditions for the attribution of a linguistic system (Premack, 1971). It is probable that nearly all mammals can discriminate spoken words and associate them with meaning, and that they are almost all capable of learning new motor responses to signal some mental state, yet no one attributes language to a dog. On the other hand, there is a real controversy as to whether apes are capable of acquiring language, and the controversy arises because apes not only manifest propositional thought in their use of language symbols (Premack, 1971; Rumbaugh, 1977; Fouts, 1973; Terrace and Bever, 1976), but, at least in some cases, appear to apply simple ordering rules to their language symbols.

As Terrace, Pititto, and Bever (1976) have shown with Nim, the ordering of gestural words is not random, but it is unclear as yet as to whether Nim generalizes orders to new grammatical elements. In apes such as Sarah (Premack, 1971) and Lana (Rumbaugh, 1977), whose words are represented by concrete, temporally stable objects, rather than by vanishing gestures, generalization of syntax is apparent. Human language, however, consists of words that vanish in time, and capacity to maintain a syntax only when representatives of words persist through time may rely on very different processes than those that permit syntactical generalization in people. The limitations of the human right hemisphere in syntactical understanding have been mentioned previously.

Perhaps "true" language necessarily includes the neurological capacity to generate oral speech. Lieberman (1975) might argue that apes may have the neurological capacity, but lack the peripheral apparatus. However, in addition to the fact that Lieberman's work has only shown that the vocal apparatus of apes is incapable of generating *certain* phonemic elements (and thus *is* capable of generating others), the peripheral argument cannot be applied to the human right hemisphere.

It is unlikely that the argument regarding whether the language of apes is "true" language can be settled without first understanding how the human right hemisphere manages the speech comprehension it does, the nature of its organization that so limits its linguistic powers compared to the left hemisphere, and why it is almost totally incapable of speech generation.

Studies of split-brain patients in collaboration with Colwyn Trevarthen (Levy and Trevarthen, 1976) suggest that the right hemisphere's cognitive propensities are ill-suited for certain aspects of language, and that it totally lacks a fundamental process necessary for speech generation (Levy and Trevarthen, 1977).

THE COGNITIVE DISPOSITIONS OF THE RIGHT HEMISPHERE

The right hemisphere of split-brain patients generally has little difficulty in following orally given instructions, but the instructions are always simple, redundant, unambiguous, and could be easily followed by a young child. On the other hand, if instructions are ambiguous, it is quite possible that each hemisphere would generate a different interpretation, appropriate to its view of the world, and these differing interpretations would provide some insight into the cognitive operations of the two sides of the brain. If, also, each hemisphere is free to take control of behavior in any given circumstance, the conditions under which the left or right side does so would yield clues regarding the dispositional differences of the hemispheres.

We administered a series of tests in which two different pictures were simultaneously shown by tachistoscopic presentation to the two sides of the brain in split-brain patients (Levy and Trevarthen, 1976), for example, a cake on a cake plate to the right hemisphere, and a bird's nest with eggs to the left hemisphere. Displayed in free vision were four choice pictures: a bird, a knife and fork, a hat with a brim, and a sewing basket filled with spools of thread.

In one condition, a patient (N.G.) was told that she would "see a picture in the machine" and that she was to point to one of the choices that was "similar to, or like in some way, or goes with" what she saw. On approximately half the trials, N.G. selected a choice that was *visually* similar to what the right hemisphere had seen (e.g., the hat in the example given), and on the other trials, she selected a choice that was *functionally* matched with what the left hemisphere had seen (e.g., the bird in the example given). Thus similarity for the right hemisphere meant that visual form was similar, but for the left hemisphere, it meant that a functional relation existed.

Tests were adminstered to three other patients, as well as to N.G., in which they were specifically told to "pick a choice that *looks like*" the stimulus, or in which they were told to "pick a choice that you would *use with* or that *goes with*" the stimulus. The appearance instruction generally elicited right hemisphere control, while the functional instruction elicited left hemisphere control.

The results of this study can leave little doubt that words do not mean the same thing to the two sides of the brain, that the right hemisphere seeks visuo-spatial invariants, while the left seeks functional relations, and that each hemisphere interprets statements in accordance with its inherent priorities, and assumes control of behavior when problems with which it is confronted depend on those cognitive operations for which it is disposed and specialized. A neurological computer whose function is more to decipher the literal characteristics of space than to determine the functional relations among concepts, and that, furthermore, manifests little propensity to guide behavior that depends on functional analysis, could have very little use for language even if it had the capacity. The inadequacy of a language system for encoding such complex structural relations as the form of a human face is widely recognized. Police artists are, after all, employed precisely for this reason.

Earlier work with these patients (Levy, Trevarthen, and Sperry, 1972) had already demonstrated that the right hemisphere was superior to the left at encoding and remembering visual forms having no verbal labels in long term memory, and, in fact, assumed behavioral control whenever purely visual matches were required. Remarkably, however, it even assumed control when the left hemisphere was superior at performing a particular type of match.

In one test, patients were asked to match a stimulus that consisted of various combinations and permutations of Xs and squares ordered into a vertical array of three components. The stimuli on this test differed from those on the other matching tests in that there were no constraints of meaning or good Gestalt, no "visual syntax," that served to keep the memory of stimulus features properly related in space. This is to say that whether the stimulus consisted, for example, of X-square-square or of square-square-X was irrelevant for keeping the pattern in memory. Neither pattern is more meaningful than the other, and neither forms a better Gestalt than the other. In contrast, a stimulus like the picture of a rose is much more meaningful than a picture consisting of petals, leaves, thorns, and stem randomly ordered in space. On the pattern-matching tests, the right hemisphere performed more poorly than the left, and its high error rate was attributable to an unusual number of permutation errors. A pattern such as square-square-X was often matched with square-X-square. Levy and Reid (1978) also found that the right hemisphere in normal individuals produced a large number of permutation errors in discriminating unconstrained three-component stimuli.

In the absence of "visual syntax," the right hemisphere appears deficient at encoding visual stimuli. The left hemisphere, in contrast, rarely makes errors in correctly discriminating visual stimuli that are easily decomposable into a small set of verbally labelable features, and almost never commits a permutation error. It is as if the right hemisphere extracts only a set of spatial relationships that serve to define a stimulus, and if no such definition exists, then features are extracted that are randomly ordered in a mental space. The left hemisphere appears to extract features to which a verbal label may be assigned and the ordering of those features appears to be maintained because they are projected onto a temporal dimension in which time is conserved. Thus, as features are committed to memory, they are time-tagged according to relational rules by the left hemisphere, but not by the right, whose world is one of predominantly spatial coordinates.

If the foregoing descriptions of right and left hemisphere cognition are accurate, it is obvious why the right hemisphere is unable to decode complex syntactical forms. The time-ordering and time-tagging necessary for such decoding calls on cognitive operations not available to the right hemisphere, and its typical lack of activation and probable relative incompetency, in the face of demands for analysis of functional relations, further reduces the probability that it could process complex grammatical structures. These deficits are seen, as described, on nonlinguistic tasks, but there is probably no stimulus that places as great a demand on the cognitive operations so deficient in the right hemisphere, as does a sentence such as *Had the man the boy loved been, if not loving, then at least kind, it is likely that the murder would not have been committed.*

It is relevant to recall that the presence of syntax in ape language is almost entirely restricted to those language systems in which a concrete, temporally persistent "word" is available to the animal. While orderings of words are not entirely random in Nim's language, his productions are very deviant from anything seen in a young child. Premack (personal communication) also reports that, though in many cognitive tasks chimpanzees can equal a 5-year-old child, they are almost totally deficient at discriminating temporal patterns having no spatially persistent referents, and perform at levels worse than a normal 2-year-old on such tasks. Efron (1963a, b) and Reid (1979) have found that the language hemisphere is dominant for and superior in temporal pattern discrimination.

It is easy to understand how the cognitive properties of the right hemisphere place such severe limits on syntax and on the understanding of abstract words that cannot be projected into a concrete, spatial domain, but the properties discussed do not explain why the right hemisphere cannot speak. Though its expressions might be limited to two or three word utterances like Nim's, and though its vocabulary would be expected to be childish, at least some minimal expressive oral language should be present, particularly under test conditions that place strong demands for it. If the sole limitations of the right hemisphere are the cognitive ones discussed, then to the extent that Nim can speak with gestures, the right hemisphere should be able to communicate orally. The fact that neither apes nor right hemispheres generate speech, strongly suggests that the human left hemisphere is uniquely capable of a language-specific process, the presence of which is generally requisite for speech generation.

A MISSING PROCESS IN
THE RIGHT HEMISPHERE

The ability to perceive, appreciate, and understand a musical composition, a painting, or a scientific discovery does not imply an ability to produce it. Capacities for apprehension are much more general than capacities for construction, and, similarly, the understanding of speech implies no ability at oral expression. The very fact that pure expressive aphasias exist, with comprehension being basically intact, demonstrates that processes additional to those needed for comprehension are required for expression. It could, of course, be hypothesized that a pure expressive aphasia results from a paralysis of the vocal apparatus, but, in fact, the symptoms of aphasia are very different from those of a motor defect and the vocal system is not paralyzed. The expressive deficit clearly derives from disruption of higher level cognitive systems nonexistent in the right hemisphere.

Since expressive aphasics and the right hemisphere of split-brain patients comprehend the meaning of words and sentences, it is unlikely that the semantic system could be disrupted. Indeed, though Levy and Trevarthen (1977) found that the left hemisphere takes control of responding when a split-brain patient is required to select a picture corresponding to a written word, the right hemisphere is perfectly capable of performing the task if information is restricted to the right hemisphere. Levy (1970) had also found that the right hemisphere cannot only easily select orally named objects, but also objects which are conceptually related to a spoken word (e.g., a toy spider in response to the word *scary*). The right hemisphere can, in addition, indicate its agreement or disagreement by a nod or head shake, that a word spoken by the experimenter describes a picture shown to it. Thus the right hemisphere is quite competent at the semantic decoding of spoken or written words.

The question that Levy and Trevarthen (1977) addressed was whether the right hemisphere could construct the sound of a word describing some object, in the absence of any requirement to articulate it. They reasoned that if the right hemisphere is unable to generate a phonetic image, it could not normally generate the articulations to produce it.

Two pictures of objects were shown simultaneously to the two hemispheres, and patients were first required to select a matching picture from among a set in free vision. On almost all trials patients matched the picture seen by the right hemisphere. When required to name the picture, they named the picture seen by the left hemisphere. If pictures were shown solely to the right hemisphere, patients could, as mentioned, accurately indicate agreement or disagreement that an object name spoken by the experimenter described the picture seen. These preliminary tests demonstrated that the right hemisphere could see and remember a picture it was shown, and could recognize whether a spoken word accurately described it. Thus the right hemisphere knows, for example, what a bee looks like and knows that the spoken word *bee* accurately describes a picture of one, while the word *toes*, for example, does not. Earlier tests (Levy, 1970) even indicated that it probably knows that a bee and a wasp share certain categorical characteristics.

In the phonetic test, patients were shown the same pairs of objects, one to each hemisphere, for which the right hemisphere had typically selected a match. However, they were now required, *not* to select a matching picture, but rather a picture of an object whose name rhymes with that of the picture seen. Thus, if a bee is seen, a picture of a key was to be selected. There were three stimulus pictures, arranged in all six permuta-

tions of pairs, consisting of a bee, a rose, and an eye. The choice pictures
were a key, toes, and a pie. Rhyming matches were made by the left
hemisphere.

Next, a single stimulus picture was projected entirely to the right hemisphere, the left hemisphere seeing nothing. Choices of a rhyming match
by the right hemisphere were completely random, with no indication that
rhyming could be performed at all. Finally, stimulus pictures were again
projected solely to the right hemisphere, with the experimenter asking,
"Does it rhyme with (the name of a choice picture)?" Whereas patients
had been perfectly capable of indicating yes or no accurately if the question was "Is it the (name of a stimulus picture)?" their responses to the
rhyming question were completely random. It was as if a spoken picture
name gave rise to an image of the appropriate picture directly, bypassing
any phonetic analysis of the word. Spoken words, it appeared, were
treated as acoustic Gestalts whose phonetic components were unanalyzed
and unknown.

Work by Zaidel (1976b) showed that the right hemisphere, upon hearing a nonsense syllable, could not select its written representative, though
if a real word were spoken, it could easily select the correct written form.
Similarly, Marin, Saffran, and Schwartz (1976) have described an aphasic
patient who has an estimated reading vocabulary of 20,000 words, being
able to understand the meaning of such words as *chrysanthemum,* but
being totally unable to recognize the meaning of phonetically spelled
words such as *klok.* When asked to select from a list all words that rhyme
with a written stimulus such as *rat,* this patient selects not only *mat, hat,
bat, cat,* etc., but also *oat!* Her "rhyming," apparently, is entirely based
on similarity of graphological patterns.

These various observations strongly suggest that the right hemisphere
is almost totally lacking in phonetic analyzers, and that while it can decode
sound to meaning, it cannot generate the phonetic image of a concept it
possesses. Though it is recognized that young children often cannot consciously access the phonetic components of the words they speak, and that
the deficits described are specifically deficits in the conscious accessing of
phonetic components of words, given the almost total expressive aphasia
of the right hemisphere, it is likely that the neurological components for
the generation of sounds of words are also missing.

In cases of infantile left hemispherectomy, it is conceivable that the right
hemisphere relies on wholistic word generation, also bypassing phonetic
construction. The fact that certain aphasics can produce clichéd expressions, well-learned children's verses, and standardized curses (*god-
damnit*), without being able to produce less fixed expressions, suggests
that speech generation can be based on articulatory Gestalts. Unless the
left hemisphere has been nonfunctional or missing from early childhood,
however, the range of expressions that could be produced by this mecha-

nism would be extremely limited. With a functional left hemisphere there is little pressure for the right hemisphere to learn speech, particularly if that speech must rely on nonphonetic articulatory constructions directly elicited by concepts, in the absence of a phonetic analyzer and a phoneme-to-articuleme translator.

Word comprehension by the right hemisphere, on the other hand, would be expected to occur automatically via the same sound–meaning associative mechanisms applied to nonverbal sounds. Vocalizations in apes are restricted to a small, finite set, much as is the set of clichéd expressions of an aphasic. The processes by which apes produce their vocalizations, aphasics, their clichés, or the right hemispheres, its occasional word, would be expected to be quite restricted in productive capacity. Just as is a written language that is based on ideograms far more confined with respect to the size of reading vocabularies acquired by its readers, than is a language based on an alphabet, so would speech that is dependent on articulatory Gestalts be much reduced compared to that based on phonetic construction.

In sum, it is being suggested that the almost total absence of spoken language by apes or the right hemisphere results from the absence of processes capable of phonetic analysis and phonetic imaging. Such processes, in turn, may depend on a system capable of ordering events in time when those events have no persistent spatial referents, and this system itself may be unique to the human left hemisphere.

SUMMARY

Observations from many sources can leave little doubt that the human right hemisphere and at least some nonhuman mammals can discriminate spoken words and associate those words with meaning. The three basic deficiencies seen in the language systems of apes and in the human right hemisphere are (a) a cognitive deficit and cognitive orientation that limit the level of abstraction of concepts which can be acquired; (b) a syntactical deficit that limits the complexity of grammatical structures which can be decoded and expressed, particularly when the words of the language have no persistent spatial referents; and (c) an almost total incapacity for phonetic analysis. It is suggested that, even in the face of these deficits, by the application of special strategies, a limited amount of "language" can be understood and expressed, the level of performance being dependent on the complexity and number of transformations necessary from real world referents to a concept, on the necessity of keeping time-ordered relationships in memory, and on the dependence of performance on phonetic analysis and imaging. The power of normal human language is attributed to special cognitive processes, unique to the human left hemisphere, that are capable of generating concepts many steps distal from real-world events, encoded in the form of abstract symbols having no analogical relation with the relations they represent, that orders events into a temporal dimension and that can reorder events in that dimension in accordance with complex relational rules, and that can decompose and compose phonetic elements, in appropriate temporal order, to understand or generate spoken words. Whether it is correct to attribute language to the right hemisphere or to apes depends on whether the special processes of the human left hemisphere are taken to be the defining characteristics of language. If they are, then regardless of the comprehensive and expressive abilities of the right hemisphere or of apes, these abilities would be recognized as deriving from quite different strategies from those utilized in normal human language, and would not be reflective of a true language system. If, on the other hand, language is defined, not by the mechanisms whereby it is comprehended or generated, but rather by its performance characteristics, then the human right hemisphere, apes, and perhaps other mammals, could be legitimately said to have language.

ACKNOWLEDGMENTS

This chapter was supported from NSF grant BNS75-23061.

REFERENCES

Bogen, J. E. The other side of the brain II: An appositional mind. *Bulletin of the Los Angeles Neurological Society*, 1969, *34*, 135–362.

Broca, P. Remarques sur le siege de la faculté du langage articulé suives d'une observation d'aphemie. *Bulletin Societie Anatomique, Paris*, 1861, *6*, 330–357.

Cutting, J. and Rosner, B. Categories and boundaries in speech and music. *Perception and Psychophysics*, 1974, *16*, 564–571.

Dax, M. Lésions de la moitié gauche de l'encéphale coïncident avec l'oubli des signes de la pensée (read at Monpellier in 1836). *Gazette Hebdomadaire de Médecine et de Chirurgie*, 1865, 2 (2ème serie), 2.

Day, J. Right hemisphere language processing in normal right handers. Unpublished Doctoral dissertation, Dalhousie University, 1977.

Dennis, M. and Kohn, B. Comprehension of syntax in infantile hemiplegics after cerebral decortication: Left hemisphere superiority. *Brain and Language*, 1975, *2*, 472–482.

Efron, R. Temporal perception, aphasia and déjà vu. *Brain*, 1963a, *86*, 403–424.

Efron, R. The effect of handedness on the perception of simultaneity and temporal order. *Brain*, 1963b, *86*, 261–283.

Eimas, P. D., Siqueland, E. R., Juszyck, P., and Vigorito, J. Speech perception in infants. *Science*, 1971, *171*, 303–306.

Fouts, R. Acquisition and testing of gestural signs in four young chimpanzees. *Science*, 1973, *180*, 978–980.

Geschwind, N. and Levitsky, W. Human brain: Left–right asymmetries in temporal speech region. *Science*, 1968, *161*, 186–187.

Hamilton, C. R. Investigations of perceptual and mnemonic lateralization in monkeys. In S. Harnad, R. W. Doty, L. Goldstein, J. Jaynes, and G. Krauthamer (Eds.), *Lateralization in the nervous system.* New York: Academic Press, 1977.

Hécaen, H. Aphasic, apraxic and agnostic syndromes in right and left hemisphere lesions. In P. J. Vinken and G. W. Bruyn (Eds.), *Handbook of clinical neurology,* Vol. IV. Amsterdam: North-Holland Publishing, 1969.

Jusczyk, P., Rosner, B., Cutting, J., Foard, C., and Smith, L. Categorical perception of nonspeech sounds by two-month old infants. *Perception and Psychophysics,* 1977, *21,* 50–54.

Kuhl, P. and Miller, J. D. Discrimination of speech sounds by the chinchilla: /t/ vs /d/ in CV syllables. *Journal of the Acoustical Society of America,* 1974, *56,* S42 (abstract).

Kuhl, P. and Miller, J. D. Speech perception by the chinchilla: Phonetic boundaries for synthetic VOT stimuli. *Journal of the Acoustical Society of America,* 1975, *57,* S49(A).

LeMay, M. Morphological cerebral asymmetries of modern man, fossil man, and nonhuman primate. In S. Harnad, H. Steklis, and J. Lancaster (Eds.), *Origins and evolution of language and speech,* Vol. 280 of the *Annals of the New York Academy of Sciences.* The New York Academy of Sciences, 1976.

LeMay, M. and Culebras, A. Human brain–morphologic differences in the hemispheres demonstrable by carotid arteriography. *New England Journal of Medicine,* 1972, *287,* 168–170.

Levy, J. Information processing and higher psychological functions in the disconnected hemispheres of commissurotomy patients. Unpublished Doctoral dissertation, California Institute of Technology, 1970.

Levy, J. Psychobiological implications of bilateral asymmetry. In S. Dimond and J. G. Beaumont (Eds.), *Hemispheric function in the human brain.* New York: Halstead Press, 1974.

Levy, J., and Reid, M. Variations in cerebral organization as a function of handedness, hand posture in writing, and sex. *Journal of Experimental Psychology: General.* 1978, *107,* 119–144.

Levy, J. and Trevarthen, C. Metacontrol of hemispheric function in human split-brain patients. *Journal of Experimental Psychology: Human Perception and Performance,* 1976, *2,* 299–312.

Levy, J. and Trevarthen, C. Perceptual, semantic, and phonetic aspects of elementary language processes in split-brain patients. *Brain,* 1977, *100,* 105–118.

Levy, J., Trevarthen, C., and Sperry, R. W. Perception of bilateral chimeric figures following hemispheric deconnection. *Brain,* 1972, *95,* 61–78.

Lieberman, P. *On the origins of language: An introduction to the evolution of human speech.* New York: Macmillan, 1975.

Marin, O., Saffran, E., and Schwartz, M. Dissociations of language in aphasia: Implications for normal function. In S. Harnad, H. Steklis, and J. Lancaster (Eds.), *Origins and evolution of language and speech,* Vol. 280 of the *Annals of the New York Academy of Sciences.* New York Academy of Sciences, New York, 1976.

Morse, P. A. Speech perception in the human infant and rhesus monkey. In S. Harnad, H. Steklis, and J. Lancaster (Eds.), *Origins and evolution of language and speech,* Vol. 280 of the *Annals of the New York Academy of Sciences.* The New York Academy of Sciences, New York, 1976.

Premack, D. Language in chimpanzee? *Science,* 1971, *172,* 808–822.

Reid, M. Cerebral lateralization in children: An ontogenetic and organismic analysis. Unpublished Doctoral dissertation, University of Colorado, 1979.

Rubens, A. B. Anatomical asymmetries of the human cerebral cortex. In S. Harnad, R. W. Doty, L. Goldstein, J. Jaynes, and G. Krauthamer (Eds.), *Lateralization in the nervous system.* Academic Press, New York, 1977.

Rumbaugh, D. (Ed.). *Language learning by a chimpanzee: The Lana Project.* New York: Academic Press, 1977.

Sperry, R. W. Lateral specialization in the surgically separated hemispheres. In F. O. Schmitt and R. G. Worden (Eds.), *The neurosciences third study program.* Cambridge, Massachusetts: The M.I.T Press, 1974.

Sperry, R. W., Gazzaniga, M. S., and Bogen, J. E. Interhemispheric relationships: The neocortical commissures; syndromes of hemisphere disconnection. In P. J. Vinken and G. W. Bruyn (Eds.), *Handbook of clinical neurology.* Vol. IV. Amsterdam: North-Holland Publishing, 1969.

Terrace, H. and Bever, T. What might be learned from studying language in the chimpanzee? The importance of symbolizing oneself. In S. Harnad, H. Steklis, and J. Lancaster (Eds.), *Origins and evolution of language and speech,* Vol. 280 of the *Annals of the New York Academy of Sciences.* New York Academy of Sciences, New York, 1976.

Terrace, H., Petitto, L., and Bever, T. Project Nim: Progress Report II. Unpublished manuscript, 1976.

Wada, J. A., Clarke, R., and Hamm, A. Cerebral hemispheric asymmetry in humans: Cortical speech zones in 100 adult and 100 infant brains. *Archives of Neurology,* 1975, *32,* 239–246.

Warren, J. M. and Nonneman, A. J. The search for cerebral dominance in monkeys. In S. Harnad, H. Steklis, and J. Lancaster (Eds.), *Origins and evolution of language and speech,* Vol. 280 of the *Annals of the New York Academy of Sciences.* The New York Academy of Sciences, New York, 1976.

Wernicke, C. *Der aphasische Symptomen Komplex.* Breslaw, Poland: Cohn and Weigert, 1874.

Witelson, S. and Pallie, W. Left hemisphere specialization for language in the newborn: Neuroanatomical evidence of asymmetry. *Brain,* 1973, *96,* 641–647.

Yeni-Komshian, G. and Benson, D. A. Anatomical study of cerebral asymmetry in the temporal lobes of humans, chimpanzees and rhesus monkeys. *Science,* 1976, *192,* 387–389.

Zaidel, E. The case of the elusive right hemisphere. Paper presented at the 13th Annual Meeting of the Academy of Aphasia. Victoria, British Columbia, 1975.

Zaidel, E. Auditory vocabulary of the right hemisphere following brain bisection or hemidecortication. *Cortex,* 1976a, *12,* 191–211.

Zaidel, E. Language, dichotic listening, and the disconnected hemispheres. In D. Walter, L. Rogers, and J. Finzi-Fried (Eds.), *Conference on human brain function.* Los Angeles: Brain Information Service/BRI Publications Office, UCLA, 1976b.

Zaidel, E. Unilateral auditory language comprehension on the Token Test following cerebral commissurotomy and hemispherectomy. *Neuropsychologia,* 1977, *15,* 1–18.

V

SOCIOCULTURAL ASPECTS

17

Individual and Social Differences in Language Use

JOHN J. GUMPERZ and
DEBORAH TANNEN

Social differences in language are those features of an individual's speech behavior which are shared by significant numbers of others and play a role in the signaling of common identity. The usual method of demonstrating this sharedness has been to focus on groups previously delimited by nonlinguistic criteria such as residence, class, or ethnic background and to isolate phonological, syntactic, or semantic indices which show a systematic relationship to the macro-sociological variables that partition such groups. Sociolinguists have argued that to study the social functioning of language the traditional methods of linguistic analysis which rely on long-term in-depth hypothesis testing between investigator and key individual informants should be abandoned in favor of survey techniques where large numbers of informants reply to predetermined lines of questioning. The claim is that only statistical abstraction from a broad sample enables the investigator to transcend variation due to personality traits and momentary performance characteristics.

305

*Individual Differences in Language Ability and
Language Behavior*

Copyright © 1979 by Academic Press, Inc.
All rights of reproduction in any form reserved.
ISBN 0-12-255950-9

Survey approaches are very successful in characterizing language usage patterns of large populations and have made key contributions to the study of processes of change and diffusion, but they do not deal with the problem of social meaning, that is, the symbolic significance of alternate linguistic choices. Students of human interaction have long been aware that successful communication of any kind relies on shared symbolic systems which are learned through previous social interaction. It is through language that the sharedness of symbolic systems is recognized and signaled. That is, we rely on shared features of language both to assess what speakers are *doing* through talk and at the same time to make judgments about them. The basic question of how such micro-social evaluations relate to the macro-social characteristics of speech gleaned from statistical abstraction is as yet unresolved.

Furthermore, the correlation of linguistic variables with social variables has begun from the assumption that social groups are identifiable and known. This, however, is an issue much in dispute in the social sciences. That is, the question of what a social group or subgroup is has been very problematic, especially in urban areas, where much sociolinguistic work has focused. Secondly, the elicitation of valid information from large numbers of speakers is a vast problem, especially since it is crucial that responses truly reflect their habitual performance and knowledge rather than being an artifact of the interview situation. The more closely we study pragmatic meaning, the more disagreement arises about interpretation and appropriateness of utterances.

We would like to suggest a way of approaching the problems outlined which (a) avoids a priori identification of social groups, but rather builds on empirical evidence of conversational cooperation; and (b) extends the traditional linguistic method of in-depth hypothesis testing with key informants, to the process of conversational inference.

A key heuristic device in linguistic research has been the concept of "starredness." That is, to discover the grammatical rules of a language, the linguist compares acceptable and unacceptable sentences in order to make hypotheses about the knowledge that speakers rely on to derive meaning from words. To achieve an understanding of discourse strategies used in conversation, we have found it useful to compare what are in effect starred and unstarred discourse sequences. A starred sequence is one in which the smooth flow of conversation has been disturbed, or there is empirical evidence that a misunderstanding has occurred: Participants show signs of discomfort or annoyance, or otherwise give indications that communication has not been successful.

Our characterization of "unstarred," that is, successful communication, is derived from recent research on conversational cooperation by ethnomethodologists (Sacks, Schegloff, and Jefferson, 1974) and on conversational rhythm by students of nonverbal behavior (Erickson, 1975). This work has shown that successful communication requires subtle and complex coordination of such elements as turn-taking, gaze direction, and establishment of rhythm. Speakers learn to use these conventions in the course of socialization through repeated interaction in the home and in networks of social relationships. Thus, to the extent that successful communication is characterized by smooth speaker change, establishment and maintenance of conversational rhythm over significant stretches of discourse, use and recognition of formulaic routines, and cooperation in the production of identifiable lines of thematic progression, to that extent it evidences shared systems of communication strategies. By contrast, when communication exhibits choppy turn-taking, lack of shared rhythm, failure to recognize and participate in formulaic routines, and inability to establish coherent thematic progression, it therefore may at times reveal differing systems of conversational strategies.

Our unit of analysis is a set of conversational exchanges which is sufficiently complete to provide a basis for applying the criteria outlined above. Ideally, we look for brief, thematically self-contained sequences; that is, sequences which, although they may be part of a larger interaction or sequentially discontinuous, nonetheless have identifiable beginnings, middles, and ends. Given knowledge of the outcome, we can then hypothesize about what contributed to it by looking at internal evidence in the form of utterances and responses. We obtain independent confirmation of our hypotheses by asking first participants and then others (a) how they interpreted utterances in the interchange; and (b) what linguistic features led them to their interpretations. This procedure furnishes concrete evidence for hypotheses about the ways in which speakers expect meaning to be communicated.

Thus we confront the problem of the symbolic significance of linguistic variables by discovering how they operate in interaction and how they serve to signal the interpretation of what is being done by the communicative act. Our hypothesis is that any utterance can be understood in numerous ways, and that people make decisions about how to interpret any given utterance or gesture based on their definition of what is happening at the time of interaction. In other words, they define the interaction in terms of a "frame" which is identifiable and familiar. We call these socially significant units of interaction *activity types*. This concept corresponds to the notions of "frame" as used by cognitive anthropologists, and "schema" or "script" as used by others in psychology and artificial intelligence (Tannen, 1979). We prefer the term "activity type" in order to emphasize that, although it is a structured ordering of event sequences and represents the speakers' expectations about what will happen next, yet it is not a "template," that is a static structure, but rather a dynamic, active process which develops and changes as the participants interact. Moreover, its basis in meaning reflects something being *done*, some purpose or goal being pursued (much as Bartlett, 1932, who originated the concept of "schema" as an organizing principle in interpreting events, stated that he preferred the term "active developing patterns"). Thus the activity type does not determine meaning but simply constrains it by channeling interpretation so as to foreground certain aspects of background knowledge and to underplay others.

Our basic assumption is that this channeling of interpretation is effected by conversational inferences based on conventionalized cooccurrence expectations between content and features of surface style. That is, constellations of surface features such as prosody, phonology, lexical choice, turn-taking conventions, interjections, idiomatic or formulaic usages, and so on, are the means by which speakers signal and listeners interpret how semantic content is to be understood and how each sentence relates to what precedes or follows. We call these features "contextualization cues" (Gumperz, 1976, 1977). For the most part, they are habitually used and perceived but rarely consciously noted and almost never talked about directly. Therefore they must be studied in process and context rather than in the abstract. Habitual use of particular groups of these cues to communicate certain meaning and serve certain interactional goals makes up an individual's "conversational strategy." Thus, in our attempt to understand strategies we focus on the systematic use of cues in conversation and their effect on the interpretation of intent.

Our procedure involves

1. Playing a tape-recorded sequence of conversation to informants and then
2. Asking what a given portion of the discourse "means".
3. The informants are then asked what it was about the utterance in the conversation that led them to that interpretation.
4. They are then asked how it would have had to be said in order for a different interpretation to have been indicated.

Social boundaries can then be empirically determined, as a result of the data gathered, based on similarity of interpretations and agreement as to which aspects of the communication led to those interpretations. Systematic attention to certain linguistic and paralinguistic aspects of conversation then yields insight into the system of cuing meaning which is operating for people who agree on certain interpretations.

To demonstrate this procedure, we will present a number of natural conversation sequences. Our examples will be given in order of increasing divergence of communicative strategies. In each case we will identify the cues that are operating. At the end, we will distinguish between those that reflect individual differences as opposed to those that characterize differences in communicative and social background. Although misunderstandings, as our chosen linguistic site, is a correlate of the starred sentence, we are not interested in "right" and "wrong" interpretations, or even "appropriate" and "inappropriate" forms per se. Rather, by studying what has gone wrong when communication breaks down, we seek to understand a process that goes unnoticed when it is successful.

EXAMPLE 1: REGENT ST.

The following interchange took place during a telephone conversation between two friends, both educated professionals of East Coast urban backgrounds now living in California. A has called B on the telephone. B is in a university office.[1]

(1) A: *Come here for dinner.*
(2) B: *OK. But I can only bring what I can pay for by check or credit card.*
(3) A: *That's a flimsy excuse!*
(4) B: *I can get something at the Coop.*
(5) A: *But that's out of your way.*
(6) B: *I'll go to your Coop.*
(7) A: *Never mind. Just come.*
(8) B: *It'll just take me 10 minutes to walk to the parking structure, then I'll leave.*
(9) A: *Oh, you have the car? I thought you were walking.*
(10) B: *Yes, I have the car.*
(11) A: *It's 2222 Regent Street.*
(12) B: *WHAT'S 2222 Regent Street?*
(13) A: *C's house. That's where I am.*
(14) B: *Oh! I thought you were home.*

This is typical of misunderstandings which arise and are cleared up every day between friends and acquaintances. The trouble lay in different assumptions at the start of the conversation. When A said, *Come here for dinner,* he was assuming that *here* referred to C's house. Since this was not made overt, B was free to assume differently, that *here* referred to A's house. Both interpretations are reasonable, given each person's perspective.

As the conversation proceeded, both parties had difficulty maintaining their lines of reasoning. When B offered to buy something at the Coop supermarket, A was confused because he knew that this was not on her way to C's house. Therefore he said (5). As a result B also became confused, because she knew that the Coop was on her way to A's house. At this point both parties were aware that something was wrong, yet neither questioned the assumptions they had made. For one thing, B thought that A might be suggesting she not bring anything because she had said (2).

[1]We are aware of the fact that situated interpretation of any utterance depends on prosody, that is, intonation and stress, and paralinguistic features such as loudness, rhythm, and pitch register. Our insights into interpretation derive in large part from studies of just these features. Our analysis of examples relies on a system of transcription which captures these conversational aspects of prosody and paralinguistics. This system has been discussed elsewhere (Gumperz and Herasimchuk, 1972; Gumperz, 1977). In the present paper, however, we will use only conventional spelling, employing capitalization as a rough indicator of emphatic stress where necessary.

Thus there was an unlikely but plausible explanation for A's odd comment. With (7), A dismissed the misunderstanding, and they agreed to let it go and move to a new topic.

The second sign of trouble came when B referred to her car. A was startled because he was only a few blocks away from where she was. He therefore stated in (9) that he expected B to walk. But B knew that A's house was not within walking distance. The misunderstanding had proceeded to a second level, where each one sensed the other was saying very strange things. Still, this interchange also went uncorrected. B's utterance of (10) was a signal that this issue would stand as it was too.

Their respective lines of interpretation became untenable, however, when A uttered (11). At this point, B had no idea whatever what A was talking about. Only then did she voice her bewilderment (12). In response, A stated what he had assumed was understood all along: That he was at C's house (13). B also stated what her erroneous assumption had been (14). This cleared up the misunderstanding.

This misunderstanding could be easily repaired, because the participants had made different choices between alternate interpretations which both could easily understand. It is interesting to see how much odd verbal behavior they were willing to put up with, before they talked about what was wrong. Rather than question their assumptions, they tried to twist the other's strange comments into a meaning that made sense. Only when this was no longer possible, did they make their assumptions overt and have the chance to see what had gone wrong. The explanation about where *here* referred to in (1) satisfied both parties, and the misunderstanding was over. In this example, there is no detectable difference in signaling systems; the problem lies in the inherent ambiguity of deictic words.

EXAMPLE 2: YOGURT DRESSING

Other misunderstandings, however, are not attributable to simple semantic ambiguity. Consider, for example, the following interchange which took place between two close friends, both East Coast urban professional men living in California. In this example, the participants were of different religious and ethnic backgrounds. A was preparing dinner.

(15) A: *What kind of salad dressing should I make?*
(16) B: *Oil and vinegar of course.*
(17) A: *What do you mean "of course"?*
(18) B: *Well, I always make oil and vinegar, but if you want we could try something else.*
(19) A: *Does that mean you don't like it when I make other dressings?*

(20) B: *No. I like it. Go ahead. Make something else.*
(21) A: *Not if you want oil and vinegar.*
(22) B: *I don't. Make a yogurt dressing.*
(23) A: *mm.*

(A prepares yogurt dressing, tastes it, and makes a face).

(24) B: *Isn't it good?*
(25) A: *I don't like yogurt dressing.*
(26) B: *Well if you don't like it, throw it out.*
(27) A: *Never mind.*
(28) B: *What never mind? It's just a little yogurt!*
(29) A: *You're making a big deal about nothing!*
(30) B: *YOU are!*

This misunderstanding ended in frustration and anger for both participants. Whereas in Example 1 the two participants made different assumptions about the referent of the deictic *here*, in Example 2, A and B had different ways of using directness and indirectness strategies. Therefore their efforts to repair the miscommunication only led to further misunderstandings of each other's intent. Of course this interchange, like all human encounters, did not occur in isolation but was influenced by both participants' moods, their previous experience with each other and with others that day and, in some sense, every day of their lives; a myriad of social and emotional factors bear upon every interchange. Nonetheless, what we want to look at is the form that the interaction takes, regardless of what emotional and other pressures led to it.

The first sign of trouble occurred when B said *of course* in (16). A indicated he not understand what this "meant," that is, what B intended to convey. However, when A asked for clarification, things did not get cleared up at all. B attempted in (18) to explain what he had meant by *of course* in (16): an ironic comment on his own habitual eating patterns, and he tried to make it clear that it was fine with him if A made another kind of dressing.

Not every speaker of English will recognize (16) as ironic. However, this interpretation is possible for many, especially those familiar with New York style. This is an example of a situation in which the analyst can reconstruct what seems like a plausible interpretation and then check it with participants. In the case of Example 2, Speaker B readily identified that (16) was an ironic response. As always, the interpretation is inextricably bound to the precise way in which the phrase was uttered, but the ironic inflection and its interpretation are meaningful only to those familiar with its symbolic significance. The very fact that such an interpretation is obvious to some and inconceivable to others is the kind of evidence we are concerned with in the present study.

To continue with our analysis: A did not (perhaps was unable to) understand *of course* as ironic; he thought it indicated that B perferred oil and vinegar. At this point, B began to realize that A did not understand his intentions. He tried to convince A that he should feel free to make something else (20). Note that (20) constitutes an intensification of the direct strategy B had used in (18). Now his direct statement has become an imperative: *Make something else.*

A, however, was still operating under his initial assumption that *oil and vinegar* expressed B's preference. Therefore he felt B was now veiling that preference in order to avoid hurting A's feelings. In a manner suggestive of what Bateson (1972) calls "complementary schismogenesis," A became more insistent on not making a different dressing (21). To make it abundantly clear that this was not his preference in fact, B "suggested" that A make a yogurt dressing, as proof of B's good faith. He intended *yogurt dressing* to stand for "something other than oil and vinegar." A however took (22) as another order; he understood *yogurt dressing* as representing "yogurt dressing." In the face of what he perceived as a demand from B, he did not voice the fact that he did not like that type of dressing.

A was now annoyed at B for telling him to make a kind of dressing A did not like. A had shown utmost consideration for B's preferences, and now B was being selfish and inconsiderate, from A's point of view. Only when A made a face after tasting the dressing did B learn that he did not like it. He then told him (26). This was even more confusing to A. First B ordered him to prepare it; then he ordered him to throw it out. Inferring that B was being capricious and domineering, A resisted complying. B saw that A had inexplicably refrained from telling the obviously relevant information about his not liking yogurt dressing and, furthermore, had stubbornly refused to rectify the situation by throwing it out. Both ended up thinking the other irrational, stubborn, difficult, and unwilling to cooperate.

B's strategy was based on the expectation that A would state his preferences without being asked. Furthermore, he expected A to take literally B's attempt to go "on record," in Brown and Levinson's (1977) sense, by lexicalizing his intent, once a misunderstanding had arisen over his use of *of course*. A continued to operate on a strategy that assumed that a preference once stated had to be honored, and therefore B would not directly state his preferences, even when pushed (see Tannen, 1975, for numerous examples and discussion of miscommunication due to directness–indirectness differences).

Although our line of argumentation may at times have the ring of literary exegesis, we do not intend our analysis to be a running account of what the text "means," but rather to suggest plausible paraphrases which make clear the operation of differing strategies and to show the signaling devices which may underlie the participants' interpretations of each other's utterances.

Applying our method of recovering expectations by subsequent questioning, we asked A what he had expected in response to (15). He told us, "Oh, something like 'Make whatever you like' or 'How about something creamy?' " In other words, he expected a kind of negotiation in which both would indirectly express preferences until a decision was reached. He did not expect to be told what to make. Therefore B's answer, *oil and vinegar*, was unexpected and A could not "understand" it. B, on the other hand, said he did not intend his response (16) as a demand. It was his ironic way of saying "Make whatever you like." B reiterated his incredulity that A did not express his dislike for yogurt dressing.

Patterns of signaling indirectness are habitual styles of communication or communication strategies, which, while they are matters of individual choice, are nonetheless influenced by family and regional background. Usages such as *of course* in the preceding example are acquired while growing up and through peer group interaction. Perhaps it is significant that A in the above example is from Boston, while B is from New York City, and that A is Catholic and B is Jewish. However, the relationship between background and habitual strategies has yet to be determined.

EXAMPLE 3: PARTY

In the above example, the fact that something was wrong was clear to both participants, to the extent that both felt frustrated and dissatisfied with the other's behavior. There are many instances, however, when both people think they correctly understood each other and that their communication was effective, but in fact their interpretations of what took place are quite different. In Tannen (1975) the following interchange between a husband and wife is reported:

(31) A: *John's having a party. Wanna go?*
(32) B: *OK.*
(33) A: (Later) *Are you sure you wanna go?*
(34) B: *OK. Let's not go. I'm tired anyway.*

At the end of this interchange, the couple did not go to the party, and both felt satisfied. However, each one thought that not going was a favor to the other. Although the participants agreed on what was being done—deciding whether to go to the party—they differed about how they expected that activity to be carried out interactionally. Perhaps A intended the opener (31), much as A in the yogurt dressing example intended his initial question, that is, the initiation of an exchange in the course of which they would jointly arrive at a decision based on preferences which would be indirectly expressed. B, however, interpreted question (31) as indicating that A wanted to go. Therefore, he agreed to do what she wanted and said *OK*.

Perhaps A was uncomfortable because the type of negotiation she had expected never took place. She asked if B was sure (33). B took her bringing it up again as an indication that she did not want to go. Therefore he agreed not to go, for her sake. Furthermore, he wanted her to feel comfortable about his giving in to her, so he said that he was *tired anyway*. A, however, now had even more evidence that he was telling her what he really wanted. That is, he was tired. In fact there are possible indications in *OK* and *anyway* that B is acquiescing; however, as has been seen in the other examples, people rarely question the indirect contextualization strategies that the other is using. They make an interpretation and stick to it and will ignore considerable discrepancies between their expectations and the other's behavior, unless and until those discrepancies become so extreme that they can no longer be integrated into participants' lines of reasoning.

EXAMPLE 4: WHO'S THE ARTIST?

In the preceding examples, the people communicating (or failing to) came from what ordinarily would be considered similar class or cultural backgrounds. When people from more obviously divergent backgrounds communicate, misunderstandings have similar effects, but their linguistic bases can be quite different.

When a house painter arrived at the home of a middle class couple in California, he was taken around the house to survey the job he was about to perform. When he entered a spacious living room area with numerous framed original paintings on the walls, he asked in a friendly way, "Who's the ARtist?" The wife, who was British, replied, "The painter's not too well-known. He's a modern London painter named—." The housepainter, looking puzzled, said, "I was wondering if someone in the family was an artist."

In this sequence, the misunderstanding did not have significant consequences. First of all, it was part of a casual encounter between strangers which was not expected to result in any action. Furthermore, the speakers were aware of the dissimilarity in backgrounds because of the differences in their "accents."

"Who's the ARtist?" is a formulaic comment that fits a paradigm often uttered by Americans being escorted around a house. That is, one might just as well say, "Who's the COOK?" on seeing a panoply of kitchen utensils on a pegboard, or "Who's the GARdener?" on looking out the window and seeing rows of tilled earth with seed packages on sticks in the ground. Such formulae often are a conventionalized way of fulfilling the expectation that a complimentary comment be made upon seeing some-one's house for the first time. The compliment in the formulaic paradigm generally initiates a routine in which the addressee indirectly acknowl-edges the indirect compliment by saying, for example, "It's just a hobby," or "I'm just a fan," or making some other self-deprecatory remark, in response to which the compliment is reasserted: "But they're really very good." The British wife in the above example was not familiar with this paradigm and its attendant routine, and therefore took the housepainter's question to reflect an objective interest in the art work. The questioner's puzzled look after her response was an indication that his question had not been understood as intended.

In recent years, linguists have come to recognize that, as Fillmore (1976) puts it, "an enormously large amount of natural language is formulaic, automatic, and rehearsed, rather than propositional, creative, or freely generated [p. 9]." As sociolinguists, we want to know how the formulaic nature of utterances is signaled. In the example given here, there are both extralinguistic and linguistic cues. The extralinguistic signals lie in the setting and the participants' knowledge of what preceded the interaction. There are at least three linguistic signals: first, the semantic content; second, the syntactic paradigm; and third, the contextualization cues such as prosody (for example, the stress and high pitch on the first syllable of "ARtist," and its marked high falling intonation). The contextualization cues here alert the listener to the possibility of a formulaic interpretation, even if the specific utterance has never been heard before. Formulaic use of language is always a problem for non-native speakers or visitors to a foreign country. It is perhaps even more of a danger, however, between people who ostensibly speak the same language but come from different social or regional backgrounds. Since they assume that they understand each other, they are less likely to question interpretations.

EXAMPLE 5: HOW'S THE FAMILY?

The following conversation is reported in Gumperz (1976). A student, B, has called a faculty member, A, on the telephone.

(35)   A: *Hello.*
(36)   B: *How's the family?*
(37)   A: *Fine.*
(38)   B: *I'll get back to you next month about that thing.*
(39)   A: *That's OK. I can wait.*
(40)   B: *I'm finished with that paper. It's being typed.*
(41)   A: *Come to the office and we'll talk about it.*

When A later refused to give B a grade without seeing the typed paper, B was annoyed, saying A was being inconsistent. B believed A had agreed to give him special consideration.

In this interchange, it had seemed strange to A that B did not begin with a greeting ("Hi") and self-identification ("This is . . ."). Whenever verbal behavior seems strange, it may be a clue that a different strategy is being used. Again, we asked participants and others to comment on the interchange. While many simply called the omission of a greeting "odd," others identified it as semantically significant. They suggested that B was using the omission to establish familiarity, and that he therefore might be asking for a favor. All these commentators were Black or had had a great deal of close social contact with Blacks. Many also spontaneously recalled personal encounters where the same technique had been used with different words for similar purposes.

A's failure to recognize the routine led to the misunderstanding. When the student and other Black informants were asked how the professor could have signaled unwillingness to give B special consideration, they said he would in that case not have answered the question, "How's the family?" Instead, he would have responded with another question, such as, "What do you want?"

In this example, it is clear that the formulaic omission of a greeting is ethnically specific; only those people familiar with urban Black culture recognize the routine. One might ask why someone would use an ethnically specific routine in an interaction with others who are not members of that "group." The fact that they do is evidence of the automatic nature of linguistic strategies. Whether or not the strategies are limited to certain groups is a matter for posthoc analysis, of which the present study is a first step.

Although the professor failed to recognize the verbal routine, his response, on the surface, was entirely appropriate, and conversation proceeded. In some cases, however, lack of familiarity with conventionalized rhetorical devices and consequent failure to recognize cues associated with them can lead to obstruction of conversational flow. This can be seen in the following example.

EXAMPLE 6: THE FINGERS OF THE HAND

Five graduate students of varying backgrounds were videotaped discussing a first-year graduate course. A difference of opinion had developed concerning the need for the course to integrate various approaches to anthropology. One of two male students in the group argued that, given the complexity of research in the field, such integration was no longer possible. Three women students, on the other hand, maintained that the connection still existed and therefore should be brought out. One of these women attempted to summarize their line of argument. Notice when she was interrupted by her friend:

(42)   A: *It's like all parts of the hand. The fingers operate independently,*
      ⌐ *but they have the same . . .*
(43)   B: ⌊ *What I would like to say is . . .*

The videotape clearly shows that A was disconcerted by B's interruption. She turned suddenly to B and uttered an expression of frustration.

When the participants in this discussion viewed the tape, B insisted that she had agreed fully with what A had said, but she had thought A was finished, and therefore had taken a turn to talk. A asserted that she had been interrupted just when she had been about to make her point based on the simile she had introduced. It may be relevant to note at this point that A is Black, from an inner-city neighborhood in Northern California, and the extended simile she was using is recognized by those familiar with Black rhetoric as fitting a formulaic paradigm for summing up an argument or commenting on what someone had said.

Elsewhere in the same discussion, A made another statement which fits a formulaic paradigm: "You hear one thing, and you read another." One indication of the formulaic nature of this expression lies in the fact that in in-group conversation only the first part of such a sequence is uttered; that is, one would say, "You hear one thing," or "It's like all parts of the hand," and stop at that, relying on the hearers' cultural knowledge to supply the rest. Our examples, however, arose in a mixed group session, and we see that A intended to complete the simile. Her intonation rose on *independently* (42), signaling that she was going to continue, and presumably any native speaker of American English would have known from this signal that she was not relinquishing the floor. While she has spoken English most of her life, B is from India. Studies we have made of in-group talk among speakers of Indian English have shown that prosodic and paralinguistic cues operate quite differently in Indian English (Gumperz *et al.*, 1978) and other varieties of English.

While different rhetorical strategies can lead to misunderstandings, cross-cultural differences, which consist of more generalized discrepancies in use of prosody and paralinguistic cues, can lead to the disruption of conversational rhythm and thematic progression. Throughout the videotaped discussion under consideration, B interrupted much more than the other participants, despite her subsequent assertion that she did not intend to do so; moreover, she was frequently interrupted by the others, who also later asserted that they had thought she was through.

EXAMPLE 7: A GIG

The following example, which took place after an ethnically mixed class, illustrates both the risks and the benefits derived from the use of shared conventions.

Student A approached his professor, B, who was surrounded by other Black and White students and said, "Could I talk to you for a minute? I'm gonna apply for a fellowship and I was wondering if you would give me a recommendation?" After the professor responded favorably, the student turned ever so slightly to take in the group as a whole and said, "Ahma git me a gig." (Rough gloss: 'I'm going to get myself some support.') Linguistically, this last sentence contrasted with the first. It represented a shift to Black phonology ("Ahma," "git," and the long [I] followed by an off-glide in [gI:g]). The prosody and tune also gave the sentence a singsong rhythm. Informants familiar with Black speech styles recognized this as a formulaic utterance. When asked to interpret it, they suggested that A's manner of saying this was a way of alluding to the dilemma often discussed among Blacks of having to get support from the establishment. The speaker was capitalizing on this shared system to justify his behavior in the eyes of his fellow-students, even though he was violating what some perceive as the constraint against using dialect in an academic setting. Many white informants, in fact, had difficulty interpreting A's remark. Unable to identify it as formulaic, they simply thought it was a lapse into the speaker's conversational style, and suggested that he was turning away from the rest of the group and addressing only the other Black students. In fact, this was not his "normal style" at all. Correct identification of the utterance as a formulaic routine depends on knowledge of a whole range of phonological and prosodic variables, as well as expectations about their cooccurrence.

EXAMPLE 8: I DON'T WANNA READ

In a taped elementary school classroom session, the teacher told a student to read aloud. The student responded, "I don't wanna read," using an intonation pattern marked by raised pitch on "I" and a drawn-out fall–rise on "read." The teacher got annoyed and said, "All right, then, sit down."

When this interchange was played to others, some said that the child was being uncooperative. Others said the child meant, "Push me a little and I'll read. I can do it, but I need to know that you really want me to." This latter group interpreted the child's statement, "I don't wanna read" in somewhat the same way as those judges who interpreted the wife's question in Example 3 ("Are you sure you want to go to the party?") as meaning that she would prefer not to go. The difference is, first, whereas

Whites generally opt for the "refusal" interpretation in the present example, Black informants generally favor the "encourage me" interpretation. Second, those who choose the latter interpretation agree that it is the child's rising intonation at the end of his sentence that led to their conclusion, and many of them furthermore volunteer the information that if the child had intended to refuse, he would have stressed "want." The two possible intonation contours, then, form a contrast set for a group of informants. On the other hand, the indirect interpretation of the wife's question in Example 3 was justified in numerous different ways by different speakers.

Just as the husband misunderstood his wife's intent and thought she was hinting that she didn't want to go, so the teacher in this example misunderstood the child's intent and thought he was refusing to read outright. She did not perceive the intonation as a significant signal; rather, she reacted to the semantic content alone and became annoyed.

The same pattern can be seen in many interchanges in which rising intonation is used in this way by speakers who employ this system. For example, note the following classroom interchange.

EXAMPLE 9: I DON'T KNOW

(44) T: *James, what does this word say?*
(45) J: *I don't know.*
(46) T: *Well, if you don't want to try someone else will. Freddy?*
(47) F: *Is that a "p" or a "b"?*
(48) T: (encouragingly) *It's a "p."*
(49) F: *pen.*

Sentence (45) was spoken with rising intonation, and therefore, in the child's system at least, implied, "I need some encouragement." The teacher missed this and thought James was refusing to try. The question in (47), in effect, had the same "meaning" (communicative function) as (45): "I need some encouragement." However, Freddy communicated his hesitance in a way the teacher expected, so she furnished that encouragement (48), and Freddy proceeded. Witnessing this interchange, James then "saw" that the teacher was willing to encourage Freddy but not him. He therefore may have logically concluded that she was "picking on him" or "prejudiced against him."

EXAMPLE 10: A BRIDGE

Our last example comes from the same discussion among graduate students as Example 9. At this point, the main topic has been the failure of

the course program to show the relationship between linguistic anthropology and social anthropology.

(50)   A: *But if you took a core that was designed by the linguistics
              department and one by the sociocultural, and both of them had
              Boas there would be some connection. Then why is it important
              in both areas? What's the difference? and I*

(51)   B: *Do you think it's because people in sociocultural sort of
              monopolize the field?*

(52)   C: *Wait a minute wait a minute*

(53)   A: *You pick what you need, you don't pick up the whole package.
              You pick out what YOU need. You don't need the whole box.*

(54)   D: *Both of them are justified. Anthropologists have their own
              emphasis, linguists have their own emphasis and . . . but ah
              there is no connection. What we need is a bridge ah . . .*

(55)   C: *Maybe the problem is that there is no faculty person that really
              has that oversight*

D finished a sentence and followed it by *ah* . . . . Then C took a turn to
speak. Speakers of American English do not see C's contribution as an
interruption. D, however, seemed annoyed at this point, and when viewing the tape afterward, he commented that he had been interrupted and
prevented from making his point. D, who is Indian, further stated that
this happened to him continually with Americans. Up until the time C
broke in (55), D had simply repeated what had been previously said. Later
on in the discussion, he did succeed in making his point, which was that,
to be successful, the course should be built on a common intellectual
foundation. He made it, however, only when an outsider intervened and
asked each participant to state his own opinion in turn.

An examination of D's use of prosody shows that the way he signaled
relationships between clauses in longer stretches of discourse differed
significantly from American conventions. D's second and third statements
in (54) were intended to contrast with each other; he was saying that
anthropologists and linguists have different emphases. Since he used the
same syntax and lexicon in both statements, the Americans would not
hear these as contrasting unless he differentiated them through prosody
(e.g., contrastive stress on *their*). D, however, used the same stress pattern
on both sentences. The Americans, using their own system, perceived this
as simply "listing." D's next two sentences were: *but there is no connection.
What we need is a bridge.* Here he put what sounds to Americans like
emphatic stress on *connection, we,* and *bridge.* Americans are therefore
likely to assume, as C did, that these two sentences represent D's main
point.

Our studies of other conversations in which all participants are of

Indian background reveal at least two rhetorical devices which operate differently from those typically used by Americans:

1. In making an argument, Indian speakers take great care to formulate the background for what they are going to say.
2. They use increased stress to signal that this is background information, then shift to low pitch and amplitude on their own contribution.

The strategy behind the cue is something like raising one's voice to get attention, then stating one's message in a low voice.

In our example, D apparently expected to be listened to attentively because he had used the repetition plus stress cues to set the stage for his contribution. Nonetheless, he was interrupted, since his American interlocutors did not share his system of signaling and therefore did not expect anything important to follow. The tragic outcome of such signaling differences lies in the judgments made by participants and observers about the intellectual quality of conversational contributions. As it stands, D's contribution sounds unoriginal, repetitive, and not logically connected. In fact, he never got to make his point at all.

CONCLUSION

All our examples involve mistaken judgments of others' conversational intent. Everywhere these misreadings were the result of different interpretations of verbal and nonverbal cues. The linguistic nature and interpretive effect of the cues, however, change progressively as the list proceeds.

In Example 1 (Regent St.), and to some extent in Example 2 (Yogurt dressing), the misunderstanding hinged on lexical interpretation. When commenting on Example 1, all informants could easily accept the possibility of both interpretations. The effect is like the changing focus of a camera lens or a picture that can be seen alternately one way or another. In contrast, when commenting on Example 2, some informants could easily accept both the literal and the ironic interpretations of *of course*, while to others the literal interpretation was the only plausible one. Furthermore, some informants understood *"How's the family?"* in Example 5 as the possible start of a certain kind of routine, and those same informants recognized that a negative statement spoken with rising intonation in response to situated requests such as those in Examples 8 and 9 can mean "I am pushable." Other respondents, on the other hand, could only see that a greeting had been oddly omitted in Example 5 and that the child was being uncooperative in Examples 8 and 9.

In the examples involving Indian speakers, moreover, the differences in use of contextualization cues operate on a more general level of interaction. They reflect prosodic and rhetorical signals which are directly attributable to differing language backgrounds and influence all aspects of individuals' speech. The differences profoundly affect their participation in conversation.

To recapitulate our discussion, our assumption has been that conversational inference is based on knowledge of (a) semantic content; and (b) habitual use and perception of surface cues which make up discourse strategies. The way these features combine to signal meaning is a matter of convention learned through previous interaction. We are returning, then, to Sapir's hypothesis that there is a direct relationship between the kind of individual cues used by speakers and the amount and kind of social interaction they have experienced. Note, moreover, that while the linguistic phenomena involved here are those studied by linguists, their communicative effect is felt at the level of conversational inference rather than the level of sentence meaning.

We suggest investigation of miscommunication as a way of recovering shared sociocultural knowledge used in conversation. In each case we ask, first, what one has to know to arrive at the interpretation made by participants or others and, second, at what level of language the signaling takes place. Our analysis yields a tentative hierarchy of signaling differences which corresponds to the subtle distinction between individual and social differences in language use.

We have found four levels of signaling differences:

1. Differing assumptions, leading to different ways of exploiting the inherent indeterminacy of verbal signals (Example 1)
2. Differences in broad strategies of operating within a shared system (e.g., types of indirectness) (Examples 2 and 3)
3. Differences in shared routines and formulaic paradigms signaled in similar ways (Examples 4, 6, 8, and 9)
4. Differences in basic contextualization conventions for signaling pragmatic salience (e.g., given and new), thematic progression, and expressiveness (Examples 6, 7, 10, and to a lesser extent 8 and 9)

The degree to which conversational cooperation is obstructed is a function of where in this hierarchy the differences occur. It is assumed that this is an implicational hierarchy, so that people with differences at Level (4) can be expected to have difference in Levels (1), (2), and (3) as well.

Level (4) differences correspond to the kinds of gross intercultural communication difficulties, as seen in Examples 6 and 10, when the Indian and American students were unable to judge when others had made their main points. Generally, in the case of Level (4) differences, ability to establish conversational rhythm, to effect smooth turntaking, to cooperate in the establishment of thematic progression, are severely impaired. Level

(3) is perhaps most typically the level of differences resulting from divergent ethnic backgrounds in modern urban societies. While miscommunications on all levels result in misunderstanding of the other's intent, conversational cooperation can still be maintained in Level (3) situations and therefore can lead to the even more disconcerting situation in which all participants erroneously believe that they have communicated successfully.

Examples 5 and 6 both contain instances in which people failed to recognize the other's use of a conventional routine. However, in the case of Example 5, (How's the Family?), where participants shared Level (4) cueing conventions, the professor was able to participate in the conversation in a way that had a semblance of cooperation. In Example 6 (The Fingers of the Hand), however, participants differed at Level (4), so the result was disruption of conversational rhythm in the form of interruptions. Someone who differed from the Black speaker on Level (3) and consequently failed to understand that a conventionalized simile was being invoked, might yet have realized that rising intonation indicated the speaker was not finished.

Our initial analysis focuses on specific conversations in context which generate hypotheses to be tested through further, more structured investigation. The crucial element of our method is that it studies interaction itself and gleans information about similarities and differences from a combination of direct observation of the data and intensive interviewing. The questioning of informants and participants about the sources of their interpretations furnishes a way to recover ordinarily unverbalized expectations.

Since responses to contextualization cues are automatic, and since talking about them (or "metacommunicating," to use Bateson's term) is almost never done, misunderstandings such as the ones discussed generally lead to conclusions not about the other perons's use of language but about his ability or intentions. This has been seen in all our examples.

To further complicate matters, inferences drawn from indirect interpretation of cues seem as "real" as those drawn from what is directly said. In retrospect, one often recalls as having been stated what at the time was inferred. Thus the husband and wife in Example 3 later had an argument in which one asserted, "We didn't go to the party because you didn't want to. You SAID you didn't want to go." The other countered "I did not. I said I wanted to. You said YOU didn't want to." To "say" something and to communicate it indirectly become merged in retrospect, both having "meaning" for the speaker and hearer in the same way.

This theory goes far to explain what has hitherto been labeled prejudice and clannishness—the tendency to feel more comfortable with those who share one's communicative system, and to perceive those people who communicate differently as having suspect intentions and negative personality traits. Thus the study of contextualization phenomena may give insight into how groups are formed, and how and why linguistic differences are maintained. Ultimately, and hopefully, these methods may, to paraphrase D in Example 10, build a bridge between macro-sociolinguistic measurement of linguistic variables and the psycholinguistic study of interpersonal relations.

ACKNOWLEDGMENTS

We are grateful to Jenny Cook-Gumperz for Example 3, and to her as well as Jane Falk, Paul Kay, and Michael Moerman for helpful comments on many points of our analysis. Adrian Bennett, Arpita Agrawal, Gurinder Aulakh, and Cheryl Seabrook assisted in the analysis of Examples 6 and 9. Thanks are also due to Walter Gorman and Karl Goldstein for supplying and repeatedly discussing Example 2. Work on this chapter was supported by NIMH Grant #MH26831-Gumperz.

REFERENCES

Bartlett, F. C. *Remembering*. Cambridge: Cambridge University Press, 1932. (Reprinted, 1977.)

Bateson, G. *Steps to an ecology of mind*. New York: Ballantine books, 1972.

Brown, P. and Levinson, S. Universals in language usage: Politeness phenomena. In E. Goody, (Ed.), *Questions and politeness: Strategies in interaction*. Cambridge: Cambridge University Press, 1977, 56–324.

Erickson, F. One function of proxemic shifts in face to face interaction. In A. Kendon, R. Harris, and K. Key (Eds.), *Organization of behavior in face to face interaction*. The Hague: Mouton, 1975.

Fillmore, C. The need for a frame semantics in linguistics. In *Statistical methods in linguistics*. Stockholm: Skriptor, 1976.

Gumperz, J. and Herasimchuk, E. The conversational analysis of social meaning. In M. Sanchez and B. Blount (Eds.), *Sociocultural dimensions of language use*. New York: Academic Press, 1975.

Gumperz, J. Language, communication and public negotiation. In P. Sanday (Ed.), *Anthropology and the public interest*. New York: Academic Press, 1976.

Gumperz, J. Sociocultural knowledge in conversational inference. In M. Saville-Troike (Ed.), *Twenty-eighth Annual Roundtable Monographs on Languages and Linguistics*. Washington D.C.: Georgetown University Press, 1977.

Gumperz, J. The conversational analysis of interethnic communication. In E. L. Ross, (Ed.), *Interethnic communication: Proceedings of the southern anthropological society*. University of Georgia Press. 1978.

Gumperz, J., Agrawal, A., Aulakh, G., and Bonte, R. Prosody in conversational inference, Manuscript, 1977b.

Sacks, H., Schegloff, E., and Jefferson, G. A simplest systematics for the organization of turn taking in conversation. *Language*, 1974, *50*, 696–735.

Tannen, D. Communication mix and mixup or how linguistics can ruin a marriage. *San Jose State Occasional Papers in Linguistics*, 1975.

Tannen, D. What's in a Frame? Surface evidence for underlying expectations. In R. Freedle (Ed.), *Discourse processes*, Vol. 2. *New Directions*. Norwood, New Jersey: Ablex, 1979.

18

Locating the Frontier Between Social and Psychological Factors in Linguistic Variation

W. LABOV

Over the past 15 years, our research on language in its social context has obtained records on the speech of approximately 4000 individuals. All but a few of these speakers have been analyzed as representatives of speech community. We have not been concerned with the uniform or invariant features of their speech, since there would be no need to conduct such wide-ranging studies to obtain that data: Our inquiries and measurements have concerned inherent variation in the vernacular and other speech styles. We have recorded data on stochastic processes, random events with stable probabilities whose outcome could not be predicted in any one case, but associated with stable probabilities.

In a first approximation to these processes, individual variation was treated as noise, and the signal-to-noise ratio has been gratifyingly high. The great majority of the variables we have dealt with have been socially determined elements of the linguistic system which individuals used to communicate socially recognized messages. The resultant array of average

327

Individual Differences in Language Ability and Language Behavior

Copyright © 1979 by Academic Press, Inc.
All rights of reproduction in any form reserved.
ISBN 0-12-255950-9

values was so regular that statisticians saw no need to apply tests of significance: Almost every individual follows the same patterns of style shifting, and internally conditioned controlled variation, and the data could be subdivided many times without any change in internal relations. Typical of these processes is the vocalization of postvocalic (r) in New York City (Labov, 1966) or Hillsboro, North Carolina (Levine and Crockett, 1966), negative concord in a variety of American dialects, or the deletion and aspiration of Spanish /s/ (Cedergren, 1973). In the most recent studies of consonant cluster simplification, 39 out of 40 Philadelphians show a remarkable, dialect-specific uniformity for the array of internal relations controlling this process.

In this type of analysis, individual cases often played a significant role. Some individual cases exemplified the basic process in an unusually revealing manner. The case of Everett Poole was archetypical of the process of local identification which determined the reversal of a sound change on Martha's Vineyard; he had left the island for a mainland university, but returned to take up a role as a leading entrepreneur on the docks of the archetypical rural community. His centralization of (ay) and (aw) was the most extreme (Labov, 1963).

In the study of the social stratification of language in New York City, individual cases also played a major role, and have often been cited in place of general charts or tables. Again, some individuals revealed the basic processes most clearly because the special nature of their social experience brought them into high relief. Molly S. was almost blind, and she and her daughter listened to the radio a great deal; they were especially sensitive to stigmatized dialect features in radio broadcasts. It was all the more revealing that she was not able to perceive the same variables in her own speech; she was a remarkable demonstration of the basic principle that the sharpest stigmatization of a social variable in the speech of others is characteristic of those who use that variable most in their own speech.

The case of Steve K. illustrated the obverse side of the same principle. Steve was an intense young man of 25 who had studied philosophy at Brooklyn College, but turned away from academic life as he adopted a strong Reichian view, seeking self-fulfillment in the awareness of his sexuality. He was unique among New Yorkers in his awareness of all five of our major linguistic variables. He believed that he had successfully reversed the pattern of style shifting towards the norms of careful speech and had returned to his earlier vernacular. Nevertheless, his array of stylistic shifting was almost identical with that of other New Yorkers.

For this variable (r), he showed a steadily increasing percentage of pronunciation of consonantal /r/ in postvocalic position as he moved from casual to careful to more formal styles. The variables (eh) and (oh) represent the degree of opening of the vowels of *last* and *lost*, respectively; as

Steve K.

	Style							
	Casual		Careful		Reading		Word list	Minimal pairs
(r)	00	→	06	→	08	→	38	→	100
(eh)	28	←	33	←	34		30	
(oh)	22	←	23	←	25	←	30	
(th)	09	→	00	→	00			
(dh)	15	→	06	→	05			

(r): Percentage of realization as /r/
(eh), (oh): Height of the vowels of *bad, lost*, etc. from 40 (lowest) to 10 (highest)
(th), (dh): Mean values of realization as fricatives ($\emptyset$), affricates (1), or stops (2) × 100

the stylistic context became more formal, Steve K.'s vowels became more open, correcting from the vernacular forms. The variables (th) and (dh) are the familiar alternation of standard fricative with nonstandard affricate and stop in *thing* and *this* respectively. As the context became more formal, his percentage of nonstandard forms dropped in exactly the same way as other speakers in the sample.

Steve K. believed that he had learned to pronounce all final *r*s in college, but that he had now returned to his vernacular pattern. But he showed the same style shifting as any other New Yorker, with steadily increasing percentage of consonantal *r* as the context became more formal. His case shows that a profound shift in social experience and ideology could not alter the socially determined pattern of linguistic variation.

Thus a number of studies of individuals served to reinforce our finding that the major social variables in language were strongly constrained by individual behavior, despite the conviction of many people that they had engaged in "individual enterprise" in language. There was a wide individual variation in placement on the use of the variables, but the individual's place in that spectrum reflected his early social experience, almost independent of his individual ideology or self-image.

Research on the Black English Vernacular in Harlem also showed considerable variation among individual speakers. The use of such linguistic rules as contraction and deletion of the copula, or consonant cluster simplification, was heavily determined by an individual's relation to the central peer group structures. Even within this relatively homogeneous group of adolescent speakers of the vernacular, it was possible to show subtle but regular patterns of variation that reflected the individual's distance from the central peer group on sociometric diagrams (Labov, 1973). One of the most remarkable demonstrations of this uniformity appeared to us in individual records of consonant cluster simplification

TABLE 18.1
Proportion of t, d Deletion in Clusters for 11 Members of the Jets in Single Interviews

	Monomorphemic (KD_{mm})		Past tense (KD_p)	
	Before consonant	Before vowel	Before consonant	Before vowel
Stanley	19/20	7/10	2/6	0/14
Rednall	25/26	5/9	2/5	0/3
Hop	18/21	4/9	5/7	1/3
Larry	36/38	2/8	5/9	0/25
Vaughn	35/42	4/11	4/12	1/16
Doug	28/30	4/8	1/3	0/3
Tyler	16/17	4/7	1/5	0/2
Its	9/15	1/1	1/4	0/3
Stevie	21/21	2/4	7/11	2/13
Turkey	11/13	0/1	3/3	2/13
Rip	11/12	1/2	2/7	1/8
Total:	229/255	34/70	33/72	7/103
%$-t,d$ Deletion:	90	49	46	07

among the Jets (Table 18.1). Here we see repeated regularity of the effects of morpheme boundary and a following consonant, even with less than five tokens in a cell. Two individuals vary from the norm of 90–95% simplification of monomorphemic clusters before a consonant: Vaughn and Its. Vaughn was thoroughly integrated into the peer group structure, but he was a recent transfer from another school where he had an outstanding academic record. He had consciously rejected that record in favor of peer group values, but his earlier social history still showed in his phonology and grammar. Its was a different and more puzzling case: He adopted the social role of a slow and stupid thinker, and he was the butt of many jokes. But several linguistic measures indicate his alignment to the rules of the more standard dialects that indicated a special capacity for drawing inferences about linguistic structures.

Though we did not penetrate further into the case of Its, we suspect that here we have reached the limits of the social determination of linguistic behavior, and have touched on psychological differences within the group.

A DEVIANT INDIVIDUAL: NATHAN B.

The other cases I have cited so far showed no clear evidence of a direct influence of individual differences in linguistic processing on the resultant linguistic behavior. Instead, individual differences in psychological orientation have led to differences in social experience and social aspirations, which in turn are reflected in predictable, socially patterned differences in behavior.

For a clear demonstration of individual difference in capacity we can consider the deviant case of Nathan B., who seriously disturbed the pattern of upper middle class speakers in the social stratification of New York City.

Nathan B., a 40-year-old political economist, used most of the sociolinguistic variables of New York City in the same way as other New Yorkers of his class. His use of postvocalic (r) was normal. But his use of (th) and (dh) was deviant in the extreme: a high frequency of stops without any downward shift in more formal styles. (A score of 200 means consistent use of the nonstandard stops.)

Nathan B.

| | Style | | | | |
	Casual	Careful	Reading	Word lists	Minimal pairs
(r)	00	09	12	23	42
(th)	88	98	88		
(dh)	107	89	114		

The (dh) and (th) figures are so deviant that they seriously affect the mean values of the other upper middle class speakers in the sample. Even with the most strenuous effort, Nathan B. could not consistently produce fricatives for (th) and (dh). This articulation problem was reflected in perception. At one point in the interview, I raised a question about *fate*. He interpreted my *fate* as *faith*, and the confusion continued until he spelled out F-A-I-T-H because he could not differentiate the two in speech (Labov, 1966, pp. 250–251).

This individual difference effectively prevented Nathan B. from playing his normal upper middle-class role. When he was attending college, he had a very high academic record; but as captain of the debating team his speech had to be delivered by someone else. As he was about to receive his Ph.D., he was told informally that he had a promising future in political science, and might have an appointment at his own university if he took corrective courses to improve his speech. As he had done many times before, Nathan B. abruptly refused to do anything of the kind. He continued to work as a writer in political science, but could not take up an academic position that required speech. Thus it is evident that Nathan B.'s special problem combined a productive and perceptive difference with an attitude that rejected any kind of corrective action. It was not simply a speech impediment.

The psychological dimension which was dimly reflected in the cases of Its and Nathan B. appears to involve sensitivity or insensitivity to the rules of other dialects, or the capacity to modify a vernacular pattern when exposed to other patterns. Our most direct encounter with this range of individual behavior occurred in the repetition tests carried out in our Harlem study in 1968.

INDIVIDUAL VARIATION IN REPETITION TESTS

There is abundant evidence in the psycholinguistic literature that young children find it difficult to repeat linguistic structures which are not in their grammars (Fraser, Bellugi, and Brown, 1963; Miller and Isard, 1963). We were somewhat surprised to discover that this was true of many speakers of the Black English Vernacular in their adolescent years. In a series of Memory Tests with the preadolescent Thunderbirds (ages 10–12) and Jets (ages 13–17) we found that certain rules were so firmly fixed in the BEV grammar that sentences were repeated back in the vernacular form. This was not a simple question of omitting inflections, but a completely different arrangement of words and word order (Labov *et al.*, 1968, pp. 310–334).

We presented these tests as a betting game, a memory test where the experimenter uttered a sentence, and the subject was to repeat it back in exactly the same words. In the final form of the test, the subject won a nickel if he repeated it correctly on the first trial, broke even if he succeeded on the second, and lost a nickel if he failed on the third and the fourth. Before the fourth repetition the experimenter said as clearly as possible, "No, you said _____, but I said [repeats the original sentence]." These tests were highly motivated, we knew the subjects quite well, and it is evident from the tape recordings that they were putting maximum effort into the task. The verbal leader of the Thunderbirds was Boot: here are three successive efforts on a sentence embodying negative concord:

SE-14:   **Nobody ever set at any of those desks, anyhow.**
Boot-1:   *Nobody never sa—No [whitey] never sat at any o' tho' dess, anyhow.*
Boot-2:   *Nobody never sat at any o' tho' dess, anyhow.*
Boot-3:   *Nobody [æs] ever sat at no desses, anyhow.*

Here are three successive efforts on a sentence involving an embedded indirect question:

SE-12:   **I asked Alvin whether he knows how to play basketball.**
Boot-1:   *I asked Alvin—I asked Alvin—I can't—I didn't quite hear you.*

Boot-2:   *I asked Alvin did he know how to play basketball.*
Boot-3:   *I asked Alvin whether—did he know how to play basketball.*

Boot had no difficulty with equally long sentences in vernacular form like *Ain't anyone here who can see it; ain't anyone here who can do it.* It is also clear that he understood and interpreted accurately the standard sentences. But whatever process was necessary to store and reproduce these sentences lost the form of the input. The translation to vernacular form may have occured in storage or in production, but in any case the standard forms could not be retrieved.

We were interested to observe that Boot was one of the most extreme of the Thunderbirds in this asymmetrical pattern, which we termed "dialect-bound." He was also the dominant figure in all vernacular verbal events; singing, ritual insults, story telling, or running off at the mouth generally. On the other hand, he was among the very worst readers of the group.

We observed an even wider range of individual differences in the adolescent Jets. Table 18.2 shows the pattern of individual repetition errors for eight members of this group. First of all, it was clear that there was considerable differentiation of behavior, even among the central group members. Second, the eight members of this group seemed to fall into two extreme types which suggested the possibility of a bi-modal distribution. Looking at total errors, for example:

Errors	0–5	6–10	11–14	15–20	21–25
Number	2	3	0	3	2

Our impression of two central tendencies was not based on these figures

TABLE 18.2
Individual Errors in Jets Memory Test

	NegConc		Yes–No Embedding		Copula		Possessive		Dummy it		Total	
	SE	NNE	SE	NNE	SE	NNE	SE	NNE	SE	NNE	SE	NNE
Stevie	1	–	–	–	1	2	1	–	–	–	3	2
Junior	–	1	–	–	1	1	–	–	–	–	1	2
Tommy	1	–	1	1	–	–	–	–	–	3	2	4
Turkey	1	1	2	–	3	1	1	–	–	–	7	2
Laundro	2	5	1	–	1	–	–	–	1	–	5	5
Tinker	2	5	4	–	4	1	1	–	1	1	12	7
Joseph	4	4	3	1	1	2	1	–	–	1	9	8
Kitfoot	5	5	4	–	4	1	1	–	1	1	15	7
Total											54	37

alone, but also on the guessing game. Three or four members of the Jets showed the same rigidity of response that Boot had shown, plainly dialect-bound. But the three best performers on the repetition tests were of a very different type. In this case, all three were verbal leaders of the group. Though they did no better at school then any other members of the Jets, they plainly showed their verbal superiority in one way or another. The most outstanding in this respect was Stevie, age 13. He talked very fast and almost continually; he was the group's best singer, and though he was only a junior member, he was the major link with the older group, who thought very well of him for his verbal abilities. Stevie's stylistic flexibility was shown in many other ways. He was the only BEV speaker who did well on the Vernacular Correction Test—that is, he was able to correct standard terms to BEV in a formal situation. We also see that Stevie used very different styles in group sessions and individual interviews, and his style shift is truly phenomenal compared to the rest of the group. For the forms of *is* we find

	is	*'s*	$\emptyset$	N
Stevie				
group sessions	12%	15%	73%	33
Single interviews	58%	13%	29%	38
All Jets				
Group session	24%	31%	45%	213
Single interviews	38%	36%	26%	500

Stevie's use of zero *is* dropped from 73% to 29%, a 44% difference, while the group average moved only from 45% to 29%, a 16% difference. Stevie thus demonstrates the unusual ability to shift his linguistic performance in a way that escapes the limitations of any one dialect. This ability is not unlimited: There is no such change in his use of *are*, or dummy *it*, or many other features. But the copula deletion rule is one of the stylistic devices that are relied on most in BEV to indicate a change of contextual style, and Stevie is able to exploit this far more than any other member.

The repetition tests shown here were replicated on larger populations by Baratz (1969), and Garvey and McFarlane (1968). The same general pattern appeared in the concentration of dialect-bound responses on certain grammatical features. These studies were carried out in classroom situations where they obtained reliable overall differences between black and white responses, but they did not isolate members of the vernacular culture from others, and no individual differences were reported. It was not possible to isolate individual differences which were due to differences in personal history—distance from the vernacular peer groups and variable exposure to the vernacular pattern—from differences in individual cognitive style and capacity. The recent studies by Day in Hawaii

(1976) also showed wide variation in individual capacity, and here it may be possible to isolate psychological parameters from social history.

We were naturally struck by the series of reports by Ruth Day on a number of other measures of a "language-bound" versus "stimulus-bound" dimension (1969, 1973a, 1973b). Whether or not replications of these tests support the existence of a bimodal pattern, they clearly demonstrate a wide range of individual differences that are closely related to the phenomena we have been studying, and may well be fundamental parameters of language-learning skill. A natural strategy is to replicate the kinds of peer-group studies that we have been carrying out with the additional insight to be gained by testing subjects for degree of dichotic fusion, categorical discrimination, and secret language learning as well as repetition tests. But in any case, it will be necessary to know as much as possible about the social history of the subjects in order to isolate psychological parameters. This might not apply to fusion tests, which do not correspond to any aspects of social experience, but it would apply to other tests of verbal manipulation, such as the learning of secret languages.

INDIVIDUAL VARIATION IN THE ACQUISITION OF THE PHILADELPHIA DIALECT

We have been alert to the importance of individual differences in cognitive style in our approach to the acquisition of the Philadelphia dialect. In connection with our study of change and variation in the Philadelphia speech community, Arvilla Payne carried out an extensive investigation of 24 families in the suburban community of King of Prussia (1975, 9176). In this new middle-class community, the dominant dialect was that of Philadelphia: Half of the residents had moved there from the city itself. The other half had arrived from other dialect areas. The high concentration of chemical, electronic, and computer-based industries had brought skilled personnel from Massachusetts, Cleveland, New York, and other regions. We had an opportunity to observe the acquisition of the local dialect by children in large families with varying degrees of exposure to their parents' dialect and the local pattern.

The major results of this study showed that children rapidly acquired the phonetic patterns of their peers, with only a few years exposure to the Philadelphia dialect: the fronting of /ow/ and /uw/ except before /1/; the centralization of /ay/ before voiceless consonants; the raising of the nucleus of /aw/ and reversal of the glide to a low back target; and the raising of tensed short a. Adults showed only sporadic acquisition of these features. The major determinants of the rate of acquisition of the phonetic patterns of the Philadelphia dialect were the age of arrival in the area, and the type of block: dominated by local speakers, mixed, or dominated by out-of-state speakers. We also observed a strong influence of the family: Children from the same family seemed to show similar rates of acquisition.

Exactly the opposite type of result appeared when we examined the more abstract phonological patterns of the dialect: the merger of /uhr/ and /ohr/in *lure* and *lore;* the merger of /er/ and /ər/ in *merry* and *Murray;* and the complex split of short *a* into tense and lax members. Children from out-of-state showed very limited acquisition of these features, and age of arrival did not have a major effect. The case of the complex distribution of short *a* was the most extreme instance. Even children who were born in King of Prussia did not learn this pattern well unless their parents were also born there.

From these results we have drawn strong conclusions about the nature of the underlying phonological system in the local dialect and the process of language learning. Here it is important to note that there were some striking individual differences. Three children showed remarkable progress in matching their short *a* patterns to the Philadelphia pattern; one in particular is a clear exception to the generalization just stated. Karen Cameron came to King of Prussia when she was 8, and was tested when she was 15. Her parents were raised in Cleveland and showed the "Northern cities" pattern of short *a* distribution, that is, all the vowels were tensed and showed a continuous distribution from [æ] to [e:ə] depending on phonetic context. Karen's remarkable achievement is shown in Figure 18.1: She maintained a pattern of phonetic distribution similar to that of her parents, but reorganized the lexical items so that one could draw a line separating those that were tense in the Philadelphia pattern and those that were not. Her mother's pattern is shown in Figure 18.2.

Figure 18.1 shows eight short *a* words that fall within the ellipse marked /æh/: the tense vowels opposed to the lax set marked /æ/. All of these fall into the classes that are tense for Philadelphians: /æhN/, short *a* before front nasals (*hands, hand, stand*) and /æhF/ before front voiceless fricatives (*after, half, laugh, pass.*) None of these word classes are represented in the lax /æ/ ellipse in low central position. Figure 18.2 uses the same word classes, treating a Cleveland speaker as if she were a Philadelphian. This is not entirely unreasonable, since the phonetic positions of most words in the single Cleveland short *a* phoneme are roughly arranged in the same way as the two-phoneme Philadelphia system: *man* is high and front, and *black* is low and central. But the details are all wrong, as shown by the five words designated by small squares: *tavern, have, alley, match* and *hang* are well up with the tense /æhN/ and /æhF/ classes while in Philadelphia they would have low central vowels. Karen Cameron has been able to rearrange the phonetic system learned from her mother into the Philadelphia pattern of Figure 18.1. In addition, Figure 18.1 shows she has acquired fronted /uw/ and /ow/ (except before /l/), the back chain shift that

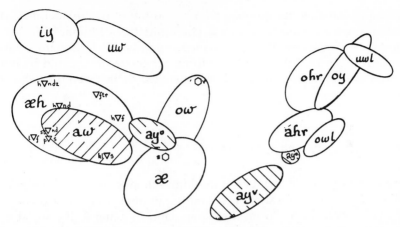

Figure 18.1. Vowel system of Karen Cameron, 15, of King of Prussia (from Payne 1976). /ay°/ = /ay/ before voiceless consonants; /ay^v/ = /ay/ before pause and voiced consonants. /owl/ and /uwl/ = allophones of /ow/ and /uw/ before final /l/.

raises /ohr/ and /oy/ to high position, and /ahr/ to mid back, and the raising of /aw/ to mid front. None of these features appear in Figure 18.2, though one token each of /ow/ and /uw/ shows Philadelphia influence in her mother's speech.

In the case of (/ay°/) in *fight, sight, life,* etc., the Cleveland pattern is not necessarily different from Philadelphia: Karen shows the same front cen-

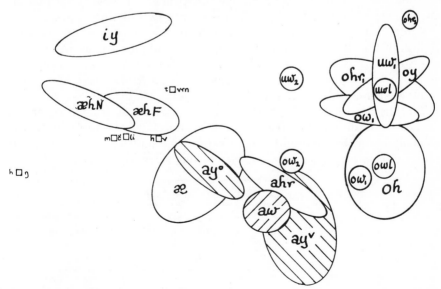

Figure 18.2. Vowel system of Anna May Cameron, 35, of Cleveland and King of Prussia (from Payne 1976). /æhF/ = /æh/ before front voiceless fricatives; /æhN/ = /æh/ before front nasals. Other symbols as in Fig. 18.1.

tralized allophane as her mother, a form also found in Philadelphia; she also shows one back (/ay°/) which is characteristic of Philadelphia but is not heard in Cleveland. Thus the evidence points to a minimal readjustment: Karen has kept the Cleveland forms whenever they could be fitted into the Philadelphia system, and only changed them when they showed no fit at all.

CATEGORICAL DISCRIMINATION

Karen was a popular member of her high school group, well integrated into the local society. But there was nothing in her social background that clearly differentiated her from the others, and in general, the social histories of the King of Prussia children rarely predicted their degree of acquisition of the local vernacular. We tested 13 King of Prussia children for categorical discrimination of short *a*, using an experimental stimulus developed in our Philadelphia study. This involved a series of ten resynthesized transformations of the natural pronunciation of the word *mad*, with a range of F^1, F^2 values characteristic of [æ] to those characteristic of the upper mid value [e:ə]. Our test sharply differentiated speakers of the New York and Philadelphia dialects, who clearly had a categorical discrimination, from speakers of other dialects with a single phoneme, who did not. We also found that a number of speakers of these other dialects failed completely to categorize the series into two distinct types.

Karen Cameron's responses to the categorical discrimination test were typical of the Philadelphia area, with a discrimination peak in both the one-step and two-step test. Her categorization crossover was shifted slightly to the higher position characteristic of the Midwestern dialect area in other speakers' tests, that is, her crossover point for the "tense" members of the class was at a higher point in the phonetic series. However, she was clearly differentiated from the other subjects by the precision of her categorization. In this randomized series, she had ten opportunities to identify each of the ten stimuli. Her results were as follows:

Stimulus #	1	2	3	4	5	6	7	8	9	10
F_1	655	621	594	571	543	515	495	471	445	424
F_2	1509	1556	1607	1662	1718	1770	1831	1886	1940	1991
No. identified as "Type 2" or tense	0	0	0	0	0	6	10	10	10	10

This result suggests that we might indeed look more closely at the precision of categorization of various subjects as reflecting an important dimension of language learning ability.

In the various studies of the speech community, we have found strong social determination of variation in linguistic behavior. The strongest single source of individual variation seems to me the dimension of "language-bound" versus "stimulus-bound," isolated most clearly by Day, and each of the individual cases that have appeared in our studies can best be understood at present in these terms.

I am particularly struck by the relationship between this dimension and the process of learning to read. The first task in learning to read clearly seems to require abilities that are highly developed in the extreme type of "stimulus-bound" individual like Stevie Wise. Such a person is quick to notice small differences and can reproduce them. The individual features of letters, and the differences between them; their relation to the standard dialect as well as the vernacular pattern; and the succession of letters in the printed chain, all require close attention to retrieval of the stimuli. On the other hand, it is well known that good readers must eventually learn to make mistakes that indicate that they are learning to ignore the less important details. We found that the better readers among the Jets and Cobras made mistakes in replacing *a* with *the* and substituting other function words that did not radically alter the meaning of the sentence. The poorer readers did not. Given the mysterious problem of understanding what good readers do in their rapid assimilation of the message on the printed page, I think we have to weigh the possibility that these abilities are similar to those developed most in the "language-bound" person. Presumably such a person takes in a small sampling of the stimuli and reproduces the larger meaning by supplying most of the structure from his own linguistic competence.

We can also see the reflection of the language-bound–stimulus-bound dimension in various approaches to the task of learning a second language. It is evident that some great polyglots master each detail of phonetics, intonation, and gesture. Other language learners stop at some plateau of referential communication, and supply the basic phonetics and prosody from their own original vernacular rules, even though they may continue to improve their command of the written language. From all of these indications, it seems clear that a deeper penetration of the psychological dimensions that underlie this first approximation to individual differences will be an important step towards our understanding of the mechanism of language learning.

REFERENCES

Baratz, J. C. A bi-dialectal task for determining language proficiency in economically disadvantaged Negro children. *Child Development*, 1969, 40.

Cedergren, H. J. The interplay of social and linguistic factors in Panama. Unpublished Doctoral dissertation, Cornell University, Ithaca, New York, 1973.

Day, R. Language acquisition in a bicultural community: A case study in bidialectalism. Paper presented at Fifth Annual Colloquium on New Ways of Analyzing Variation, Washington, D.C., October, 1976.

Day, R. S. Temporal order judgments in speech: Are individuals language-bound or stimulus-bound?" Paper presented at the Ninth Annual Meeting of the Psychonomic Society, St. Louis, November, 1969.

Day, R. S. Digit-span memory in language-bound and stimulus-bound subjects. Paper presented at the 85th Meeting of the Acoustical Society of America, Boston, April, 1973a.

Day, R. S. On learning "secret languages." Paper presented at the Eastern Psychological Association Meeting, Washington, D.C., May, 1973b.

Fraser, C., Bellugi, U., and Brown, R. Control of grammar in imitation, comprehension, and production. *Journal of Verbal Learning and Verbal Behavior*, 1963, *2*, 121–135.

Garvey, C. and McFarlane, P. T. A preliminary study of Standard English speech patterns in the Baltimore City public schools. Report No. 16, John Hopkins University, Baltimore, 1968.

Labov, W. The social motivation of a sound change. *Word*, 1963, *19*, 273–309.

Labov, W. *The social stratification of English in New York City*. Arlington, Virginia: Center for Applied Linguistics, 1966.

Labov, W. The linguistic consequences of being a lame. *Language in Society*, 1973, *2*, 81–115.

Labov, W., Cohen, P., Robins, C., and Lewis, J. *A study of the non-standard English of negro and Puerto Rican speakers in New York City*. Cooperative Research Report 3288, Philadelphia: U. S. Regional Survey, 204 North 35th Street, 1968.

Levine, L. and Crockett, H. J., Jr. Speech variation in a Piedmont community: Postvocalic *r*. In S. Lieberson (Ed.), *Explorations in sociolinguistics* [Sociological Inquiry 36, No. 2]. (Reprinted as Publication 44, *International Journal of American Linguistics*, 1966.)

Miller, G. and Isard, S. Some perceptual consequences of linguistic rules. *Journal of Verbal Learning and Verbal Behavior*, 1963, *2*, 217–228.

Payne, A. The re-organization of linguistic rules: A preliminary report. *Pennsylvania Working Papers on Linguistic Change and Variation I*, *6*, 1975.

Payne, A. The acquisition of the phonological system of a second dialect. Unpublished Doctoral dissertation, University of Pennsylvania, 1976.

Index